D1107634

The Imperial Frontier in the Tropics, 1865–75

By the same author

COLONIES INTO COMMONWEALTH

(*Blandford Press*)

The Imperial Frontier
in the Tropics, 1865–75

A STUDY OF BRITISH COLONIAL POLICY
IN WEST AFRICA, MALAYA AND THE SOUTH PACIFIC
IN THE AGE OF GLADSTONE AND DISRAELI

W. DAVID McINTYRE

PROFESSOR OF HISTORY,
UNIVERSITY OF CANTERBURY, NEW ZEALAND

MACMILLAN
LONDON · MELBOURNE · TORONTO
ST MARTIN'S PRESS
NEW YORK
1 9 6 7

© W. David McIntyre 1967

MACMILLAN AND CO LTD
Little Essex Street London w c 2
also at Bombay Calcutta Madras Melbourne

THE MACMILLAN COMPANY OF CANADA LIMITED
70 Bond Street Toronto 2

ST MARTIN'S PRESS INC
175 Fifth Avenue New York NY 10010

Library of Congress catalog card no. 67–19403

PRINTED IN GREAT BRITAIN

Contents

List of Maps

Preface

THIS book attempts to bridge a gap which exists between general and theoretical works about imperialism and those area studies and national histories which are now making it possible to see western expansion in perspective. I have, it is true, written 'from within the blinkers of imperial history' (as one distinguished Africanist would say), but I have tried, so far as I can, to measure up to the requirements of the regional experts. The result is a series of 'case-studies' concerning British expansion in West Africa, Malaya and the South Pacific which attempts to fit certain remote and widely scattered experiments into the wider story of mid-Victorian imperialism.

I wish to acknowledge most gratefully the generous help given by many people. Her Majesty the Queen granted permission for me to consult the Royal Archives at Windsor. Lord and Lady Brabourne lent me the Brabourne Diaries and Miss Cecilia Goodenough lent Commodore Goodenough's Journal. The Earl of Kimberley allowed me to consult the Kimberley Papers, then at Wymondham Hall, Norfolk, and Lieut.-Col. R. P. F. White of the National Registry of Archives not only arranged the visit but provided transport. The National Trust allowed me to consult the Disraeli papers at Hughenden Manor. The Cabinet Office (Historical Section) gave permission to quote from the Gladstone Cabinet Minutes in the British Museum. I also received most valuable help, over many months, from the staffs of the Public Record Office, the British Museum, the Institute of Historical Research, the Methodist Missionary Society archives, the British Transport Commission archives, the Royal Geographical Society and the libraries of the Colonial Office, the War Office, the Royal Commonwealth Society, Rhodes House, the School of Oriental and African Studies and the University of Nottingham.

A number of scholars read earlier drafts or gave me the benefit of their expert knowledge. I wish to thank Dr I. M. Cumpston, Mr G. B. Milner and Mr D. H. Jones of the University of London, Dr D. Cooms of the University of Ghana, Mr Robert I. Conhaim of the University of California, Los Angeles, the late Dr C. F. Goodfellow of Rhodes University, Dr Wong Lin Ken of the University of Singapore, Dr W. P. N. Tyler of Massey University, the late Mr Kingsley Roth of Cambridge and Dr C. C. Eldridge of Edinburgh University.

I owe special debts of gratitude to Professor D. G. E. Hall and Professor C. D. Cowan of the London School of Oriental and African Studies, who supervised most carefully my work for the Ph.D. thesis out of which this book has grown. Finally, I wish to pay particular tribute to Professor J. A. S. Grenville, of the University of Leeds, who, during several delightful years when I was his assistant lecturer at the University of Nottingham, read and revised my work, and criticized and encouraged, with such insistence, good humour and insight, that I learnt to forge a book from the raw material of a thesis. To all these, and to my wife (who read the proofs and put up with much else besides), I would like to record my grateful thanks. The shortcomings of the present work are mine, not theirs.

W. DAVID McINTYRE

Christchurch, N.Z.
March 1967

Abbreviations

GENERAL

Ad.	Admiralty	L.O.	Law Officers
A.D.C.	Aide-de-Camp	Maj.	Major
Adj.	Adjutant	min(s).	minute(s)
Brig. Maj.	Brigade Major	N.S.W.	New South Wales
Brig.	Brigadier	N.Z.	New Zealand
Brig.-Gen.	Brigadier-General	P.R.O.	Public Record Office
C.O.	Colonial Office	R.A.	Royal Artillery
Comm.	Commodore	Rear-Ad.	Rear-Admiral
encl.	enclosed	S.S.Assoc.	Straits Settlements
F.O.	Foreign Office		Association
gov.	governor	St.	Street
Govt.	Government	Treas.	Treasury
I.O.	India Office	W.O.	War Office
Is.	Isles, Islands		

PERIODICALS

A.H.R.	*American Historical Review*
C.H.B.E.	*Cambridge History of the British Empire*
C.H.R.	*Canadian Historical Review*
C.M.	*Camden Miscellany*
C.S.	*Camden Society*
C.S.S.H.	*Comparative Studies in Sociology and History*
Econ.Hist.Rev.	*Economic History Review*
H.J.	*The Historical Journal*
H.S.A.N.Z.	*Historical Studies Australia and New Zealand*
J.A.H.	*Journal of African History*
J.A.L.	*Journal of African Law*
J.B.S.	*Journal of British Studies*
J.C.P.S.	*Journal of Commonwealth Political Studies*
J.E.H.	*Journal of Economic History*
J.M.B.R.A.S.	*Journal of the Malayan Branch of the Royal Asiatic Society*
J.S.E.A.H.	*Journal of South East Asian History*
N.C.M.H.	*New Cambridge Modern History*
P.H.R.	*Pacific Historical Review*
P.M.H.	*Papers on Malayan History*
P.M.S.	*Papers on Malay Subjects*

R.A.H.A.	Report of the American Historical Association
R.M.S.	Renaissance and Modern Studies
S.C.A.	Survey of Commonwealth Affairs
S.L.S.	Sierra Leone Studies
T.A.P.S.	Transactions of the American Philosophical Society
T.G.C.T.H.S.	Transactions of the Gold Coast and Togoland Historical Society
T.R.H.S.	Transactions of the Royal Historical Society
T.R.U.S.I.	Transactions of the Royal United Service Institution

The Imperial Frontier
in the Tropics

'WE have been of late much perplexed by a new word, "Imperialism", which has crept in amongst us.' With these words the fourth Earl of Carnarvon, speaking to a large Edinburgh audience in 1878, entered upon a discussion as to the 'meaning and value of the word Imperialism', which has continued from his day to this. In the course of his lecture he found it easier to say what imperialism was 'not' than to define what it was. In particular was he at pains to refute analogies which were then being drawn between the Roman Empire and the mid-Victorian British Empire. In one respect, however, Carnarvon admitted that they could be compared. Every great empire, he declared, was confronted by 'similar difficulties of frontier — the same arguments for and against — the same provocations real or supposed — the same questions as to the key of the position — the same temptation of those on the spot to acquire territory'.[1] These remarks highlighted an important, though comparatively neglected, aspect of imperial affairs.

Amid all the clamour over Disraeli's diplomacy in the Eastern Question, which made 'imperialism' a pejorative word for many people, and amid all the soul-searching about Britain's relationship with her self-governing colonies, aroused by Gladstone's first Government, the 'difficulties of frontier' tended to be forgotten. Carnarvon was one of the few men who could speak of them with authority.

The reason for this was that four years earlier, as Secretary of State for the Colonies, he had launched three experiments which were of tremendous significance for the history of the British Empire

[1] From an address entitled 'Imperial Administration' to the Edinburgh Philosophical Institution on 5 Nov. 1878. Printed in *Fortnightly Review* (Dec. 1878), 23, p. 760. Reported also in *The Times*, 6 Nov. 1878.

in the tropics. In West Africa, the tiny settlement of Lagos was added to the forts along the Gold Coast to form a new Crown Colony, and a new authority was assumed in the region known as the Gold Coast protectorate; in the Malay States, the first British Residents were appointed, and in the South Pacific the annexation of Fiji gave Britain her first possession in this part of the world outside the Australasian colonies. Although the three experiments, which were launched in 1874, were widely separated geographically, they were all inaugurated by the same ministers in London, at roughly the same time, and they all formed part of the general problem which Carnarvon later alluded to in his lecture — that of the expansion of the frontiers of empire.

The experiments were, in reality, the result of a reappraisal of Britain's role in the three tropical regions which was conducted by the Colonial Office under the first Earl of Kimberley, Gladstone's Secretary of State for the Colonies from July 1870 until the Liberal Government fell in February 1874. During Kimberley's tenure of office the growth of British involvement in the three areas, interacting with the particular developments of regional history, had raised the general question as to whether further British intervention should follow. While Kimberley himself was reluctant to move and wanted to avoid the extension of British responsibilities, Edward Knatchbull-Hugessen, who became his parliamentary under-secretary in January 1871, was an 'imperialist' and urged Kimberley to intervene. Indeed, Knatchbull-Hugessen, who sensed the mood of the House of Commons, insisted, time and again, that any withdrawal of British influence might be politically dangerous in view of public opinion at home.

He had good grounds for his fears. But it is as well to remember that the British public rarely took much interest in the development of colonies, unless something jarred — a sudden disaster, a need for military expenditure, a humanitarian outcry. The dramas of British expansion at Isandhlwana, Majuba Hill, Tel-el-Kebir, Khartoum, Pendjeh, Omdurman and Mafeking stirred such emotions among the later Victorians that one begins to suspect that they became the outlet for the vicarious adventures of an increasingly well-ordered society. But, just because British society tended to react to colonial affairs in this fitful way, public opinion did not affect colonial policy continuously. A succession of serious problems reached the headlines, opinion became roused, the issues were faced, and then, after a little while, the interest of everybody, save a tiny minority, faded away.

Something like this occurred in the years 1873 and 1874. Gladstone's Government was becoming increasingly unpopular because so many interests were offended by his Irish, Army, educational and licensing reforms. Gladstone, in fact, resigned after the defeat of the Irish University Bill by three votes on 12 March 1873, and only continued in office because Disraeli refused to form another minority Government. In July 1873, irregularities in the General Post Office and Treasury led to a vote of censure and the transference of Lowe from the Exchequer to the Home Office. While the Liberal Government encountered these growing political difficulties at home, which made it feel 'shaky not only politically but physically',[1] it also had to face crises on the frontiers of British influence in West Africa, Malaya and the South Pacific. Because its attention was directed to the problems in these regions and because Knatchbull-Hugessen's warnings were heeded, Gladstone's Government contemplated some significant changes on the frontier in the tropics.

During the spring and early summer of 1873, Kimberley, the Colonial Secretary, studied the problems of the three tropical regions and finally made a series of important recommendations. He decided to reverse the policy which had been tried for eight years in West Africa. He planned to attempt firmer administration in the Gold Coast and to intervene with force against the powerful kingdom of Ashanti. He adopted a proposal for the appointment of Residents in certain of the Malay States. He also urged Gladstone to annex the Fiji Islands. Gladstone, on his part, consented to the appointment of officers to 'inquire and report' on each region. But, before any final decisions were taken in these matters, Disraeli came to power after his victory in the general election of February 1874. The new policies, therefore, were left to the Conservative Government.

Thus, far from Disraeli initiating an imperial 'forward movement' in 1874, his Government merely went ahead with policies worked out by their Liberal predecessors. Undue significance has been given to the effect of the Conservative victory of 1874 upon colonial policy. It used to be suggested that the experiments in the tropics were part

[1] Kimberley, 'Journal of Events during the Gladstone Ministry, 1868–1874', ed. by E. Drus, *C.M.* (1958), xxi, p. 37.

of a 'new imperialism' which Disraeli launched.[1] The new policies
were, in fact, the culmination of a period of tentative innovation
rather than the beginning of a forward movement. It is, moreover,
of very great significance that Carnarvon, who actually inaugurated
the experiments, deliberately avoided the appearance of a 'forward
movement'. It was 'impossible to appropriate every territory and
every island', he maintained; and he pleaded for 'some breathing
time before we are required to act on a large scale'.[2] The idea of a
'forward movement' itself, therefore, requires some redefinition, for
the colonial experiments with which it has been identified were not
part of a comprehensive scheme of colonial expansion. Carnarvon
tried to minimize the significance of the new experiments, by insisting
that each case had been judged on its merits. Perhaps, for this reason,
historians have tended to neglect the crisis of decision over the frontier
in the tropics in 1873–4, which led to major landmarks in the development of the British West African colonies and in the assumption of
British control in Malaya and the Pacific islands.

What makes the crisis so interesting is that most of the politicians
and civil servants in Whitehall who were involved in the decision-
making began to perceive, if rather dimly, that a general problem was
involved in each case — the problem of expansion into new areas.
They now began to wonder uneasily where the process might end.
This dilemma was perhaps recognized most clearly by Lord Blachford,
who, better known as Sir Frederic Rogers, was permanent under-
secretary in the Colonial Office from 1860 to 1871 and, whilst there,
had tried hard to ward off the assumption of new responsibilities in the
tropics. The experiments were launched after Rogers's retirement,
and did not meet with his approval. While writing to a former
colleague in 1875, he predicted further expansion: 'We have Suez

[1] The role of the Liberal Govt. in the three experiments is recognized in
P. Knaplund, *Gladstone and Britain's Imperial Policy*, London, 1927, p. 137,
and C. E. Carrington, *The British Overseas*, Cambridge, 1950, p. 534.
Greater emphasis on Disraeli's impact is given by H. E. Gorst, *The Earl of
Beaconsfield*, London, 1899, p. 227; J. A. Froude, *The Earl of Beaconsfield*,
London, 1905, pp. 238–9; R. Muir, *A Short History of the British Common-
wealth*, London, 1922, vol. ii, pp. 591–4; P. T. Moon, *Imperialism and
World Politics*, New York, 1933, pp. 35–36, 295; A. P. Newton, *A Hundred
Years of the British Empire*, London, 1940, pp. 232–3.

[2] To a deputation on 29 Apr. 1875. *The Times*, 3 May 1875.

with Egypt in the distance — Perak with Siam in the distance — Fiji with Oceania in the distance, and Ashanti with Central Africa in the distance'.[1]

But Rogers, apprehensive though he was, could hardly have imagined the long-term consequences of the experiments. In terms of future military intervention, international rivalry, economic development, administrative experiments and racial and moral issues, the modern history of Ghana, Nigeria, Sierra Leone, Singapore, Malaya and the British possessions in the South Pacific raised issues even more formidable than the subtle riddle of Britain's changing relationship with Canada, Australia, New Zealand and South Africa, about which the mid-Victorians seemed so obsessed. The origin of these problems forms an important chapter in the early history of the 'New Commonwealth' as distinct from that of the 'Dominions'.

The experiments in the tropics, therefore, were not part of a 'forward movement' so much as an outcome of the 'frontier' problem. It was a problem which had long been experienced in some form in India and South Africa. There, as in the tropics, the frontier of British influence stretched beyond the frontier of sovereignty. In trying to stabilize the narrower frontier, the three experiments, which are the subject of this book, were born.

What is meant by the frontier in the tropics? Clearly it was not the frontier of American historiography — that receding area of free land and westward march of settlement, which in 1893 was sufficient to 'explain American development' for Frederick Jackson Turner.[2] The abundance of land for settlement and the comparatively small indigenous population of the American West bears little comparison with the three tropical regions. Nor is the application of Turner to South Africa altogether relevant. As one distinguished historian has already pointed out, 'The Indians of North America were hunters before they were cultivators; the Bantu races were above all else graziers and cultivators'.[3] There were also many more Africans on

[1] Blachford to Taylor 9 Dec. 1875. G. E. Marindin, *Lord Blachford's Letters*, London, 1896, p. 365 (hereafter referred to as Marindin).

[2] F. J. Turner, 'The Significance of the Frontier in American History', *R.A.H.A.* (1893), p. 199.

[3] C. W. de Kiewiet, *British Colonial Policy and the South African Republics, 1848–72*, London, 1929, pp. 113–14.

the frontiers of the Cape and Natal than there were Indians in the
American West.   Unlike America and South Africa, the three
tropical regions (apart from Fiji) had no European settler problem.

Nor, again, were the frontiers of India a precise parallel with the
tropical frontier. 'What I call *a frontier*', wrote Sir Alfred Lyall in
1891, 'is the utmost political boundary projected as one might say
beyond the administrative boundary.'[1]   This sort of definition is
theoretically appropriate to the three tropical regions; but Lyall was,
in fact, thinking primarily in terms of military protection along a vast
defensive frontier stretching from the Persian Gulf to Burma. More
recently, Sir Keith Hancock, in examining the economic development
of West and South Africa, used a different concept of frontier which
he defined as 'the moving fringes of an expansionist society'.[2]   But
the frontier in the tropics cannot be adequately explained in any of
these terms.

The frontier in the tropics was a vague zone, adjacent to (or, in the
case of the Pacific islands, strategically related to) territory under
British sovereignty.   Within this zone a great variety of British
activities had developed — missions, trade, treaty relations, military
intervention, protection, and even in some cases settlement, administration and jurisdiction.   By the year 1873, relations between the
British colonies and the adjacent states had reached the point where
it was generally felt that the internal conditions of the latter posed
serious threats to the security of the colonies.   In other words, Britain
had, in each case, already become 'involved', in various ways, with
the neighbouring tropical societies.

In West Africa, for example, she was entangled in rivalries, which
she little understood, between a number of African states; in Malaya,
civil wars in the Malay States led to increased piracy at sea which
damaged the trade of the Straits Settlements; in the South Pacific,
internal dissension in islands where Europeans and Americans had
settled gave rise to rumours that foreign intervention was about to
take place close to Australia and New Zealand.   At the same time,
some British subjects embarrassed the nation's conscience by kidnapping

[1] A. Lyall, 'Frontiers and Protectorates', *The Nineteenth Century* (Aug.
1891), 174, p. 31.
[2] W. K. Hancock, *Survey of Commonwealth Affairs*, London, 1942, vol. ii,
pt. 2, pp. v–ix.

Pacific islanders for work on plantations. By 1873 the Colonial Office had to face, in these regions, the sort of decision which had previously been posed in South Africa and India. The frontier had to be stabilized. The alternatives frequently urged were new annexations or withdrawal of existing involvement. When it finally came to a decision, neither of these suggestions were followed (except in the one case of Fiji). Instead, a vague middle-of-the-road notion of paramountcy was conceived, and experiments in new forms of 'informal empire' were conducted.

This frontier problem, although alluded to by Carnarvon in his famous Edinburgh lecture in 1878, did not impress itself upon the public imagination as did the contemporary quest for the 'consolidation' or 'confederation' of the English-speaking colonies.[1] It is true that it became a major issue of late-Victorian diplomacy. With the growth of French and German, and later American, Belgian and Italian activity in the colonial field, there was intense rivalry from the 1880's to the First World War. By this time many leading statesmen were deeply preoccupied with the problem. In the early 1870's, however, statesmen were only beginning to realize the logical consequences of expansion in the tropics; and the idea of European power rivalries extending into the jungles was not taken very seriously at home. Indeed, when France attempted to gain some advantage over Britain in West Africa in the late 1860's, Sir Frederick Elliot of the Colonial Office could only express his pained surprise. 'Friendly European Nations ought to avoid *elbowing* each other . . . in such countries as Africa.'[2] In this period most of the writers who ventured to contribute to colonial affairs confined themselves almost completely to the problem of the relationship between Britain and her self-governing colonies; they did not discuss the possibilities of expansion.

Only a few commentators recognized the importance of the frontier in the tropics. The best-known was Charles Dilke. His *Greater*

[1] For a discussion of the debate on this subject in the years 1869–72, see C. A. Bodelsen, *Studies in Mid-Victorian Imperialism*. Copenhagen, 1924, pt. ii, and R. Koebner and H. D. Schmidt, *Imperialism. The Story and Significance of a Political Word, 1840–1960*, Cambridge, 1964, chs. 3–5.

[2] Min. by T. F. Elliot 14 Nov., on Gov. Blackall to Carnarvon 11 Oct. 1866. C.O. files in the P.R.O.: Sierra Leone correspondence, C.O. 267/287.

Britain, published in 1868, was an immediate popular success and probably contributed to the revival of interest in empire which occurred at the end of the 1860's. Most of the book was about the English-speaking world — the settlement colonies and the United States — and it propounded a frankly racialist theory in which he predicted that what he termed the 'dearer' races would destroy the 'cheaper peoples'.[1] But Dilke also wrote about those areas under British power and influence which he defined as 'dependencies'. He believed that if the Australasian colonies, for example, were given their independence trade with them would continue, but that if India and Ceylon were abandoned they would fall into anarchy. Dependencies were 'a nursery of statesmen and warriors' without which the British would 'irresistibly fall into natural sluggishness of thought'. Britain's interests in Asia and Africa imparted 'width of thought and nobility of purpose' and offered the chance of 'planting free institutions among the dark-skinned races of the world'.[2]

Dilke, in fact, produced some of the most influential notions in the whole mythology of Britain's role in the world, which were to be cherished for nearly a century. What is also significant is the clear distinction between 'colonies' proper, and those places which were the scene of entirely different experiments in British control. Sir Charles Adderley labelled this distinction the difference between the 'Grecian' and 'Roman' elements of the British Empire.[3]

Arthur Mills was another writer who showed himself to be aware of the problem of the frontier in the tropics. He was one of the colonial experts in Parliament, and his first impact on the Empire was made as chairman of the Select Committee on imperial defence in 1861. In an article entitled 'Our Colonial Policy', which he published in the *Contemporary Review* in 1869, he too drew the distinction between 'our attempts to govern coloured races' and the 'everyday phases of our colonial policy'. Unlike Dilke, he clearly disapproved of the notion of a British civilizing mission. He criticized attempts to transplant British institutions on to the Gold Coast. He lambasted

---

[1] C. W. Dilke, *Greater Britain: a Record of Travel in English-Speaking Countries during 1866 and 1867*, London, 1868, ii, p. 405.

[2] Ibid. pp. 394–406.

[3] C. B. Adderley, *Review of 'The Colonial Policy of Lord John Russell's Administration' by Earl Grey, 1853*, London, 1869, ii, p. 193.

what he called the 'petting and patronizing policy' towards other races, and caricatured the signing of treaties with rulers in the tropical regions as 'a mere diplomatic pastime carried on between the Queen's representative and a set of tattooed and feathered chieftains'.[1]

Herman Merivale's article on 'The Colonial Question in 1870' provided a third example of the distinction between 'colonial' and 'frontier' problems. It was mainly concerned with the problems of relations between England and the large self-governing colonies; but he, too, referred to the frontier question. He did so in a more constructive way than the others. He reminded his readers of the refusal to annex Fiji in 1861, and discussed the special problems of relations with the original inhabitants in New Zealand and South Africa. He recalled (although he was a bit out of date with his facts) that the Government of India held 'dependencies in the Malay Peninsula', and he ended his essay with a very coherent view of what today would be called 'informal empire' in Asia.

> I will finish with a few hasty glances at another great field of national development — almost an empire, in all but name — with which our connection seems as yet in its infancy. By actual possession here and there; by quasi-territorial dominion, under treaties, in other places; by great superiority of general commerce and the carrying trade everywhere, we have acquired an immense political influence in all that division of the world which lies between India and Japan. . . .[2]

Merivale saw very clearly the type of frontier zone which existed in West Africa, in Malaya and in the South Pacific. More significantly, he also realized that they gave rise to conflicts of departmental responsibility in Whitehall. He therefore proposed that a single 'Minister' or 'Governor-General' should be appointed to co-ordinate British policy in his Asian frontier zone, rather like the later High Commissioner in South-East Asia. Merivale's was the most constructive public discussion of the frontier problem in the early 1870's. A few writers, therefore, realized that, as well as the much debated problem of relations between Britain and the self-governing colonies, there were new and intractable questions which would have to be faced in

[1] A. Mills, 'Our Colonial Policy', *Contemporary Review* (June 1869), p. 232.
[2] H. Merivale, 'The Colonial Question in 1870', *Fortnightly Review*, n.s. (Feb. 1870), 7, p. 175.

the tropics. Most of the discussion, it should be noted, was in some-what abstract terms. Merivale, in his article in 1870, and Carnarvon, in his Edinburgh lecture in 1878, were two of the very few men interested in empire who based their theories upon solid practical experience of work in the Colonial Office.

Most of the mid-Victorian writers, and indeed many modern historians of imperialism, have one thing in common: lacking direct experience of colonial problems, they theorize. Historians have been eager to find comprehensive explanations for the origins and development of imperialism. Their conclusions are usually theoretical and controversial, sometimes polemical.[1] The approach of this book is different. It seeks to describe, in as great a detail as the sources permit, one of the elements of imperialism which Carnarvon outlined in his famous lecture. It provides a series of case-studies of the process of decision-making on the subject of that expansion of the imperial frontier in the tropics which was taking place at the moment when Disraeli replaced Gladstone as prime minister.

[1] See Koebner, *Imperialism*, for a survey of the changing usages of 'imperialism'.

PART ONE

The Formulation of Colonial Policy

THE three experiments launched in 1874 appear, at first sight, to represent clear reversals of British policy. After constantly repeating a doctrine of non-intervention, the British Government decided to intervene in the Gold Coast, Malaya and Fiji, and to exercise greater influence there in the future. This expansion, however, came as a response to particular crises in the tropics, not as part of preconceived plans made at home. Probably the most crucial element in this response was the attitude of the man on the spot.

The governor of a minor mid-Victorian Crown Colony, or the consul in a Polynesian island, was a very isolated functionary. In West Africa he would have no telegraphic communication with England until 1886. The cable to Singapore was not opened until 1871, and extended to Australia in the following year. Personal consultation between these representatives and the Government at home was, of necessity, confined to interviews at the Colonial Office during infrequent leaves of absence. The Secretary of State for the Colonies did not travel around the Empire in the nineteenth century.

Decision-making in the mid-Victorian Empire depended on correspondence across half the globe. Instructions, sent out in the form of despatches from the Secretary of State, sometimes took months before they arrived. Major policy decisions had to be made on the basis of factual reporting and advice from the man on the spot a long time after it had been tendered. Thus a governor, if he was energetic, could have an immense effect on the development of policy and he could, and did, sometimes commit the home Government. Moreover, this position of influence was underlined by two important factors.

The first of these was the element of discretion which was deliberately incorporated into his instructions. For, while British policy in the regions under discussion was generally one of restraint and non-intervention, a loophole was always provided for local action in particular circumstances. The loophole arose from the problems of security. British policy was, in fact, one of 'non-intervention — *unless* the safety of the colonies was endangered'. This was a vague, infinitely flexible qualification, which was utilized frequently by the man on the spot.

The second factor which contributed to his influence was the cumbersome manner in which the response to colonial events was handled at home. Major decisions were always rendered in the dignified impersonality of 'the opinion of Her Majesty's Government'. It is worth considering what this phrase meant. Was it merely a seemly constitutional formula which signified a real unanimity of purpose, or did it hide a series of muddled improvisations ? Edward Cardwell once complained to Gladstone, in the thick of one of the crises in 1873, about 'our form of government, which seldom very clearly defines responsibility . . .'.[1] Who was really responsible, one must therefore ask, for the making of British policy in West Africa, Malaya and the South Pacific ?

[1] Cardwell to Gladstone 19 Sept. 1873. *Gladstone Papers*, British Museum, Add. MS. 44120, 135.

1. *Influences at Home*

It would be wrong to assume that the policies which led to the three experiments in the tropical empire were made in the Colonial Office. However able and influential the Secretary of State might have been, and however expert was his staff of civil servants, the forces which moulded colonial policy came as much from outside the Office as from within. The Colonial Office was only the focal point where ideas from many sources were reconciled. At one extreme stood low-ranking, hard-pressed, often not very well qualified, officials who faced the mundane tasks of administration in the tropics; at the other, there was public opinion at home — vague, unpredictable, and usually in reality the opinion of a few interested parties or enthusiasts.

Besides the Colonial Office there were, broadly speaking, five significant sources of influence on policy: the prime minister and the queen; other Government departments; Parliament; interested parties and pressure groups; and finally the colonial governors, officials and special commissioners, who were the men on the spot. These might be termed the 'external' determinants of colonial policy.

THE PRIME MINISTERS: GLADSTONE AND DISRAELI

Gladstone and Disraeli both considered colonial policy in the light of general attitudes which had been formed as responses to the major revolution in colonial affairs which had been accomplished during the 1830's and 1840's with the adoption of free trade and responsible government. Gladstone possibly had acquired a more detailed knowledge of these matters because his nine months of office in the Department of War and Colonies in 1835 and 1845 spurred him to make certain somewhat theoretical studies of colonization.[1] Nevertheless, Disraeli evidently gave considerable thought to colonial affairs too, particularly in the period after he became Leader of the Opposition

[1] Gladstone was appointed by Peel as parliamentary under-secretary for the colonies for three months in 1835, and again as Secretary of State for six months in 1845. His theoretical studies included *Colonies and Colonization*, 1835, and *Our Colonies*, 1855, which are reprinted in pt. ii of Knaplund, *Gladstone and Britain's Imperial Policy*.

in the House of Commons. He became interested in colonies not so much for their own sake, but because he believed, for a time, that colonial issues might provide him with a sturdy stick with which to beat the Russell administration.[1] Gladstone, on the one hand, approved of the revolution which had been accomplished in colonial policy by the middle of the century, while Disraeli, without wishing to reverse it, regretted that the destruction of the old colonial system was not accompanied by any attempt at 'reconstructing' the colonial relationship.

The views of Gladstone and Disraeli on the subject of empire, however, have long been something of a puzzle to historians. Any assessment of their attitude is complicated by the obvious fact that 'ideas' have to be tempered by circumstance once a politician gains office. It should be remembered, therefore, that Gladstone's and Disraeli's acts as premier did not necessarily fulfil the principles they had worked out in their earlier years. Gladstone, after taking office in 1868, tended to concentrate on Irish affairs, although he was seriously diverted in his second ministry by the crises in Egypt, the Sudan, Central Asia, the Niger, the Congo and South Africa. Disraeli, who took office in 1874 determined to restore Britain's position as a great Power, found his chief opportunity in the Eastern Question, although he too was embarrassed by the turn of events in Central Asia and South Africa. Neither premier, then, could, or wished to, treat the details of colonial policy as their major concerns. Nevertheless, their general approach to colonial questions, however much tempered by circumstances, is of considerable interest and importance.

It is remarkable, moreover, that while the two statesmen focused their thought on parallel aspects of empire in their earlier careers, they tended, in most cases, to come to diametrically opposite views. They were both impressed with the 'moral' aspects of empire. To Gladstone this meant a moral responsibility, implied by the possession of colonies, to provide for the extension of good laws.[2] Disraeli, on the

[1] W. F. Monypenny and G. E. Buckle, *The Life of Benjamin Disraeli, Earl of Beaconsfield* (revised ed. in 2 vols.), London, 1929 (henceforth abbreviated to Buckle). See letters to Stanley 17 Dec. 1849 (i, pp. 1049–50), 28 Dec. 1849 (i, pp. 1051–3) and 19 Oct. 1850 (i, p. 1151).

[2] *Colonies and Colonization* and *Our Colonies*, quoted in Knaplund, op. cit., pp. 178 and 199.

other hand, was impressed by the 'moral' effect that displays of British power had on the maintenance of British 'prestige', particularly its impression on the imagination of 'oriental people'.[1] Both leaders saw the connexion between self-government and self-defence. If, for Gladstone, independence was the ultimate destiny of colonies, they could never reach the 'full possession and enjoyment of freedom'[2] until they were responsible for their own defence. This in turn, he felt, ensured that newly independent communities would pursue pacific policies, since 'the burdens of war were the providential preventives of war'.[3] Disraeli considered that when self-government was granted the matter of defence had been treated too carelessly, and he realized that this continuing anomaly had led to serious embarrassment because of Britain's involvement in Canadian defence at the time of the American Civil War.[4]

Both statesmen realized the inevitability of territorial expansion. To Gladstone 'lust for territory' was one of the 'greatest curses of mankind',[5] and in general he set himself against expansion, even though he later found himself presiding over numerous accessions of territory. Disraeli was not alarmed that 'imperial characteristics' were part of the 'destiny of man', and he noted that even the United States had expanded to the Pacific coast.[6] He believed that Britain 'must get possession of the strong places of the world' if she was to maintain her power.[7] Both leaders, again, took considerable interest in the 'frontier' of American history, as the end product of an earlier phase of colonization. Gladstone noticed the democratizing influence of the frontier, and sensed a 'tendency of the colonial system towards republicanising the world'.[8] Disraeli was so impressed by the workings of the North-West Ordinance in successfully including new states on

[1] See his views on the Abyssinian expedition of 1867–8. Buckle, ii, pp. 384–6.
[2] Speech on the Canadian Railway loan, 1867. Third series *Hansard*, vol. 186, column 754. See also his view to the committee on colonial defence, 1861. Knaplund, op. cit., pp. 87–89.
[3] 15 Apr. 1851. Ibid. p. 87.
[4] Disraeli to Adderley 26 Jan. 1862. Buckle, ii, p. 63.
[5] *Our Colonies*. Knaplund, op. cit., p. 193.
[6] Speech on the Address, 1863. Buckle, ii, pp. 66–67.
[7] Speech on the Ionian Is., 1863. Buckle, ii, p. 69.
[8] *Colonies and Colonization*. Knaplund, op. cit., p. 183.

an equality with the original thirteen in Congress that he toyed with the idea of making it the model for a new British Imperial Parliament.[1] Finally, both men were agreed that colonial policy should always remain subordinate to the wider aims of Britain's external relations. To Gladstone the fulfilment of international obligations was more important than the particular interests of individual colonies. Disraeli regarded the maintenance of British power in general as the best defence of all Britain's interests. This, in very bald summary, then, represents what could be called the theoretical differences between Gladstone and Disraeli on colonial policy.

Although during the 1860's and 1870's neither leader made the initiation of new colonial policy his major preoccupation while in office, it is remarkable that they both remained extraordinarily faithful to their own ideologies. Thus Gladstone in his 1868–74 ministry supported the withdrawal of the garrisons from Canada, Australia and New Zealand, tried to halt expansion and military intervention in Africa, Asia and Polynesia, resisted certain Canadian demands in the interest of better relations with the United States, and tried to deny Australians the right to make reciprocal tariffs for fear of violating Britain's commercial treaties. In other words, the themes of non-expansion, free trade, responsible government and self-defence can still be traced in Gladstone's general attitude, even though in the circumstances he very often failed to get his way. On this point historians now seem to be generally agreed.

Disraeli, on the other hand, is still the subject of violent controversy, which revolves, in particular, around the significance of his famous Crystal Palace speech in 1872. Historians who accept Disraeli's own argument suggest that Gladstone's 1868–74 ministry saw the 'climax of anti-imperialism',[2] and that it was Disraeli who checked the ebbing tide by making, at the Crystal Palace, what George Buckle

[1] Disraeli to Derby 18 Dec. 1851. Buckle, i, p. 1050.
[2] A. L. Burt, *Imperial Architects*, London, 1913, pp. 115–18; R. L. Schuyler, 'The Climax of Anti-Imperialism in England', *Political Science Quarterly* (Dec. 1921), p. 537 (reprinted in 1945 as ch. vii of *The Fall of the Old Colonial System*, New York); Bodelsen, *Studies in Mid-Victorian Imperialism*, pp. 7–8, 79; C. D. Allin, *Australasian Preferential Tariffs and Imperial Free Trade* (University of Minnesota Studies in the Social Sciences, 19), Minneapolis, 1929.

called 'the famous declaration from which the modern conception of
the British Empire largely takes its rise'.[1] Bodelsen, however, pointed
out that the remarkable amount of interest in empire which was
suddenly manifested in the years before the Crystal Palace speech,
particularly 1869–70, was a bipartisan movement which grew as a
reaction to the publication of a number of despatches by Granville to
the governors of Canada, British Columbia, New Zealand and the
Cape. The significance of the Crystal Palace speech, for Bodelsen,
lay in Disraeli's annexation of the new movement to the Conservative Party. But, while asserting that Disraeli 'initiated the connexion
between Imperialism and Conservatism', Bodelsen emphasizes that
Disraeli did not himself start the new interest in empire.[2] Professor
Koebner has taken this argument a stage further by suggesting that
Disraeli 'had no particular affection for or interest in the colonial
Empire', that his concern in 1872 was 'new and unexpected', that
the renown of the Crystal Palace speech 'is utterly unjustified'.[3]
'It is quite a mistake', he goes on, 'to believe that the Crystal Palace
speech inaugurated an ideological link between Empire champion-
ship and Conservatism. . . . A distinctive conservative attitude to
Empire questions was scarcely in evidence before the second Salisbury
administration.'[4]

Certain aspects of the new view, however, are open to question, as
for instance Koebner's assertion that 'an attempt to ante-date the
"imperialism" of Disraeli and to understand his pertinent utterances
made from 1872 onwards as the outgrowth of life-long convictions
would be futile'.[5] So much of the Empire section of the Crystal
Palace speech does echo Disraeli's views from the 1830's that a re-
consideration of these earlier statements is, surely, not to be ruled
out.

Perhaps the ground may first be cleared by reviewing two earlier
statements of Disraeli which have misled many writers — his famous
supposedly anti-colonial remarks about the 'millstones' and the
'deadweights'. 'These wretched Colonies will be all independent,
too, in a few years, and are a millstone round our necks' (in 1852),[6]

[1] Buckle, ii, p. 535.   [2] Bodelsen, op. cit. pp. 120–3.
[3] Koebner, *Imperialism*, pp. 107–9.   [4] Ibid. p. 111.
[5] Ibid. p. 110.
[6] Disraeli to Malmesbury 13 Aug. 1852. Buckle, i, p. 1201.

and 'what is the use of these colonial deadweights which *we do not govern*? . . . Leave the Canadians to defend themselves; recall the African Squadron; give up the settlements on the west coast of Africa' (in 1866).[1] Time and again these excerpts have been quoted as Disraeli's view of the Empire before it appeared that it might make a popular movement, when he then made the Crystal Palace speech as a skilful jump on to the now popular bandwagon. What better illustration, runs the argument, of Disraeli's opportunism?

It should be pointed out that both statements referred to the same problem, on which Disraeli had quite consistent views. In general, it was the problem of the anomaly of self-governing colonies for which there were still imperial responsibilities; in particular, they referred to the problem which Canada caused in Britain's relations with the United States. In 1852 the issue was fisheries, in 1866 the Fenian attacks.[2] In both cases the Conservatives were briefly in office and facing embarrassing questions of foreign policy which stemmed from the involvement in Canada, and the possibility of major military expenditure in the unlikely, though possible, event of war between Canada and the United States. Surely a more correct interpretation of Disraeli's meaning could be paraphrased thus: These colonies, in view of our anomalous relationship, are an embarrassment. We cannot go back now on the grant of responsible government, but we can never ultimately defend Canada against the United States of America. In the short run we will have to stand up to the Americans, but in the long run we should let the Canadian provinces become fully autono-

[1] Disraeli to Derby 30 Sept. 1866. Ibid. ii, pp. 210–11.
[2] *Fisheries*: The failure to achieve a reciprocal trade agreement between British North America and the U.S.A. in 1849 brought a long-standing fishery dispute to a head. By a convention of 1818 the U.S. had renounced the right to fish within three miles of British North America's coastline, but the precise nature of the three-mile limit was disputed. Americans took it as a line always parallel to the coast; the British measured the three miles from a line drawn from headland to headland. In 1852 both Govts. sent gunboats to enforce their 'rights'.

  Fenians: In 1866 Irish-Americans of a revolutionary secret society tried to attack Britain, in the interest of Irish freedom, by invading Canada. On 31 May 1866 several hundred Irish crossed the border at Niagara, won the Battle of Ridgeway on 1 June, and then returned to the U.S. See L. B. Shippee, *Canadian–American Relations, 1849–1874*, New Haven, 1939.

mous, since we should not have potentially costly obligations to them when we cannot decide on their policies. The reference to West Africa in 1866 concerned the possibility of quick economies in the budget. The naval squadron was becoming redundant as the export of slaves was finally suppressed, and the withdrawal of most of the West African settlements was something which had just been advocated by a Select Committee of Parliament.

The statements should be read in this quite specific way and not be taken to represent a general aversion to the Empire.[1] Indeed, although Disraeli fully accepted the revolution in colonial policy that Gladstone had welcomed, and persuaded his party to abandon its opposition to free trade and responsible government, it is nevertheless quite clear that Disraeli had viewed these changes at the time they were *made* with considerable misgiving. He refused to join his Tory colleague Adderley's 'Society for the Reform of Colonial Government'.[2] As he watched free trade and the 'commercial principle' supplant 'our colonial system', Disraeli sought, around 1850, some method of 'reconstructing' the Empire. He thought the Conservative Party ought to produce their 'own colonial system', that 'consolidation' of the colonial Empire might become a great Conservative principle.[3] To this end he toyed with two ideas in particular: a customs union with the colonies, and making the colonies an integral part of the United Kingdom with colonial representation in Parliament. Nothing came of these ideas at the time, and the Conservative leader, Lord Derby, remained sceptical. Moreover, after 1860, Disraeli concentrated his thoughts on the rather wider implications of his search for a Conservative imperial principle. He was increasingly impressed by the significance of extra-European developments such as the rise of

[1] See also S. R. Stembridge, 'Disraeli and the Millstones', *J.B.S.* (1965), 5 (1), 122–39.

[2] Adderley invited Disraeli to join the Society's council in Adderley to Disraeli 12 Dec. 1849. *Disraeli Papers*, Hughenden Manor, B/xxi/A/69 (consulted by courtesy of the National Trust). Disraeli called them the 'Colonial Dilettante Society'. Disraeli to Stanley 28 Dec. 1849. Buckle, i, p. 1051. The Society minute-book is in the Birmingham Public Library, *Norton Papers*, 1007 (consulted by courtesy of the Librarian).

[3] Speech on the repeal of the Malt Tax, 1850. Buckle, i, p. 1069; letter to Stanley 28 Dec. 1849. Buckle, i, p. 1051.

the United States, the potential growth of Japan, the Westernization
of China and Britain's power in India. At the same time he sensed
that he was living, by the 1860's, in a sort of watershed of world
affairs. 'An immense suspense in foreign affairs', he wrote in 1861,
'but what questions!';[1] or again in 1862, 'It is a privilege to live in
this age of rapid and brilliant events.'[2] In it he envisaged Britain
viewing her role as a Power in a world-wide context. He argued, for
example, in 1859 that

> The day is coming . . . when the question of the balance of power cannot
> be confined to Europe alone . . . Remember always that England, though
> she is bound to Europe by tradition, by affection, by great similarity of
> habits . . . is not a mere Power of the Old World. Her geographical
> position, her laws, her language and religion, connect her as much with
> the New World as with the Old.[3]

Again, in 1866, he insisted that 'England is no longer a mere European Power; she is the metropolis of a great maritime Empire,
extending to the boundaries of the farthest ocean'.[4] In other words
Disraeli continued to cherish the idea that the Empire had a major
part to play in Britain's role as a Power, and also in the principles of
the Conservative Party, even though he was not very successful, in
practice, in finding a plausible method of 'consolidation' or 'reconstruction' which would make a popular party rallying-cry.

When, however, the movement of interest in empire occurred in
the years 1869–70 — mainly, it appeared, as a response to policies
which were being followed by Gladstone's Government (however
unjustly these might have been interpreted) — Disraeli must have
felt that here, at last, was the possibility of fulfilling his long-standing
dream. Thus ideas of imperial federation, colonial representation in
Parliament, an imperial *zollverein* and a colonial council, which were
mooted by the denizens of the Royal Colonial Institute, must have
found a ready response in a politician who had himself already been
thinking along these lines. At the Crystal Palace he at last found a
fruitful atmosphere for the acceptance of Conservative principles for

---

[1] Disraeli to Mrs Brydges Williams 16 Mar. 1861. Buckle, ii, p. 60.
[2] Disraeli to Mrs Brydges Williams 9 Dec. 1862. Ibid. ii, p. 65.
[3] Speech at Aylesbury, 1859. Ibid. i, p. 1631.
[4] Speech on the Sleswick-Holstein question, 1866. Ibid. ii, p. 201.

the reconstruction of the Empire, and he simply repeated the ideas he had first tried out over twenty years before:

> self-government, in my opinion, when it was conceded, ought to have been conceded as part of a great policy of Imperial consolidation. It ought to have been accompanied by an Imperial tariff, by securities for the people of England for the enjoyment of the unappropriated lands which belonged to the Sovereign as their trustee, and by a military code which should have precisely defined the means and the responsibilities by which the Colonies should be defended, and by which, if necessary, this country should call for aid from the Colonies themselves. It ought, further, to have been accompanied by the institution of some representative council in the metropolis, which would have brought the Colonies into constant and continuous relations with the Home Government.[1]

It is true that Disraeli was not being original — the ideas were not new to the speaker himself; it is true that he was being opportunist, in the sense that he was reviving his earlier ideas at a time when he knew they would find ready acceptance; but it is surely not correct to suggest that this represents a new-found conversion to the cause of empire which was inconsistent with his earlier pronouncements on the subject.

The specific influence of the prime minister on the details of colonial policy was rarely exerted. It has to be emphasized that since the experiments in the tropics were essentially on the fringes of British external policy, both Gladstone and Disraeli had a relatively small part in the ultimate decisions. Although Gladstone's carefully preserved Cabinet papers and his letters to the queen indicate that colonial questions often took a considerable amount of the Cabinet's time,[2] they also show that, while policy in the Gold Coast and Fiji was

[1] Crystal Palace speech, 24 June 1872. Ibid. ii, p. 535.

[2] Gladstone's 'Cabinet Minutes' (British Museum, Add. MSS. 44637–41) consist of papers passed about the Cabinet table during meetings, e.g. lists of members present, items of business discussed, some memos. and drafts of despatches. Although there is little detail on colonial affairs, there are useful indications that certain matters came before the Cabinet and at what times. Further valuable information is in the accounts which were sent, almost daily, to the queen, which are preserved in the *Royal Archives*, Windsor Castle, A 39–46 (consulted by the gracious permission of Her Majesty the Queen).

discussed quite frequently, other parts of West Africa, the Straits Settlements and Malay States (except in one matter relating to Sumatra) were not. Disraeli convened fewer Cabinets than Gladstone, and we know much less, as yet, of what went on in them, his accounts for the queen, for example, being less helpful than Gladstone's.[1] But, although it would appear that colonial topics did not have such a prominent place as under Gladstone, in what Lord Derby, the Foreign Secretary, called his 'bill of fare' for a group of November meetings in 1874, Fiji and the Gold Coast were the most important colonial matters listed.[2] Even so, Carnarvon had to go ahead with the annexation of Fiji without a Cabinet discussion. In the same way, he did not, it would appear, tell the Cabinet that he was going ahead with the Resident system in Malaya, although in 1875 the Cabinet treated the Perak War as a major crisis.

A comparison of the two premiers shows that Gladstone took more interest in the details of departmental administration and he often demanded information from Kimberley when developments in the tropics looked dangerous politically or were likely to cause new expenditures. He admitted, however, to Kimberley that he was rather hazy on many colonial matters, and he once confessed to a naval officer that he always confused Hawaii with Tahiti.[3] Disraeli's only major intervention in the details of frontier policy occurred as the result of a hostile debate in the House of Commons in 1874, when he forced Carnarvon to consider the abolition of slavery on the Gold Coast. Disraeli, however, suffered badly from gout in 1874 and during the early part of his ministry was severely embarrassed by Cabinet divisions over the Ritualist Controversy.[4]

---

[1] While Gladstone's Cabinet met frequently during the parliamentary session, Disraeli avoided meetings in 1874 because of disunity over the Public Worship Regulation Bill. He tended to have an occasional full week of Cabinets when whole meetings were devoted to particular ministries. His reports to Queen Victoria were intended to convey the general spirit or the chief topics of the meeting rather than trouble the queen with minor matters. See *Royal Archives*, A 47–50.

[2] Derby to Disraeli 13 Oct. 1874. *Disraeli Papers*, B/XX/S/936.

[3] *Commodore Goodenough's Private Journal*, i, entry of 18 June 1873 (MS. consulted by courtesy of Miss Cecilia Goodenough, M.A.).

[4] Buckle, ii, pp. 653–71.

THE QUEEN

Queen Victoria took little interest in minor questions of colonial policy, but she conducted a voluminous correspondence with her ministers and certainly made her views on important issues known. She insisted on being informed about colonial affairs, and on occasion rebuked the Secretary of State for failing to keep her up to date.[1] As she considered imperial affairs, three general themes constantly reappeared in her letters. She was '*always* for *keeping up England*', for maintaining the position of a great Power, and for being militarily prepared.[2] She deprecated the arrogant manner of her countrymen towards non-European peoples, particularly in India: 'coloured races should be treated with every kindness and affection, as brothers, not — as, alas! Englishmen too often do . . .'.[3] She was also against taking on potentially dangerous and compromising responsibilities. She was, for example, opposed to the annexation of Fiji at first, for fear of becoming responsible for what she believed was still a 'population of cannibals',[4] and she was against acquiring new responsibilities in West Africa which were likely to lead to wars and loss of life.[5] On the other hand, she deprecated abandoning territory if it meant 'bartering' her subjects. Her attitude was thus governed by generous human impulses.

Her attempts at interference with policy, however, did not influence her ministers, except when she recommended someone for a colonial post[6] or suggested a name for a new colonial possession. It was the queen, for example, who insisted on retaining the name Fiji rather than Carnarvon's 'Oceana' and Disraeli's 'national, historical, stately

[1] Queen Victoria to Carnarvon 15 Nov. 1868. G. E. Buckle (ed.), *Queen Victoria's Letters*, 2nd ser., London, 1926, i, p. 373.
[2] Queen Victoria to Marchioness of Ely 21 Sept. 1879. Ibid. iii, pp. 47–48. See also Queen Victoria to Beaconsfield 28 July 1879. Ibid. iii, pp. 37–38.
[3] Queen Victoria to Carnarvon 24 Dec. 1874. Ibid. ii, p. 361.
[4] Gen. Ponsonby to Derby 12 Apr. 1874 (copy). *Royal Archives*, P/24/99.
[5] Ponsonby to Carnarvon 30 Oct. 1874 (copy). Ibid. P/17/17.
[6] See correspondence with Gen. Biddulph over employment for Capt. Speedy in 1873–4 in *Kimberley Papers*, Wymondham, A/40 (consulted by courtesy of the Earl of Kimberley).

and picturesque' title of the Windsor Isles.[1] Her most characteristic contribution was to suggest amendments to the wording of instructions to governors and commanders-in-chief, and she took a particular interest in military operations, like the Ashanti expedition of 1873–4, as she did in army affairs generally.

THE FOREIGN OFFICE, THE SERVICES AND THE TREASURY

Some of the other Departments of State played an important role in the making of colonial policy. They, indeed, were probably responsible for much of the criticism which was made of the policy-making machinery, since it was inter-departmental wrangles which caused the major delays of Victorian Whitehall. The reason for this was that responsibility for policy was, in many matters, very ill-defined. This was particularly true of questions concerning the South Pacific, where Foreign and Colonial Office roles were generally rather confused. The Treasury and the War Office could easily frustrate a Colonial Office initiative by objecting to expenditure or by refusing to supply armed force. On the other hand, the Foreign Office sometimes advocated more positive action in cases where the Colonial Office was laggard.

The attitude of the Foreign Office to British policy in the three regions was governed, in the first place, by general considerations of foreign policy, such as the fostering of friendly relations in Europe with her neighbours France and the Netherlands, the protection and encouragement of British trade, and the suppression of the slave-trade. In some cases the first of these aims ran counter to the tendency of officials in the tropics to regard the French and the Dutch as inveterate rivals. The same attitude was taken to the Germans immediately after the founding of the Empire. While Bismarck was at pains to disavow colonial ambitions, and the Foreign Office was disposed to accept his disclaimer, British colonists, administrators, traders, missionaries and naval officers frequently displayed alarm at the prospect of imminent German intervention in the tropics.

Apart from such general considerations, the Foreign Office pursued some more particular aims in each area. In West Africa it combined

[1] Carnarvon to Victoria 26 Nov., Disraeli to Victoria 30 Nov., and Ponsonby to Carnarvon 1 Dec. 1874. *Letters*, ii, pp. 358–9.

humanitarian and commercial ends by its efforts to secure the super-
session of the slave-trade by 'legitimate commerce' — a policy with
which Lord Palmerston had been particularly associated.[1] In South-
East Asia the prime aim was to provide for the security of the trade
route to China, and after that to ensure adequate rights for British
traders in the Indonesian islands by negotiations with the Dutch. In
mainland South-East Asia, by recognizing the territorial integrity and
suzerainty of China and Thailand, it sought to check the spread of an
exclusive French commercial sphere from Cochin-China and Cambodia.[2] In the South Pacific, consuls had been appointed to watch
over the interests of British traders and missionaries, and the Government undertook, through the efforts of the Navy, to punish crimes by
British subjects outside the Australasian colonies, but it is difficult to
detect any long-term aims of foreign policy in the Pacific other than
the maintenance of the *status quo*.[3]

As well as these general trends, however, one can detect in the
Foreign Office approach to two of the regions what might be called a
'progressive' attitude, which contrasted sharply with that of the
Colonial Office. The impression is strong that in its handling of
relations with European Powers in West Africa and South-East Asia
the Foreign Office generally followed a policy the objective of which
was the recognition by other nations of spheres of preponderance,
which would simplify the conduct of international relations. In this
way it was hoped that friction would be avoided and that the interests
of British traders could be secured by negotiation.

[1] See R. Robinson and J. Gallagher, *Africa and the Victorians*, London,
1961, ch. ii; J. D. Hargreaves, *Prelude to the Partition of West Africa*,
London, 1963, chs. i and ii; K. O. Dike, *Trade and Politics in the Niger
Delta 1830–1885*, Oxford, 1956; C. Lloyd, *The Navy and the Slave Trade*,
London, 1949.

[2] See C. D. Cowan, *Nineteenth Century Malaya. The Origins of British
Political Control*, Oxford, 1961, prelude; N. Tarling, 'British Policy in the
Malay Peninsula and Archipelago 1824–71', *J.M.B.R.A.S.* (1957), 30 (3),
no. 179; D. G. E. Hall, *A History of South-East Asia*, London, 1955, chs.
27 and 34.

[3] See J. M. Ward, *British Policy in the South Pacific, 1786–1893*, Sydney,
1948; J. I. Brookes, *International Rivalry in the Pacific Islands 1800–1875*,
Berkeley and Los Angeles, 1941; W. P. Morell, *Britain in the Pacific
Islands*, Oxford, 1960, ch. iv.

In certain areas the Foreign Office encouraged the expansion of British influence and sometimes saw fit to advocate the annexation of territory. The Colonial Office, on the other hand, which had all the burden of supervising the day-to-day expenditure and administration of colonies, took a much more cautious view. A vivid example is provided by the case of Lagos, where the Foreign Office, prompted by Palmerston, urged annexation in 1861 against the wishes of the Secretary of State for the Colonies, who did not want any more difficult possessions in West Africa.[1] It should be remembered, moreover, that there was no device like the later nineteenth-century Foreign Office protectorate, which could provide a middle way between informal empire and full sovereignty. Indeed, it was because of the search for such a middle way that the three experiments under discussion were born.

The two examples where the Foreign Office took a much broader view than the Colonial Office would suggest that the diplomatists already wished to see some attempt to 'partition' West Africa and South-East Asia. The Foreign Office, for instance, welcomed the French proposal in 1866 for exchanging the small British colony of the Gambia for some French footholds to the east. This project provided for the drawing of a line across the coast delimiting the British and French spheres on the West African coast, and it might well have led to a neat partition of West Africa at a later date. However, Kimberley, as Colonial Secretary, allowed the opportunity to pass because of opposition in the Gambia.[2] Similarly, in South-East Asia during the 1860's, the Foreign Office accepted the spread of Dutch influence in Sumatra provided concessions were secured for British traders, and it supported the maintenance of Thailand's influence over her tributary Laos and Malay States to north and south, in order to check the spread of French influence. The Colonial Office, on the other hand, here accepted the advice of officials who opposed the Dutch and

[1] J. F. Ade Ajayi, 'The British Occupation of Lagos 1851–61. A Critical Review', *Nigeria Magazine* (1961), 69, pp. 96–105; R. Gavin, 'Nigeria and Lord Palmerston', *Ibadan* (June 1961), pp. 24–27; W. D. McIntyre, 'Commander Glover and the Colony of Lagos, 1861–73', *J.A.H.* (1963), 4 (1), pp. 59–60; C. W. Newbury, *The Western Slave Coast and Its Rulers*, Oxford, 1961, ch. iii.

[2] See below, pp. 104–9.

Thais because they were more concerned with the narrow interests of the colony of the Straits Settlements.[1] In the South Pacific, however, the roles of the two departments were reversed. The Foreign Office took no great interest in the region, and allowed Kimberley, who as Colonial Secretary was naturally concerned with the views of the Australasian colonies, to make most of the major decisions. In one notable instance the Cabinet accepted his advice in 1871 of according *de facto* recognition to a new régime in Fiji, but the British consul was never even told of this decision officially by the Foreign Office for over a year.[2]

If there were differences with the Foreign Office as to the aims of British policy, there were also important controversies over its execution with the armed services, whose aid was frequently needed. The whole problem of imperial strategy and colonial defence involved many branches of government, in particular, of course, the War Office. In 1861 a Select Committee of Parliament on defence expenditure had devoted a good deal of its discussion to the relationship between the self-governing colonies and the mother country, and, as part of the general reorganization of defence which followed, the imperial garrisons were withdrawn from those parts of the Empire. This change was virtually completed during the Gladstone Government.[3] In these discussions the three tropical regions did not figure prominently, although the strategic value of Singapore and Fiji was noted. The defence of the tropical colonies was, in fact, a neglected topic. But the War Office's attitude to these possessions could be of great importance when troops had to be paid for out of slender Crown Colony revenues, or where reinforcements were not forthcoming in a crisis. Then, dispute with the War Office was all too common.

The usual complaint of the Colonial Office was that the military authorities were too wrapped up in their regulations. During a

---

[1] See below, pp. 164–7.   [2] See below, pp. 233–9.
[3] W. C. R. Tunstall, 'Imperial Defence 1815–1870', *C.H.B.E.*, Cambridge, 1940, ii, pp. 827–36; Knaplund, *Gladstone and Britain's Imperial Policy*, pp. 125–30; de Kiewiet, *British Colonial Policy*, pp. 211–12; C. P. Stacey, *Canada and the British Army 1846–1871*, London, 1936, chs. 9 and 10; A. J. Harrop, *England and the Maori Wars*, London, 1937, chs. 13 and 16; R. L. Schuyler, *Fall of the Old Colonial System*, ch. vi.

squabble, for example, which lasted from 1868 to 1872 over the
provision of a small garrison to guard the Straits Settlements, Sir
Frederic Rogers, the permanent under-secretary for the colonies,
scoffed that the War Office only thought about how many sentries
would be needed and 'how many men were necessary to give these
sentries five nights in bed out of six'.[1] The War Office, in fact,
fearful of submitting English regulars to the tropical sun, would only
agree to allow them to do sentry-duty in Singapore if they were trans-
ported in horse-drawn buses. Rogers commented dryly, 'the British
army is not comprised as to be available for the necessities of tropical
dependencies'.[2] Another example of army pettiness occurred in Fiji,
where the War Office would only provide a small detachment of
Royal Engineers to assist the new Government after annexation on
the condition that its equipment was purchased from colonial revenues.
The request was complied with. But when in 1876 the governor
requested the Army's help against some cannibal tribes, the detachment
commander insisted that reinforcements would first have to be secured
from India, the Cape, or Mauritius.[3] When, moreover, this unhelpful
officer left Fiji, his unit carried off the equipment which had been
paid for by the colony. Kimberley also found the War Office very
reluctant to send reinforcements to the Gold Coast in the early stages
of the Ashanti War in 1873.

On the whole, however, matters improved during Gladstone's
Government when Cardwell and Sir Garnet Wolseley began to reform
the organization of the War Office. Many of the younger officers
eagerly rushed forward to volunteer for service with Wolseley in the
Ashanti War. The Ashanti expedition of 1873–4 and the Perak
expedition in the Malay Peninsula of 1875 were waged with forces
(in each case roughly a brigade in strength) far in excess of requirements.

The Admiralty's attitude to the tropical possessions was rather like
the War Office's when it came to co-operation with colonial Govern-

[1] Rogers to Lady Rogers 9 Aug. 1868. Marindin, p. 274.
[2] Min. by Rogers 17 Nov. on Ord to Kimberley 6 Sept. 1870. C.O.
MSS. in P.R.O.: Straits Settlements correspondence, C.O. 273/39.
[3] Gordon to Carnarvon 18 Nov. 1876. A. H. Gordon, *Fiji. Records of
Private and Public Life 1875–80*, Edinburgh, 1897–1912, ii, p. 224.

ments. Service in the West African Squadron was understandably unpopular because of the climate, but although the Admiralty was always glad to borrow Government steamers from the colonies for its expeditions in the Niger region,[1] it was very reluctant to allow naval vessels to help the colonial Government in the Gambia.[2] There were frequent quarrels between West African governors and commodores, and Sir Arthur Kennedy complained that, having to administer possessions scattered along a thousand miles of coast, he was entitled to better co-operation from the Navy than he was receiving. But his remonstrances had little effect: in 1870 he could not even collect the solitary official from Bulama Island when it was handed over to Portugal. The Colonial Office agreed that the governor was 'very much left in the lurch by the Admiralty'.[3] Sir Arthur Gordon had similar trouble in Fiji with naval officers who were over-zealous in their interpretation of regulations about transporting civil officials in Her Majesty's ships. By way of contrast, the Straits Settlements Government found that local naval units readily answered calls for action from the governor; this is to be explained, perhaps, by the strong 'pirate-chasing' traditions of Malay waters.

The influence of the Treasury on colonial policy is difficult to assess precisely, since the department's explicit role in the three areas was relatively small. The Treasury's general influence was, of course, felt in all realms of government and Professor de Kiewiet went so far as to assert that 'It is hardly an exaggeration to say that the Treasury and the exigencies of the British budget have made as much colonial history as the Colonial Office itself'.[4] Yet this view may have been unduly influenced by the undoubtedly hostile feeling which the Colonial Office staff felt towards the Treasury.

The colonies, it is true, had to pay for themselves: grants in aid

[1] Ad. to C.O. 23 Feb. 1871. Sierra Leone correspondence, C.O. 267/313.
[2] Ad. to C.O. 5 Sept. 1872. Gambia correspondence, C.O. 87/103.
[3] Min. by Rogers 23 Aug. on Kennedy to Granville 4 July 1870. C.O. 267/306.
[4] de Kiewiet, *British Colonial Policy*, pp. 8–9. A full study of the role of the Treas. has been made by Ann Burton, 'The Influence of the Treasury on the Making of British Colonial Policy 1868–1880', D.Phil. thesis, Oxford, 1960.

were exceptional, and this rigidity was a source of frustration. Sir Frederick Elliot complained bitterly that

> the real source of the darkness and confusion which pervade all these
> African finances has been the arbitrary way in which, with no reasons
> assigned, the Treasury has for some years overruled by its sheer will
> every successive attempt from this Office to look the affairs in the face and
> make some reasonable settlement.[1]

It has been argued, on the other hand, that Treasury control was only the operation of Parliament's control over the nation's finances.[2] Following this view, and noting that correspondence between the two departments seemed perfectly cordial and routine, one could say that the Treasury merely exercised a wise discretion over public expenditure. There is, however, a rather more fundamental point. Sir John Wood pointed to the crux of the problem when he said that the Gladstonian Treasury was interested in 'regularity and prudent administration' rather than 'policy'.[3] The Foreign and Colonial Offices, which after all were not the major spending departments like the War Office and the Admiralty,[4] were interested in questions which sometimes

[1] Min. by Elliot 20 Dec., on Pine to Cardwell 13 Nov. 1864. Gold Coast correspondence, C.O. 96/65.

[2] Sir John Wood, 'Treasury Control', *Political Quarterly* (1954), 25 (4), pp. 370–81.   [3] Ibid. p. 377.

[4] Statement of Expenditure, 1870–1. *Parliamentary Papers*: *Accounts and Papers* (1871), xxxvii, pp. 44–48.

Services

Army	£14,085,400
Navy	9,767,171
Abyssinia Exped. of 1868	300,000
Credit: war in Europe	2,000,000
	26,152,571

Foreign Office

Office	77,814
Embassies	73,970
Diplomatic service	294,919
Consular service	275,520
Slave Trade	5,747
	727,970

had a global significance, while the Treasury was interested in scrutin-
izing the details of expenditure. Thus to the former a controversy
over the cost of an additional clerk in a consulate was infuriating, when
to the latter it was all in a day's work. The Colonial Office could
hardly be accused of extravagance in the three tropical regions. When
new colonies like the Straits Settlements and Fiji came within its
purview, financial considerations were naturally the first major preoccupation of the staff. The Secretaries of State of both parties
accepted the need for economy. Lowe, as Chancellor of the Exchequer, once wrote to Kimberley: 'I am always most anxious to
meet your wishes because I believe you are really anxious for economy'.[1] Carnarvon insisted, when Gordon was reluctant to reduce
expenditure in the new colony of Fiji, that the governor 'must be
told in the plainest — though of course in very civil — terms that
he must carry out all the proposed reductions'.[2]

Yet there can be no doubt that the Treasury was regarded as the
bogyman of mid-Victorian Whitehall. Maybe the civil servants were
to blame; the Colonial Office claimed that its letters never reached
the Lords of the Treasury.[3] Treasury clerks sometimes received
higher salaries than the rest of the civil service, and they were said
to constitute 'the worst dressed and most highly spirited department

---

Colonial Office	
Office	34,933
Grants in aid	71,624
Orange R. Terr. & St. Helena	6,019
Emigration	14,545
Coolie emigration	1,260
Treasury chest	18,393

146,774

It was because of this distribution of expenditure that Disraeli justified
Foreign and Colonial Secretaries being in the House of Lords, and ensured
that the service ministers were in the House of Commons. Disraeli to
Richmond 18 Feb. 1874. Buckle, ii, p. 627.

[1] Lowe to Kimberley 30 Oct. 1872. *Kimberley Papers*, PC/A/13.

[2] Min. by Carnarvon 28 Mar. on Gordon to Carnarvon 14 Jan. 1877.
Fiji correspondence, C.O. 83/13.

[3] H. L. Hall, *The Colonial Office*, London, 1937, p. 269.

of state'.¹ The commonest complaint was about the tone of Treasury
letters. 'What a peremptory letter from one office to another' was
a typical comment.² One of the bitterest critics was Edward Knatchbull-Hugessen, himself a former junior Lord of the Treasury, who
lambasted the 'petty parsimonious spirit', the 'blundering stupidity'
and 'miserable pettyfogging proceedings' of his former Office.³ He
was particularly incensed when, after the tragedy of a governor who
died only a few weeks after setting foot in West Africa, Kimberley
suggested that the widow might be repaid the £175 stamp duty on
her husband's commission. The Treasury replied regretting that
there were no funds for such repayments, and this led Knatchbull-
Hugessen to exclaim, 'It is this niggardly, parsimonious treatment of
public servants — not always accompanied by the courtesy of language
which might soften the weight of the blow — which discredits the
department which controls the finance of this country'.⁴ Kimberley
usually gave way over small matters, but he disliked the Treasury's
'silly petulancy'.⁵ This was undoubtedly the sort of reputation the
Gladstonian Treasury had with contemporaries.

Yet the only two serious cases of Treasury interference in the
working out of the three experiments under review concerned the
South Pacific, which was the area where departmental responsibilities
were particularly blurred. It was largely Treasury delay, in the years
from 1863 to 1869, which led to the abandonment of an attempt to
provide consular jurisdiction in Fiji. While this was being debated,
the Treasury once took over a year to answer a Foreign Office letter,⁶
and when the matter was eventually revived in 1871 the Foreign
Office had to resort to the shift of getting half the scheme approved
and working before allowing the Treasury to find out that further

¹ Wood, op. cit. p. 375.

² Min. by Barrow on Treas. to C.O. 31 Jan. 1871. C.O. 267/313.
See also W. A. Baillie Hamilton, 'Forty-four Years at the Colonial Office',
The Nineteenth Century (1909), 65, pp. 610–12.

³ Hall, op. cit. pp. 33–35.

⁴ Min. by Knatchbull-Hugessen 18 June, on Treas. to C.O. 12 June
1873. Colonies General: C.O. 323/314.

⁵ Min. by Kimberley 1 Feb., on Treas. to C.O. 31 Jan. 1871. C.O.
267/313.

⁶ F.O. MSS.: Pacific islands consular correspondence, F.O. 58/124,
pp. 69 and 91.

expenditure would have to follow. Much more serious was the Treasury's whole attitude to a genuine attempt to check kidnapping of Pacific islanders by British subjects. In 1862 a Bill to empower colonial governors to subpoena witnesses from outside the colonies had to be dropped because the Treasury would not sanction the expense. Even after some blatant cases of kidnapping and a growing public outcry in England caused the matter to be reopened in 1871, the Treasury tried to pass any costs for prosecutions on to the Australasian colonies. 'This seems to me to be governing an Empire in the spirit of a subordinate department of the Inland Revenue Office,' exclaimed Rogers.[1] In the end Kimberley succeeded in getting the Cabinet to reverse the Treasury decision.

Nevertheless, the Treasury was not really to blame for this attitude of stringency; the drive for economy came from Parliament and the electorate. Gladstone, for example, still tried to resist the annexation of Fiji in 1874 because he envisaged 'disagreeable and distorted phantoms stalking' across the House of Commons in the shape of 'new Votes in the Estimates'.[2] But there was probably some justification in Carnarvon's lament that, when matters seemed settled and the Treasury reopened them on the grounds of expense, then in 'every moment of my available leisure I should be obliged to carry on a controversy with the Treasury on a matter of the smallest detail'.[3]

PARLIAMENT AND PRESSURE GROUPS

The influence of Parliament on colonial policy was not only exercised through its restraint on expenditure. By questions, requests for the publication of correspondence with governors, or by the moving of resolutions and votes of censure, members of both Houses could embarrass the Colonial Office. In a few cases they directly influenced policy in this way. There was, moreover, a general increase in parliamentary interest in colonial questions during this period; Fiji, in particular, provided a lively topic for debate. The period when

[1] Min. by Rogers 2 Jan. 1871 on Treas. to C.O. 30 Dec. 1870. New South Wales correspondence, C.O. 201/560. See below, pp. 241–6.
[2] 3 *Hansard*, 221, col. 1287.
[3] Hall, op. cit. p. 36.

colonial debates emptied the House of Commons was drawing to a close. The three tropical regions sometimes became political issues in the late 1860's and early 1870's. Palmerston, over the Gold Coast in 1864, Gladstone, over Fiji in 1872 and 1873, and Disraeli, over the Gold Coast in 1874, required all their debating skill to overcome the hostility of the House. In some cases parliamentary agitation led to immediate decisions. The day after the Fiji debate of 1872 the Colonial Office pressed a new Fiji policy on the Foreign Office.[1] A motion censuring the Government's Malay States policy by Lord Stanley of Alderley in the House of Lords in May 1874 forced Carnarvon to make up his mind as to future policy.[2] A Commons debate on slavery in the Gold Coast in July 1874 was responsible for the Government's decision to abolish domestic slavery in the colony and protectorate. Fear of hostility in Parliament was one of the reasons why Disraeli's Government dropped the project of exchanging the Gambia with France in 1876.[3] Parliament, therefore, played an important role in the experiments of 1874, in some cases, indeed, a vital one.

The influence of Parliament, however, was really the work of a small group of enthusiasts. By forcing the Colonial Secretary to defend policies which otherwise might have been decided without public debate, they were able to make some impact on the formulation of policy. In the House of Lords the Duke of Manchester, Lord Stanley of Alderley, the third Earl Grey, and ex-colonial governors like the Marquis of Normanby and the Earl of Belmore took an interest in colonial problems. In the House of Commons the leading enthusiasts were men like Sir Charles Adderley, Arthur Kinnaird, Admiral Wingfield and Admiral Erskine, Baillie-Cochrane, Arthur Mills, Robert McFie, Robert Torrens and Robert Fowler, many of whom had resided in the colonies. One of the most successful of them, who provides a vivid example of a minor politician who could force the Colonial Office to reconsider problems in the tropics, was Alderman (later Sir) William McArthur, Liberal member for Lambeth. He earned the sobriquet of 'patron saint of the Fiji Islander'.[4]

[1] See below, pp. 246–50.   [2] See below, pp. 298–9.
[3] See below, pp. 285–9.
[4] Sir Wilfred Lawson in the House of Commons, 4 Aug. 1874. 3 *Hansard*, 221, col. 1296.

The son of a Methodist parson from Donegal, McArthur was a successful woollen-draper of Londonderry who transferred his head office to London in the 1850's, when business with his brother's firm in Sydney expanded. He was a leading Wesleyan and a member of the Aborigines Protection Society. His brother, Alexander McArthur, was a prominent Methodist and politician in New South Wales, and it was his marriage to the daughter of the Rev. W. B. Boyce, president of the Australian Methodist Conference and then general secretary of the Wesleyan Missionary Society in London, which brought William McArthur into missionary circles.[1] This persistent philanthropist succeeded in getting a West Africa debate in 1871 and a Fiji debate in 1872. In 1873 he managed to embarrass the Colonial Office and the Government twice: in February by calling for the publication of instructions for a new administrator on the Gold Coast — before the Colonial Office had written them; and in June by threatening to propose a motion in favour of the annexation of Fiji. In the latter case the Cabinet's decision to send the Goodenough–Layard Commission to Fiji was an abortive attempt to avert McArthur's motion.[2]

The clue, then, to Parliament's influence lies in the efforts of zealots of this kind. In addition to them, sometimes allied with them, were other individuals and pressure groups. Through Parliament, by deputations and publicity, or simply by letters to the Colonial Office, they sometimes played a very important part. The parliamentary zealots usually spoke for some group: McArthur for the Wesleyans, Kinnaird for Scottish Presbyterians, Stanley of Alderley for the Straits Settlements Association. Sir Charles Adderley spoke for the controversial governor, Sir John Pope-Hennessy, a former Tory Member of Parliament.[3] On the whole the pressure groups represented

[1] T. McCullagh, *Sir William McArthur, K.C.M.G. A Biography*, London, 1898, pp. 66–67.

[2] Kimberley to Gladstone 11 and 12 June 1873. *Gladstone Papers*, 44225/49 and 53.

[3] When Adderley asked the C.O. to lay before Parliament Pope-Hennessy's proposal for uniting Labuan and the Straits Settlements, the head of the Eastern Dept. wondered how Adderley knew about it. 'Mr. Hennessy told him,' wrote Herbert in a min. on the question, received 16 Feb. 1872. Labuan correspondence, C.O. 144/39.

economic or humanitarian interests, but each would make use
of the arguments of the other on occasions. Thus, although the
movement for the annexation of Fiji, which was conducted in 1873
by the Fiji Committee, was mainly inspired by humanitarian motives,
it also deployed commercial, strategic, even chauvinistic arguments.
The Straits Settlements Association proclaimed itself as a constitution-
alist body to defend the independence of the Singapore Supreme Court,
but in fact it was a pressure group for the houses which traded there.
Another group, the Gambia Committee, was able to mobilize so much
opposition in 1876 that the Government dared not put the revived
Gambia exchange project to Parliament. This committee was the
usual mixture of missionary, humanitarian, merchant, or simply
'imperialist' elements.[1] Motives were always mixed: 'Commerce,
Christianity and Civilization' was the battle-cry of a whole host of
Victorian special interests.

In assessing how effective these pressure groups were in influencing
policy, it is useful to discover what the Colonial Office thought of
them. It would appear that the department, in fact, considered the
relative weight to be given to pressure groups fairly carefully. A
leading Gold Coast firm, which advocated total withdrawal of government from the Coast in 1874, could be ignored because it was dis-
credited by allegations of trading with the enemy during the Ashanti
War.[2] The Gambia merchants, who fought the idea of cession to
France, were fairly respectfully treated as 'watchdogs'.[3] The Straits
Settlements Association, on the other hand, so persistently attacked
the governor in Singapore that after two years of it the permanent
under-secretary of the Colonial Office was led to say 'the time has
arrived when the Association may be relieved of the supervision of the
Col[onial] Office'.[4] Again, in 1872, he wanted to 'rebel against the

[1] See Royal Colonial Institute to F.O. 12 Jan. 1876. F.O. MSS.:
correspondence with France, F.O. 27/2227.

[2] F. and A. Swanzy supplied arms to Ashanti from their trading-factory
at Assini, west of the protectorate. Hargreaves, *Prelude to the Partition*,
p. 174.

[3] Min. by Kimberley 26 May, on Pope-Hennessy to Kimberley 21 May
1872. Gambia correspondence, C.O. 87/102.

[4] Min. by Herbert on S.S. Assoc. to Granville 31 Jan. 1870. Straits
Settlements correspondence, C.O. 273/30.

tyranny'[1] of the unremitting pen of the editor of the *West African Herald*, London spokesman for discontented inhabitants of the West African colonies. The New Guinea Association of 1875, in spite of 'a varnish of piety', was regarded as little better than 'a filibustering expedition'.[2] Established societies were well known and treated accordingly. The missionary societies met with patience and respect in the Colonial Office, but the Aborigines Protection Society was known to pass on a good number of exaggerated charges. The reception given to financial interests varied from the great respect shown to Mr Seymour Clarke, manager of the Great Northern Railway, who represented tin and telegraph interests in South-East Asia, to Herbert's comment that some New Guinea land speculators were nothing but 'scoundrels'. On the whole, the Colonial Office attitude to this type of commercial venture in tropical lands was: 'Go at your own risk — and don't expect British officials to come and bail you out!'

In two cases, however, non-parliamentary activity by pressure groups played a very significant role. In one, the passage of the Kidnapping Act in 1872, it was attended by great publicity; in the other, the decision to intervene in the Malay States in 1873, it was very much behind the scenes. In the first case, the news of the murder of Bishop Patteson in the South Seas, which reached London in December 1871, opened the gates to floods of publicity after a particularly frustrating year of responsibility-dodging in Whitehall. In less than a month, the Cabinet decided to meet the kidnapping problem with legislation.[3] In the second case, the Colonial Office was virtually blackmailed into intervening in the Malay States. Between 1868 and 1873, promoters in London and Singapore bombarded the Colonial Office with proposals relating to tin concessions in Selangor in western Malaya, and for a telegraph extension from Burma to Australia through the Indonesian archipelago. The Colonial Office gave them a patient hearing but remained non-committal in the face of demands for a statement which might assure investors that their money would be safe in the Malay States. Early in 1873, Kimberley, quite independently of these

[1] Min. by Herbert 30 May, on Fitzgerald to Kimberley 25 May 1872. Lagos correspondence, C.O. 147/26.

[2] Carnarvon to Cairns 30 Oct. 1875, private (copy), *Carnarvon Papers*, in the P.R.O gifts and deposits: P.R.O. 30/6/6, p. 32.

[3] See Ch. 8 below.

interests, decided that civil war in western Malaya called for some
intervention. He was still uncertain what form that intervention
should take when, out of the blue, a letter from Singapore was produced by the London interests hinting that the ruler of Selangor might
request a German protectorate. It is unlikely that this was anything
more than a threat, but it had the desired effect. Kimberley suddenly
viewed the matter with great urgency. British paramountcy in the
Peninsula seemed threatened, and, after a careful study of past relations
with the Malay States, Kimberley produced his well-known suggestion
of the Residents.[1] This is sufficient proof that the letters from cranks,
committees and commercial houses, which are always filed last in the
Colonial Office papers, deserve the careful attention of historians who
seek the springs of British policy.

GOVERNORS, MINOR OFFICIALS AND SPECIAL COMMISSIONERS

Returning, finally, to the role of the man on the spot, it must be emphasized that his influence can scarcely be over-estimated. Ultimate
decisions, of course, always lay with the home Government, its authority based, in the last resort, on the electorate. A governor could always
be censured, even recalled. But once in Government House he, in
fact, exercised the widest discretion. This is well illustrated by a
notorious case where a governor was at cross-purposes with the
Secretary of State — Sir William Jervois's policy of expansion in
Perak in 1875. He launched an ambitious new scheme of government before reporting to the Colonial Office, and when things went
wrong he ordered a brigade of troops into action before his superiors
at home had a clear understanding of what was at stake — and this at
a time when a telegraph to Singapore existed.[2] Jervois was severely
censured, and most of his policy was reversed, but he made a spirited
defence which amounted to a personal insult to Carnarvon. Yet, after
all this, he was not recalled, nor was his promotion jeopardized.

In each of the three tropical regions the man on the spot had an
important influence on the development of policy from 1870 to 1874.
Put quite simply, their technique was to exceed their instructions and

[1] See Ch. 6 below.

[2] It is true that the cable between Penang and Madras did break down at
a crucial moment and contributed to the delay. See Ch. 10 below.

report a *fait accompli*, which was then usually approved. Sir Andrew Clarke's Pangkor Engagement, which provided for the appointment of the first Residents in Malaya, was the most outstanding case. But Commodore Goodenough, who was sent to Fiji to investigate the requests for annexation, fulfilled his job by accepting the cession of the islands — a Reuter's report of which reached London two months before the Report supporting it. General Wolseley was sent to the Gold Coast in 1873 to see what could be done to defeat the Ashantis without a major expedition, but he asked for British battalions before he could have time to try alternative methods. Captain Strahan, governor of the new Gold Coast colony in 1874, when asked to report on the possibility of abolishing slavery, replied by reporting a scheme for abolition, which, in anticipation of approval, he had already begun to implement. Even a minor official could have a far-reaching influence. The 'Resident idea' for the Malay States, for example, received its greatest advocacy from a temporary lieutenant-governor of Penang, who was borrowed from Ceylon while others were on leave, and who turned up in London himself just as Kimberley was changing his mind about intervention. In Fiji, naval officers intervened on their own initiative to keep the peace in 1873 to the extent that they were described as constituting a 'virtual protectorate'. In all these matters the role of the man on the spot was, in effect, decisive.

Colonial governors who were formerly Members of Parliament were another interesting source of pressure. John Pope-Hennessy, a mercurial Irishman, was always the champion of the underdog. As a former well-known Member of Parliament, he had his defenders in the House of Commons.[1] Sir James Fergusson, another ex-Tory Member of Parliament and a former under-secretary in the India Office, missed the active political life while he was governor of New Zealand from 1873 to 1875,[2] and he infuriated the Colonial Office by

[1] See J. Pope-Hennessy, *Verandah. Some Episodes in the Crown Colonies 1867–1889*, London, 1964.

[2] Sir James Fergusson (1832–1907). After serving in the Crimea he represented Ayrshire, 1854–7 and 1859–68, and was parliamentary under-secretary for both Home and India Offices. He became gov. of S. Australia in 1868 and of N.Z. in 1873. For his views on the colonies see Goodenough's *Journal*, i, entry of 28 Sept. 1873; Fergusson to Disraeli, Adelaide, 2 Dec. 1872. *Disraeli Papers*, B/xxi/F/106 and 12 May 1874. B/xxi/F/107.

his open encouragement of Julius Vogel's visionary schemes for expansion in the Pacific. Samuel Blackall, once a Liberal Member, became governor of Sierra Leone. When Palmerston came under fire over West African policies in 1864, Blackall's despatches were designed to provide replies to the criticisms which had been made in the House of Commons, and his suggestion of a unified governorship-in-chief was in fact adopted.[1] Sir Arthur Gordon, who was given the task of building the Crown Colony of Fiji, had been private secretary to his father, Lord Aberdeen, when he was prime minister; he was a Member of Parliament from 1854 to 1857, and was also private secretary to Gladstone in the Ionian Islands. His colonial career satisfied a craving for grandeur rather than strictly material ends.[2] In Fiji from 1875 to 1880 he demanded almost entire freedom of action, which Carnarvon on the whole granted him. Yet all the while Gordon regularly corresponded with Gladstone, who attacked Carnarvon's decision to annex the islands.[3]

Thus, although the influence of certain governors who had political contacts at home, or even had something of an independent reputation, became a little too overpowering for the Colonial Office, one cannot avoid the conclusion that the civil servants spent as much time convincing themselves of the wisdom of a particular governor's own policy,

[1] Samuel Wensley Blackall was Liberal Member for Longford from 1847–51, gov. of Dominica from 1851–7, and became gov. of Sierra Leone in 1862. C. Fyfe, *A History of Sierra Leone*, Oxford, 1962, p. 318. See despatch Blackall to Cardwell 21 Sept. 1864. C.O. 267/281.

[2] It is probable that Gordon would not have taken the Fijian governorship had he not also expected to become High Commissioner for the W. Pacific. In 1876 he told Carnarvon he could not be tempted away from England again except for an Indian presidency, the governorship of Ceylon, the gov.-generalship of Canada or a proposed gov.-generalship in the West Indies. (Gordon to Carnarvon 8 Sept. 1876 (private). P.R.O. 30/6/39, p. 100.) Gordon in fact went to N.Z. in 1880 where he found he had no influence. See D. K. Fieldhouse, 'Autochthonous Elements in the Evolution of Dominion Status: the Case of New Zealand', *Journal of C.P.S.* (1963), 1 (2), pp. 89–93. See also J. K. Chapman, *The Career of Arthur Hamilton Gordon, First Lord Stanmore 1829–1912*, Toronto, 1964.

[3] P. Knaplund (ed.), 'Gladstone–Gordon Correspondence, 1851–1896. Selections from the private correspondence of a British Prime Minister and a Colonial Governor', *T.A.P.S.* n.s. (1961), 51 (4), pp. 62–81.

and then defending it, as they did in thinking ahead and instructing their governors clearly what to do. This is what made the man on the spot the key influence among the many diverse factors which focused on the department which formally was responsible for colonial affairs.

2. The Mid-Victorian Colonial Office

THE British Empire was administered, before 1876, from dilapidated premises, now demolished, which used to close the St. James's Park end of Downing Street.[1] They were, in the words of a distinguished civil servant, 'less like a centre of State affairs than a decent lodging-house'.[2] In 1870, the entire establishment numbered only sixty-seven, including messengers, and the whole burden of looking after the far-flung mid-Victorian Empire was borne by the Secretary of State, the parliamentary and permanent under-secretaries, an assistant under-secretary, a legal adviser and about a dozen departmental clerks.[3]

One of the latter, William Baillie Hamilton, who joined the permanent staff in 1865, later wittily described his first impressions on entering the office:

> I had pictured the Colonial Office to myself as a dignified abode of mystery, excitement, and *la haute politique*, where I should be entrusted with weighty secrets, and where, in plain English, I should be able to 'fancy myself' as an active participator in some of the most important and delicate affairs of State. Instead of this, I found myself in a sleepy, and humdrum office, where important work was no doubt done, but simply because it had got to be done; where there seemed no enthusiasm, no *esprit de corps*, and no encouragement for individual exertion. And, what to my foolish imagination seemed worst of all, I very soon began to realise that the Colonial Office did not occupy the position in the eyes of the world that even I was able to feel that it ought to have . . . The Colonies were simply a bore. They were there somehow, and they had got to be maintained, but at as little expense and with as little trouble as possible. They might now and then provide the subject for abstract

---

[1] No. 14 Downing St. was first used in 1798, but by the 1870's colonial administration had encroached on other available spare rooms in Downing St. D. M. Young, *The Colonial Office in the Early 19th Century*, London, 1961; Hall, *Colonial Office*, p. 48.

[2] H. Taylor, *Autobiography, 1800–1875*, 2 vols., London, 1885, ii, p. 34.

[3] J. Bramston, 'The Colonial Office from Within', *Empire Review* (Apr. 1901), p. 283. In 1870 the legal adviser became a second assistant under-secretary, and a third was appointed in 1874.

discussion, and might even come in useful occasionally for political purposes; but they were not recognised as constituting an integral factor in the life of the nation, and they just had to take their chance.[1]

It was quite true that colonial affairs rarely made headlines. To a colonial governor who had been worried by criticisms of his policy in Parliament, the permanent under-secretary observed that his anxiety was needless as no one would read 'that part of the proceedings *because it relates to a Colony*'.[2] In the years 1870–1, however, new personalities made a significant impact in the Colonial Office. The period, in Hamilton's view, marked the 'beginning of a new era'. He claimed this was the result of Robert Herbert's appointment as permanent under-secretary in 1871.[3] Kimberley's arrival as Secretary of State in the previous year has also been singled out as the sign of a 'minor revolution' in colonial policy.[4] But there were other personalities who had a major part to play. It is worth considering, therefore, to what extent changing personalities in the Colonial Office were responsible for this apparent revival of the department.

There were five different Secretaries of State in the period from 1865 to 1875, but responsibility for the experiments in the tropics, with which we are primarily concerned, lies with Kimberley and Carnarvon, who between them ruled for eight years. As Cardwell, Buckingham and Granville did not conduct a major reappraisal of Britain's position in the three regions they can be discussed briefly.

CARDWELL, BUCKINGHAM AND GRANVILLE

Edward Cardwell has won a prominent place in English history. The Army reforms which he initiated at the War Office from 1868 to 1874 bear his name. But it is now generally forgotten that he laid the

[1] Baillie Hamilton, 'Forty-four Years at the Colonial Office', p. 601.

[2] Min. by Herbert 31 Jan. 1878 on Gordon to Carnarvon 30 Nov. 1877 C.O. 83/14.

[3] Baillie Hamilton, op. cit. p. 604.

[4] G. Greenwood, *Australia: A Social and Political History*, Sydney, 1955, p. 136; see also Allin, *Australasian Preferential Tariffs*, p. 105, where it is suggested that Kimberley's appointment 'reflected a significant change in the course of imperial relations'; and G. W. Rusden, *History of New Zealand*, London, 1883–96, ii, p. 605, who suggests that Kimberley 'earned a new reputation for Downing Street'.

foundations for these reforms while serving as Secretary of State for
the Colonies from 1864 to 1866.[1] At the Colonial Office he impressed his colleagues with his clarity of thought and the hard-headed
and industrious way in which he conducted the affairs of the department.[2] He was, in fact, responsible for two major changes of colonial
policy which are usually credited to others. It was Cardwell who
decided to accept Canadian confederation, and then ruthlessly forced
the unwilling maritime provinces into the Dominion.[3] He also
inaugurated the policy of withdrawing the imperial garrisons from the
self-governing colonies. This was completed in 1871, and made his
military reforms possible.[4]

Yet in some ways Cardwell's popular reputation is not inappro-
priate. He scarcely followed what could be termed a 'colonial' policy
at all; he viewed the Colonial Office's work as a branch of Britain's
domestic administration, to be conducted in the interests of the mother
country. He encouraged Canadian autonomy and colonial self-defence
because Britain's responsibilities were thereby reduced. He was averse
to expansion in Africa and elsewhere, although he did not approach
specific problems in a doctrinaire spirit. Therefore he was important
for the imperial frontier in the tropics as an exponent of the doctrine
of qualified restraint. In 1865, for example, he saw to it that the
Select Committee on West Africa's prohibition of further expansion
was qualified so that minor extensions could be made which led to
more efficient administration and defence in the existing colonies.[5] In

[1] See R. Biddulph, *Lord Cardwell at the War Office. A History of His
Administration, 1868–1874*, London, 1904; G. Wolseley, *The Story of a
Soldier's Life*, London, 1903, ii, pp. 271–2; A. B. Erickson, 'Edward
Cardwell — Peelite', *T.A.P.S.*, Philadelphia, 1959. For a more critical view
of his Army reforms, see B. Bond, 'Prelude to the Cardwell Reforms, 1856–
1868', *T.R.U.S.I.* (1961), 106 (622), pp. 229–36, and 'The Effect of the
Cardwell Reforms in Army Organisation, 1874–1904', ibid. (1960), 105
(620), pp. 515–24.

[2] Marindin, pp. 226 and 253.

[3] P. B. Waite, 'Edward Cardwell and Confederation', *C.H.R.* (1962), 43,
pp. 17–41; C. Martin, 'British Policy in Canadian Confederation', ibid.
(1932), 23, pp. 3–19; J. A. Gibson, 'The Colonial Office View of Canadian
Confederation 1856–1868', ibid. (1954), 35 (4), pp. 279–313.

[4] Schuyler, *Fall of the Old Colonial System*, pp. 228–32.

[5] *Accounts and Papers* (1865), v, p. iii.

the following year, similarly, he rejected a request for the annexation of Basutoland with the injunction that it could not be entertained unless 'some overruling necessity' left no other choice.[1]

Carnarvon succeeded Cardwell when the Conservatives took office in July 1866, but resigned eight months later when he and Salisbury opposed the 1867 Reform Act. The Duke of Buckingham, who then took over the Colonial Office, made no major policy changes. He continued Cardwell's policy of withdrawing the garrisons, in spite of loud protests from New Zealand. He went ahead with the expansion of the Dominion of Canada by supporting the plan of incorporating the Canadian West into the Confederation.[2] His most important act, perhaps, was to persuade the Cabinet that Cardwell's conditions for the annexation of Basutoland were fulfilled.[3] He contributed little towards the tropical empire, taking such a negative attitude to West Africa that he delayed the project for the exchange of the Gambia. In presiding over the transfer of the Straits Settlements from the responsibility of the India Office, he decided to apply the policy of 'non-intervention — unless the safety of the colonies was endangered' in the neighbouring Malay States.

Granville, however, who took over in December 1868, was a much more interesting figure, and remains one of the most controversial Colonial Secretaries in British history. He presided over, so it is claimed, the 'climax of anti-imperialism', and he was the Secretary of State who had to face Carnarvon's famous charge in the House of Lords in 1870 that there were 'whispers abroad that there is a policy on foot to dismember this Empire.... If there is such a policy, in God's name let us know it; if there be not, let it be disavowed.'[4] As Gladstone's closest political associate, Granville probably somewhat elevated the status of the Colonial Office, but accounts by contemporaries differed on his effectiveness as Colonial Secretary. Rogers thought he was 'the pleasantest and most satisfactory chief of those under whom I served', but this was, no doubt, because he delegated many of the

---

[1] Cardwell to Wodehouse 9 Mar. 1866.

[2] Harrop, *England and the Maori Wars*, chs. 13 and 16; J. Galbraith, *Hudson's Bay Company as an Imperial Factor, 1821–69*, Berkeley and Los Angeles, 1957, ch. 18.

[3] de Kiewiet, *British Colonial Policy*, p. 223.

[4] 3 *Hansard*, 199, col. 209.

decisions to Rogers.[1] Kimberley thought Granville was 'slipshod', trusted too much to the 'chapter of accidents', was 'singularly ignorant of the details of the questions he has to deal with' and 'an indifferent departmental Minister'.[2] Indeed, Granville admitted to his private secretary that 'People think I am a very idle man; I am sorry to say it is quite true'. After five years as his private secretary, Arthur Godley remembered 'comparatively little work and a great deal of time most agreeably spent in conversations and occupations which had nothing whatever to do with politics'.[3]

However, Granville's somewhat tarnished reputation as Colonial Secretary is not based on imputations of laziness so much as on the reputation which he earned for toughness. It was argued that the crisis of opinion about empire, which occurred about 1869–70, was a response to Granville's treatment of the colonies. New Zealanders felt he was driving them out of the Empire, Canadians believed he wanted them to proclaim their independence, the Cape Colony Government was offended when he pushed them unwillingly towards responsible government, British Columbia felt that he jostled them, rather too quickly, towards confederation. It is, indeed, true that there are about a dozen despatches in Granville's name which are, in some sense, susceptible to the interpretation that Granville was eager for the separation of the self-governing colonies and the prevention of expansion elsewhere. Yet when Granville publicly disavowed any intention of dismembering the Empire in 1870 he was not deceiving his hearers. The 'tough' despatches which he signed were in every case drafted by Sir Frederic Rogers,[4] and the fact that so many issues came to a head

1 Marindin, p. 264.   2 Kimberley's 'Journal', p. 31.
3 A. Godley, *Reminiscences*, London, 1931, pp. 102–4.
4 The drafts of Granville's chief 'stiff' despatches, listed chronologically, can be found as follows: 21 Mar. and 25 Mar. 1869 (confidential) to N.Z. in C.O. 209/215; 21 May 1869 to N.Z. in C.O. 209/210; 14 June 1869 to Canada in C.O. 42/678; 17 June and 14 Aug. 1869 to British Columbia in C.O. 60/36; 21 Aug. 1869 to N.Z. in C.O. 209/211; 7 Oct. 1869 to N.Z. in C.O. 209/212; 10 Jan. 1870 to Canada in C.O. 42/678; and 25 Mar. 1870 to N.Z. in C.O. 209/216. Granville, far from writing these despatches, sometimes slightly toned down Rogers's language. Rogers in fact admitted: 'The ways of N[ew] Z[ealand] politicians are to me so provoking that I do not quite trust myself as a judge'. Granville, it should be noted, fully approved of the despatches which went in his name.

during Granville's tenure of office was a coincidence. The policies he followed had usually been started several years earlier, and had been endorsed by the Conservatives, including Disraeli's own first Government. When it came to the three tropical regions, Granville's contribution was small. He continued the policy of 'non-intervention — unless the safety of the colonies was endangered' in the Malay States; he permitted the acquisition of the Dutch possessions on the Gold Coast in the interests of uniformity, but in the South Pacific he took very little interest.

KIMBERLEY AND CARNARVON

Kimberley and Carnarvon, the ministers who were so important for the development of British policy in the tropics, between them administered the Empire from July 1870 until February 1878. Kimberley is now beginning to emerge from undeserved, but understandable, obscurity,[1] while Carnarvon is better known through Hardinge's biography, and because he incurred Disraeli's antipathy.[2] Both Kimberley and Carnarvon were among the leading public figures of their day; they both served as Lord-Lieutenant of Ireland, and were also offered the Viceroyalty of India. But neither was of the usual type of Victorian peer who became a party war-horse in the House of Lords. Kimberley was a Whig, who believed in 'that tacit understanding

[1] E. Drus's edition of his 'Journal' and her 'The Colonial Office and the Annexation of Fiji', *T.R.H.S.*, 4th ser. (1950), 32, pp. 98–110; Cowan, *Nineteenth Century Malaya*; D. Coombs, *The Gold Coast, Britain and the Netherlands 1850–1874*, Oxford, 1963; B. Hamilton, *Barbados and the Confederation Question, 1871–1885*, London, 1956; A. Ross, *New Zealand Aspirations in the Pacific in the Nineteenth Century*, Oxford, 1964; O. W. Parnaby, *Britain and the Labor Trade in the Southwest Pacific*, Durham, N.C., 1964; J. D. Legge, *Britain in Fiji, 1858–1880*, London, 1958; E. Thio, 'British Policy in the Malay Peninsula, 1880–1909', unpublished Ph.D. thesis, London, 1956; Chapman, *Arthur Hamilton Gordon*; and Goodenough and Brabourne manuscript journals.

[2] A. H. Hardinge, *The Life of Henry Howard Molyneux Herbert, fourth Earl of Carnarvon, 1831–1890*, ed by Elizabeth, Countess of Carnarvon, London, 1925; see also C. W. de Kiewiet, *The Imperial Factor in South Africa*, Cambridge, 1937, and C. F. Goodfellow, *Great Britain and South African Confederation, 1868–1881*, Cape Town, 1966.

between the leaders on both sides which has much more to do with the
smooth working of our complex political system than superficial
observers, who only see the outside of public affairs, imagine'.[1] Carnarvon was certainly in agreement with Kimberley in deploring doctrinaire partisanship and he looked to the day when colonial affairs,
in particular, would cease to be party questions.[2] On many aspects
of colonial policy there was only a narrow area of difference between
Kimberley and Carnarvon in the crucial period 1872–5.

The respective positions in the Cabinet, however, were somewhat
different. Kimberley and Gladstone understood each other especially
well, and Kimberley was usually able to get his way. Although Gladstone was remarkably conscientious in his efforts to understand the
details of colonial policy, he rarely overruled his Secretary of State.
Between Carnarvon and Disraeli, on the other hand, there was mutual
suspicion, stemming from their disagreement over the Reform Act of
1867. Yet as the Conservative expert on colonial affairs, Carnarvon
was the obvious choice for Secretary of State, and in 1874 Disraeli
seemed to flatter him in order to win his loyalty. He relied on Carnarvon's judgement in the matters awaiting decision in 1874 and told
him that they 'will only give you fresh opportunities for distinguishing
yourself'.[3] But soon after the three experiments in the tropics were
launched, Disraeli began to have doubts about Carnarvon's policies.
Already by 1876 he was telling his friends of 'Twitters' blunders' and
relations between them were considerably strained long before Carnarvon's final break with Disraeli over the Eastern Question in 1878.[4]
Another important contrast between Kimberley and Carnarvon was
their apprenticeship in office. While they both had considerable experience in Britain's external relations, and had, indeed, already en-

---

[1] Kimberley's 'Journal', p. 1.

[2] After W. E. Forster associated himself with the 'imperialist' movement
by his famous address in Edinburgh, *Our Colonial Empire*, 1875, Carnarvon
wrote to him saying, 'it gives me the sort of assurance that the time has come
when colonial policy may be very greatly, at least, taken out of the category
of party questions'. 3 Dec. 1875. *Carnarvon Papers*, P.R.O. 30/6/43,
p. 314.

[3] Disraeli to Carnarvon 12 Apr. 1874 (private). P.R.O. 30/6/11, p. 8.

[4] Disraeli to Lady Bradford 26 Apr. 1876. Buckle, ii, p. 815, and 27
Sept. 1878. Ibid. ii, p. 1292.

countered the problems of West Africa, South-East Asia and the South Pacific on which they had to decide in the 1870's, it is significant that Kimberley had approached them from the Foreign Office, where he had served in Palmerston's Government, while Carnarvon had previously been in the Colonial Office. Thus Kimberley was more sensitive, though not always far-seeing, in diplomatic and strategic matters, while Carnarvon was more concerned with Britain's moral responsibilities.

Kimberley was forty-four when he took over the seals of the Colonial Office on 6 July 1870. His diplomatic career had been widened by a few years as under-secretary in the India Office, and by his two years' service in Ireland.[1] He entered Gladstone's first Cabinet as Lord Privy Seal, where Knatchbull-Hugessen considered him as 'a very good, hardworking man in an idle place'.[2] He was subsequently in all Gladstone's Governments and fulfilled his lifelong ambition when Rosebery made him Foreign Secretary in 1894. Never a popular figure, he was dubbed by a journalist 'a statesman of peculiarly solid and trustworthy type'.[3] Although he was a poor public speaker, he gained a reputation of being the Liberals' 'best man in the Lords',[4]

---

[1] John Wodehouse, third Baron Wodehouse, first Earl of Kimberley. Born 7 Jan. 1826; went to Eton 1838 and took a first in classics at Oxford 1847. First spoke in House of Lords 1858; under-secretary in the F.O. 1852–6; British envoy to St. Petersburg 1856–8; returned as under-secretary in the F.O. 1859–61; resigned on Russell's elevation to the House of Lords in 1861, and turned down Newcastle's offer of the gov.-generalship of Canada in the same year. Special envoy to Denmark in 1863 during the Sleswick-Holstein question. In Apr. 1864 he became under-secretary in the I.O., but in Nov. went as Lord-Lieut. to Ireland, where he remained until June 1866. In Gladstone's first ministry he was Lord Privy Seal until he went to the C.O. in July 1870. Gladstone offered him the Viceroyalty of India in 1880, but he served instead as Colonial Secretary until taking over the I.O. in Dec. 1882, where he returned in the third and fourth Gladstone ministries. He was Foreign Secretary from Mar. 1894 to June 1895, and was twice leader of the House of Lords. Died 1902. The most complete account may be found in the introd. by Ethel Drus to his 'Journal', pp. vii–xii.

[2] E. Knatchbull-Hugessen, *The Political Diary of Lord Brabourne 1858–1888*, iii (1867–9), p. 448.

[3] T. H. S. Escott, *Pillars of the Empire*, London, 1879, p. 174.

[4] A. E. Gathorne-Hardy, *Gathorne-Hardy, First Earl of Cranbrook. A Memoir*, London, 1910, ii, p. 377.

and he was regarded as 'a most powerful member of every Cabinet in which he sat'.[1]

Purely as an administrator Kimberley had very high abilities. The few comments that survive from his contemporaries suggest that he was one of the most efficient departmental ministers of the second half of Victoria's reign. Arthur Godley rated Kimberley a good second best after Gladstone.[2] Sir Garnet Wolseley regarded him as a 'strong' minister, and Lord Dufferin thought he was 'one of the ablest of our public men'.[3] In Knatchbull-Hugessen's 'order of talent' of the Liberal Cabinet, Kimberley stood fourth after Gladstone, Lowe and Granville. Beside Chichester-Fortescue, who thought he was going to get the Colonial Office, one colleague thought Kimberley was like 'a whale to a sprat'. By 1871 Knatchbull-Hugessen wrote in his diary 'as things look now, Kimberley stands a good chance of being one day Prime Minister'.[4] Thus Kimberley's ability undoubtedly impressed itself on all who saw him at work.

Yet at the same time there are indications of a rather cold, aloof side to Kimberley's personality. He despised oratory, and much preferred the man who could sway a 'cold critical audience'[5] like the Lords. Sir Arthur Gordon, who disliked Kimberley, thought he was 'the sort of man to *not* do a thing, all the more because he is asked to do it'. Gordon, on the other hand, was quite wrong when he charged Kimberley with never giving his 'full attention' to colonial affairs.[6] Godley was impressed by Kimberley's shrewd, businesslike application, and his courageous self-confidence once his mind was made up. It is in these qualities that we find Kimberley's contributions to the problems under discussion in this book. He believed that the Secretary of State should see all the important despatches, and he often personally drafted the major despatches to the governors in the three tropical regions. His grasp of detail is well illustrated by some brilliant sum-

---

[1] Godley, *Reminiscences*, p. 158.

[2] Ibid. p. 157.

[3] Wolseley, *Soldier's Life*, ii, p. 271; A. C. Lyall, *Life of the Marquis of Dufferin and Ava*, 2 vols., London, 1905, i, pp. 23–24.

[4] *Brabourne Diary*, iv (1870–3), p. 526.

[5] M. E. Grant Duff, *Notes from a Diary, 1886–1888*, London, 1900, i, pp. 130–1.

[6] Gordon, *Fiji*, iv, p. 316; Chapman, *Arthur Hamilton Gordon*, p. 153.

maries of issues which he made for the prime minister. All in all, Kimberley's conscientious application to business, and his sensitivity to diplomatic implications, played an important part in the reawakening of the Colonial Office, and in particular in causing a thorough re-appraisal of British policy in the tropics. By the end of 1873, however, Kimberley admitted that he was 'dried up' and weary of office.[1]

Carnarvon, who took over on 21 February 1874, after Disraeli's election victory, had first served in the Colonial Office during Derby's short Government in 1858–9.[2] Then, as a twenty-six-year-old par-liamentary under-secretary, he made a mark as a 'very able, clear-headed, cool and remarkably good and quick writer'.[3] In 1859, when Bulwer-Lytton was ill, and Merivale, the permanent under-secretary, was away, Carnarvon virtually had charge of the department. In this way he encountered as early as 1859 the three main problems on which he had to decide in 1874: the question of the annexation of Fiji, the problems of the future administration in the Gold Coast and of expansion in South-East Asia. At this early stage he formed the opinion, as Kimberley did, that the political heads of the office should see 'all that is done'. He tried to follow this rule in 1874, when his private secretary, calling at his house at 10 a.m., would find him 'at a very large table with a mass of correspondence he had already read'.[4]

Thus Carnarvon was quite as conscientious as Kimberley, but he was also more warm-hearted and imaginative. Kimberley apparently

---

[1] Kimberley to Gladstone 22 Sept. 1873. *Gladstone Papers*, 44225/105.
[2] Henry Howard Molyneux Herbert, fourth Earl of Carnarvon. Born 24 June 1831. As a child was taken on visit to Turkey; went to Eton in 1844 and Christ Church 1849, where he took first-class honours. Made a tour of the Levant in 1852; on conclusion of the War made a tour of Crimean battlefields; and in 1859 made his first speech in the House of Lords. Parliamentary under-secretary for the colonies from Feb. 1858 to Jan. 1859. High Steward of Oxford University, 1859. Further travel in the Mediter-ranean in 1860. In June 1866 became Colonial Secretary but resigned after the 1867 Reform Bill. Returned as Colonial Secretary in 1874 but resigned in 1878 over Disraeli's policy during the Eastern Question. Chairman of the Commission on Imperial Defence, 1879. Lord-Lieut. of Ireland, 1885–6. Visited S. Africa and Australia in 1887–8, but declined Rhodes's offer of the chairmanship of the British South Africa Co. Died 1890.
[3] Herman Merivale quoted in Hardinge, *Carnarvon*, i, p. 113.
[4] Sir Herbert Jekyll quoted in ibid. iii, p. 317.

never entertained visitors from the Empire, while Carnarvon's house, Highclere, became a notable centre of hospitality for colonial politicians.[1] Carnarvon was the better public speaker; his performances in the Lords have an attractive modesty of style, and he was known as an 'exceedingly ready, quick and courteous debater'.[2] While Kimberley penned particularly incisive despatches, Carnarvon's tended to be rather rambling and informal by contrast. Sir Arthur Gordon, although a Liberal, much preferred Carnarvon of the two because he treated him 'as a gentleman which his predecessor did not', and because he was grateful for Carnarvon's frequent private letters of encouragement.[3]

Carnarvon was also much more ambitious than his predecessor. Rogers felt he had a wish to 'shine before the public and to distinguish himself in the ordinary sense of the word. His failing was rather too much self-consciousness, and a disposition to be caught in showy schemes.'[4] One suspects, too, that he was more headstrong than Kimberley. His private secretary thought he was 'inflexible' once his mind was made up. It is, therefore, perhaps not surprising that he resigned twice over disagreements with Disraeli. It would seem, in fact, that Carnarvon's personality made him a rather awkward Cabinet minister, while his real enthusiasm for colonial problems made him an excellent choice for the Colonial Office. His genuine devotion to his subject is evident from the large private correspondence he encouraged with governors, and the great care he took with deputations, and in preparing major policy statements. Carnarvon's warm-hearted imagination, therefore, was another factor in the making of colonial policy.

THE PARLIAMENTARY UNDER-SECRETARIES

Turning now to the five parliamentary under-secretaries during our period, we find that only one was of major significance; two were interesting, but uninfluential, figures, and two were completely insignificant.

[1] Escott, *Pillars*, pp. 22 and 173.   [2] Ibid. p. 22.
[3] Gordon to Carnarvon 28 Aug. 1876 (private). *Carnarvon Papers*, P.R.O. 30/6/39, p. 96.
[4] Marindin, p. 263.

W. E. Forster, who served for seven months under Cardwell in 1865–6, was a Yorkshire manufacturer from a Quaker background, who impressed Rogers as a 'rough diamond' and a hard worker.[1] He was primarily interested in franchise and social reform, but as an ardent opponent of slavery, who had once worked with his uncle, Fowell Buxton, he took an interest in colonial questions. He was one of the first Liberals to be associated with the movement for consolidating the Empire which appeared in 1869–70.[2] Although he made no major contribution to the development of policy in the tropics, he took part in the investigations of the parliamentary Select Committee on West Africa in 1865, and when he joined the Colonial Office shortly afterwards he showed himself reluctant to give up any foothold in Africa which might assist in the ending of slavery.

Charles Adderley, who succeeded him when the Conservatives took office in 1866, took the opposite view. He was largely responsible for the appointment of the 1865 Committee and was its chairman. While in office he pressed tirelessly for the abandonment of the West African possessions. It would be fair to say, however, that, although he was one of the most active colonial zealots for thirty years, Adderley did not make a great impact in the Colonial Office.

He was a survivor of the colonial reformers who were associated with Wakefield, Molesworth and Buller in the later 1840's, and was one of the very few of their number to receive major office. He had been secretary of the Society for the Reform of Colonial Government which met weekly during the parliamentary sessions in 1850–1 to plan its strategy of pressure on the Russell administration.[3] He was also one of the most prolific writers on colonial affairs[4] and kept up a constant correspondence with Disraeli, who nevertheless was careful

[1] Rogers to Kate 25 Nov. 1865. Ibid. p. 258.

[2] See T. Wemyss Reid, *Life of the Right Honourable William Edward Forster*, London, 1888, pp. 57–71, 211–16, 372–4.

[3] See Society's minute-book, *Norton Papers*, 1007, Birmingham Public Library.

[4] *Some Reflexions on the Speech of Lord John Russell on Colonial Policy*, 1850; *Letter to the Right Honourable Benjamin Disraeli on the Relations of England with the Colonies*, 1861; *Review of 'The Colonial Policy of Lord John Russell's Administration' by Earl Grey*, 1853, 1869; *Our Relations with the Colonies and Crown Colonies*, 1870.

not to associate himself publicly with Adderley's views. On the face of it, Adderley appears somewhat inconsistent, in some cases advocating abandoning colonies, as in West Africa, in others opposing withdrawal, as in the case of the Orange River Sovereignty; and his constant insistence on the withdrawal of imperial garrisons and the granting of autonomy to the settlement colonies left him open to the charge of separatism. He seems, indeed, to be more in the Gladstonian tradition than a supporter of consolidation, which Disraeli was to make the Conservative ideal.

Yet Adderley thought more deeply on colonial questions than most of his contemporaries, and his general attitude was perfectly consistent when considered in the light of his basic distinction between colonies of settlement and other dependencies. He believed passionately that colonies of English settlers should have complete self-government and that Britain's future relations with these colonies need not be based either on imperial federation or complete independence: 'between the alternatives of dependence and separation lies the real secret of a lasting connexion — that of common partnership'.[1] His placing of South Africa in this category accounts for his support of expansion there while he was proposing withdrawal elsewhere.

On the subject of Britain's possessions in the tropics, Adderley's mind was open. He would judge individual cases on their merits:

> The advantage to England of such dependencies . . . consists in their assistance to commerce, encouragement of enterprise, or in furthering and extending Imperial interests throughout the world.
>
> Such possessions the Sovereign of Great Britain holds for special purposes, and may, if those objects cease to exist, abandon, cede, or exchange at any time, only fulfilling engagements made, and securing interests created. They are not extensions of empire, like national settlements . . .[2]

He believed that such possessions were not suited to the English constitution, and should be ruled by a system of 'autocracy on the spot'.[3] Some of them he had doubts about retaining at all, such as the Straits Settlements outside Singapore, or the West African settlements, which he thought could be disposed of to France and Liberia. But

---

[1] Adderley, *Review*, p. 420.   [2] Ibid. p 195.   [3] Ibid. p. 375.

while Adderley had some influence over Carnarvon and Buckingham on New Zealand and South African issues,[1] he did not gain his way about the tropics while he was in office. By the outbreak of the Ashanti War in 1873 he even admitted to Disraeli that disengagement from West Africa was getting very difficult. 'It looks as if the English were destined just now to open up Africa,' he exclaimed, 'but it's an awful destiny.'[2]

William Monsell was quite insignificant as under-secretary in the early years of the Liberal Government from 1868 to 1870: Rogers had no confidence in his ability to represent the Colonial Office in the House of Commons.[3] Similarly, James Lowther, the Tory under-secretary in 1874, was a poor representative of the department. He was better known as a sportsman, and he seemed to spend his time rewriting Herbert's minutes in rather more rumbustious (and more readable) form. He no doubt regarded Carnarvon's feelings of moral responsibility for non-European peoples as the sort of 'negrophilist claptrap' which he abhorred.[4]

EDWARD KNATCHBULL-HUGESSEN

The most important of the parliamentary under-secretaries in the mid-Victorian era was Edward Knatchbull-Hugessen. He held office from 1871 to 1874 and became one of the earliest Liberal 'imperialists'. As the Colonial Office representative in the House of Commons during the period of great uncertainty about Liberal intentions in colonial policy he built up a reputation as a very able parliamentarian. Gladstone, however, did not share in the admiration of Knatchbull-Hugessen. Thus when he was dropped from Gladstone's second

[1] See Harrop, *England and the Maori Wars*, pp. 297–310; de Kiewiet, *British Colonial Policy*, pp. 222–3.

[2] Adderley to Disraeli 23 Jan. 1873 (?). *Disraeli Papers*, B/xxi/A/124.

[3] William Monsell (1812–94). Appointed Postmaster-General in 1871 and raised to the peerage as Baron Emly in 1874. See Marindin, p. 278.

[4] Min. by Lowther 26 Mar. on F.O. to C.O. 10 Mar. 1877. C.O. 83/15 See R. Lucas in *Dictionary of National Biography*, suppl. ii, vol. 2, p. 483.

Government and given a peerage in 1880, he turned against the Liberals. In 1885 he was one of the first Whigs to go over to Salisbury as a result of Gladstone's withdrawals in South Africa and the Sudan.[1]

Knatchbull-Hugessen entered the Colonial Office in January 1871 feeling that he had 'not been well treated'.[2] As a Whig protégé of Palmerston he had received his first office in 1859 as a junior Lord of the Treasury.[3] His duties were those of an assistant Whip in the House of Commons; so, not satisfied with this lowly office, he frequently threatened to resign. Although Gladstone, as Chancellor of the Exchequer, gave him some responsibilities in the Treasury in 1865, and Russell appointed him parliamentary under-secretary for the Home Office in 1866 (where he returned under Gladstone in 1868), Knatchbull-Hugessen felt very aggrieved that many other politicians were promoted above his head. When Bright's resignation from the Board of Trade in December 1870 reawakened his hopes, he suggested to Gladstone that he should be entrusted with the responsibility of a Government department in the House of Commons. But all Gladstone could offer was the Colonial Office under-secretaryship, which was accepted only grudgingly as it was not coupled with a Privy Councillorship.[4]

'One reason for my acceptance', he recorded, 'was friendship for, and good opinion of, Kimberley, with whom I am sure to do well.'[5] He later wrote that 'During my whole tenure of office under Kimberley no two men could get on better'.[6] Although their relationship was cordial and, as we shall see, fruitful, Kimberley was strangely silent about Knatchbull-Hugessen. When, however, in 1880 the latter attacked the Government which had elevated him during his first session in the House of Lords, Kimberley was furious.[7]

---

[1] *The Political Diary of Lord Brabourne 1858–1888* (consulted by courtesy of Lord and Lady Brabourne) is a bound typescript in 8 vols. compiled by Lord Brabourne in the 1880's from his 'Political Journal' (which, unfortunately, he did not keep in the years 1870–4 because of pressure of business), his 'ordinary diary', his correspondence and other memos. See ibid. vii (1882–5), pp. 1225–6, for his change of party.

[2] Ibid. iv (1870–3), p. 516.   [3] Ibid. i (1857–65), p. 46.

[4] See correspondence in *Gladstone Papers*, 44111, 24–46, and *Brabourne Diary*, iv, pp. 506–16.

[5] Ibid. iv, p. 519   [6] Ibid. iv, p. 583.

[7] Ibid. vi (1880–1), p. 948.

Beside Kimberley and Carnarvon, Knatchbull-Hugessen was of much lesser stature. But he had had plenty of experience as a junior minister in the 1860's; he was an effective under-secretary both inside the Colonial Office and in Parliament in the early 1870's, and his subsequent political demise is, on the face of it, surprising. It certainly stemmed from Gladstone's attitude to him, but probably not, as Knatchbull-Hugessen himself later suspected, because of mere personal antipathy.

Knatchbull-Hugessen had a reputation for being a political wag — as those who suffer his puns in the Colonial Office files have cause to know. When *Vanity Fair* published a hilarious cartoon of him in 1870, he was dubbed 'a promising apprentice . . . an adept in the genial and jovial intercourse which does so much to hold parties together'.[1] He also published several volumes of fairy stories while serving in Gladstone's Government and later believed that his chances of high office were thereby damaged because Gladstone considered 'writing Fairy Tales for children as "frivolous"'.[2] He had also contributed, during the years 1866–8, to *The Owl*, a journal which he regarded as 'good natured and never vulgar',[3] but which was, in fact, a rather daring London gossip-sheet. Gladstone's verdict on Knatchbull-Hugessen was that he was 'a good fellow, a clever fellow, a very good speaker; But he . . . has never earned a reputation as a hard worker'.[4] His disapproval of Knatchbull-Hugessen was, however, over much more fundamental issues than these.

Knatchbull-Hugessen became genuinely interested in colonial affairs. He regarded the job of a subordinate member of the Government as 'no sinecure'.[5] He was sensitive to the feeling of the House of Commons on the Empire, and on more than one occasion he embarrassed the prime minister by identifying himself in the House with the movement of imperial sentiment which had developed in the years 1869–71. Although Granville had denied categorically that the Liberals had any intention of abandoning the colonies, Knatchbull-Hugessen realized that the colonial policy of Gladstone's ministry was still being watched vigilantly by the colonial zealots in Parliament,

---

[1] *Vanity Fair*, 11 June 1870, p. 331.
[2] *Brabourne Diary*, vi, p. 927.   [3] Ibid. ii (1866–9), p. 353.
[4] Gladstone to Granville 24 Oct. 1873 (copy). *Gladstone Papers*, 44543/3.   [5] *Brabourne Diary*, iv, p. 481.

especially Robert McFie, the Member for Leith Burghs. It is easy to understand, moreover, that Gladstone's own position must have appeared somewhat equivocal to them. He honestly endorsed all the denials that his Government wanted to dismember the Empire, and in the case of the Gambia, the one colony which the Government tried to get rid of, he personally promised the House of Commons that the project would be put to Parliament. On the other hand, Gladstone's general ideas about empire, as we have seen, included a belief in the inevitability and desirability of colonial independence. Most of the leading members of his Cabinet subscribed to this view, although they believed that the process should be gradual and that their role was to ensure that separation was amicable.

Therefore Gladstone certainly did not sympathize with that part of the new movement of imperial interest which sought to define the colonial relationship, or to 'consolidate' the ties of empire. Knatchbull-Hugessen, who had the task of defending the Government's colonial policy in the House of Commons, received clear proof of Gladstone's attitude in 1871.

The occasion for this was a debate on 12 May 1871 when McFie called for the appointment of a royal commission to consider how the 'most cordial inter-connection' between Britain and the colonies might be created.[1] Knatchbull-Hugessen as the spokesman for the Colonial Office began his rebuttal by stating the Liberal policy clearly: 'The Government wished to retain the Colonies; but they wished to retain them bound to this country by ties of kindred and affection'. But in his next sentence he declared, 'They were sometimes taunted with having told the Colonies that they might go free if they pleased'; and this was greeted with loud cheers from the Conservative benches. Knatchbull-Hugessen said he understood those cheers. By the end of his speech he had so far associated himself with the new movement as to say 'there had sometimes floated before his mind a vision of a confederation of all English speaking people'.[2] Gladstone was obviously shocked to hear this from a member of his own Government, and he immediately told him in no uncertain terms. 'I made a speech which I supposed was successful — as it was much cheered,' Knatchbull-Hugessen recorded in his diary:

---

[1] 3 *Hansard*, 206, cols. 750 ff.   [2] Ibid. col. 767.

Gladstone, however, is not fond of speeches in favour of our Colonial empire, and remarked to me that I had spoken 'an excellent bit of *bunkum*'. Not very encouraging! Of late years there has been a cry, by no means just, that 'the liberals would like to give up the Colonies', which cry I set myself to disprove wherever and whenever I can, for it is mischievous and untrue as regards the great body of the Liberal Party. But if sentiments of loyalty to the Colonial Connection are termed 'Bunkum' by the Liberal Prime Minister, the task will be difficult.[1]

But Knatchbull-Hugessen was not deterred by Gladstone's rebuff. He knew that most of the charges which were being made about the Government's colonial policy were wrong, but he also realized that Gladstone's attitude contributed to the suspicions. They were the suspicions which Disraeli began to use for political advantage in his Manchester Free Trade Hall speech on 3 April 1872, when he suggested that the colonies would 'in due time, exercise their influence over the distribution of power'.[2] Knatchbull-Hugessen's aim was to nullify Disraeli's advantage as much as possible.

In the month after Disraeli's speech, an incident of even greater significance occurred in the House of Commons. McFie tried once again, on 31 May 1872, to get a royal commission on colonial policy. Knatchbull-Hugessen replied by hinting that the colonial zealots did their cause a disservice by their constant repetitions. But if the Leader of the Opposition were to raise general questions of colonial policy, Knatchbull-Hugessen suggested the House might listen with more respect. 'Hit us fairly in the face here; but don't stab us in the back at Conservative banquets.' He reminded the House that the Government's policy was to strengthen Britain's links with the colonies. He had stated it clearly in answer to McFie's first motion. The prime minister had then been sitting next to him and would have

---

[1] *Brabourne Diary*, iv, p. 558. Gladstone expressed the same view in 1873 when, during the Post Office scandal, Knatchbull-Hugessen was briefly considered as a possible Postmaster-General. Gladstone was attracted by the possibility of Granville's brother, Lord Edward Leveson-Gower, as under-secretary for the colonies since he would not 'talk the Bunkum in which, on that subject, the House too much delights'. A. Ramm, 'The Political Correspondence of Mr. Gladstone and Lord Granville 1868–1876', *C.S.*, 3rd ser. (1952), LXXXII, ii, p. 418.

[2] Buckle, ii, 531.

C 2

corrected him if he was wrong. He knew that the speech had been popular in the colonies.

Who was Knatchbull-Hugessen trying to challenge — Gladstone or Disraeli? The prime minister had not corrected him in public during the 1871 debate, but privately had called the speech 'bunkum'. Now Knatchbull-Hugessen not only repeated his views, but announced that he would be the last man to stay in a Government which followed a policy of 'separation'. He would sooner join the backbenches behind Disraeli, he declared, than represent such a policy from the Treasury bench.[1] Neither Gladstone nor Disraeli contributed to the debate. But one senses that Knatchbull-Hugessen was hinting that the prime minister should stop equivocating, and that Disraeli should lay his cards on the table. Three weeks later, in the Crystal Palace speech of 24 June 1872, Disraeli came out into the open. Possibly Knatchbull-Hugessen's invitation in the House of Commons may have prompted him to elaborate on some of the hints he had made at Manchester.

Gladstone's feelings about Knatchbull-Hugessen may be imagined. Their rift became public only a day after the Crystal Palace speech. In the House of Commons William McArthur called for a protectorate in the Fiji Islands and also complimented Disraeli's speech at the Crystal Palace. Knatchbull-Hugessen once again showed his sympathy with the Government's critics while he was supposed to be putting his party's case. As *The Times* commented next day, 'officially bound to curse he ended up by nearly blessing' McArthur's motion. This time Gladstone had to intervene in the debate to clarify the Government's policy.[2] After these incidents Gladstone's mistrust of Knatchbull-Hugessen is understandable — even if the prime minister's failure to appreciate the positive side of his tactics may be criticized.

Knatchbull-Hugessen's contribution to colonial policy was not confined to his attempts to quieten opposition in Parliament.[3] Within the Colonial Office he took issue with Kimberley on the question of

---

[1] 3 *Hansard*, 211, cols. 933–4.

[2] For the Fiji debate, 25 June 1872, see 3 *Hansard*, 212, cols. 19–217. See below, pp. 247–50.

[3] For complimentary comments on his ability see S. Childers, *Life and Correspondence of Rt. Hon. Hugh C. E. Childers, 1827–1896*, London, 1901, i, pp. 211–12.

the frontier in the tropics. In the years 1871–3 he repeatedly challenged the policy of 'non-intervention — except in emergencies'. Kimberley at first appeared to disregard Knatchbull-Hugessen's lengthy
and insistent advice. In fact, in the crucial summer of 1873, the latter practically ceased to offer any and contemplated resigning again.[1]

One thing stands out clearly from their disagreements. Knatchbull-
Hugessen stated more clearly and persistently, almost passionately,
one feels, than anyone else the British dilemma in West Africa,
Malaya and the South Pacific. Briefly, his contention was this:
Britain was 'involved', one way or the other, in these tropical lands.
She had never followed a consistent policy in the past; still worse, she
had never made it clear to the African, Malay or Fijian populations
what her real intentions were. She now faced a choice between
complete withdrawal or the assumption of further responsibilities and
the pursuit of a consistent policy. He believed that failure to resolve
this dilemma had created a form of stalemate — 'since the Policy of
HM's Govt. would not allow for extension and Public Opinion would
certainly not [permit] . . . abandonment'.[2] Knatchbull-Hugessen's
point was this: 'It is idle for us to halt between two opinions'.[3] He
repeatedly pressed this view in the minutes he prepared from 1871 to
1873 on the issues relating to the three tropical regions. Sometimes
he wrote at great length; at other times he summed up his opinions
with glacial brevity. Eventually Kimberley accepted Knatchbull-
Hugessen's view. In 1873 he admitted that in West Africa, for
example, 'we have fallen between two stools'.[4] The persistence of
Knatchbull-Hugessen therefore played an important part in the new
approach of the Colonial Office in the early 1870's.

THE PERMANENT OFFICIALS

It is difficult to generalize about the role of the civil servants. They
frequently appeared in the guise of defenders of governors who had

[1] See Kimberley to Knatchbull-Hugessen 10 Aug. 1873: 'I trust you
are not serious in talking of making your bow'. *Brabourne Diary*, iv, p. 639.
[2] Min. by Knatchbull-Hugessen 12 Jan., on Goldsworthy to Kimberley
4 Jan. 1873. C.O. 147/29.
[3] Min. 6 Aug., on Simpson to Pope-Hennessy 5 June 1872. C.O. 87/102.
[4] Min. by Kimberley 23 Sept. on Cooper to administrator-in-chief 29 July
1873. C.O. 87/105.

incurred the displeasure of the Secretary of State. But apart from
this, the general attitude and prejudices of the permanent under-
secretaries in particular are worth investigating, for the Victorian
Colonial Office was served, with remarkable continuity, by some of
the most notable civil servants of their day. For over half a century
the office was held by only four men — Sir James Stephen (1836–47),
Herman Merivale (1847–59), Sir Frederic Rogers (1860–71) and
Robert Herbert (1871–92). Almost as influential were the assistant
under-secretaries, Sir Henry Taylor and Sir Frederick Elliot. As
Baillie Hamilton dated his 'new era' from the change-over from
Rogers to Herbert, some attention must be paid to their attitudes.

ROGERS AND HERBERT

Rogers was by training a lawyer and a scholar. After Eton and
Oxford and a call to the Bar in 1831, he became a Fellow of Oriel in
1840. He was a Liberal and High Churchman, and a close friend of
Gladstone and Newman.[1] For a time he was a leader writer on
The Times. In 1844, at the age of thirty-three, he received from
Gladstone his first official appointment as Registrar of Joint Stock
Companies. He first joined the Colonial Office in 1846 but was
quickly transferred to the Land and Emigration Board, from which
he also advised the Colonial Office on legal matters. He returned to
Downing Street as permanent under-secretary in 1860. When he
retired in 1871 it was said that 'he probably had no equal among civil
servants'. Lord Kilbracken described him as 'a man of extra-ordinary
intellectual power, possessing an immense knowledge of a great variety
of subjects; a delightful companion, and, with all this, modest and
humble to a fault'.[2] Modesty was not always a quality so evident
in his official work. According to Knatchbull-Hugessen, Rogers
'scarcely ever wrote a despatch . . . without administering a snub
to some unhappy Colony'.[3] George Higinbotham, the Australian

---

[1] For the fullest account of Rogers see W. P. N. Tyler, 'Sir Frederic Rogers,
Permanent Under-Secretary at the Colonial Office, 1860–1871', unpublished
Ph.D. thesis, Duke, N. Carolina, 1962. See also Marindin; J. Morley, *The
Life of William Ewart Gladstone*, London, 1903, i, pp. 54, 59 and 307;
Godley, *Reminiscences*, p. 74.

[2] Godley, op. cit. p. 74.   [3] *Brabourne Diary*, iv, p. 669.

politician, was particularly irate, and suggested that while the Australian Governments thought they were self-governing he believed they were really ruled by 'a person named Rogers. He is the Chief Clerk in the Colonial Office.'[1] For this reason Higinbotham proposed in 1869 that the colonial Governments should by-pass the Colonial Office by communicating directly with the British Government. Rogers's lengthy and scarcely legible minutes show the cold analysis of a legal mind; even when he had nothing to suggest he still took a few pages of foolscap to say so. But Rogers was clearly actuated by firmly held convictions.

It is perhaps significant that the three experiments in the tropics were begun after Rogers had retired. He was what came to be called a 'separatist', convinced that the colonies of settlement were destined for independence. The only 'moral difficulty' in this for him was the question of 'the protection of coloured races, who are always exterminated by Anglo-Saxons in temperate climates, and yet are incapable of receiving more than an illusory share in the Government'.[2] This was one of the very problems which arose in the three areas under discussion and Rogers had obviously not reached any decided conclusions about resolving it. However, it was evident from his comments before retirement that, although he would have preferred territory close to British colonies to be acquired by Britain rather than other nations, he was generally opposed to taking on further responsibilities in the tropics. Several years after Carnarvon had inaugurated the three experiments, Rogers wrote, 'I still look with a certain distrust on our accessions of responsibility in West Africa, Fiji, the Straits and South Africa'.[3] His experience in the administration of colonial affairs made him unprepared for the new tropical empire which forms the subject of this book.

Robert Herbert's background was quite different, and left him more adaptable in the face of new problems. He went to Eton and Oxford with his cousin, Carnarvon, and after a promising Oxford career where he took a second in classics and gained an All Souls fellowship, he

---

[1] E. E. Morris, *A Memoir of George Higinbotham*, London, 1895, p. 183.

[2] Autobiographical fragment, written about 1885. Marindin, p. 295.

[3] Blachford to Taylor 28 May 1877. Ibid. p. 380. It is difficult to agree with Knaplund (*Gladstone and Imperial Policy*, p. 134) that Rogers, like Knatchbull-Hugessen, 'lent a willing ear to requests for new annexation'.

became Gladstone's secretary in 1855. The break in this conventional career came in 1858 when he went out to the new colony of Queensland as Colonial Secretary. With the immediate grant of responsible government in 1860 Herbert received a seat in the Legislative Assembly and he was later premier of the colony. Returning home in 1867 he spent two years at the Board of Trade and joined the Colonial Office in 1870 as assistant under-secretary. He succeeded Rogers in 1871.

Herbert was the first permanent under-secretary with personal experience of the Empire east of Suez, and Knatchbull-Hugessen felt that in his relations with the self-governing colonies Herbert did 'as much good as his predecessor did harm'.[1] But his experience also made him more flexible than Rogers on questions of expansion in the tropics. It would be wrong simply to dub him as an 'expansionist',[2] but in the case of New Guinea, in particular, his first-hand experience in Queensland made him eager for annexation. He fully accepted the 1874 experiments elsewhere: after Sir Andrew Clarke's negotiations with the Malay States he wrote, 'We are now obliged to interfere frequently on the [Malayan] Coast', and after the Ashanti War was over in the Gold Coast he confessed, momentarily, that he was 'not at all sure that the annexation of the whole Protectorate' might not be necessary.[3] This colonial experience and interests, combined with flexibility of outlook, imperturbable resolution and great personal charm, made Herbert an important force within the Colonial Office. A contemporary called him 'the ideal colleague' to whom 'the hill Difficulty does not exist'.[4] Another was impressed by Herbert's coolness:

> officially he does not know the meaning of the words hurry or discomposure. Tidings of colonial revolution might arrive without causing him visible excitement and would simply suggest themselves as incidents — all coming in a day's work — each to be dealt with in its proper turn.[5]

---

[1] *Brabourne Diary*, iv, p. 670.

[2] R. B. Pugh, 'The Colonial Office, 1801–1925', *C.H.B.E.* iii, p. 744, suggests Herbert was 'the first expansionist Under-Secretary'.

[3] Min. by Herbert 2 May on Clarke to Kimberley 24 Feb. 1874. Straits Settlements correspondence, C.O. 273/75; min. by Herbert 17 Apr. on Fitzgerald to Carnarvon 13 Apr. 1874. C.O. 96/114.

[4] Grant Duff, *Notes from a Diary*, ii, p. 337.

[5] Escott, *Pillars*, p. 121.

His contribution to the problems under review was large, especially in the affairs of the South Pacific. Here his flexibility played an important part in the search for a suitable policy on the frontier in the tropics.

Besides the under-secretaries the only other influential members of the Colonial Office staff were the principal clerks responsible for correspondence with regional divisions — the so-called 'heads of departments'. They, and a few others, were sometimes influential in particular cases where their specialized study led them to carefully argued conclusions. The internal organization of the office went through a significant change at this time.[1] The individuals most concerned with the changes in the tropics were Charles Cox (Eastern Department), William Dealtry (Australian and North American), Sir George Barrow (African, until he retired in 1872) and two rising young clerks in the African Department, Augustus Hemming and Edward Fairfield. Two examples of the way in which their studies could weigh heavily with the Secretary of State may be seen in the effect of Fairfield's Gold Coast memoranda in 1874,[2] and a New Guinea memorandum in 1875 by William Malcolm,[3] who was the recently appointed third assistant under-secretary. It was only in 1872, however, as a result of Herbert's adoption of the Northcote–Trevelyan principle, that minute-writing was not restricted to the senior level of the office. Hemming, who joined the office in the

[1] With the transfer of the Straits Settlements from the I.O. in 1867, and the confederation of Canada at the same time, it was possible to regroup the four geographic depts. (West Indies, North American, Mediterranean and African, and Australian and Eastern) as follows: West Indies, North American and Australian, African and Mediterranean, and Eastern. When Taylor, who had long handled West Indian business, retired in 1872, Herbert organized the office into two depts. only (apart from a big 'General' dept. for financial, legal, parliamentary business, etc.): West Indian, Eastern and North American ; and Australian, African and Mediterranean. In 1874 the work was again split into three: West Indian and Eastern, North American and Australian, and African and Mediterranean. In 1879 under Hicks-Beach it was split into four again: Eastern, West Indian, North American and Australian, and African and Mediterranean. The most important trends of the period were (1) the emergence of the separate Eastern Dept., (2) the decline in the size of the West Indian Dept., and (3) the increase in African business. For civil service aspects of the C.O. see Pugh, *C.H.B.E.* iii, pp. 739–45. For Rogers's contribution see Tyler, op. cit. pp. 33–37.

[2] See below, pp. 280–1.   [3] See below, pp. 349–50.

hey-day of Taylor and Rogers, recalled that 'the idea that a youngster from public school or university or even from a Board school, presuming to spoil official paper and waste official time by the expression of his crude and undigested "views" and "suggestions" is enough to make these eminent men turn uneasily in their graves'.[1]

In short, 'the stagnant waters of the Colonial Office were stirred up by an occasional breath of life' in the early 1870's, not simply, as Baillie Hamilton claimed, by Herbert's advent, but by a combination of Kimberley's conscientiousness, Knatchbull-Hugessen's persistence, Carnarvon's warm-hearted imagination, Herbert's flexibility, the detailed studies of up-and-coming clerks like Fairfield, as well as the urgency of the crises on the frontiers of empire in the tropics.

ADMINISTRATIVE METHODS

Before these crises, and the official response to them, are examined, there are four general characteristics of the Colonial Office's methods and attitude which are worthy of note.

The first is the prevalent Victorian method of policy-making by 'inquiry and report'. The obvious technique for putting off a decision, or for satisfying a sincere lack of information, was to instruct a governor or special commissioner to visit the scene of action to inquire and report. That is why in the three regions the man on the spot had such importance. Their significance was heightened, moreover, by a habitual tendency of the men on the spot to prejudge and exceed their instructions. In the three most important cases of officers specially commissioned to inquire and report in 1873 — Wolseley in the Gold Coast, Clarke in Malaya and Goodenough in Fiji — these officers did exactly that; they acted first and reported afterwards.

Secondly, it is clear that the Colonial Office imperfectly understood the complex local history of the three tropical regions. Because of the remoteness of the areas, and because Downing Street depended for its information on governors' despatches, the selectiveness of a governor's information — even a delay in the mails — would produce a heightened sense of crisis. Information about the Malay States, in particular, was kept from the Colonial Office by a succession of governors

[1] A. W. L. Hemming, 'The Colonial Office and the Crown Colonies', *Empire Review* (July 1906) (66), p. 350.

until major difficulties had arisen. On the other hand, officials near the scene of trouble were often prone to panic. Australian politicians were alarmed by reports of 'anarchy' or 'imminent foreign intervention' in Fiji. Most of the military interventions of the period, in Selangor (1871), the Gold Coast and Ashanti (1873–4), and Perak (1875) were in much greater force than sober military appreciation might have indicated. The exception was Sir Arthur Gordon's 'little war' in the Fijian mountains in 1877, when he deliberately avoided the appearance of 'a war between whites and natives'.[1] Ignorance of regional history also caused the Colonial Office to get its priorities wrong. In 1871–2, for instance, when they faced a dangerous breakdown of law and order on the west coast of Malaya, the Colonial Office staff expended a lot of nervous energy over Governor Ord's relations with the Maharaja of Johore, the one ruler with whom Britain had, in fact, fairly satisfactory relations. Similarly, in spite of the formidable number of problems in West Africa, a boundary dispute with Liberia, and much fun at its expense, seem to have taken an unwarrantable amount of Colonial Office penmanship.

Thirdly, an element of racial superiority was very evident in this period. The political units of the three regions were, to the Victorians, 'native states' — usually 'uncivilized' or 'barbarous' states. Within the Colonial Office, officials usually preferred the rather neutral word 'native' and Herbert once had to rebuke a senior official for his 'planter' attitude to West Indians;[2] but English public men less concerned with the day-to-day exercise of British responsibilities often displayed a contemptuous racialist attitude. Lord Halifax spoke impatiently of what was to be done with 'these Coast niggers',[3] and Lord Stanley once asserted in the House of Commons that the life of one British officer was 'measured by any rational standards of comparison, worth more than the merely animal existence of a whole African tribe'.[4]

[1] Memo. of Jan. 1877 quoted in A. H. Gordon, *Story of a Little War. Letters and Notes written during the Disturbances in the Highlands of Viti Levu, Fiji, 1876*, Edinburgh, 1879, p. xiv.

[2] The official in question was Sir Julian Pauncefote, then an assistant under-secretary in the C.O. See Hamilton, *Barbados and the Confederation Question*, p. 20.

[3] Halifax to Kimberley 21 Dec. 1873. *Kimberley Papers*, A/52.

[4] 3 *Hansard*, 177, col. 550.

Wolseley regarded West Africans as 'so many monkeys'.[1] Fijians
were thought to be 'cannibals', and Sir Arthur Gordon, whose Fijian
policy was remarkably benevolent, admitted (rather surprisingly) to
some settlers, 'My sympathy for the coloured races is strong; but my
sympathy for my own race is stronger'.[2] A very typical attitude among
the European community in the Straits Settlements was stated by a
Singapore official: 'the innate superiority of the ordinary Englishman
in his sense of honour and justice, is sufficient to dominate the inferior
character of the Malay'.[3] Even in a matter of administration of
justice, Knatchbull-Hugessen could write: 'Of course all men are held
equal before the law but it is a mistake to suppose that you can treat
Chinese as if they were English. . . .'[4] Kimberley once alluded to the
question of trial by jury in Sierra Leone with the quip: 'A jury of
English is a tolerable institution — a jury of Irishmen often intolerable
— a jury of blacks I should say always intolerable'.[5] This sort of attitude was often half-humorously stated, but was, in reality, deep-seated,
and was one which Gladstone, Disraeli and Carnarvon tried to repress.

    Finally, the Colonial Office attitude to German rivalry requires
comment, since a new concern was evident in the Office for a time after
the Franco-Prussian War. Although in the years before and immediately after the foundation of the German Empire Bismarck deliberately discouraged schemes of colonial expansion, this did not prevent
German residents abroad, traders, missionaries and naval leaders from
producing various colonial projects.[6] Bismarck refused an offer of

---

[1] Wolseley to his wife 27 Sept. 1873. Quoted in G. Arthur (ed.), *The
Letters of Lord and Lady Wolseley, 1870–1911*, London, 1923, p. 10.

[2] Gordon, *Fiji*, i, p. 183.

[3] C.O. Confidential Print: Eastern, C.O. 809/1, p. 246.

[4] Min. by Knatchbull-Hugessen 18 June, on Ord to Kimberley 4 May
1872. C.O. 273/57.

[5] Min. by Kimberley 19 Nov., on Kennedy to Kimberley 19 Oct. 1871.
C.O. 267/312.

[6] See W. H. Dawson, *The German Empire, 1867–1914, and the Unity
Movement*, London, 1919; M. E. Townshend, *The Origins of Modern
German Colonialism, 1817–1885*, New York, 1921; W. O. Aydelotte,
Bismarck and British Colonial Policy, Philadelphia, 1937; M. Jacobs,
'Bismarck and the Annexation of New Guinea', *H.S.A.N.Z.* (1951), 5 (17),
pp. 14–17; S. Masterman, *The Origins of International Rivalry in Samoa,
1845–1884*, London, 1934, ch. 3.

Fiji in 1869, and he ordered the consul in Samoa to cultivate good relations with the Americans there. But in spite of the official attitude, the appearance of German gunboats in South-East Asia and the South Pacific in the years 1870 to 1872 gave rise to rumours of German intervention in Malaya, Fiji, New Guinea and Samoa. For this reason British merchants, missionaries, naval officers and colonial servants became increasingly suspicious of German intentions.

The Colonial Office was at first quite unperturbed about all these rumours, but by 1872 there was a significant change of attitude. Rogers was not in the least bit worried by German actions. In 1867 he believed a German colony in New Guinea would be 'a very good thing for the Australians'.[1] In 1870 he thought that if Fiji could be reduced into 'Berlin order it would be useful',[2] and his attitude to the rumour that a North German harbour was sought in Malaya was: 'let her by all means'.[3] At this stage Herbert thought the entry of the North German Confederation into the Pacific would help to keep the balance of naval power there.[4]

The change of attitude in 1872 stemmed largely from Knatchbull-Hugessen's and Herbert's response to the rumours of German activity. It is difficult to see when Knatchbull-Hugessen's aggressive attitude began. In January 1871, when he heard a rumour that Germany might acquire Liberia, where her merchants had been established for thirty years, he thought the acquisition 'would probably be a general benefit'.[5] By July 1872, however, he was noting the dangers to Australia of a German Fiji. Kimberley also seemed to change his mind. In 1872, in face of rumours about Samoa, he was content to let the Germans have 'this questionable luxury',[6] but the suggestion of a German protectorate in Selangor in 1873 prompted him to urgent action where he felt Britain's position as the 'paramount power'[7] in the

[1] Min. by Rogers 3 Aug., on Young to Buckingham 31 May 1867. C.O. 201/542.

[2] Rogers to Hammond 4 Feb. 1870. F.O. 58/119, p. 206.

[3] Min. by Rogers 20 July, on F.O. to C.O. 14 July 1870. C.O. 273/42.

[4] Memo. by Herbert 10 May 1870. C.O. 201/562.

[5] Min. by Knatchbull-Hugessen 27 Jan. 1871 on Kennedy to Kimberley 28 Dec. 1870. C.O. 267/307.

[6] Min. by Kimberley 12 Apr. 1872 on W. H. Weld (extract) 25 Dec. 1871. C.O. 201/572.

[7] Kimberley to Gladstone 10 Sept. 1873. *Gladstone Papers*, 44225/103.

Malay Peninsula was challenged. Herbert took a similar view of the South Pacific in 1875 and advocated a policy of quietly acquiring 'paramount influence' in the Pacific to forestall the United States, Germany and France.

It is impossible to generalize from these isolated comments, and after the annexation of Fiji, and official German denials of ambition for Samoa and New Guinea, Carnarvon was satisfied. Nevertheless, there were plenty of Germans who were agitating for colonies, and a good number of British traders and missionaries and Australasian colonists who publicly expressed their fear of German expansion. Thus, whatever the truth of the rumours, the possible rivalry of a new colonial power had a noticeable part in the background of the three experiments in the tropics.

PART TWO

The Dilemma

BRITAIN faced a crisis of decision over the frontier in the tropics in 1873. Gladstone's Government found itself confronted by some perplexing dilemmas. As one of the colonial zealots had written five years earlier, it was 'almost impossible for a great Power like England to push itself' in frontier regions 'without extending or being implicated'.[1] In 1873 Kimberley advised Gladstone that the time for extension had come. He recommended a series of significant changes in British colonial policy.

Why did Kimberley make these decisions? The answer is that they mark the culmination of a reappraisal of Britain's policy which had become imperative. The circumstances of each decision were different, but the basic dilemma was the same. Should the Government, in the face of intractable problems on the frontier in the tropics, remain passive, withdraw, or extend British control? There was no doubt, by 1873, that existing policies were inadequate.

In West Africa the Colonial Office found that it could not withdraw from existing settlements as had been recommended by a Select Committee of Parliament in 1865. The reappraisal of British policy in Malaya followed the transfer of the Straits Settlements from India Office to Colonial Office control in 1867. In subsequent years the problems of the Malay Peninsula demanded more and more of the Colonial Office's attention. Finally, the rejection of an opportunity to annex the Fiji Islands in 1863 left the question of Britain's future relations with the islands of the South Pacific open. The evident desire of Australia and New Zealand for British control to be extended forced Kimberley to reconsider British policy in the 1870's.

[1] Sir Charles Adderley 22 Apr. on Blackall to Buckingham 30 Jan. 1868. C.O. 147/14.

In each of the tropical regions Britain's possessions were strictly limited. On the frontiers, the traditional policy was one of deliberate restraint, of non-intervention in the affairs of the states outside British territory. Yet non-intervention proved to be a surprisingly elastic concept. Several Colonial Secretaries admitted that there were circumstances where it might be advisable to intervene. They qualified the policy of restraint and followed, in practice, a policy of non-intervention — except in emergencies. Britain's policy in the tropics may be described as a frontier doctrine of qualified restraint.

In consequence, Britain intervened several times before 1873. On these occasions she became involved because she 'took sides' in existing local disputes. Complicated dynastic rivalries, civil wars or power struggles within the societies adjacent to the British possessions in West Africa, the Straits Settlements and the South Pacific were thought to constitute a threat to British territory or to invite interference by other nations. By 1873 the one permissible ground for intervention was all too evident.

In the Colonial Office there was by this time a confirmed advocate of expansion. Edward Knatchbull-Hugessen, the parliamentary under-secretary, had in times past stressed the ambiguity and weakness of the frontier doctrine of qualified restraint. He now demanded an extension of British influence. He argued that 'public opinion' as reflected in the House of Commons required the adoption of such a course. He remembered the feeling of the House during the crisis of opinion in 1869–70, when the Government's policies in Canada, New Zealand and South Africa had caused a fear that Gladstone was about to abandon the colonies. He had borne the brunt of subsequent suspicions of Liberal colonial policy. He was convinced that defeat or withdrawal in the tropics would lead to hostile resolutions in Parliament.

In forthright minutes in 1873, Knatchbull-Hugessen urged Kimberley to advance. Kimberley was undoubtedly impressed by the urgent need for decision. During the course of 1873 he made a number of major recommendations to the prime minister. In February he decided to abandon the 1865 Committee's policy in West Africa. That same month he advised Gladstone to annex Fiji. By July he had come to the conclusion that new policies would have to be worked out for Malaya.

It is true that immediate action was not taken. In each case, high-ranking officers were appointed to inquire and report as to whether intervention would be desirable. Their reports did not reach the Colonial Office until after the Liberal defeat in the general election of February 1874. But Kimberley's own mind was already made up. He had conceded the need for some expansion. What led him, we must ask, to this decision?

3. Contradictory Aims in West Africa: the Cardwell Policy, 1864-5

ON 17 June 1864 Vice-Admiral Sir John Hay rose in the House of Commons to make a furious onslaught upon Lord Palmerston's Government. Clutching in his hand some letters from a brother who had just died on military service in the Gold Coast, Hay spoke with intense emotion as he moved a motion of censure on the Cabinet: 'The men who have betrayed Denmark and truckled to Germany . . . who have alienated France and irritated Russia . . . who have convulsed China and devastated Japan; the same men who ten years ago sent a British army to perish of cold, of hunger, of want of shelter in a Crimean winter . . . have now sent British troops to perish of fever, of thirst, and of want of shelter on the burning plains and fetid swamps of Western Africa.'[1] Only a year before Palmerston's death, the great statesman, who had once challenged the crowned heads of Europe and had dominated the British political scene for the past decade, was thus angrily denounced and forced to defend his 'benevolent crotchet'. He replied, with a hint of the old aggressive fire, that if England became responsible for protecting 'tribes of men' the honour of the country sometimes demanded steps to 'make that protection not an empty word but a reality'.[2] But many of his hearers were not impressed. Admiral Hay's motion of censure was rejected by the slender margin of seven votes.

The Government won the day. But Palmerston's narrow escape was only the beginning of a memorable debate about colonial policy. The whole of Britain's involvement in West Africa was soon to be challenged. Realizing this, Cardwell, the Secretary of State for the Colonies, immediately decided to make a thorough investigation of

[1] 3 *Hansard*, 175, col. 1962.
[2] Ibid. col. 2017.

Britain's position in West Africa.[1] In 1865 the inquiry became public. When Charles Adderley, the Conservative colonial reformer, demanded the appointment of a Select Committee of Parliament, Cardwell consented to Parliament's scrutiny of his department's policies.[2] The motion of censure over the Gold Coast was, therefore, only the first spark in what became a blaze of publicity and criticism for the British West African settlements. Why did the West African settlements become the subject for political controversy? The answer seems to be that by 1865 many people regarded these minute colonial possessions as a rather curious legacy from the past, whose future usefulness was questioned.

Every phase of Britain's three-centuries-old relationship with the Guinea coast had left its mark. Elizabethan adventurers, the chartered companies of the seventeenth century and the slave-traders had all built forts, and occupied them intermittently, at the mouth of the River Gambia and along the Gold Coast. Philanthropists had colonized the Sierra Leone peninsula with freed slaves at the end of the eighteenth century. Traders, missionaries, naval officers and consuls had worked to open up the Niger region since the 1840's.

Despite all these interests and activities British sovereignty was still confined to four tiny coastal settlements. Bathurst, in the west, lay on an island at the mouth of the Gambia, which had been occupied since the end of the Napoleonic Wars.[3] Sierra Leone had been taken over by the Crown in 1808. Some forts on the Gold Coast were constituted a third Crown Colony in 1850,[4] and Lagos, the most easterly settlement, was annexed in 1861. The early Victorians may have dedicated themselves to the mission of displacing the slave-trade

[1] Lord de Grey to Captain Clarke, R.E., 18 June 1864 quoted in R. H. Vetch, *The Life of Lieutenant-General the Honourable Sir Andrew Clarke*, London, 1905, p. 83.

[2] Adderley's formal motion requesting the Select Committee came before the House of Commons on 21 Feb. 1865, but he had made his views clear in 1864. See W. S. Childe-Pemberton, *The Life of Lord Norton: Rt. Hon. Sir Charles Adderley, 1814–1905*, London, 1909, pp. 187–9. Cardwell gave instructions to his Commissioner, Col. Ord, on 25 Oct. 1864. *Accounts and Papers* (1865), xxxvii, pp. 289–90.

[3] McCarthy's Is., 150 miles up-river, was also purchased in 1820.

[4] Ord found five forts occupied in 1864 — Dixcove, Cape Coast Castle, Anomabu, Winneba and James Fort, Accra.

of West Africa by promoting a 'legitimate commerce', but they were never able to agree as to the best method of achieving this noble aim. The confusion of their policies was mirrored in the jumble of Crown Colonies, 'protectorates' and 'informal empire' which they haphazardly created.

The most irksome feature about West Africa was that the value of Britain's trade stood almost in inverse ratio to the degree of her political influence. She therefore derived least profit from the very areas which caused her the most trouble. In the Gold Coast, where British political influence was greatest, trade was very small.[1] In the Niger Delta, on the other hand, where Britain held no territory, trade was valued at over a million pounds a year.[2] Here the Government had always preferred the methods of 'informal empire'. British power in the Bights of Benin and Biafra had steadily increased from the formation of the Anti-Slave Squadron of the Royal Navy in 1810 and the discovery of the mouth of the Niger in 1830, until, with the appointment of a consul in 1849, British interference so disrupted the states of the Delta that consular and naval officers could exercise considerable power. But there were no annexations.[3]

[1] Value of trade 1860–5:

		1860	1861	1862	1863	1864	1865
Gambia	Imp.	£73,138	109,581	99,825	172,965	135,777	128,808
	Exp.	109,137	136,837	154,443	141,673	148,157	138,693
Sierra	Imp.	172,726	168,070	144,269	209,106	190,441	368,545
Leone	Exp.	304,394	213,204	268,814	295,853	201,808	237,240
Gold	Imp.	112,454	162,970	145,100	76,955	no Blue Books	
Coast	Exp.	110,457	145,819	102,086	53,764		
Lagos	Imp.	no figures			171,138	120,796	114,284
	Exp.				158,341	166,903	175,636

Memo. by Edward Fairfield 21 Jan. 1874 in C.O. Confidential Print: African 40, C.O. 806/3, p. 4. Ord's report of the 1865 trade figures gave a very misleading picture because of the Ashanti War.

Ord estimated that expenditure on the Settlements was: Civil, £12,000; Military, £130,000; Naval, £157,000.

[2] Estimate in memo. by Consul Charles Livingstone 8 Dec. 1871. F.O. MSS.: Slave Trade files, F.O. 84/1343; the value of palm oil imports into the U.K. was estimated at between £1½ million and £2 million by Capt. Andrew Clarke in 1864. 'Confidential memo. on the British Possessions on the West Coast of Africa', W.O., Confidential Print: W.O. 33/13/1387, p. 92.

[3] See Dike, *Trade and Politics in the Niger Delta*.

Piecemeal expansion of this kind led to confusion in Whitehall. Two Departments of State, the Foreign Office and the Colonial Office, found themselves ruling rival little West African empires. At Lagos, where their spheres overlapped, they were sometimes at cross-purposes.[1]   However, the conflicts were gradually sorted out and a general understanding emerged whereby the Foreign Office looked after relations with the states in the region of the River Niger, and the Colonial Office became responsible for policy in the states immediately adjacent to the colonies.[2]

In 1864 these untidy, complicated, unloved and not particularly profitable responsibilities provided such fuel for political controversy that they demanded the careful attention of Cardwell, the Colonial Secretary.   In 1865 they engaged the Select Committee of Parliament for three weeks.   In the course of these inquiries the politicians discovered the problem of the frontier in West Africa.   They became acutely aware of Britain's tendency to expand in three regions: the Gold Coast protectorate, the Lagos protectorate and the vicinity of Sierra Leone.

THE GOLD COAST PROTECTORATE

The controversy in 1864 began over the Gold Coast and for a decade events on the Gold Coast were to have a profound effect on British policy in West Africa.   The Gold Coast was the most hazardous commitment, although British sovereignty was confined to a few coastal trading forts.   Cape Coast Castle, occupied since the seventeenth century, was the most important.   Interspersed among the British forts were others owned by the Netherlands.

Beyond the seaboard, however, there lay the 'protectorate'.   Extending inland for about 50 miles to the River Pra, and reaching along the coast for about 300 miles from the Tano to the Volta, the protectorate was an ill-defined area, which also included enclaves of Dutch influence.   After attempting to grasp the meaning of the protectorate in 1865, the Select Committee could only admit that it was 'not defined by treaty but only implied' and that the frontiers of British

---

[1] Min. by Rogers 8 Sept., on F.O. to C.O. 5 Sept. 1863.   C.O. MSS.: Lagos correspondence, C.O. 147/5.   Cf. Adderley's *Review*, p. 213.

[2] A procedure described in Meade to Enfield 5 Jan. 1872.   F.O. 84/1360.

influence were 'wholly indefinite and uncertain'.[1]   Here was Britain's
largest political involvement in West Africa. What did it really mean?

The protectorate was not, in this case, a way of forestalling other
European Powers in the manner of the Asian and African protectorates of the later nineteenth century.[2]   The French, the Germans
and the Portuguese were not interested in the Gold Coast in this
period. The protectorate was, in reality, the political and judicial
legacy of the most remarkable early-Victorian empire-builder in West
Africa, Captain George Maclean. It was his device for keeping the
peace in the vicinity of the British forts.

Britain had become reluctantly involved in African politics because
of the expansion of the powerful Ashanti kingdom. The Ashantis had
by the early years of the nineteenth century subjected many of the
coastal states near the forts. Although Britain had defeated the
Ashantis in 1826, the Government attached no great value to the
area. Indeed, they tried to abandon the forts; but pressure from
merchants who were interested in the Gold Coast led to their retention.
Captain Maclean then appeared on the scene, and for nearly twenty
years worked to pacify the region.[3]   He was a stolid, patient, hard-
headed Scot, who earned the trust both of the Ashanti and the coastal
peoples. Through his personal influence a type of British paramountcy
grew up in the Gold Coast which was taken to imply that the Fante
and the neighbouring states would be supported by Britain against the
Ashanti — hence the name 'protectorate'. Maclean became the
chief element in a tripartite system of mediation between Ashanti,
the coastal states and the British traders.

Within the states of the protectorate Maclean's influence went
deeper. The inhabitants submitted disputes to his jurisdiction, and a
semblance of legality was given to his system in 1844. In that year
the British Government granted him extra-territorial jurisdiction over
British subjects outside the forts. At the same time, some, but not all,
of the African rulers signed the Bond, by which they consented to

[1] *Parliamentary Papers: Reports from Committees* (1865), v, p. 10.
[2] See below, Ch. 13, for a discussion of the legal aspects of 'protectorate'.
[3] The forts were governed by a committee of three merchants in London
with a parliamentary grant of £4,000 a year. Maclean was officially 'President of the Council' at Cape Castle, but styled himself 'Governor of His
Britannick Majesties Settlements' on the Gold Coast.

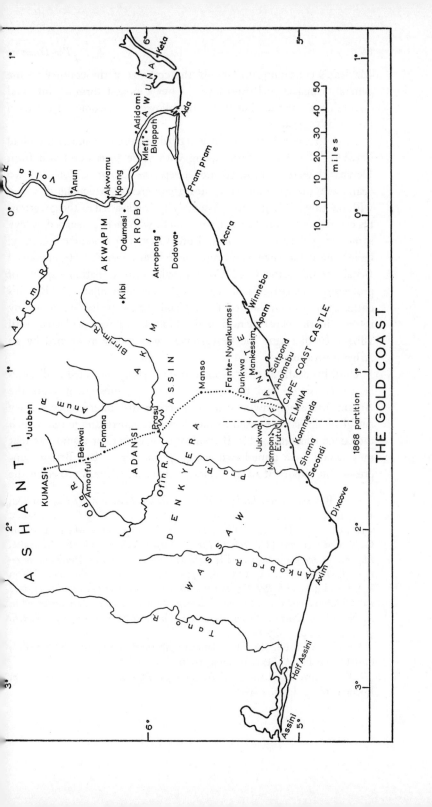

THE GOLD COAST

Maclean's continuing to 'mould the customs of the country to the general principles of British law'. Thus a modest form of 'informal empire' was created; but it was not allowed to become a burden on the British taxpayer.[1]

In 1850 a novel experiment was tried to raise revenue in the Gold Coast.[2] The British forts (along with some forts purchased from Denmark) were constituted into a separate Crown Colony. Two years later the governor convened a conference, which he dignified with the title of 'Legislative Assembly'. It consisted of the governor, his council and a number of Fante chiefs, who were persuaded to levy a modest poll tax. At home, Lord Grey, the Colonial Secretary, hailed the conference as a 'rude negro Parliament'. He envisaged Britain training the Gold Coast peoples into a 'nation capable of protecting themselves and managing their own affairs'.[3] But his enthusiasm was not shared in England. Few politicians took any interest in the experiment and the Gold Coast was neglected until 1864. In that year the Government was rudely awakened by an Ashanti invasion.

Until his death in 1847, Maclean successfully mediated in disputes between Ashanti and the coastal states. In subsequent years the Ashanti had ever-growing cause to resent British interference. They had given up claims to their former coastal conquests and to rent which they once claimed for the British forts, in return for assurances that they would have unmolested access to the coast. But Britain suppressed the export of slaves by sea. Above all, Britain protected the

[1] See B. Cruikshank, *Eighteen Years on the Gold Coast of Africa*, London, 1853, i, pp. 170–5; W. E. F. Ward, *A History of the Gold Coast*, London, 1948, ch. 9; J. D. Fage, 'The Administration of George Maclean on the Gold Coast 1830–44', *T.G.C.T.H.S.* (1952–55), i; G. E. Metcalfe, *Maclean of the Gold Coast. The Life and Times of George Maclean, 1801–1847*, Oxford, 1962, pp. 143–78, 294–318. The text of the 'Bond' is in J. J. Crooks, *Records Relating to the Gold Coast and Settlements from 1750 to 1874*, Dublin, 1923, p. 119; legal aspects of the protectorate are discussed in A. N. Allott, 'Native Tribunals in the Gold Coast 1844–1929', *J.A.L.* (1957), i (3), pp. 163–8.
[2] See F. Wolfson, 'British Relations with the Gold Coast, 1843–1880', unpublished Ph.D. thesis, London, 1950.
[3] Earl Grey, *The Colonial Policy of Lord John Russell's Administration*, London, 1853, ii, pp. 284–7.

states such as Assin, Akim and Denkyera, which lay on the Ashanti routes to the sea. Here Ashanti travellers were often molested, and tension was endemic.

In 1863 the ruler of Ashanti, the Asantehene Kwaku Dua I, could restrain his war-chiefs no longer. The British governor, Richard Pine, granted asylum to a runaway Ashanti slave-boy and a man fleeing from justice. Repeated requests for their extradition, and categorical assurances that they would not be executed, were rebuffed.[1] In March 1863 three Ashanti armies marched into the protectorate and Britain's noble, neglected experiment in peace-making and nation-building was placed in jeopardy.

The Ashanti War of 1863–4 was a fiasco for Britain. A small force of 400 men of the West India Regiment was scraped together from the other settlements, but their commander was too timid to attack the Ashanti. The governor tried to rally resistance, but he fell ill. As the rainy season set in in the autumn of 1863 the Ashanti armies retired from the protectorate, but they were undefeated and were still a potential threat. The governor, therefore, planned to strike a blow at the Ashanti capital to forestall a further invasion. At first his suggestion was rejected by the Secretary of State; but in December 1863 he changed his mind and agreed to provide reinforcements for a march on Kumasi.

The offensive against Ashanti was never made. Detachments of the West India Regiment, which were sent to the Ashanti border to await reinforcements and prepare for the attack, languished in the rains through the early months of 1864, suffering growing casualties from malaria and yellow fever. Over half the officers were struck down and thirteen out of sixty-four died.[2] As news of demoralization and confusion reached England, the Opposition in Parliament challenged the Government in the House of Commons and decisively affected Britain's West Africa policy.

On 20 May 1864 Sir John Pakington denounced the proposed invasion of Ashanti as 'wild and visionary . . . hopeless and impossible'.[3]

[1] See Ward, op. cit., pp. 205–13; Wolfson, op. cit., 63–67; W. W. Claridge, *A History of the Gold Coast and Ashanti*, London, 1915, pp. 503–29; F. C. Fuller, *A Vanished Dynasty — Ashanti*, London, 1921, pp. 91–97.

[2] Statement of casualties. *Accounts and Papers* (1864), xli, pp. 161–3.

[3] 3 *Hansard*, 175, col. 546.

Only three days later, Cardwell, the Colonial Secretary, cancelled the operations.[1] Sir John Hay's motion of censure failed on 17 June, but its import was not lost on Cardwell. On the day after the debate he made it known that a commissioner would be sent to make a full inquiry in West Africa.[2] On 23 June he issued an order that British troops could not be used against future Ashanti attacks. If the protectorate was to continue, the governor was to confine his efforts to encouraging the chiefs to unite and providing arms and advice.[3] British protection of the Gold Coast protectorate was virtually withdrawn.

THE LAGOS PROTECTORATE

The Ashanti War did more than strike a blow at the Gold Coast protectorate in 1864. The Lagos protectorate, over 300 miles away to the east, was also affected. On the day Cardwell called off the Ashanti expedition, he also cancelled an 'energetic policy'[4] which he had recently approved in the Yoruba states on the mainland. Lagos underwent the same critical scrutiny as the Gold Coast as a result of the Ashanti War.

The Lagos protectorate was a much more modest affair than Maclean's creation on the Gold Coast. Cardwell's commissioner discovered in 1865 that it did not 'involve the responsibilities' which existed in the Gold Coast system.[5] At the same time the acquisition and development of the minute Lagos colony and protectorate provided a good example of the muddled way in which Britain pursued her mission of spreading 'Commerce, Christianity and Civilization' in West Africa and became involved in African politics.

From the 1840's Britain tried, in the Niger region, to pursue Fowell Buxton's dream of saving Africa by 'calling forth her own

[1] Cardwell to officer-administering-the-government 23 May 1864. *Accounts and Papers* (1864), xli, p. 157.
[2] de Grey to Clarke 18 June 1864. Vetch, *Life of Clarke*, p. 83.
[3] Cardwell to Pine 23 June 1864. *Accounts and Papers* (1864), xlix, pp. 864–5.
[4] Cardwell to Freeman 23 May 1864. See draft of cancelled despatch by Cardwell, filed with Freeman to Newcastle 9 Apr. 1864. C.O. 147/6.
[5] Ord to Cardwell 9 Mar. 1865. *Accounts and Papers* (1865), xxxvii, pp. 308–13.

resources'.[1]   But early attempts at following this policy up-river failed disastrously, and the pioneering trading efforts of Laird and Baikie were disappointing.   A more promising ground for Buxton's ideas was found at Abeokuta, the capital of the Egba state.   Here slaves, who had been recaptured by the Royal Navy and educated in the mission schools of Sierra Leone, emigrated back to their homeland and called for both the Wesleyan and Church Missionary societies to follow them.   In the 1850's Abeokuta was enthusiastically publicized in England as the 'Sunrise in the Tropics' and the missionaries ensured that Britain supported the Egba against their predatory rivals, the kings of Dahomey, Porto Novo and Lagos.   Palmerston appointed a consul to watch over Britain's growing interest in 1849, and John Beecroft, his choice, proved to be an empire-builder in the tradition of Maclean.   A masterly exponent of 'informal empire', he came to be regarded by African rulers as a sort of 'de facto Governor of the Bights of Benin and Biafra'.[2]

But as in the Gold Coast, interference with African politics led to unexpected complications.   In 1851 the consul and the missionaries combined to interfere in a long-standing dispute over the Lagos kingship and helped to install an amenable ruler.   By their intervention they not only took sides in what appeared to be a purely local dispute, but they soon unwittingly committed the British Government to one of the parties in a major struggle for power in this part of West Africa. In 1853 a separate consulate was created in Lagos.   The first incumbent contrived to turn the island into an 'anomalous protectorate' and he began to draw up ambitious plans for furthering British influence in Dahomey and Yorubaland.[3]

The creation of the Lagos consulate led to a significant change in British policy.   The consul's duty was to foster British interests.

[1] T. F. Buxton, *The African Slave Trade and Its Remedy*, London, 1840, ii, p. 518.

[2] Dike, *Trade and Politics in the Niger Delta*, p. 128.   The consulate was at Fernando Po until 1872 when it was moved to Old Calabar.

For events in the Lagos hinterland see S. Johnson, *History of the Yorubas*, Lagos, 1924, pp. 200–93.

[3] S. O. Biobaku, *The Egba and their Neighbours 1842–72*, Oxford, 1957, chs. 1 and 2;   C. W. Newbury, *The Western Slave Coast and Its Rulers*, Oxford, 1961, chs. 3 and 4;   A. A. B. Aderibigbe, 'Expansion of the Lagos Protectorate, 1863–1900', unpublished Ph.D. thesis, London, 1959, ch. 1.

Thus his activities came to be dictated more and more by the needs of
Lagos traders rather than those of the missionaries at Abeokuta. He
soon began to suggest that Britain should annex Lagos. In 1860 a
struggle for power broke out among the successor states of the former
Yoruba empire which is known as the 'Ijaye War'.[1] Palmerston,
the prime minister, who feared the French might step in, insisted that
Britain should 'strike while the iron is hot'.[2] In 1861, Docemo,
King of Lagos, ceded his lands to Britain. A twenty-year tradition
of working through African agency at Abeokuta was cast aside.
British influence now became based, as it was on the Gold Coast, on
a port under British sovereignty.

The frontier problem immediately became evident. Where, it was
asked, should the borders of the new possession be drawn? The
existence of domestic slavery, which was illegal on British soil, made it
expedient to restrict British territory to the narrowest limits — as on
the Gold Coast. But a host of intractable problems immediately led
the new Government into extensions outside Lagos Island. Customs
duties were wanted for revenue, so the governor claimed Badagry to
the west, and Palma and Leckie to the east, as parts of the ceded
territory. 'Protection' was extended to the town of Ikorodu, on the
north shore of the lagoon, because it was the terminus of an important
trade route from Ibadan and the interior. Relations with Abeokuta
deteriorated because the Egba resented the British *volte-face* and the
governor of Lagos claimed that Igbessa and Otta on the mainland
belonged to Lagos. Finally, after French traders at Porto Novo to the
west avoided British duties by engineering a French protectorate in
1862, the acting governor, Commander Glover, stepped in to block
the French by creating his own 'protectorates' north-west of Lagos
at Addo and Oke Odan, and then negotiating a line between the French
and British spheres. It became abundantly clear, after only two years
at Lagos, that the frontiers of British influence were moving, once
more, beyond the frontiers of sovereignty.

[1] For the best account see pt. ii of J. F. Ade Ajayi and R. S. Smith, *Yoruba
Warfare in the Nineteenth Century*, Cambridge, 1964.
[2] Min. by Palmerston 19 May 1861. F.O. 97/433. Also on the annexa-
tion of Lagos, J. F. Ade Ajayi, 'The British Occupation of Lagos, 1851–61',
Nigeria Magazine (1961), 69, pp. 96–105; R. J. Gavin, 'Nigeria and Lord
Palmerston', *Ibadan* (June 1961), pp. 24–27.

The Colonial Office was puzzled and displeased by the appearance of a Lagos protectorate. But they had not reckoned on the man on the spot. John Hawley Glover was a domineering personality who was regarded by his admirers as Britain's greatest West African pro-consul since Maclean.[1] A product of one of those evangelical service families, which provided so many minor empire-builders before the coming of the big capitalists and professional administrators, he prob-ably heard tales of Africa from his father, the Rev. Frederick Glover,

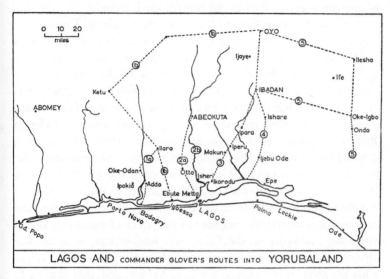

LAGOS AND COMMANDER GLOVER'S ROUTES INTO YORUBALAND

who had served on the Gold Coast in 1826 before he was ordained. At the age of twelve Glover left the vicarage to enter the Navy as a cadet. For seventeen years he saw something of British power in action. After serving in the Levant, the Cape and China, he fought in Burma, and took part in the Baltic operations during the Crimea. Then, at the age of twenty-eight, he volunteered for service in Dr Baikie's second ascent of the Niger in 1857 — the expedition during which the Rev. Samuel Crowther planted the Niger Mission.

[1] Forster and Smith to Kimberley 3 Aug. 1872. C.O. MSS.: Gold Coast correspondence, C.O. 96/95. For Glover see Lady E. Glover and R. Temple, *The Life of Sir John Hawley Glover*, London, 1897, and McIntyre, 'Commander Glover and the Colony of Lagos, 1861–73', *J.A.H.* (1963), 4 (1), pp. 57–79.

Glover's first experience of Africa was of great significance for his future role at Lagos. One of the major aims of the Niger expedition was to divert some of the trade which normally went north across the Sahara by entering into relations with the Muslim states north of the Niger. Baikie believed they were engaged in an international race with France, who, he feared, would expand from Algiers and Senegal and dominate the entire Sudan. Baikie argued that both Lagos and the Niger 'must be secured for us' and 'Lagos must be the great base of operations as it is the especial port for the interior'.[1]

Accident, however, forced Glover into the vicinity of Lagos. The Niger expedition was wrecked up-stream in October 1857 and Glover had to travel overland to Lagos on three occasions. Some unfortunate, if rather obscure, experiences at the hands of the Egba on these journeys caused him to reject Britain's traditional pro-Egba policy. He became convinced that the Ibadans were 'the flower of the Yoruba people' and he supported those at Lagos who wanted to change Britain's alliance.[2] After Lagos was annexed Glover joined the first colonial Government. His official position was harbour-master. But he twice administered the Government when the governor was on leave and he emerged as the dominant influence in the new colony.

Glover was at Lagos from the start of the new colony, then, and became the most notable exponent of the policy of expanding British influence, and opposing the Egba. He was, in fact, as much pro-Ibadan as his predecessors were pro-Egba. He failed to appreciate, what the modern historian of the Egba has revealed, that Ibadan, by striving to re-establish an Oyo empire, 'was upsetting the balance of power' in Yorubaland, and was using the British régime at Lagos as a pawn in its strategy.[3]

Englishmen who thought they understood Yoruba affairs believed that analogies could be drawn with the 'middlemen' states of the Niger Delta and the Gold Coast. In their view the Egba and their ally Ijebu Ode were 'monopolizing' the trade with the interior. As the Yoruba Wars severely damaged the trade of Lagos the colonial

[1] Baikie to Malmesbury 2 Mar. 1859. F.O. MSS.: consular correspondence, Africa, F.O. 2/31.

[2] Glover to Baikie 20 July, encl. in Baikie to Malmesbury 6 Aug. 1859. F.O. 2/32.

[3] Biobaku, *The Egba*, p. 72; Ajayi, *Yoruba Warfare*, ii, ch. 3.

Government's response took the form of an attempt to revive trade by opening alternative routes to Ibadan, and beyond to Oyo, Ilorin and the Niger. From 1863 Lagos diplomacy was directed towards dislodging the Egba and Ijebu from a position athwart the Lagos line of communication from Ikorodu to Ibadan. Cardwell was about to add his support to Glover's policy in 1864 when the Ashanti War caused a dramatic revision of his attitude. The Lagos protectorate had to be reviewed along with the rest of the West African settlements.

SIERRA LEONE AND 'INFORMAL EMPIRE' ON THE WINDWARD COAST

While Beecroft, Maclean and Glover were establishing their modest spheres of influence east of Cape Palmas, the colonies to the west appeared to be more static. The Gambia was simply the terminus of a trading inlet. Apart from occasional intervention to protect some small accessions of territory on the river banks opposite Bathurst the colony's influence was small.[1] Sierra Leone was still centred on the mountainous Freetown Peninsula, which had been settled in the eighteenth century. Small tracts of land, which had been acquired on the Bullom Shore opposite Freetown and in the Rokel river, were sparsely populated. The Colonial Office was relieved to hear in 1864 that there was 'no protectorate, nor anything analogous'.[2]

By the 1860's, however, appearances had become deceptive. Sierra Leone began to embark on a policy of expansion. Another potentially dangerous frontier problem soon became evident and led to rivalry with Liberia, Portugal and France. But, as in the eastern settlements, the initiative did not come from the home Government. This time it came from the Sierra Leonians.

A unique society had grown up in the colony, which began to have an influence far beyond its borders. The population of former slaves from England, North America and the West Indies was substantially increased after the 1820's by recaptured slaves released from slaving-ships by the Royal Navy. With its British laws, its churches, schools and growing businesses, Sierra Leone became a fragment of African

[1] Hargreaves, *Prelude to the Partition*, pp. 49–53.
[2] Ord to Cardwell 9 Mar. 1865. *Accounts and Papers* (1865), xxxvii, p. 10.

Victoriana and was regarded as a centre for spreading 'civilizing influences' along the coast.[1]

But population-growth and commercial success led to territorial expansion. Even the Colonial Office admitted that Sierra Leone was 'a very cramped colony'.[2] There were frequent skirmishes with neighbouring chiefdoms, and in 1860 Koya, on the eastern frontier, was annexed. In the following year Sherbro Island, lying 50 miles to the south, was added, along with some ill-defined territory on the mainland shores of the Sherbro estuary. A long dispute with the Republic of Liberia over the Gallinas region soon followed the Sherbro cession.[3]

The most significant scene of Sierra Leone expansion was in the 'northern rivers': the 300-mile stretch of coastline between the colony and the Gambia, where numerous rivers drained from the Fouta Djalon highlands. Here two islands had been annexed, the Îles de Los and Bulama in the Bissagos archipelago. But Bulama was claimed as part of the decrepit colony of Portuguese Guinea. The cession of the island to a British sailor, along with some territory on the mainland between the Geba and Rio Grande, was a long-standing bone of contention between Britain and Portugal. When Bulama was formally incorporated into Sierra Leone in 1860, Portuguese protests were renewed.

Trade was more important to the Sierra Leonians than territory. Therefore the chief regions which attracted their attention were the river estuaries, particularly the Mellacourie, where colonial merchants built up a valuable trade. In support of their efforts, a number of treaties were signed with rulers in the region, who agreed to suppress the slave-trade, protect the colonial merchants and submit disputes to the governor in return for small 'stipends'. Thus, like Maclean on the Gold Coast, the governors of Sierra Leone found that a modest influence as arbitrator helped to keep the peace beyond the confines of the colony.

[1] A detailed study of the 'recaptive' community is found in C. Fyfe, *A History of Sierra Leone*; for the wider influence of the former slaves see J. F. Ade Ajayi, *Christian Missions in Nigeria 1841–1891. The Making of a New Elite*, London, 1965, ch. 2.

[2] Min. by Elliot 16 Feb. 1861 on Hill to Newcastle 19 Dec. 1860. C.O. MSS.: Sierra Leone correspondence, C.O. 267/268.

[3] Fyfe, op. cit., pp. 250, 307–8, 320–1, 362–3, 384, 412.

Here, in the northern rivers, Sierra Leone met the challenge of France. French traders from Senegal had built up a useful trade in

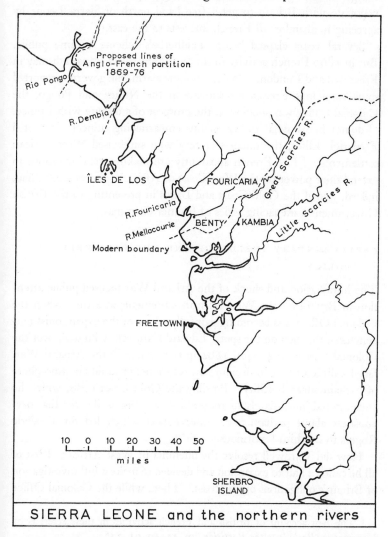

SIERRA LEONE and the northern rivers

the Nunez and Pongo rivers, and gradually competed with the British in the Mellacourie. Louis Léon Faidherbe, the ambitious governor of Senegal, who dreamt of controlling the Senegal and the Niger, envisaged the Nunez as a secondary route to the Niger headwaters. He

planned a military post in the Nunez and a Political Resident in the
Pongo. In 1863 he made a far-reaching proposal that France should
negotiate with Britain to get a free hand north of Sierra Leone by
agreeing to abandon all French interests to the east.[1]

Several years elapsed before Faidherbe's scheme became public.
But in 1860 French activity in the 'northern rivers' caused dismay in
Freetown and London.[2] When, in some alarm, the governor reported
some suspicious French movements in the Nunez and Pongo, the
Colonial Office was shocked at the prospect of a dispute with France.
'I do not know what to say on this embarrassing subject,' lamented
Frederick Elliot, the under-secretary who supervised West African
settlements. 'The French apparently are making great exertions to
extend their power on the West Coast of Africa.'[3] Sierra Leone had,
indeed, joined the Gold Coast and Lagos in presenting to the British
Government a menacing series of frontier dilemmas.

PARLIAMENTARY INFLUENCE AND THE CARDWELL
POLICY

The humiliation and shock of the Ashanti War focused public attention in Britain on the West African settlements at a time when the
Colonial Office was becoming painfully aware of the expansionist tendencies of the men on the spot. Edward Cardwell, who took over the
Colonial Office on 4 April 1864 in the middle of the Ashanti War,
faced a difficult task in deciding on future policy amid an atmosphere
of parliamentary hostility. Possibly the Gold Coast crisis, which he
encountered immediately he took office, was responsible for that ner-
vousness about parliamentary intervention which led Sir Frederic
Rogers to call him 'enormously safe'.[4]

How did Cardwell resolve the dilemma in West Africa? First of
all he called a halt to expansion and decided to make a full investigation
of Britain's obligations on the coast. Then, while the Colonial Office

---

[1] The best account of British and French activities in these rivers is by
Hargreaves, *Prelude to the Partition*, pp. 41–49, 91–136.

[2] Fitzjames to Newcastle (private and confidential) 21 May 1860. C.O.
267/266.

[3] Min. by Elliot 16 Feb. 1861 on Hill to Newcastle 29 Nov. 1860.
C.O. 267/268.   [4] Marindin, p. 226.

prepared to meet a Select Committee of Parliament in 1865, he listened with an open mind to criticisms and suggestions. He must have been perplexed by the conflicting advice which he received.

Captain Andrew Clarke of the Royal Engineers, a survivor of the Ashanti War, made a scathing attack on Britain's policy on the coast. As one of the staff officers sent out to prepare for the reinforcements which never came, Clarke had assisted the governor at Cape Coast Castle. In June 1864 he prepared a confidential memorandum for the War Office in which he called for a drastic reduction of Britain's responsibilities. He regarded the colonies in West Africa as a 'costly and profitless experiment'.[1] He pointed out that relations with African rulers, which had been opened for the purpose of trade, had developed into extensions of 'quasi-British authority'. Apart from Sierra Leone a few trading-stations would, he believed, fulfil Britain's needs.

> Lawful commerce will best be promoted by confining the operation of English influence and interference to that exercised by a Consul or mercantile agent, and not by endeavouring to force, by military power and the machinery of a colonial government, our institutions and laws upon a people to whom they are neither suited nor applicable.[2]

Clarke's forthright criticisms made such an impact on Cardwell that he considered sending him to West Africa to conduct the Colonial Office's inquiry.[3]

Clarke's views were, however, those of a soldier with limited knowledge of the Gold Coast, gained during a humiliating emergency. Not everyone was so pessimistic. Samuel Blackall, the governor of Sierra Leone, was prompted to offer more constructive criticisms to Cardwell after reading an account of the Gold Coast debates in Parliament. Blackall agreed with Clarke that the protectorates should be abandoned. They were 'anomalous, absurd and dangerous': anomalous, because toleration of slavery compromised British principles; absurd, because it was impossible to protect them; and dangerous because African rulers were likely to embroil unsuspecting British officers in their own petty quarrels. But while he agreed that Britain should keep to the

---

[1] Clarke, confidential memo.: 'British Possessions on the West Coast of Africa' (June 1864), W.O. 33/13/1387, p. 69.

[2] Ibid. p. 77.   [3] Vetch, *Life of Clarke*, p. 83.

coast, fostering her interests by treaties with African states, and possibly by a general agreement with France, he did not advocate complete non-expansion. 'Judicious extensions of territory' along the seaboard near the colonies would, in Blackall's view, contribute to the financial self-sufficiency of the settlements. He also proposed uniting all the settlements under a single governor-in-chief, preferably a soldier with diplomatic experience.

Blackall's comments impressed the Colonial Office. They were 'extremely well worth considering from beginning to end' said Rogers.[1] Colonel Harry Ord, the governor of Bermuda, whom Cardwell selected as the commissioner to report on West Africa, studied Blackall's despatch before he received his own instructions.[2] But Ord had views of his own. He had already been on the Gold Coast twice before and was regarded as the department's 'expert' on the region.[3] His report in March 1865 was more optimistic than either Clarke's or Blackall's.

Ord was against withdrawing from the settlements and he defended the protectorates. He believed the existence of small British territories did more than contribute to the suppression of the slave-trade

[1] Min. by Rogers 15 Oct., on Blackall to Cardwell 21 Sept. 1864. C.O. 267/281.

[2] Ibid. Min. by Barrow 14 Oct. 1864.

[3] Harry St. George Ord (1819–85). Commissioned in R.E., 1837; served at Chatham, Woolwich and Ireland; in the West Indies, 1840–5; and at home in 1845–54, ending up as Adj. of the R.E. depot at Chatham. Visited W. Africa and Ascension Is. Dec. 1849–Sept. 1850 inspecting military and naval works. During the Crimean War he was Brig. Maj. of the British force under Brig.-Gen. Harry Jones, which took part in the Baltic campaign of 1854. At the siege of Bomarsund Ord volunteered for regimental duties in addition to staff work and he gained a brevet majority and a mention in despatches. Although he returned to regimental duty, he spent most of the rest of his life in the Colonial Service. In 1855–6 he conducted an inquiry on the Gold Coast; in 1856 he went to The Hague to negotiate over the Gold Coast; in 1857 he went to Paris and The Hague for the same purpose. He was Lieut.-Gov. of Dominica 1857–8 and was then seconded to the Colonial Service. Gov. of Bermuda, 1861–7 (during which time he visited W. Africa, 1864–5); gov. of the Straits Settlements, 1867–73, and gov. of W. Australia. 1877–9, K.C.M.G., 1867. For his early career see his Record of Service, W.O. 25/3913/111, and *London Gazette*, 1. Sept, 1854, p. 2699. He is often incorrectly referred to as 'Sir Henry' and 'Orde'.

and the development of legitimate commerce. Human sacrifice had been abolished in the settlements, oppressive aspects of African law had been mitigated in the Gold Coast protectorate, and the lot of domestic slaves had improved. Ord challenged many of the recent criticisms. He accepted Blackall's proposal for a grouping under a single governor-in-chief at Sierra Leone. He suggested that precedents existed in the West Indies.[1]

Colonel Ord and Captain Clarke represented diametrically opposed views as to Britain's future role in West Africa. Clarke wanted a drastic reduction of territory; Ord was reluctant to give up any foothold. They were both interrogated by the Select Committee of Parliament, which met under Adderley's chairmanship in 1865. The remarkable thing is that, although their advice was quite contradictory, the Committee tried to do justice to both their points of view. It was unable to recommend immediate withdrawal from any of the colonies. But it insisted that, in the interests of economy and uniform policy, a single governor-in-chief should rule all the settlements. The governor was then to aim at withdrawing eventually from all the colonies except Sierra Leone.[2]

In reaching their conclusions, the Committee found that Lagos and the Gambia seemed to present comparatively simple problems. Lagos was the most recent acquisition and it was hoped that an African ruler could soon be restored. McCarthy's Island, the inland station up the Gambia, was already unoccupied, and the colonial Government was ordered to confine itself to the mouth of the river. But the Gold Coast protectorate was a much more baffling problem. Having decided not to give military help to the protectorate states again, the Colonial Office tried to argue before the Committee that Britain had no legal obligation to defend them. Colonel Ord could not accept this contention. He maintained that Maclean had always contemplated 'using influence' to keep the peace, and that as Ashanti now regarded the coastal states as 'identified' with Britain the government would not be morally justified in standing aside if there was another invasion.[3]

[1] Ord to Cardwell 9 Mar. 1865, *Accounts and Papers* (1865), xxxvii, pp. 290–320.

[2] Report of the Select Committee on the West African settlements 26 June 1865. *Reports from Committees* (1865), v, p. iii.

[3] Ibid. pp. 25–26.

Sir Benjamin Pine, a former governor, looked ahead idealistically and
proposed training the inhabitants for self-government, 'so that in a
given time, it might be half a century, and it might be a century, we
should be free to a great extent'. He would start by 'making them
drain their towns'.[1] Confronted with such conflicting advice the
Committee found itself unable to recommend abandoning the protectorate immediately, but it established that there was no obligation to
protect it.

The report of the 1865 Committee is the most quoted document in
the history of the West African settlements. It tried to embody two
fundamentally different ideas. On the one hand Fowell Buxton's
tradition was revived and it became the general policy to encourage
'civilization' through African agency. Extensions of British territory
and responsibilities were to cease, and Africans were to be encouraged
to exercise 'those qualities which may render it possible for us more
and more to transfer to them the administration of all the Governments
with a view to our ultimate withdrawal from all, except, probably
Sierra Leone'.[2] Self-governing African states were to be the agents
of British influence, rather than colonies under British sovereignty.
It might, in fact, appear from this that the doctrines of the 'New
Commonwealth' of the mid-twentieth century have a long pedigree.
But significant qualifications were added which soon led to such
doctrines being forgotten for nearly a century.

New settlements were forbidden. But an amendment which Cardwell added to the original draft of the Report provided that the new
policy could not 'amount to an absolute prohibition of measures which,
in particular cases, may be necessary for the more efficient and eco-
nomical administration of the settlements we already possess'.[3] The
Report was a compromise. It called for a policy of 'non-intervention
— except in special cases'. There was always the saving-clause to fall
back on. An element of flexibility was deliberately retained by the
Colonial Secretary. Similar loopholes for local discretion were pro-

[1] Report of the Select Committee on the West African Settlements 26 June
1865. *Reports from Committees* (1865), v, p. 148.   [2] Ibid. p. iii, clause 3.
[3] Ibid. Compare with Adderley's original draft before Cardwell's amendments were included, p. xv, clause 50, and p. xvi, clause 3 (with amendment).
For the best analysis of the Committee see Hargreaves, *Prelude to the Partition*,
pp. 64–78.

vided for the men on the spot in South-East Asia and the South Pacific. The Colonial Office wanted to avoid taking on new responsibilities, but obviously it did not want to tie its hands completely. It subscribed to the frontier doctrine of qualified restraint.

THE CARDWELL POLICY IN ACTION

How successful was the Cardwell policy in West Africa? The Colonial Office made a real attempt to follow it until 1873. Frederick Elliot, the assistant under-secretary, constantly reminded his political superiors of the 1865 Report until his retirement in 1868.[1] Adderley, the Conservative, and Granville, the Liberal, both made resolute attempts to follow Cardwell's aims. But the conflicting principles inherent in the policy were difficult to reconcile. By 1871 Kimberley and Knatchbull-Hugessen found they were increasingly hard to follow.

The failure of Cardwell's policy has been variously interpreted by historians. A distinguished Nigerian authority claims that within a decade of 1865 'the logic of the facts drove the British government towards a vigorous policy of economic and political expansion not only on the coast but in the West African interior'.[2] But this can hardly be maintained. Where is the evidence for a vigorous policy by the Government in the early 1870's? Even in the most valuable trading region, the Niger Delta, the *status quo* was maintained. Although war between Bonny and Opobo cut Britain's trade by half in 1871, Granville, as Foreign Secretary, refused to intervene. The Foreign Office insisted, in the early 1870's, that the system of trading through the delta 'middlemen' states should be retained as the 'established custom of the oil rivers'.[3]

What is more certain is that by 1874 the idea of quitting the British colonies on the west coast was all but abandoned. Edward Knatchbull-Hugessen and some of the younger civil servants like Fairfield and

[1] Thomas Frederick Elliot. Joined the C.O. as a clerk in 1825. Secretary to the Canadian Commission of Inquiry 1836. Agent-general for Emigration 1837; later chairman of Colonial Land and Emigration Board. Returned to the C.O. in 1847 as assistant under-secretary. Retired Dec. 1868. K.C.M.G. 1869.   [2] Dike, *Trade and Politics in the Niger Delta*, p. 81.
[3] Granville to Livingstone 25 Jan. 1871 (copy). F.O. 84/1343. Derby to Hartley 21 May 1874 (copy). F.O. 84/1401.

Hemming placed great emphasis on Britain's moral responsibilities. The most ardent Foreign Office exponent of Britain's 'duties' in West Africa was William H. Wylde, head of the commercial and consular department.[1] He argued forcefully against a Treasury attempt in 1873 to cease payments to Masaba, Emir of Nupe, who had undertaken to protect British traders in the middle reaches of the Niger.

> We have probably done more within the last 20 years to open up Africa to European Traders than had been achieved in the century previous, and it would be bad policy now for the sake of a few pounds to risk the closing of one of the principle high ways into the interior of Africa.[2]

But while members of both the Foreign Office and the Colonial Office proclaimed moral duties in West Africa and deprecated withdrawal from the settlements, policy-makers of both political parties were reluctant to incur new responsibilities.

By 1873, however, Kimberley had to admit that the Cardwell policy had failed. The 1865 Committee had recommended withdrawal from all the settlements except Sierra Leone. It was still open for Kimberley to fulfil these recommendations when he took office in 1870. Negotiations were well advanced for the cession of the Gambia to France, but he broke them off. He did manage to check the expansion of Lagos in 1872, but he decided a year later that it was impossible to quit Lagos. At the same time he abandoned the self-government aspects of Cardwell's policy in the Gold Coast and began to work out new arrangements for making the chiefs agents of firmer British rule.

He could not have chosen a worse moment. Ashanti had just renewed its attacks on the protectorate. Kimberley therefore finally set Cardwell's orders of 1864–5 aside and called for armed intervention

---

[1] William Henry Wylde became a supernumerary clerk in the F.O. in 1839. He went with his father, Col. Wylde, on a mission to Spain and Portugal, 1846–7, and became an assistant clerk in the Office in 1859. In 1865 he was a member of the Slave Trade Instructions Commission and was appointed head of the Commercial and Consular Dept. of the F.O., sometimes called the 'Slave Dept.', which dealt with the African and Polynesian business. In 1872 he conducted an inquiry into consular establishments. Retired 1880.

[2] Min. by Wylde 28 Mar., on C.O. to F.O. 22 Mar. 1873. F.O. 84/1382.

against Ashanti.   He summed up the failure of the Cardwell policy
when he wrote in September 1873:

> when we tried to get rid of it [Gambia] with what a clamour we
> were met.   One good thing may come out of the Ashantee war that some
> definite policy must be agreed upon by Parliament as regards these
> African Settlements.   The report of 186[5] was neither one thing or the
> other;   and as usual we have fallen between two stools.[1]

The essential contradictions of the 1865 policy were finally appreciated in full.   How this happened in the case of each colony must now
be followed in detail.

[1] Min. by Kimberley 23 Sept. on Cooper to administrator-in-chief. 29
July 1873, C.O. MSS.: Gambia correspondence, C.O. 87/105.

4. Contradictory Aims in West Africa: the Failure of the Cardwell Policy, 1865-73

The first and most promising attempt to put Cardwell's policy into effect was made on the windward coast. The sudden and startling possibility of Anglo-French rivalry in the region between Sierra Leone and the Gambia presented an excellent chance of fulfilling the recommendations of the Select Committee.

A minor war broke out in the Mellacourie region while the Committee was sitting. It concerned a dispute over the succession to the Moriah chiefdom and was regarded by Sierra Leonians as an opportunity for extending British influence. In August 1865 Colonel William Chamberlayne, the acting governor, proposed that Britain should step in and annex the region. But the suggestion came so soon after the 1865 Committee that Cardwell had no alternative but to reject it.[1] His refusal to annex the Mellacourie region left the way open for the French.

Some Bordeaux merchants had already requested their Government to protect French commerce in the northern rivers from extensions of the Sierra Leone customs. Governor Faidherbe had been planning direct intervention by France. Now, between 1865 and 1867, his successor, Pinet-Laprade, signed treaties with the rulers of the Nunez and Pongo rivers, where there was little British trade, then moved on to make agreements with both sides in the Moriah succession dispute.[2]

---

[1] Chamberlayne to Secretary of State 19 Aug. 1865. C.O. 267/284. Cardwell to administrator 22 Sept. 1865 (draft).

[2] Hargreaves, *Prelude to the Partition*, pp. 129–36; and 'The French Occupation of the Mellacourie 1865–67', *S.L.S.* (1957), 9, pp. 3–15; R. Catala, 'La Question de l'échange de la Gambie Britannique contre les Comptoirs Français du Golfe de Guinée de 1866 à 1876', *Revue d'Histoire*

Sierra Leonian fears were realized. French 'protectorate and suzerainty' suddenly appeared to be established in the Nunez, Pongo, Fouricaria and Mellacourie estuaries. Small French posts were built at Boké and Binty, and French anchorage dues were collected.[1]

News of the French action reached London in 1866 to find the Colonial Office surprised and hesitant. Frederick Elliot, the supervising under-secretary, was clearly shocked by the possibility of international rivalry:

> The French ought not to be coming in with Protectorates or other pretensions so near to our Settlement of Sierra Leone; Friendly European Nations ought to avoid *elbowing* each other . . . in such countries as Africa.[2]

Adderley, however, was now parliamentary under-secretary, and looking for a chance to implement his ideas. He welcomed the French advance: 'What could we wish for more than that the French should undertake these Protectorates'.[3] But Sierra Leone merchants objected to paying French duties. After a year the Foreign Office suddenly woke up to the fact that the French encroachments 'were more extensive than we were aware of'.[4]

The French were really much less concerned with their new position in the Nunez–Mellacourie region than with the hinterland of Senegal. They were more interested in Britain's possession of the Gambia than in Sierra Leone. Faidherbe's suggestion that France should try to obtain the Gambia from Britain by offering all France's interests lying to the east, in exchange, had been shelved. But the

---

des Colonies, 1948, 35, pp. 114–18; B. Schnapper, *La Politique et le Commerce Français dans le Golfe de Guinée de 1838 à 1871*, Paris, 1961, pp. 227–39.

[1] Blackall to Carnarvon 22 Mar. 1867; French treaties enclosed in Blackall to Buckingham 27 June 1867. C.O. 267/290.

[2] Min. by Elliot 14 Nov., on Blackall to Carnarvon 11 Oct. 1866. C.O. 267/287.

[3] Ibid. Min. by Adderley 14 Nov. 1866.

[4] In F.O. to C.O. 30 Apr. 1867 (C.O. 267/291) Lord Stanley suggested that Britain had no grounds for protesting against the French action. But after studying the French treaties the F.O. woke up to their implications, and suggested in F.O. to C.O. 6 Aug. 1867 that Britain should negotiate with France to ensure equal entry of British ships in the rivers.

publication of the report of the Select Committee in 1865 revived interest in the idea in Paris. The French ambassador in London made some discreet inquiries. In March 1866 the French Government formally proposed that the Gambia should be exchanged for three small posts on the Ivory Coast. Later they revised their offer and suggested that their post at Gabon might make a better exchange.[1]

Here was the first concrete opportunity for abandoning one of the West African settlements. Adderley naturally welcomed the proposal as a perfect chance of implementing the 1865 policy in the Gambia. Buckingham, the Secretary of State, thought the time was not ripe,[2] but Adderley refused to be put off. He tried to link the Gambia exchange with the question of the rivers north of Sierra Leone. Sir George Barrow, the head of the Africa Department, had always suspected that the French move in the Mellacourie was really designed to force Britain out of the Gambia. Adderley wanted to take advantage of the French advance. When the Foreign Office asked for Colonial Office comments on a proposal for getting some safeguards for British traders in the Mellacourie, Adderley revived the Gambia exchange project. But Buckingham again turned it down.[3] It is somewhat ironical that the chairman of the 1865 Committee failed to sustain his policy while in office during a Conservative ministry.

With the accession of Gladstone's Government at the end of 1868, the prospect of an Anglo-French agreement brightened. Granville determined to apply Cardwell's policy. He informed the newly appointed governor, Sir Arthur Kennedy, who called for resistance to French expansion, that the British Government should have 'no such desire for the extension of their own political influence in the vicinity of S[ierra] Leone as would lead them to oppose the establishment of a French Protectorate'.[4] As long as British traders were given adequate

[1] Catala, op. cit., pp. 121–2. The stages of the negotiations are summarized in memo. by Hemming 8 Oct., on Grant to Carnarvon 6 Oct. 1874. Gambia correspondence, C.O. 87/107.

[2] Mins. by Adderley 11 May, and Buckingham 13 May on F.O. to C.O. 5 May 1868. C.O. 87/90.

[3] Mins. by Adderley and Buckingham 26 Nov., on F.O. to C.O. 22 Nov. 1867. C.O. 267/291.

[4] Granville to Kennedy 1 Apr. (draft) after F.O. to C.O. 23 Mar. 1869. C.O. 267/303.

safeguards, Granville approved of the idea that Britain and France should draw a line across the coast, and so, in effect, partition West Africa into separate spheres of influence.

Governor Kennedy soon became an ardent exponent of the exchange project. The seemingly insuperable problems raised by religious wars in the Gambia led him to revive the idea of giving up the colony. Therefore Sir Frederic Rogers made an ingenious suggestion. The Colonial Office was becoming convinced that the Dutch enclaves on the Gold Coast ought to be eliminated — for reasons to be discussed later. The Dutch Government was eager to co-operate, although King William III of the Netherlands was opposed.[1] Why not, suggested Rogers, exchange the Gambia for the French posts on the Ivory Coast (lying to the west of the Gold Coast) and give them to the Dutch in return for their Gold Coast forts ? Granville liked the idea,[2] but Governor Kennedy's aims were somewhat different.

The governor was always more interested in getting the French out of their new positions *north* of Sierra Leone. He suggested partitioning the coast at the line of the River Dembia. Such an agreement would permit a modest expansion of British territory between Sierra Leone proper and the Îles de Los, but would eliminate all British claims to the north, including the Gambia.[3] Clarendon, the Foreign Secretary, supported the proposal, which was put to the French Government in February 1870. After four years of disappointment the French were delighted at the prospect of gaining the Gambia.

Unfortunately, the British Government had neglected public opinion, which had recently been aroused by Granville's so-called 'separatist' policy in New Zealand and Canada. While the British and French Governments were confident that the exchange would soon be settled, and the respective governors began conferring at Bathurst, opposition to the exchange was engineered by a successful pressure group of merchants in Britain. Its first victory was marked by Gladstone's admission to the House of Commons on 10 June 1870

[1] See below, pp. 121–3.
[2] Min. by Barrow 2 Apr. (with marginal comment by Rogers), on Kennedy to Granville 13 Mar. 1869. C.O. 87/91. Mins. by Barrow 21 May, and Rogers 24 May, on Kennedy to Granville 29 Apr. 1869. C.O. 267/300.
[3] Kennedy to Granville 29 Apr. 1869. *Accounts and Papers* (1870), 1, p. 543.

that no colony could be ceded to another state without Parliament's approval.[1]

In the middle of the political crisis caused by the Gambia exchange project Kimberley became Secretary of State for the Colonies. Only a week after seeing his first file of Gambia correspondence he received a deputation of merchants who traded in the colony. He agreed to consider an estimate of what they would lose if the French took over the Gambia.[2] On 15 July 1870, the day after Kimberley's interview, there were debates in Parliament and some of the colonial zealots in the House of Commons grasped a chance of making a general attack on the Liberal Government's colonial policy.[3]

Kimberley was extremely fortunate that two excuses for delay were readily to hand. The Government's Law Officers decided that legislation would be necessary before the Gambia could be given up, and it could not be fitted into the session.[4] More important, the Franco-Prussian War broke out and negotiations were suspended. Kimberley never allowed them to resume while he was at the Colonial Office. The clamour which he faced during his first week in the office obviously made a deep impression. He decided to retain the Gambia. In 1871 he gave up trying to abandon McCarthy's Island, which had been explicitly recommended in 1865.[5] When the French revived the exchange project in August 1871, Kimberley regretted having to end negotiations which had been 'conducted in a most friendly spirit between the two governments'. But there had been so much opposition he did not think they could resume.[6] The French

[1] 3 *Hansard*, 201, col. 1843.

[2] There appears to be no record of this interview, but the date is certain from Edmund Wodehouse to Meade 13 July 1870 (copy in *Granville Papers*, P.R.O. 30/29/55, p. 178) and from Monsell's statement in the Commons. Hints of what passed can be gleaned from mins. by Kimberley (17 July, on Brown to Kimberley 12 July, and 4 Aug., on Chown to Kimberley 30 July 1870. C.O./87/98) and from Monsell's speech, 3 *Hansard*, 203, col. 366.

[3] Ibid. cols. 351–67.

[4] Min. by Kimberley 16 July, on L.O. to C.O. 13 July 1870. C.O. 87/98*a*.

[5] Min. by Kimberley 10 May, on Kennedy to Kimberley 11 Apr. 1871. C.O. 87/99.

[6] Min. by Kimberley 20 Aug., on F.O. to C.O. 14 Aug. 1871. C.O. 87/101.

Government tried again in May 1873, but met with the same polite refusal.[1]

Having decided to abandon the Cardwell policy in the Gambia, Kimberley considered how best he could provide for its future security. Knatchbull-Hugessen had by now become his parliamentary under-secretary, and began to demand a more consistent policy in the Gambia. Traders on the river should either be told they could have no Government protection at all, or, he argued, force should be regularly paraded: 'It is idle for us to halt between two opinions'.[2] This was a theme often repeated by Knatchbull-Hugessen about West Africa in the next two years. It was an opinion Kimberley also came to accept. The Gambia decision marked the beginning of Kimberley's conversion. It represented the first important set-back for the Cardwell policy.

LIMITING THE FRONTIERS OF SIERRA LEONE, 1870–3

Although the Gambia was not given up, the expansion of Sierra Leone was successfully curtailed in several places, and one portion of the colony was relinquished. Bulama was handed back to Portugal after international arbitration.

A naval officer, who was sent to report on the island in 1865, suggested that it should either be abandoned altogether, or some territory on the mainland should be occupied to make the settlement pay. Bulama might then, he claimed, grow to become a rival port to Bathurst or Bissau.[3] But the Colonial Office could not accept such a proposal. Elliot still cherished an exalted code of behaviour for European Powers in Africa. They avoided 'planting thorns in each others' sides' and he regretted having 'thrust ourselves at the heart' of Portuguese Guinea.[4] He advocated complete withdrawal from Bulama. Adderley naturally saw another opportunity for fulfilling the recommendations of the 1865 Committee.[5]

[1] Min. by Kimberley 31 May, on F.O. to C.O. 23 May 1873. C.O. 87/106.
[2] Min. by Knatchbull-Hugessen 6 Aug., on Simpson to Pope-Hennessy 15 June 1872. C.O. 87/102.
[3] Lieut. Layard's report on Bulama, dated 16 Jan. 1866. C.O. 267/289.
[4] Min. by Elliot 14 Jan., on F.O. to C.O. 9 Jan. 1865. C.O. 267/285.
[5] Mins. by Adderley 20 Mar., on F.O. to C.O. 21 Dec. 1866 (C.O. 267/288); 20 June, on Blackall to Buckingham 28 May 1867 (C.O. 267/290); and 3 July, on F.O. to C.O. 26 June 1867. C.O. 267/291.

There was some hesitation in the Colonial Office because the Portuguese were thought to be unreliable over the suppression of the slave-trade. But the dilemma had to be faced. In 1867 Stanley, the Foreign Secretary, agreed that the Anglo-Portuguese dispute should go to arbitration.[1] The case was adjudicated by the President of the United States, who upheld the Portuguese case. Bulama was finally handed over in 1870.[2] It was the one clear, if rather obscure and forgotten, success of the Cardwell policy.

Liberia was another target for British expansionists. Ever since the occupation of Sherbro in 1861, Sierra Leone and the Republic had disputed over the Gallinas region, which lay between them.[3] Humanitarians in England suggested that Britain should annex the area.[4] Liberian pretensions were certainly resisted. But in 1871 Winwood Reade, the well-known explorer, proposed that the governor of Sierra Leone should become consul in Liberia. Under his influence the Republic could then 'gradually become a British protectorate'. The Colonial Office was appalled by Reade's proposal. Kimberley's answer was emphatic: 'I am quite opposed to any extension of our obligations on the African Coast, already more than sufficiently onerous'.[5] Knatchbull-Hugessen even welcomed a suggestion that Germany might acquire Liberia.[6] In the vicinity of Sierra Leone, then, Kimberley rigidly adhered to Cardwell's policy.

There were, however, 'imperial visionaries' within the colony, who were not aware of Kimberley's unmistakable stand on the question of expanding frontiers. They seem to have been given a good deal of encouragement by the men on the spot. The Legislative Council voted funds in 1871 for an expedition to travel 120 miles inland to Falaba, and then on to search for the headwaters of the Niger. Although Kimberley approved the expenditure, he once again ex-

[1] Mins. by Adderley, on F.O. to C.O. 4 Dec. 1867.

[2] F.O. to C.O. 11 May 1870. C.O. 267/309. Cf. Hargreaves, *Prelude to the Partition*, pp. 83–85.

[3] Ibid. pp. 45–47, 85–88; Fyfe, *History of Sierra Leone*, pp. 307, 320, 362.

[4] Alfred Churchill (African Aid Society) to Newcastle 31 Mar. 1864. C.O. 267/282.

[5] Reade's letter to Lord Enfield encl. in F.O. to C.O. 14 Apr., and min. by Kimberley 18 Apr. 1871. C.O. 267/313.

[6] Min. by Knatchbull-Hugessen 27 Jan. 1871 on Kennedy to Kimberley 28 Dec. 1870. C.O. 267/307.

pressed his disapproval of 'the annexing tendencies of Governors'.[1] Another mission was sent to Falaba in 1872, when the remarkable Afro-West Indian, Edward Blyden, was appointed 'Agent to the Interior'. His expedition led to proposals for extending British influence into the Scarcies river in order to channel the Falaba trade through the colony.

Knatchbull-Hugessen did not want to let the opportunity of gaining an advantage pass, but Kimberley disliked a dog-in-the-manger policy. If Britain did not want the territory, he thought the French should not be kept out as long as there were safeguards for traders. He asked the governor if some method of bringing the chiefs of the region under British influence might not be possible, such as the appointment of a British 'Agent'.[2] In 1873 Governor Pope-Hennessy visited the area and supported the idea. Nothing was done to put it into practice, however, because the Colonial Office became preoccupied with another Ashanti War.

The new crisis on the Gold Coast diverted attention from Sierra Leone at a significant moment. Blyden was about to produce his most grandiose vision. After penetrating to the heart of Fouta Djalon in 1873 he proposed the appointment of a consular agent at Timbo, the capital. Later he went on to suggest that Britain should gain control of the headwaters of the Niger. Khedive Ismail of Egypt was about to gain control of the Nile valley, he argued; Britain should acquire western Sudan. Kimberley could not take this seriously. The suggestion reached London at a critical moment in the Ashanti War. Kimberley was confident that

> Just now the British public don't seem much disposed to projects such as 'taking charge of Western Soudan', a project of considerable magnitude, not to say audacity.[3]

Not only was Blyden's proposal contrary to the 1865 policy and quite

[1] Min. by Kimberley 17 Apr., on Kennedy to Kimberley 29 Mar. 1871. C.O. 267/310.
[2] Mins. by Knatchbull-Hugessen 3 Oct., and Kimberley 8 Oct. on Blyden's report 26 Mar., encl. in Pope-Hennessy to Kimberley 1 Sept. 1872. C.O. 267/316.
[3] Min. by Kimberley 5 Dec., on Blyden to Kimberley 22 Oct. 1873. C.O. 267/324. A booklet on the Timbo Expedition is encl. in Harley to Kimberley 22 May 1873. C.O. 267/320.

impracticable during the Ashanti War; it was also difficult to relate to the general trend of Britain's West African policy, which was to concentrate on the coast, and to encourage African states.

Thus the Cardwell policy prevailed at Sierra Leone. Bulama was given up, the Gallinas and Liberia were resisted, and grandiose projects of expansion in the interior were rejected. But there had been one major failure. The most promising chance of abandoning a settlement had, in the case of the Gambia, been lost.

COMMANDER GLOVER AND THE EXPANSION OF LAGOS, 1865–72

Only two years after the rejection of the Anglo-French exchange agreement, which would have fulfilled Cardwell's policy in the Gambia, a somewhat similar decision was made over Lagos. Here again, one of the colonies from which the 1865 Committee had recommended withdrawal was retained because of a decision by Kimberley.

Why did Cardwell's policy fail at Lagos ? The answer is to be found in Glover's dispute with the Egbas.[1] Glover believed that his chief duty was to keep open the trade routes leading to Lagos. When the Ijaye War interrupted trade Glover tried to mediate between the contestants. Cardwell called halt to his efforts in 1864 while Britain's policy was under review. Cardwell's investigator, Colonel Ord, realized that Glover was biased towards Ibadan, but Ord and Glover probably knew each other from Crimean days and, on the whole, Ord defended Glover's régime at Lagos.[2] The Select Committee of Parliament severely criticized his interference in Yoruba affairs and hoped that a 'Commandant' could be appointed at Lagos until an African ruler could be restored.[3]

The man on the spot was not deterred. While the Committee

---

[1] See above, pp. 92–93.

[2] Ord to Cardwell 9 Mar. 1865. *Accounts and Papers* (1865), xxxvii, pp. 308–13. Ord and Glover were certainly friends later in life (Lady Glover, *Life of Glover*, pp. 305–13). They had both served in the Baltic campaign during the Crimean War, when Ord was Brig. Maj. of the British military detachment, and Glover served as senior lieut. of the *Rosamond*.

[3] *Reports from Committees* (1865), v, p. 15.

deliberated in London, Glover took the law into his own hands. The Egba were still threatening Ikorodu, Lagos's port on the lagoon for the Ibadan trade. After an ultimatum on 29 March 1865, Glover sent in 150 men of the West India Regiment, supported by his Hausa police force from Lagos, and drove off the Egba.[1] Thus one of the first tasks facing Samuel Blackall, the first governor-in-chief of the West African Settlements, was to warn Glover of the Cardwell policy. Lagos was not to be abandoned immediately, but intervention on the mainland was to cease.

For a short while it seemed that the Lagos Government would fall in with Cardwell's policy. Blackall visited the colony, listened to missionaries, who represented the Egba case, and agreed that Glover was too much pro-Ibadan. He made a 'gesture' by repealing Glover's restrictions on trade to Abeokuta and communicated with the Egba in friendly terms.[2] In 1866, while Admiral Patey briefly ruled at Lagos, a flourishing trade with Abeokuta resumed.[3] But Glover returned as administrator in November 1866. He resumed his inter-ference in mainland affairs, and treated contemptuously the very elements in Abeokuta who might have been suitable instruments of the Cardwell policy.

In a number of the coastal regions of West Africa there existed in this period a growing literate class of 'new men'. They have been variously called 'educated Africans', 'scholars', 'creoles', 'recaptives', the 'new élite'.[4] They were distinguished from the majority of their fellow countrymen because they had often become detached from traditional society by their contact with Europeans, their trading interests, by wars, slavery, or by residence abroad in Brazil, Sierra Leone, Great Britain, the West Indies or the United States. After

[1] Glover to Cardwell, 5 Apr. 1865. C.O. 147/8; Biobaku, *The Egba*, p. 76; Ajayi, *Yoruba Warfare*, pp. 119–20.

[2] Blackall to Cardwell 3 Mar. 1866; Glover to Cardwell 10 Mar. 1866; Blackall's correspondence with the Egba in Blackall to Cardwell 21 Mar. 1866. C.O. 147/11.

[3] Biobaku, op. cit., pp. 81–82.

[4] See Ajayi, *Christian Missions in Nigeria*, chs. 2, 4, 5 and 6; Biobaku, op. cit., ch. 7; J. D. Hargreaves, *A Life of Sir Samuel Lewis*, Oxford, 1958; Fyfe, *History of Sierra Leone*; D. Kimble, *A Political History of Ghana. The Rise of Gold Coast Nationalism 1850–1928*, Oxford, 1963, chs. 2, 3, 5 and 6.

education in mission schools, they often embraced certain European ideas and manners, and occasionally Christianity. They were employed in the British colonies in their own trade, as clergymen, Government officials and members of the Legislative Councils. From among this class the leaders of several self-government movements emerged in the 1860's, who are now seen as the early progenitors of modern African nationalism. 'Africa for the Africans' was an inevitable cry as Europeans ventured inland from the coast, but it came not only from rulers, like the kings of Dahomey, who tried to insulate themselves from European power, but also from the 'new men' who wished to adopt many European ideas provided they were unaccompanied by alien rule.

The 'new men' might well have fitted the requirements of Buxton's theory about 'African agency' and the 1865 Committee's recommendations about self-government. Yet with few exceptions, British officers were contemptuous of these incipient 'nationalist' movements. One governor stigmatized the leaders of such a movement on the Gold Coast as 'characterless mulattoes'.[1] British rule in the interiors of the Gold Coast and Nigeria in a later period often tended to strengthen the power of traditional authority rather than foster the African classes most receptive to European ideas. Commander Glover was an early exponent of this attitude. The 'new men' who emerged in Abeokuta in 1865 were largely responsible for the virulence of his hostility to the Egba state.

A group of educated Sierra Leone emigrants, led by George W. Johnson, formed the Egba United Board of Management to promote a new sort of traditional government in Abeokuta with European bureaucratic trappings.[2] Whether Johnson had contact with Africans who appeared before the 1865 Committee, or was in any way influenced by its recommendations, is not clear. Certainly, rumours circulated about Lagos in 1865 that the colonial Government was to be withdrawn.[3]

Johnson and his followers were confident enough to challenge Glover's boundaries. They insisted that Lagos had no right to territory on the mainland. They demanded that Glover should withdraw

[1] Gov. Kennedy to Kimberley 9 Jan. 1872. C.O. 96/92.
[2] Biobaku, op. cit., pp. 79–80; Ajayi, op. cit., ch. 6.
[3] Glover to Cardwell 5 Apr. 1865. C.O. 147/8.

his garrison. Glover maintained Johnson had no authority to speak for Abeokuta, that the 'independence' of Otta must be preserved, and that a negotiated boundary should be drawn. Glover's intransigence probably contributed to the 'outbreak' against the Europeans at Abeokuta on 13 October 1867 — the *Ifole* — and the expulsion of the European missionaries and traders a year later.[1] After a quarter of a century of contact, Britain's relations with Abeokuta were severed.

At first, Glover did not respond violently. His interference in Egba affairs stopped. He concentrated on developing the port of Lagos, and he went exploring the River Volta in the Gold Coast with Sir Arthur Kennedy. Glover also knew that the Egba were disunited among themselves following the death in 1868 of the regent — a brother of the founder of the Egba state. In fact, when one of the parties in the Egba succession dispute approached Glover, it even seemed that Abeokuta was, at last, suing for peaceful relations with the colony.[2] Glover went on leave in 1870 hoping that a better era was about to dawn.

Yet in 1871, when he returned from leave, Glover suddenly tried to sway the destiny of the Yorubas. The reason may probably be found in reports he read while at home about the effects of Khedive Ismail of Egypt's invasion of the upper Nile on the trade of the Sahara. Glover remembered Baikie's dreams on the 1857 Niger expedition — his own first introduction to Africa. He began to envisage 'Lagos becoming the port of Central Africa, a rival of the ports of Tripoli and Bengazi'.[3] Beside this 'imperial vision' the rival Yoruba states in the immediate vicinity of Lagos became a frustrating nuisance to Glover. He decided to bend them to his will.

Glover was convinced that the Egbas and Ijebus were trying to monopolize the interior trade. He feared that Ibadan would go to war to reopen the direct routes to Lagos, and so he determined to

[1] Biobaku, op. cit., pp. 83–84; Ajayi, op. cit., pp. 201–4. Yonge to Buckingham 28 Oct. and 13 Nov. 1867. C.O. 147/13; Blackall to Buckingham 15 Dec. 1867 and Kennedy to Buckingham 30 Oct. 1868. C.O. 147/14.

[2] Glover, 30 Oct. 1869, suggested that after 'a four years' interval' the Egba were trying to enter into friendly relations with Lagos. Encl. in Kendall to Granville 11 Nov. 1869. C.O. 147/15.

[3] Kennedy to Kimberley 4 Oct. 1870. C.O. 147/18; Glover to Kimberley, London, 21 Dec. 1870. C.O. 147/19.

create alternative routes in order to keep the peace. Lieutenants were despatched to organize routes to the north-west, through Igbessa, Ilaro and Ketu, and to the east, by way of Ode and Ondo.[1] He believed the existence of such alternative routes would force the Egba and Ijebu routes open. Otherwise, he felt, war was imminent. The emergency also provided an excuse for annexing Porto Novo, where rival factions had been contending for power since the French abandoned their 'protectorate' in 1864. Glover linked Porto Novo to his Yoruba diplomacy by suggesting that it was the last port where the Egba could exchange slaves for arms. He claimed that 'the peace of the Yoruba country for years to come' hung on the question of its annexation to Lagos.[2]

Glover's forceful policy came dramatically to a head in 1872. The Egbas claimed all the Lagos territory except for the island itself — a claim which, if conceded, might have led to Britain's withdrawal. Glover, therefore, threw caution to the winds. Ignoring the home Government, he continued his blockade of Porto Novo, pressed on with his road-opening diplomacy, and passed an order empowering himself to prohibit trade to the mainland as an aid to his policy. He prepared to defend his frontiers. He intended to hold out even though in 1872 trade from Lagos was brought to a standstill. He believed that, in the long run, Lagos would never be viable unless there was free access for trade inland.[3]

EDWARD KNATCHBULL-HUGESSEN AND THE RETENTION
OF LAGOS, 1872-3

Glover's dramatic and unauthorized action forced the Colonial Office to reconsider Britain's whole position at Lagos. By 1872 the expanding frontier could no longer be ignored. The Cardwell policy had, in reality, been based on the frontier doctrine of qualified restraint. Successive Secretaries of State had reiterated the same theme: no

[1] Glover to administrator-in-chief 7 Sept. 1871. C.O. 147/21, with map (now filed in P.R.O.: MR 389 (5)); Glover to Kennedy 18 Oct. 1871. C.O. 147/21.
[2] Glover 1 Nov., in Kennedy to Kimberley 15 Nov. 1871. C.O. 147/21.
[3] Glover to Kimberley 3 Feb. 1872; Glover to Kendall 17 Feb. 1872; Pope-Hennessy to Kimberley 27 Apr. 1872. C.O. 147/23.

interference in Yoruba affairs — *except* when the safety of the colony was at stake. In the knowledge that he was permitted this discretion, Glover had pressed ahead. His request for the annexation of Porto Novo in 1872 forced his superiors in London to review their attitude.

Unfortunately the Colonial Office was divided over the Lagos issue. Herbert and Knatchbull-Hugessen, who were both new-comers to the Office, tended to support Glover. Kimberley was 'altogether against' Glover's expansionism: 'On similar grounds of philanthropy we might be called upon to annex Dahomey, Ashantee, Abeokuta, and for anything I see . . . the greater part of Africa'. He rejected Glover's alternative idea of appointing a Resident in Porto Novo. 'Africa is a large continent', he wrote, 'and our extensions may be limitless if we are to provide for the peace of the interior.'[1]

Kimberley determined to curb Glover. He even considered recal-ling him. But Kimberley decided instead to send a new governor-in-chief, who was about to go to West Africa, to caution Glover. In April 1872, therefore, it seemed very likely that a serious attempt would be made to follow the Cardwell policy at Lagos. Yet at this very moment Knatchbull-Hugessen began to express serious mis-givings. And when the new governor-in-chief actually began to put the policy into practice, the Colonial Office was so shocked by his methods that it rapidly reconsidered the Cardwell policy at Lagos.

The new governor was John Pope-Hennessy. He was probably the only enthusiastic supporter of the Cardwell policy to receive an official appointment in West Africa during the period when it might have been tried. In Sierra Leone he achieved popularity by repealing the House Tax.[2] His support for university education in West Africa accorded well with the aspirations of the 'new men' who were becoming prominent in commerce and the missions.[3]

Pope-Hennessy was, in fact, one of the most controversial figures of the Victorian colonial service. A mercurial Irishman, he had become

---

[1] Mins. by Kimberley 11 Dec., on Kennedy to Kimberley 15 Nov. 1871 (C.O. 147/21) and 5 Mar., on Glover to Kimberley 13 Feb. 1872. C.O. 147/23.

[2] Fyfe, *History of Sierra Leone*, pp. 388–9.

[3] Booklet of correspondence between Blyden and Pope-Hennessy, Free-town, 1872, encl. in Pope-Hennessy to Kimberley 28 Dec. 1872. C.O. 267/317.

so well known after being elected Tory Member of Parliament for King's County in 1859 that he only missed office in Derby's Government in 1866 because he lost his seat. Disraeli tried to get him the first colonial governorship of the Straits Settlements, but the job went to Colonel Harry Ord, one of the key figures in the policy-review of 1865. Pope-Hennessy had to be satisfied, as his first colonial appointment from 1867 to 1869, with the post of administrator of the tiny island of Labuan off the north coast of Borneo. Wherever he went in the Empire he quarrelled with subordinates and fought for the underdog. At Labuan he suspended his own father-in-law — Hugh Low, later one of the greatest Residents in Malaya.[1] In 1872, Pope-Hennessy swept through the West African settlements like a tropical storm — quickly and destructively.

He reached Lagos on 24 April 1872. A few days' experience convinced him of the iniquity of Glover's policy. The Porto Novo blockade was withdrawn, the Egba were given friendly assurances. The governor listened to the Egba case and he disavowed Glover's actions. He also arranged for Docemo, the former King of Lagos, to be given a part in the island's government. When he finally left Lagos on 9 July 1872 Pope-Hennessy was convinced that he had achieved a 'friendly understanding with the Egbas' and that trade would soon revive. Glover was sent home.[2]

Pope-Hennessy's sweeping descent upon Lagos undoubtedly shocked the Colonial Office. They wanted to restrain Glover. They had no idea that Pope-Hennessy would take the 'self-government' clauses of the 1865 Report literally and commence 'handing over' to the Africans of the Lagos region. Kimberley thought the governor was unfair to Glover, and anticipated trouble.[3] Herbert, wisely ignoring the personal recriminations which ensued, thought the lesson of the affair was that colonial administrators should be made to understand that they

---

[1] See memo. by Lord Salisbury in *Carnarvon Papers*, P.R.O. 30/6/10, p. 1; Pope-Hennessy, *Verandah*; Hamilton, *Barbados and the Confederation Question*, pp. 44–46, and app. 13.

[2] For a discussion of the way the C.O. tried to maintain that Glover had not really been 'dismissed' see my article, 'Commander Glover and the Colony of Lagos, 1861–73', *J.A.H.* (1963), 4 (1), p. 72.

[3] Min. by Kimberley 6 Aug., on Pope-Hennessy to Kimberley 24 June 1872. C.O. 147/23.

were supposed to govern their colonies efficiently and not interfere in the affairs of the African states on their frontiers.

Glover's dismissal found the Colonial Office leadership once more divided. Kimberley supported Herbert's view and enunciated two general principles. First, that Britain would have to accept what he believed was the *status quo* in the trade of the Lagos region:

> The Lagos people sell to the Jebus [*sic*] and Jebus to their neighbours and the neighbours to the interior and vice versa to the coast. This is the custom of whole countries in the interior and the Governor must not interfere.

Secondly, in her political relations with African states, Britain had to be impartial and pacific:

> We should be satisfied as a rule with cultivating friendly relations with all the surrounding tribes, and when we endeavour to feel our way to direct intercourse with tribes further in the interior should do so with much caution, and not attempt to force on such intercourse by coercive measures.[1]

He still believed that Pope-Hennessy's intentions were right — only his methods were too rash. Knatchbull-Hugessen, however, not only took up Glover's case, but he began to see its implications for the West Africa colonies as a whole.

Knatchbull-Hugessen now insisted that Britain's mission in West Africa could not be fulfilled by standing 'with our hands folded and shrinking from any combat with native habits, ignorance and prejudices'. Kimberley replied by confessing, 'I am . . . less combative than Mr. Hugessen, and am not prepared for a crusade in W. Africa on behalf of trade, civilization and Christianity'.[2] But Kimberley did not deter his under-secretary. Soon Knatchbull-Hugessen went as far as to assert that Glover had been right. And in November 1872 a letter was received from the Rev. David Hinderer, on leave from Ibadan, who also supported Glover.[3]

When it became evident that the roads to Lagos remained closed,

[1] Ibid. Mins. by Herbert 3 Aug., and Kimberley 6 Aug., on Pope-Hennessy to Kimberley 25 June 1872.
[2] Mins. by Knatchbull-Hugessen 10 Oct., and Kimberley 12 Oct., on Charles Leigh Clare to Kimberley, Manchester, 3 Oct. 1872. C.O. 147/25.
[3] Hinderer to Kimberley 1 Nov. 1872. C.O. 147/26.

I.F.T.—E

and Henry Fowler, Glover's successor, called for a 'quiet blockade' to force them open, even Kimberley began to waver. He narrowed his criticism now to Glover's partiality. Knatchbull-Hugessen pressed his case. Eventually Lagos would have to be expanded or abandoned. Meanwhile he hoped that they could avert a crisis 'since the policy of H.M.'s Govt. would not allow for extension and Public Opinion would certainly not [permit] its abandonment'.[1]

By the beginning of 1873 Kimberley and Knatchbull-Hugessen were in fundamental disagreement over Lagos. At the same time they had to face a new set of problems raised by the Fante Confederation movement on the Gold Coast. There was also a distinct possibility of another Ashanti invasion. As crisis followed crisis the arguments within the Colonial Office all began to focus on the basic principles of Britain's West African policy. On 23 February 1873, in a long, forceful minute, Knatchbull-Hugessen castigated the Cardwell policy. Britain's predicament on the coast, he argued, arose 'from the inherent viciousness of the whole system . . . to do neither one thing or the other — to leave boundaries undefined — jurisdiction uncertain and administrators uninstructed' was to court confusion. Africans were 'uncertain of our intentions towards them — even doubtful whether we desire or intend to keep Lagos'. He blamed the 1865 Select Committee for the 'half and half policy of Great Britain — occupying territory as if she were ashamed of it . . . coaxing one day and threatening the next'. Above all, he maintained that whatever the Government's policy had been '*Public Opinion* will not permit the withdrawal of British Authority from the W. Coast of Africa'.

Like Glover, Knatchbull-Hugessen would have preferred to see all the seaboard in British hands and the Yoruba states compelled by force to keep an open door for trade. But he knew Kimberley would not permit the annexation of Porto Novo. He suggested: (1) that the borders of the Lagos colony should be clearly defined, and within them domestic slavery should be forbidden; (2) that the remaining 'Protected Territory' should be governed through African rulers 'securing their adhesion and fidelity by a moderate stipend, and establishing district courts . . .'; and (3) that an attempt should be made at creating stability in the Yoruba states by offering stipends to

[1] Min. by Knatchbull-Hugessen 12 Jan., on Goldsworthy to Kimberley, London, 4 Jan. 1873. C.O. 147/29.

the rulers of Abeokuta and Ijebu, provided they maintained open roads for traders.

Knatchbull-Hugessen's blend of frank, long-term appreciation and practical compromise finally convinced Kimberley. 'I put out of the question retirement from Lagos. The place must be held by force if necessary.'[1] He decided to return to the boundaries approved by Cardwell in 1864, before the 1865 Committee — British sovereignty at Lagos, Badagry, Leckie and Palma, the rest of the ceded territory to be 'protected' only, because of the existence of domestic slavery. A new governor would be appointed.

Lagos, then, would not be abandoned. Although Glover's expansionism was checked and a passive policy prevailed, Cardwell's 1865 policy had received its second major set-back. Although there was still great uncertainty as to Britain's future at Lagos during the rest of the Gladstone Government, the colony was not given up. Kimberley's new policy was stillborn because the Colonial Office was diverted in 1873 to more pressing problems on the Gold Coast.

ANGLO–DUTCH TERRITORIAL CHANGES ON THE GOLD
    COAST, 1868–72

The contradictory features of the Cardwell policy were revealed in their most dramatic form on the Gold Coast. Although Governor Blackall accepted the Select Committee's conclusion that the British forts should ultimately be abandoned,[2] the Gold Coast was in fact the scene of the most notable territorial acquisitions during the period of the Cardwell policy.

In 1868 the coastline was partitioned into British and Dutch spheres of influence. In 1872 all the Dutch possessions were ceded to Britain. Both accessions could be justified by Cardwell's saving-clause permitting minor extensions of territory which contributed to the efficiency and economy of existing colonies. But the territorial changes provoked a violent reaction from the Gold Coast states.

---

[1] Mins. by Knatchbull-Hugessen 23 Feb., and Kimberley 25 Feb., on Pope-Hennessy to Kimberley 30 Dec. 1873. C.O. 147/24. A large portion of the text of Knatchbull-Hugessen's min. is printed in my 'Glover and Lagos', p. 75.

[2] Blackall to Secretary of State 19 May 1866. C.O. 96/71.

Paradoxically, the changes prompted a number of the literate 'new men' of the Gold Coast to promote incipient nationalist movements, which might have fulfilled the self-government aspects of the Cardwell policy. They also caused a revival of Ashanti hostility, and ultimately they led to the abandonment of the Cardwell policy.

The Anglo-Dutch partition agreement of 1868 was designed as a minor fiscal and administrative 'tidying-up' and had been under discussion for over twenty years. It was made without any reference to the African states which it affected. The existence of customs-free Dutch forts interspersed among the British forts rendered the collection of duties difficult, and enclaves of Dutch 'protectorate' inland led to jurisdictional disputes. All previous attempts to solve these problems had broken down over points of detail.

By 1864 the Dutch realized that Netherlands Guinea was an expensive legacy from the past. The Minister for Colonies offered it to Britain in return for British support of Dutch expansion throughout Sumatra. The offer was not taken up, but it was probably the origin of a series of Anglo-Dutch suggestions about a possible bargain over Sumatra and the Gold Coast. In 1867, however, an Anglo-Dutch convention provided for joint tariff policies on the Gold Coast and for a division of the coast at the Sweet river, which lay between Elmina and Cape Coast Castle. The Dutch received the forts to the west of the line, while Britain took over to the east. The change had been under discussion for so long that it was greeted by the Colonial Office with considerable relief.[1]

The only misgivings were voiced by Adderley. On the eve of the exchange he reminded his colleagues of the 1865 Report. He believed that the solution to Britain's problems lay 'in the direction of withdrawing, not in entering into fresh treaties and engagements'.[2] He continued to press for the abandonment of the Gold Coast, as he had of the Gambia, throughout his period of office. It was unfortunate that Adderley made little impression. The 1868 exchange had wide-

---

[1] Text of treaty in *Accounts and Papers* (1867), lxxiv, pp. 371–6. See Coombs, *Gold Coast, Britain and the Netherlands*, ch. 2; cf. my article, 'Disraeli's Election Blunder: The Straits of Malacca issue in the 1874 Election', *R.M.S.* (1961), 5, pp. 77–82.

[2] Min. by Adderley 18 Jan. 1868 on Blackall to Buckingham 14 Dec. 1867. C.O. 96/74.

spread repercussions in the Gold Coast. It led eventually to a major campaign against Ashanti.

The Anglo-Dutch exchange set off a complex chain reaction. The Dutch had to use force to occupy some of their new possessions. The protectorate states thereupon formed an alliance to resist the Dutch and defend themselves. The Dutch soon found their settlements so untenable that they decided to give them up to Britain in 1872. The cession was opposed by the rulers of Ashanti, which caused the Fante and other protectorate states, who were still afraid of Ashanti power, to support an incipient nationalist movement in the protectorate.

The crucial factor linking all these developments was a historical link between the Dutch and Ashanti, who had captured the 'rent notes' for Elmina in the eighteenth century. From that time the Dutch had made regular payments to Ashanti, where they recruited soldiers for service in Netherlands India, carried on some trade, and sometimes maintained an agent. Ashanti found Elmina convenient as an outlet to the sea, and had extremely close relations with its inhabitants. The Elminas were therefore hated and feared by the Fante as a symbol of the menace of Ashanti power.[1] The Anglo-Dutch agreements of 1867 and 1872 totally disregarded all these well-established facts of Gold Coast history and sparked off a series of crises. For this reason historians have castigated the exchange of forts in 1868.[2]

The inhabitants around the British forts to the west of Elmina did not want Dutch rule. At Kommenda they resisted the Dutch take-over in February 1868 and suffered bombardment from the sea. When the protectorate states rose against the Dutch, they were joined by Wassaw and Denkyera, who also felt betrayed by Britain. Soon a large Fante army surrounded the Dutch at Elmina. The whole Gold Coast seemed to be in turmoil.

The British settlements were also endangered. Herbert Taylor

[1] Dutch–Ashanti relations are discussed in Coombs, op. cit., pp. 8–12.

[2] Ward, *History of the Gold Coast*, p. 231: 'Never was there a greater political blunder'; Claridge, *History of the Gold Coast and Ashanti*, i, pp. 560–2: 'a monumental piece of folly and injustice'; Coombs, op. cit., p. 48: 'the event proved a monstrous blunder'; Kimble, *Political History of Ghana*, p. 224: 'The whole transaction was a severe set-back to European prestige'.

Ussher, who governed the British forts (his title was 'Administrator'), was afraid to help his Dutch counterpart for fear that the
Fante might attack the British forts.[1] Some of the 'new men', who
were promoting a form of Fante nationalist movement, demanded an
end to the British connexion.   Ussher knew that the Ashanti would
intervene to save their allies in Elmina.   He even feared the possibility
of French intervention.[2]   He believed that the only way to solve the
crisis was to buy out the Dutch on the Gold Coast and gain a free hand
in the region.   Then, he felt, local African rivalries could be settled by
arranging an alliance between the Elminas and the Fante.   But he did
not appreciate the deep-rooted enmity of the Fante and the Elminas.
He lost his temper with the Fante when they rejected his plan, and
severed relations with them.

When the news of the Elmina crisis reached London, Adderley
felt that his opinion had been vindicated.   He thought Ussher was
'too figity' and had 'too much idea of building up our prestige'.[3]
Adderley was still convinced that it would be far better for Britain to
quit the Gold Coast altogether.   Why, in the face of the crisis, was
Adderley's advice set aside?   Part of the answer may be found in the
crucial hiatus among policy-makers at all levels which occurred at the
end of 1868.

On the coast, Herbert Ussher departed on leave, and in his absence
Sir Arthur Kennedy, newly appointed governor-in-chief, visited the
Gold Coast.   Kennedy completely reversed Ussher's policy.   Impressed by the 'general bearing, intelligence and comparative civilisation' of the Fante, compared with what he called the 'wholly barbarous
and uneducated' Elminas, with their close ties with Ashanti, Kennedy
ordered William H. Simpson, who acted in Ussher's place, to con-
ciliate the Fante.[4]

[1] Ussher to Kennedy (confidential) 16 Feb., in Kennedy to Buckingham
26 Feb. 1868.   C.O. 96/76.

[2] Ibid. Kennedy to Buckingham 27 Mar. 1868.   Rumours that the French
claimed land on the Gold Coast spread after some French naval officers
engaged on survey work visited the ruins of an old French trading-fort.
F.O. to C.O. 8 June 1868.   C.O. 96/78.

[3] Min. by Adderley 17 Aug., on Kennedy to Buckingham 28 July 1868.
C.O. 96/76.

[4] Kennedy to Buckingham 7 Nov. 1868 (and confidential same date).
C.O. 96/77.

At home, the Liberals came to power. Sir George Barrow, the head of the African Department, was beginning to accept the view that there would be no peace on the Gold Coast unless the Dutch left. But Granville, the Secretary of State in the incoming Government, seriously considered implementing the Cardwell policy. He was shocked by the expense of a colony where British influence was obviously declining. He saw no reason for keeping the Gold Coast. He gave warning that its officers might find their posts abolished. Even when Governor Kennedy came round to the view that the Dutch should go, Granville stood firm. He was influenced by Elliot, who was about to retire from being assistant under-secretary. As he briefed Granville on West Africa, Elliot described the Gold Coast as the 'most noxious and worthless' of the settlements. With 'no Slave Trade to suppress . . . no legitimate commerce to encourage', Britain's role there was questionable.[1]

The Cardwell policy was about to prevail on the Gold Coast, when Granville changed his mind in 1869. Two things were responsible for his dramatic *volte-face*. He realized that the Gambia exchange was a more promising way of following the Cardwell policy. He thought that the acquisition of the Dutch Gold Coast might assist.[2] He learned that the Dutch colonial minister wanted to give up Elmina, and so negotiations were reopened at The Hague.[3] They finally bore fruit in 1872, when the Dutch gratuitously ceded their Gold Coast possessions to Britain. There were three years of delay before the completion of the cession because Ashanti claimed Elmina, and sent a small force into the town (which will be discussed later) and because some rather complex arrangements were made whereby the Dutch sent the treaty to the States-General along with two other Anglo-Dutch colonial agreements.[4]

The Colonial Office believed that the acquisition of Elmina was

[1] Ibid. Mins. by Barrow 2 Dec., Elliot 2 Dec., Monsell 12 Dec., and Granville 12 Dec. 1868; min. by Granville 24 Dec. on Treas. to C.O. 15 Dec. 1868. C.O. 96/78.

[2] See above, pp. 104–9.

[3] Clarendon to Granville 5 Oct. 1869. *Granville Papers*, P.R.O. 30/29/55, p. 38; Coombs, *Gold Coast, Britain and the Netherlands*, pp. 57–65.

[4] The 'links' with the Sumatran and Surinam treaties are discussed in my article, 'Disraeli's Election Blunder', pp. 87–93.

quite compatible with the Cardwell policy. Kimberley, who completed the negotiations, explained to Gladstone that it was 'by no means a case of extending our responsibilities, to which I should be most averse, but of relieving us from a serious embarrassment'.[1] Governor Pope-Hennessy, who went to take possession of Elmina, was told that the object of the change was 'not the acquisition or the extension of British power, but the maintenance of tranquillity and the promotion of peaceful commerce on the Coast'.[2]

The cession of Dutch Guinea was effected on 6 April 1872 when Governor James Pope-Hennessy received Admiral de Ruyter's baton, symbol of Dutch rule for over two centuries. Pope-Hennessy, who had just got rid of Glover from Lagos, sent Ussher, the administrator, home on 'sick leave', after finding plenty of fault with his administration. The new governor seemed to have gone out 'as a new broom to sweep clean places that have become foul', said Knatchbull-Hugessen, and 'the old brooms and old housemaids had better away'.[3] Britain now had the Gold Coast to herself. The escape-clause in the Cardwell policy had been utilized yet again; a minor extension of territory had been made in the hope of bringing peace to the Gold Coast.

Hope soon gave way to perplexity and despair. The cession of Elmina exacerbated Britain's difficulties with Ashanti. The Government desperately wanted peaceful relations with the powerful inland nation. Some members of the Colonial Office even welcomed the idea of Ashanti gaining access to the sea.[4] But the Ashantis bitterly resented Britain's policy along the coast. The cession of Elmina reinforced their antagonism. The Colonial Office seemed to forget that the causes of the Ashanti War of 1863–4 had not been removed. The Ashantis still regarded themselves as in a state of war with the Gold Coast Government. The new difficulty over Elmina only added to tensions which had existed for a decade.

[1] Kimberley to Gladstone 14 Oct. 1870. *Gladstone Papers*, 44224/88.
[2] Kimberley to Pope-Hennessy 12 Feb. (draft instructions), after F.O. to C.O. 29 Jan. 1872. C.O. 96/95.
[3] Min. by Knatchbull-Hugessen 6 June, on Pope-Hennessy to Kimberley 6 May 1872. C.O. 96/93.
[4] Memo. by Rogers 27 Jan. (explaining the Gold Coast background for Knatchbull-Hugessen), after Kennedy to Kimberley 2 Jan. 1871. C.O. 90/87.

ANGLO-ASHANTI HOSTILITY, 1865–72

Anglo–Ashanti hostility was the inevitable result of the misunderstand-
ings which occurred when totally different cultures came into contact.
It was a pattern repeated thousands of times on the frontiers of empire
in the nineteenth century. Occasionally a remarkable individual like
Maclean could be accepted briefly as a mediator. But usually British
officials on the Gold Coast grossly misunderstood Ashanti under-
takings. Ashanti felt that Britain failed to stand by the 1831 treaty.
Such a misunderstanding had caused the war of 1863–4. Ashanti
received no satisfaction at this time and the chiefs were only dissuaded
from making another attack by their paramount ruler, the Asantehene.

In the years after the 1863–4 war, Ashanti traders continued to be
molested in protectorate states like Assin, which lay on the Ashanti
route to the sea. Although by the end of 1865 the administrator
believed that the Ashanti danger was over and confidentially expected
that peaceful trade would revive,[1] Ashanti hostility remained. They
merely gave up the direct approach. In the late 1860's they turned
to harass the protectorate in the Volta river region. During the
period when the Anglo-Dutch exchanges were stirring up trouble
around Elmina and the western protectorate, Ashanti threatened the
region of the Volta.

British influence in this part of the Gold Coast had always been
weak. After the Danish possessions were acquired in 1850 the extent
of the protectorate in the east was never defined. In the 1860's the
Volta states engaged in a fierce battle for the control of the palm oil
trade, not unlike the rivalries of the Niger Delta. Ada, on the west
bank, with assistance from Accra, vied with Awuna on the east shore,
which was supported by Akwamu further north. The King of
Akwamu requested help from Ashanti, and the asantehene seemed
eager to exploit the situation. By the end of 1866 Accra merchants were
crying in alarm that three thousand Ashantis were aiding Akwamu.[2]

[1] Conran to Cardwell 8 Sept. and 9 Oct. 1865. C.O. 96/68.
[2] Min. by Barrow 8 Feb. 1867 on Blackall to Carnarvon 26 Dec. 1866.
C.O. 96/72; copies of Accra Confederacy to Fante Confederation 14 Oct.
and 21 Sept., in Solomon to Boyce 22 Nov. 1869. *Methodist Missionary
Society Archives*, Gold Coast incoming letters 1868–71; see also F. Wolfson,
'British Relations with the Gold Coast', pp. 120–7.

E 2

Ashanti pressure in the eastern Gold Coast was resisted by the British administrators. Without authority from home they determined to help the eastern states of the protectorate. Small detachments of troops were sent to Accra and Ada.[1] Ussher sent Thomas Birch Freeman, an English-born mulatto, who was former superintendent of the Wesleyan mission, as commissioner to the Volta region, to make a treaty of friendship and commerce with Akwamu. If authority had been forthcoming from home, Ussher would have appointed Freeman as magistrate for the area, in the hope that the 'protectorate' could be reasserted in the Volta.[2]

In Kumasi, the Ashanti capital, Ashanti hostility to Britain intensified. The peaceable asantehene, Kwaku Dua II, was succeeded in 1867 by Kofi Karikari, who soon became the ogre of Victorian nurseries. Ashanti pressure on the protectorate increased. They not only took part in the local rivalries of the Volta. They now prepared to assist the Elminas in case they were attacked in the uproar which had followed the Anglo-Dutch exchange of 1868. Kofi Karikari despatched two armies southwards, whose precise purpose remains somewhat obscure. His uncle, Akyempon, led a small force to assist the Elminas. The war-chief Ado Bofo led reinforcements to the Ashanti army in the Volta. The asantahene himself prepared to advance by the direct route across the Pra.[3] By the time Sir Arthur Kennedy, the governor-in-chief, visited the Gold Coast in October 1868, Elmina and the Volta were potential danger spots for the colony.

Kennedy, however, was ignorant of the latest Ashanti moves, and he discountenanced the danger. Akyempon had not got very far; the central attack did not materialize. The governor could concentrate on the immediate menace in the Volta. After steaming 45 miles up-stream in November 1868, accompanied by Commander Glover from Lagos, Kennedy persuaded Ada and Awuna to sign a treaty. He dreamt optimistically of opening up a vast new area for trade.[4] But

[1] Conran to Cardwell 10 Mar. 1866. C.O. 96/70.
[2] Akwamu treaty 28 Apr., encl. in Yonge to Buckingham 15 Oct. 1867; Yonge to Buckingham 15 Oct., and Buckingham to Blackall 23 Nov. 1867. C.O. 96/74. See A. Birtwhistle, *Thomas Birch Freeman, West African Pioneer*, London, 1950, p. 101.
[3] Ward, *History of Gold Coast*, p. 236.
[4] Kennedy to Buckingham, Accra, 14 Dec. and 3 Dec. 1868. C.O. 96/77.

when William H. Simpson, the acting administrator, followed up Kennedy's mission with a visit to Akwamu early in 1869, he found that place still 'swarming with Ashantees'. He was virtually held prisoner himself for a few days.[1] By the spring of 1869, then, Simpson was quite convinced that another major Ashanti War was imminent. He claimed that four armies were descending upon the protectorate. Gallantly he planned to rally the defences of the protectorate states and to reassert British influence on the Gold Coast.[2]

The Colonial Office's reaction to these alarms was at first quite different from that of the man on the spot. Although they were busily utilizing Cardwell's saving-clause to make territorial extensions in the west, they adhered to the letter of the 1865 Report in the eastern protectorate. They declined to assert British influence in the Volta region. Accra merchants who petitioned for help met the same response in Whitehall as those who ventured in New Guinea and the Malay States in the same period:

> persons who trade at remote places must understand that they are to settle their own quarrels and that they are not to expect the intervention of British Forces.[3]

Yet, just as at Lagos and elsewhere, the loophole for local action was eventually utilized. It is very significant that, even while they tried to prevent intervention, politicians of both parties admitted that it was difficult to maintain a policy of restraint in all circumstances. Adderley, who did not waver in his desire to get rid of the Gold Coast settlements, saw that even modest interference could lead to widespread expansion. He opposed the appointment of Freeman as magistrate in the Volta because he thought the creation of a 'travelling arbitrator' would be 'tantamount to assuming the Sovereignty' of the region and would 'involve us in administering laws and recognizing customs of which we disapprove, if not in the actual disputes and wars of the tribes'.[4] During Carnarvon's brief period of office in 1866–7

[1] Simpson to Kennedy, Akwamu, 2 Mar., in Kennedy to Granville 15 Mar. 1869. C.O. 96/79.
[2] Ibid. Simpson, Accra, 22 Mar., in Kennedy to Granville 14 Apr. 1869.
[3] Min. by Elliot 11 July, on Blackall to Carnarvon 20 June 1866. C.O. 96/71.
[4] Min. by Adderley 12 Nov., on Yonge to Buckingham 15 Oct. 1867. C.O. 96/74.

the policy of qualified restraint was reaffirmed. He would sanction no interference 'in favour of one tribe or against another except it be a clear case of necessity for the safety of the settlement'. He had no desire to use this discretion against the Ashantis. Carnarvon regarded them as 'the dominant race and almost certain ultimately to subjugate their neighbours'.[1] But after the Liberals took office in 1868 there was a hardening of Britain's policy. Although the Cardwell policy was still frequently invoked, it is significant that the loophole was definitely used. Ashanti pressure increased to such an extent that the Colonial Office began to fear that the settlements *were* in danger.

By 1869 the Colonial Office was thoroughly alarmed and confused about the Gold Coast. As the Elmina danger continued in the western part of the protectorate, and Ado Bofo's army pressed on in the Volta region, William Simpson, the administrator, seemed to be on the verge of drastic measures. 'We are clearly drifting into war,' wrote Granville in July 1869.[2] He ordered Simpson to hold his hand in the Volta, while the Dutch were persuaded to quit Elmina.

If Granville thought he could stave off the Ashanti attack, he was doomed to disappointment. Ado Bofo's army continued to advance in the east and captured European members of the Basle mission at Anun who were carried off to Kumasi as hostages. The Ashanti success in the Volta caused a group of protectorate states to unite together into one of the incipient nationalist movements known as the 'Accra Confederacy'.[3] At Elmina, in the west, the entry of Akyempon's force by the end of 1869 further complicated and prolonged the Anglo-Dutch negotiations.[4] In fact, Britain and the Netherlands concluded their arrangements for the cession under the shadow of another Ashanti War. Kimberley took over the Colonial Office in July 1870 to face a grim prospect on the Gold Coast. At first he tried

[1] Min. by Carnarvon 13 Oct., on Blackall to Carnarvon 19 Sept. 1866. C.O. 96/72.

[2] Min. by Granville 23 July, on Kennedy to Granville 1 June 1869. C.O. 96/80.

[3] Copies of letters of the Accra Confederacy encl. in Solomon to Boyce 22 Nov. 1869. *Meth. Miss. Soc.*, Gold Coast incoming letters 1868–71.

[4] Kennedy to Granville 24 Jan. 1870. C.O. 96/84. Coombs, *Gold Coast, Britain and the Netherlands*, pp. 55, 85–94, 117.

to be faithful to Cardwell's principles here, as he did in Lagos.[1] He realized that the Elmina cession would affect Britain's relations with Ashanti, and he was prepared to appease the latter to prevent a war.

But Kimberley gradually gave way to the men on the spot. He abandoned an attempt to halt efforts by the local government to open up the River Volta. He objected at first to a proposal for stationing a gunboat in the river because it was contrary to the spirit of the Cardwell policy.

> The point seems to me this. Is the maintainance of a steamer on the Volta really indispensable for the protection of the territories for which we are now responsible, or is it wanted only to extend our influence ? In the *former case* I should not refuse my consent. I am most reluctant to assume any fresh responsibility whatever on the African coast.[2]

Yet he did not, in fact, veto the gunboat project. Fortunately, the Volta ceased to be his major problem, for in September 1871 Ado Bofo retired to Kumasi.

Elmina, meanwhile, was rapidly becoming Britain's Achilles heel in West Africa. What would the asantehene do ? Instead of leaving the coast in peace, the departure of the Dutch looked like leading to an Ashanti War. When Ussher notified the asantehene that Britain was negotiating for the cession, Kofi Karikari objected. He claimed that Elmina was his 'by right'.[3] His uncle, Akyempon, who was already stirring up trouble within Elmina, told the inhabitants of the town that if the English occupied the town, Ashanti would invade the protectorate.

What should Kimberley do in face of the Ashanti threats ? If the Colonial Office had few misgivings over the desirability of the cession, they had plenty of anxieties about Ashanti intentions. They accepted a Dutch denial of the Ashanti claim to Elmina, but they insisted that Akyempon should be expelled from the town before the transfer.

---

[1] 'I am most reluctant to assume any fresh responsibilities whatever on the African coast.' Kimberley 2 Dec., on Kennedy to Kimberley 2 Nov. 1870. C.O. 96/85.

[2] Ibid.

[3] Kofi Karikari to Ussher, Kumasi, 24 Nov. 1870, encl. in Kennedy to Kimberley 2 Jan. 1871. C.O. 96/87.

Kimberley was ready to continue the Dutch rent-payments for Elmina. He agreed with Knatchbull-Hugessen that the Ashanti ruler should be 'squared'.[1] But the prolonged presence of Akyempon in Elmina caused even the pugnacious Knatchbull-Hugessen to warn: 'do not let us drift into an Ashanti war. Better abandon the idea of taking the Forts.'[2] Kimberley seriously considered not occupying the forts after the cession. He was prepared to go a long way to mollify the Ashanti. But no one wavered in their conviction that the Dutch should go.

While the Colonial Office pressed on with the negotiations, the man on the spot made considerable efforts to keep the peace with the warlike Power in the north. Arrangements were made for exchanging the captured German missionaries for Ashantis who were in the custody of protectorate states. An envoy from Cape Coast Castle, J. E. Crawfurd, who met Kofi Karikari on 5 August 1871, reported that the asantehene had rescinded his claim to Elmina.[3] But Kofi Karikari was merely biding his time. He continued to prevaricate over the exchange of the missionaries, who were not handed over. What was not known in London (until it was too late) was that a determination to go to war against the British was already firmly fixed. As early as December 1871 the King of Elmina had sent his brother to Kumasi to report that the British were going to take Elmina, and the Ashanti chiefs, who were convinced that the town was theirs, had then demanded war. Kofi Karikari told the envoy that he would march to the coast in January 1872 and pull down the English flag.[4]

The attack was delayed. But the Fante and other protectorate states were sure an Ashanti invasion would follow the cession. They had already taken measures to unite and to defend themselves. These, in turn, caused trouble in the protectorate. It is ironical, therefore, that just as the Kumasi chiefs were about to launch their attack in 1872, the Colonial Office's attention was diverted to new develop-

[1] Min. by Knatchbull-Hugessen 11 Feb., on Kennedy to Kimberley 25 Jan. 1871. C.O. 96/87.

[2] Ibid. Min. by Knatchbull-Hugessen 7 Mar., on Kennedy to Kimberley 9 Feb. 1871.

[3] J. E. Crawfurd 7 Aug., encl. in Kennedy to Kimberley 28 Oct. 1871. C.O. 96/89.

[4] Thomas Lawson to Harley 14 Apr., in Harley to Kimberley 1 May 1873. C.O. 96/98.

ments within the protectorate. There the Cardwell policy was about to receive the penultimate blow.

THE FANTE CONFEDERATION, 1868–72

The Government's attention was directed away from the Ashanti menace by the rise of a Fante nationalist movement in the protectorate. The movement was probably inspired by the self-government clauses of the 1865 Report. Although, as we have seen, the Colonial Office had tried hard to follow Cardwell's policy, and gave way reluctantly over the retention of the Gambia and Lagos and the acquisition of Elmina, when they were presented with an opportunity of fulfilling the recommendations about self-government in the Gold Coast their reaction was sharp, contemptuous and decisive. They fully endorsed the attitudes of the men on the spot.

The first example of their treatment of African aspirations was seen in the banishment of King Aggery of Cape Coast. Aggery, a Wesleyan, was enstooled in February 1865 and cordially offered to co-operate with the administrator. But he began to challenge the growth of British jurisdiction on the Gold Coast.[1] In September 1865 Joseph Martin, who represented Aggery before the Select Committee, returned to the Gold Coast, and the self-government clauses of the 1865 Report were hailed as a victory for Aggery's supporters. They renewed their protests against the colonial Government. Their methods were peaceable and were confined to petitioning.

The British response, at all levels, was vehement. Aggery was declared 'insolent', 'insubordinate', 'impudent' and 'offensive'. By 1866 Colonel Conran found his protests 'seditious', and he deposed Aggery. The Colonial Office upheld his action, even though the legal adviser admitted that the banishment was for reasons of 'public safety' rather than law. Each member of the Colonial Office dismissed Aggery with contemptuous phrases. Cardwell asserted that 'in return for protection we expect deference to our authority'.[2] Two years earlier he had virtually disavowed any obligation to protect the Gold Coast! The upshot was that Aggery was banished to Bulama

[1] Blackall to Secretary of State 19 Apr. 1866. C.O. 96/71.
[2] Ibid. Min. by Cardwell. 21 May 1866.

Island and only allowed back to Cape Coast on renouncing the kingship in 1869.[1]

Some of Aggery's followers later supported the Fante Confederation movement, which has been regarded as one of Britain's greatest 'lost opportunities' in Africa.[2]   It began as a by-product of the Anglo-Dutch exchange of 1868.   Partly to assist Kommenda, Denkyera and Wassaw in their resistance to the Dutch in the western part of the protectorate, and partly to defend themselves against the Ashanti, who were expected to intervene on behalf of Elmina, a council of chiefs, and their educated advisers, met in 1868 at Mankessim, a traditional Fante religious centre.   Ussher, the British administrator, tried to disperse the council.   He warned them not to indulge in 'treasonable practices'.   He feared that the whole protectorate was in jeopardy and that the Fante might attack the British forts since their allegiance had been shaken by the Anglo-Dutch exchange.   He maintained that the 'new men' were 'misrepresenting' the 1865 Report to the chiefs.   His solution to the crisis would be for Britain to gain 'undivided control' of the coast and arrange an alliance between Elmina and the Fante.   When the latter refused this, Ussher severed relations with them, and called for strong measures against them.[3]

As has already become clear, important policy changes occurred in 1868 because new personalities came in at all levels.   When Governor Kennedy visited the Gold Coast in October 1868 he was impressed by the Fante.   Simpson, in Ussher's absence, decided to meet the Confederation leaders.   By openly recognizing the Mankessim council he hoped to substitute Government influence for that of the 'new men', and perhaps to organize a 'union for self-defence among the Protectorate nations'.

Simpson agreed that political advance of some sort was necessary on the Gold Coast, but under Government auspices.   Not surprisingly he was given an ovation when he visited Mankessim in April 1869.

[1] The fullest account of Aggery's banishment is in Kimble, *Political History of Ghana*, ch. 5.

[2] Ward, *History of the Gold Coast*, p. 255.

[3] Ussher to Yonge 5 Dec., in Blackall to Buckingham 14 Dec. 1867. C.O. 96/74; Ussher to Blackall 6 Feb., in Kennedy to Buckingham 12 Feb. 1868; Kennedy to Buckingham 30 Mar. 1868; Ussher to Kennedy 6 Apr., in Kennedy to Buckingham 16 Apr. 1868.   C.O. 96/76.

He believed that by humouring the talk of self-government, agreeing that the 1868 exchange had been wrong, and by warning the Fante not to molest Ashanti travellers, he re-established British influence in the protectorate. Ussher returned from leave at the end of 1869 to find, as he thought, that the Confederation movement had collapsed.

The British officials were disappointed. In 1871 the movement revived in slightly different form. It now attracted a larger group of the 'new men', and it was treated with contempt by the British administrator. The new movement, which met at Mankessim in October 1871, drew up a constitution for the 'New Fanti Confederacy'. In November, a National Assembly elected two chiefs as joint 'King-Presidents', along with some of the educated 'new men' as ministers. The combination of traditional and modern authority envisaged was somewhat similar to the Egba United Board of Management at Abeokuta, and the Accra Confederacy in the eastern Gold Coast. The Confederation aimed at furthering the interests of the country by doing 'every good which British philanthropy may have designed for the good of the Gold Coast, but which we think it is impossible for it at present to do for the country at large'.[1] Some experiments were made at taxation in the Mankessim region.

The movement was peaceable, and not markedly anti-British. But Charles S. Salmon, acting for Ussher (who was again away because of ill-health), panicked. 'This is a dangerous conspiracy,' he reported, and he arrested the leaders. Governor Kennedy considered the movement was 'Absurd and impractical'. He dismissed its leaders as 'bankrupt and characterless mulattoes' and claimed that the movement was not supported by the people.

These rather hysterical reports about the Fante movement were read by the Colonial Office in 1872 with growing dismay. 'Is it treason', asked Herbert pointedly, 'to negotiate a federation beyond the limits of our settlement?' Even if the movement ought to be nipped in the bud, he failed to see why the leaders should be arrested.

[1] Kennedy to Buckingham 7 Nov. 1868; Simpson to Kennedy 5 Dec. 1868. C.O. 96/77; Simpson to Kennedy 5 May, in Kennedy to Granville 26 May 1869. C.O. 96/80; New Fante Confederation to Kennedy 24 Nov., encl. in Kennedy to Kimberley 16 Dec. 1871. C.O. 96/89. The best account of the Fante Confederation is in Kimble, op. cit., ch. 6. See also Ward, op. cit., pp. 246–55.

The legal adviser confirmed the view that there was nothing illegal about the movement. Knatchbull-Hugessen even reminded Kimberley of the Cardwell policy: 'if they are now honestly seeking to develop those qualities [of self-government], with what face can we arbitrarily oppose them?' Kimberley agreed that Salmon had made a 'great blunder'. Yet the administrator was censured very mildly. The Government did not want to stamp out legitimate projects, wrote Kimberley, but the 'protecting power' must be consulted.[1] In spite of his misgivings, Kimberley upheld the views of the man on the spot.

Kimberley rather hoped that the supporters of the Fante Confederation movement would raise the matter in Parliament, so that the Colonial Office could state its views publicly.[2] He was not disappointed, but he was in for a rude shock. A short political controversy occurred over the Fante Confederation which caused him to abandon the Cardwell policy for the third time.

Members of Parliament emphasized the obvious point that the Fante Confederation appeared to fit in very well with the Cardwell policy. On 25 February 1872 Alderman McArthur warned Knatchbull-Hugessen privately that he thought the Confederation was a 'most important movement', and that he would raise the matter in the House of Commons. Knatchbull-Hugessen could only put McArthur off by promising him that Pope-Hennessy, the new governor-in-chief, was going to inquire and report on the Confederation movement.[3] Unfortunately for the Colonial Office Pope-Hennessy happened to take the self-government parts of the Cardwell policy seriously. Kimberley's method of silencing McArthur soon rebounded upon him.

Even before he reached the Gold Coast, Pope-Hennessy, interpreting Kimberley's instructions literally, ordered Ussher to tell the Confederation leaders that the British Government was prepared to consider 'a properly matured scheme for the formation of a native council of Kings and Chiefs to assist the Governor', if it had unanimous

[1] Mins. by Herbert 5 Jan., Holland 6 Jan., Knatchbull-Hugessen 9 Jan., Kimberley 11 Jan., and Kimberley to Kennedy 16 Jan. 1872 on Kennedy to Kimberley 16 Dec. 1871. C.O. 96/89.

[2] Min. by Kimberley 2 Feb., on Kennedy to Kimberley 2 Jan. 1872. C.O. 96/92.

[3] Ibid. Min. by Knatchbull-Hugessen 26 Feb., on Salmon to Kennedy 3 Jan. 1872.

support.   When he reached the Gold Coast in April 1872 Pope-Hennessy went even further.   He announced that he would 'be glad to foster any effort' for better government among the Fante and that he 'entirely approved of some parts of their scheme'.

The most striking thing Pope-Hennessy discovered was that the Fante leaders realized all too clearly Britain's basic dilemma in West Africa.   If Britain was not to quit the Gold Coast, as recommended in the 1865 Report, the Fante leaders believed that the only alternative to recognizing the Confederation was expansion of colonial rule. Britain would have

> to take over the whole country and govern it as vigorously and on the same system and principles as it does in Her [Majesty's] other Colonies, but not permit us to be governed and ruled in the shameful and neglectful way in which we have been for years past.

Pope-Hennessy agreed.   He pointed out for Kimberley's benefit that there was only one alternative to the Confederation — 'a firm extension of Her Majesty's authority, combined with the development of municipal government in the coastal towns, and the use of chiefs as judicial instruments in the interior.[1]

Pope-Hennessy's report on the Fante Confederation placed the Colonial Office in a most embarrassing position.   In July 1872 McArthur had already called for the recognition of the Confederation.[2] Now Pope-Hennessy insisted that the alternative to fulfilling the self-government parts of the Cardwell policy was to violate Cardwell's injunction against expansion.   'This is contrary to the policy of H.M.Govt. hitherto,' wrote Kimberley, who found himself in another awkward dilemma.[3]   A decision was urgently needed.   McArthur gave notice in February 1873 that he would ask for the publication of Pope-Hennessy's despatches.   He also wanted to know what instructions had been sent to the administrator of the Gold Coast about the Confederation.   The Colonial Office was quite unprepared to answer, as the instructions had not even been drafted.   Knatchbull-Hugessen persuaded McArthur privately to postpone his question for a fortnight.

[1] Pope-Hennessy to Kimberley 15 Mar. 1872.   C.O. 96/92; Pope-Hennessy to Kimberley 29 Oct. 1872.   C.O. 96/94.

[2] 3 *Hansard*, 213, col. 36.

[3] Marginal note on Pope-Hennessy to Kimberley 29 Oct. 1872.   C.O. 96/94.

A decision about the Fante Confederation could not be avoided. The contradictory features of the Cardwell policy could not be reconciled. Therefore, Knatchbull-Hugessen boldly stated his views. He attacked the 'absurd system of "Protectorate"' by which the Government never knew how much authority it had, and lacked the power of enforcement. He thought the self-government recommendations of the 1865 Committee had made matters worse. He blamed the 1865 Report for the present troubles on the Gold Coast, in the same way as he had in the Lagos case a month earlier. He insisted that 'in the present tone and temper of the British mind, no abandonment of territory would, in my view, be permitted by Parliament, or sanctioned by Public opinion'. He proposed that Britain's position on the Gold Coast should be 'more accurately defined and more certainly established'. The same alternatives existed in the Gold Coast as they did at Lagos — withdrawal to the forts, or expansion of the territory under Crown Colony rule. Knatchbull-Hugessen felt there was no middle course. He preferred expansion.

Why, it may be asked, did he reject the Fante Confederation as a middle course ? The reason is that, like most of his colleagues, he was contemptuous of the 'new men'. He said that the 'educated Africans' of the Gold Coast should be completely disregarded except for the purpose of employment as petty Government servants. He concluded his forthright minute by insisting that Britain, having undertaken responsibilities, could not 'in honour or in justice to her own character evade them, nor can the will stand still to watch the progress of events'.[1]

Kimberley accepted Knatchbull-Hugessen's argument. Maybe in the future, he wrote, Africans would be

> fit to govern themselves without our aid, and it may be proper to keep this in view, but for a long time to come our withdrawal would destroy all hope of improvement of the natives, who would speedily return to all their worst customs; and all prospect would be lost of opening the interior to commerce. Such a result would commend itself neither to philanthropists nor traders. For all present practical purposes therefore we may dismiss the question of retiring from the Coast.[2]

---

[1] Min. by Knatchbull-Hugessen 18 Feb. 1873 on McArthur's question (received in C.O. 14 Feb.). C.O. 96/104.

[2] Ibid. Min. by Kimberley 20 Jan. 1873.

In Kimberley's words, the Cardwell policy stood finally condemned. In the Gambia, Lagos, and now in a third case, the Gold Coast, Kimberley had decided to retain the West African Settlements and govern them as best he could. He rejected the Fante Confederation and decided to try governing the Gold Coast through the chiefs.

He did not want to turn the protectorate into a Crown Colony. It might have to be defended against Ashanti, and domestic slavery could not be ignored. A year earlier he had contemplated trying to end slavery by negotiation with the chiefs. Now he decided that the 'day is far distant when we can venture to meddle with it'. For the time being, he decided,

> we must keep within the line of a Protectorate, defining by agreement with the chiefs what are to be the powers and obligations of the Protecting State, and what on the other hand are to be the obligations of the natives towards us.

With this in mind he drafted instructions for Colonel Harley, the new administrator, outlining a scheme of what in a later period would probably have been called 'indirect rule'.

The main features of Kimberley's plan were as follows: (1) *Defence and Foreign Relations*: the chiefs were to make no treaties without British consent. Britain would defend the seaboard, but the protectorate states were to defend themselves. Britain might support some form of confederation. (2) *Finance*: revenue would be raised by customs duties and chiefs would be paid stipends to keep open roads. (3) The *external slave trade* was to be prohibited. (4) *Jurisdiction*: a system of courts would be created throughout the protectorate with the consent of the chiefs; and (5) *Education*: 'as much as can be spared' would be spent on vernacular education to qualify Africans for employment in subordinate Government posts.[1] The plan looks very much like a redefinition of Maclean's system. But the instructions were, in fact, never sent. In the middle of the Colonial Office's deliberations came the news of the Ashanti invasion. Cardwell's policy perished in the heat of war.

[1] Ibid., draft for Harley.

ASHANTI INVASION IN 1873

While the review of Britain's role at Lagos and the Gold Coast was being made in February 1873, the Ashantis were preparing to settle their grievances by force. The campaign began on 9 December 1872.[1] It destroyed Kimberley's new plans for the protectorate, and once again called into question Britain's whole future in the region.

Ashanti followed a familiar strategy. With small flanking attacks to east and west, the main force followed the traditional route to Cape Coast Castle. The Ashanti army crossed the Pra on 22 January 1873 and by early February it was only twenty-four hours' march from the coast. A large Fante army was rebuffed on 10 March and a more stubborn stand was broken at Dunkwa on 14 April.[2] Protectorate resistance collapsed, and the British forts prepared for defence.

Yet the Ashanti advance, now 150 miles from base, lost its impetus. The invaders, estimated at about thirty to forty thousand, suffered from casualties, hunger and disease.[3] In May 1873 they turned west into Denkyera, where they encamped at Jukwa, 15 miles from Elmina. Here on 5 June they routed a Fante attempt to dislodge them. On 13 June a small force of 3,000 Ashantis engaged British forces on the outskirts of Elmina. A period of stalemate then set in and, because of continued suffering, the Ashanti retreat began in October 1873. By 29 November the main body had retired into Ashanti territory. The invasion was in fact a more serious version of what had occurred many times before. Poor generalship and primitive logistics had

---

[1] F. A. Ramseyer and J. Kühne, *Four Years in Ashantee*, ed. by Mrs Weitbrecht, London, 1875, p. 205.

[2] C.O. to W.O. 12 May 1873. W.O. files in P.R.O.: W.O. 32/826, file 076/224. Many items of the 076 serial are now missing, but they were summarized in a Confidential General Sketch, 'Measures taken at home', by the Intelligence Branch, 13 Apr. 1874. Copy in *Wolseley Papers*, W. 13 (consulted by courtesy of the W.O. Library).

[3] 'Report on Invasion', Capt. Brett, 19 Apr. 1873. W.O. 32/826, file 076/233. When Kühne was released from captivity in 1874 he confirmed that Dunkwa was the peak of Ashanti success. Shortly after the victory he met Kofi Karikari, and saw him dance with joy in the street. After reports of sickness and defeat reached Kumasi there was no more dancing. W. W. Reade, *The Story of the Ashantee Campaign*, London, 1874, p. 103.

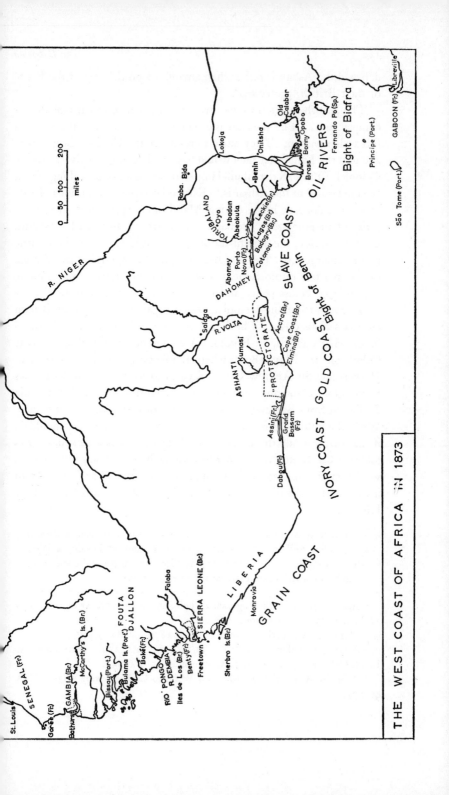

THE WEST COAST OF AFRICA IN 1873

defeated the Ashantis rather than any efforts on the part of the Fante or their British 'protectors'.

The British reaction to the invasion was, at first, remarkable for its complacency. The men on the spot refused to believe there was a full-scale invasion. They failed to reinforce the Gold Coast garrison, and told the Fante that they would have to defend themselves. In the Colonial Office Knatchbull-Hugessen was alone in calling for a 'severe lesson' to the Ashantis.[1] Kimberley remained cautious. Little at all was done at home during March and April 1873 in spite of Knatchbull-Hugessen's demand for a strong line with Ashanti. Colonel Harley, the administrator on the Gold Coast, could do little in the emergency. He banished the pro-Ashanti King of Elmina, called up a few reinforcements from Lagos and Sierra Leone, and he even sent 50 Hausa police under a British officer to stiffen the Fante.[2]

By May 1873 the Colonial Office began to realize that Britain faced a serious crisis. The Fante collapse at Dunkwa was followed by growing publicity in Britain. A conference was held at the War Office on 10 May 1873, when Kimberley, Cardwell, Goschen, Herbert and Sir Andrew Clarke decided to send 100 Royal Marines to the Gold Coast and to transfer four companies of the West India Regiment from Barbados.[3] But a change of policy was not intended. When the military commander at Cape Coast asked what he should do if the town outside the walls of the British fort was attacked, he was told that Cardwell's 1864 order forbidding direct military intervention would stand. A suggestion, from an officer in the War Office, of an invasion of Ashanti by way of the River Volta, was rejected by Kimberley:

> If we wish to weaken ourselves we cannot adopt a better course than to spend a few millions in conquering Ashantee, and establishing a West African Empire. It is to be hoped no Gov[ernmen]t will be ever mad enough to embark on so extravagant an enterprise.[4]

---

[1] Min. by Knatchbull-Hugessen 27 Feb., on Pope-Hennessy to Kimberley 10 Feb. 1873. C.O. 96/96.

[2] Harley to Kimberley 20 and 21 Mar. 1873. C.O. 96/97.

[3] Mins. of conference, W.O. 32/826, file 076/219. Instructions to Lieut.-Col. Festing, the Marine Commander, in 076/255.

[4] Min. by Kimberley 28 May, on W.O. to C.O. 22 May 1873. C.O. 96/107.

As he read that Ashanti no longer threatened the forts he must have felt that his policy was vindicated.

Bad news arrived on 10 July to shake Kimberley's complacency. He learned of the Fante rout before Jukwa and the Ashanti attack on Elmina.[1] 'An end to all peace and quiet for the unlucky Colonial Office.'[2] Kimberley finally realized that Britain could not stand aloof. He decided to intervene. First, he called for immediate reinforcements. At a War Office conference on 15 July 1873 he pressed 'very unwilling' military men to send 200 more Marines and to alert a wing of an infantry battalion at home.[3] There was even some talk in London of sending 'Chinese' Gordon to vanquish the Ashantis.[4] Secondly, it was decided to launch a full-scale expedition to invade Ashanti. This decision was taken during the last days of July and the first two weeks of August 1873. It is remarkable that the decision was largely the work of Kimberley and the War Office, with very little consultation with Gladstone and the Cabinet.

THE DECISION TO INTERVENE AGAINST ASHANTI IN 1873

The decisive turning-point of the Ashanti War came after the arrival of the dramatic news on 10 July 1873 of the Jukwa and Elmina battles. But if Kimberley decided to intervene, he was still uncertain precisely what action to take when he sought Cardwell's advice on 26 July:

> The questions seem to be: can any active measures be taken against the Ashantees during the rainy season? If so, within what limits, and of what nature?. . .
>   Of course if the Ashantees attack our forts, the course is simple, to repel them, but if they do not attack what then? We cannot leave them quietly in occupation of the Protectorate. Public opinion would not allow us to do so, if we ourselves desired it: and all the trade of our settlements is practically destroyed by the presence of the invading force, so that if things are left in their present position, the settlements will be merely a

---

[1] *The Times*, 10 July 1873, p. 10. A correspondent's report dated Free-town, 29 May 1873.

[2] Kimberley's 'Journal', p. 39.

[3] Ibid. p. 40; 3 *Hansard*, 217, cols. 267–8, 308.

[4] *The Times*, 16 July 1873; see also Lord Elton, *General Gordon*, London, 1954, pp. 144–5; Reade, op. cit., p. 145.

heavy burden on the Imperial Treasury. Are we to contemplate an
attack on Coomassie and could we assemble a force sufficient for that
purpose?[1]

The service departments had been commendably active and were
ready with their advice. They had already begun to plan an expedition
against Ashanti.

As early as May 1873 Cardwell instructed Sir Garnet Wolseley,
the assistant Adjutant-General, to draw up a war plan for an attack on
Ashanti.[2] Wolseley proposed that he should be appointed governor of
the Gold Coast and there train an African force to clear the Ashantis
from the protectorate. He would then rush about two battalions of
British regulars to the River Pra, along a road with ready-made
staging-posts, so they would be fresh to invade Ashanti and strike at
the capital, Kumasi. On 1 August 1873 Cardwell informed Kimberley that Wolseley was 'now ready to capture Coomassie'.[3]

A strikingly different plan of campaign had emerged in the Admiralty. Goschen, the First Lord, had the benefit of Commander
Glover's local experience and passed the result on to Cardwell. On
29 July, Glover personally put his plan to Cardwell. Glover, who

[1] Kimberley to Cardwell 26 July 1873, *Cardwell Papers*, P.R.O.
30/48/5/33, pp. 48–51. A week earlier Kimberley, in a message for the
queen, suggested, 'it is far better that the Ashanti should come within reach
of our forts and ships where they can receive a severe lesson'. Kimberley to
Gen. Ponsonby 17 July 1873. *Royal Archives*, F. 6/11.

[2] This memo. has not been found and therefore can only be roughly dated.
In May 1873, when there was growing publicity in Britain, Lieut.-Col.
Evelyn Wood found Wolseley poring over Dutch maps of Ashanti and was
told 'there was a king there who required a lesson to bring him to a sense of
the power of England' (E. Wood, *From Midshipman to Field Marshal*,
London, 1906, i, 254–5). Wolseley's biographers say, 'As soon as difficulties
arose on the Gold Coast, Sir Garnet prepared for Mr. Cardwell a memo. on
the situation' (F. B. Maurice and G. A. Arthur, *The Life of Lord Wolseley*,
London, 1924, pp. 61–2). Wolseley himself wrote, 'Mr. Cardwell had in
confidence already informed me that he would like me to go there should it
be determined to undertake active operations against the invading Ashanti.
. . . I submitted privately to Mr. Cardwell a rough outline of a military
scheme . . .' (*A Soldier's Life*, ii, pp. 262–3).

[3] Cardwell to Kimberley 1 Aug. 1873 (copy), *Cardwell Papers*, P.R.O.
30/48/5/33, p. 60.

had built up an effective armed police force of Hausas while he was at Lagos, was willing to raise an African force in the Accra and Volta region. He would attack Ashanti in the flank and rear using the River Volta, part of which he had explored. He was supported in this scheme by Sir Andrew Clarke, who had greatly impressed Cardwell in 1864, and as Director of Works at the Admiralty was available for advice on the Ashanti War.[1]

On the day after the interview with Cardwell, Glover wrote formally offering his services to the Colonial Office. After the unfortunate Lagos affair Kimberley was naturally very reluctant to employ Glover again in West Africa. But at a Cabinet meeting on 2 August 1873 Glover's plan was evidently accepted by the Government.[2] Gladstone thought it was a good one. The prime minister also made a private note that a 'frontal assault' on Kumasi might also have to be considered later, but he did not inform the queen of this.[3] Kimberley saw Glover on 4 August 1873 and commissioned him to lead a flanking expedition against Ashanti employing African troops and using the Volta route.[4]

Yet it must be emphasized that Glover's expedition was, from the start, a *flank* operation.[5] The most significant decision was the appointment of Wolseley to lead an overland march on Kumasi. Moreover, the decision was taken without another Cabinet meeting, for Wolseley was appointed governor and commander-in-chief of the Gold Coast on 13 August 1873 when the Cabinet was dispersed.[6] Cardwell's influence must have been of great importance, for although Kimberley supported the Wolseley plan keenly, once the decision had been taken, he only accepted it after considering a much more moderate alternative proposed by Sir Andrew Clarke, who did not want to use

[1] Lady Glover, *Life of Glover*, pp. 149–52.

[2] Herbert to Glover 2 Aug. 1873. Letter-book in *Glover Papers*.

[3] Gladstone to Kimberley 14 Aug. 1873. *Kimberley Papers*, A/52; Cabinet Min. 2 Aug. 1873. *Gladstone Papers*, 44641/189; Gladstone to Queen Victoria 2 Aug. 1873. *Royal Archives*, A.46/51.

[4] *Brabourne Diary*, iv, pp. 634–5.

[5] Glover was appointed 'Special Commissioner to the Native Chiefs of the Eastern District'. Gladstone specifically used the phrase 'flank movement' in his letter to the queen. Kimberley referred to a 'powerful diversion'. Kimberley to Ponsonby 15 Aug. 1873. *Royal Archives*, F. 6/15.

[6] Wolseley, *A Soldier's Life*, ii, p. 267.

British troops to invade Ashanti, and who probably would have re-affirmed the Cardwell policy once the war was over. Gladstone would probably have preferred Clarke's scheme. Three years later, after Sir Arthur Gordon's 'little war' against mountain tribes in Fiji, an associate of Gladstone's suggested that some such limited effort should have been used against the Ashantis.[1]

The Wolseley expedition, then, was really a decision of Kimberley and Cardwell. Knatchbull-Hugessen, the harshest critic of the Card-well policy and the keenest exponent of a tough line with Ashanti, seems to have had no part. He was going through one of his periodic bouts of disillusionment and was contemplating resigning.[2] The Cabinet, which dispersed at the end of the parliamentary session on 5 August 1873, was not consulted as a body on the decision. Kim-berley simply informed Gladstone, after Wolseley's appointment, that a final decision on the actual 'frontal assault' on Kumasi would depend on the general's appreciation when he reached the Gold Coast. Gladstone admitted his ignorance of the Ashanti question, but he could not understand why Britain should always be at odds with them. He hoped

> This miserable war will not be without some compensation, if it slackens the precipitate zeal of McArthur and Co. for the annexation of Fiji, or if it abates the disposition of John Bull to put his head hereafter into a noose.[3]

Gladstone soon became alarmed at the scale of military preparations, however, and although the decision to undertake active intervention

[1] Like Wolseley's memo., Clarke's cannot be found in the Gold Coast records. However, there is in the *Glover Papers* (Royal Commonwealth Soc.) a memo. written on Singapore Govt. note-paper signed by Clarke, dated 11 Aug. 1873, initialled by Cardwell: 'written by Sir A. Clarke at my request'. In this, Clarke says that if an attack upon Kumasi is decided do, regular troops might be needed; but he is convinced that sufficient forncs could be raised in the protectorate. See also from Vetch, *Life of Clarke*, p. 115, and A. E. H. Anson, *About Others and Myself, 1745–1920*, Lonon,e 1920, p. 324.

[2] *Brabourne Diary*, iv, p. 639, for text of letter from Kimberley dated 10 Aug. 1873: 'I trust you are not serious in talking of making your bow. You would not I am sure turn your "backside" to Coffee Calicalli.'

[3] Gladstone to Kimberley 21 Aug. 1873. *Kimberley Papers*, A/52.

had been made between 26 July and 2 August, the final endorsement of the decision to invade Ashanti had to wait until November when the Cabinet decided to sanction the despatch of British battalions.[1]

By then Kimberley and Cardwell had to counter considerable Cabinet opposition. Although they must have realized that an expedition by British troops to Kumasi was part of Wolseley's plan from the start, the plan as they presented it to Gladstone was that Wolseley would use the forces already available and those he could recruit locally to strike a blow against Ashanti, and *only* to request the British troops if they were absolutely necessary. Kimberley felt 'It is a hateful affair, but I feel sure that the only safe policy is to deal with it quickly and thoroughly'.[2]

He instructed Wolseley to warn the asantehene that an expedition was preparing in case he did not quit the protectorate. The aim should be a new treaty with Ashanti, possibly on the lines of Maclean's 1831 treaty. Kimberley also suggested that a Resident or consul should again be appointed in Kumasi.[3] Wolseley's instructions were dated 10 September 1873, the same day that Kimberley sent Gladstone his instructions to Sir Andrew Clarke, soon to become governor of the Straits Settlements, in which he suggested appointing Residents in Malaya. Although Gladstone was not happy about the wide military discretion granted to Wolseley, and Goschen now confessed to 'very great qualms'[4] about the plans, the general sailed with his staff from Liverpool on 12 September.

Gladstone, who had taken over the Treasury on 1 August following the Post Office crisis, was 'aghast' at the cost of the war preparations. A hospital ship and 15 miles of railway equipment were being made ready, and he naturally began to suspect a full-scale war. Cardwell tried to ease the prime minister's conscience:

We have not (as Northcote argues) involved the country in a war without calling Parliament together. We are in a war forced upon us . . .

[1] For a more detailed treatment of the policy decisions in London see my article, 'British Policy in West Africa: The Ashanti Expedition of 1873–4', *H.J.* (1962), 5 (1), pp. 26–46.

[2] Kimberley to Gladstone 18 Aug. 1873. *Gladstone Papers*, 44225/79.

[3] Kimberley to Wolseley 10 Sept. 1873 (draft). C.O. 96/108.

[4] Goschen to Kimberley 8 Sept. 1873. *Kimberley Papers*, A/52; Goschen to Cardwell 10 Sept. 1873. *Cardwell Papers*, P.R.O. 30. 48/5/27, p. 115.

existing long before Parliament broke up. I believe the steps we have
taken have averted a storm of indignation, which would have burst forth
if these ill tidings had arrived, and no such steps had already been taken.
    As regards the tramway . . . I do not regard it as pledging us to an
expedition into the Ashanti territory.[1]

But Kimberley and Cardwell decided they should seek the authority
of the Cabinet. On 4 October 1873, two full months after agreeing
to the Glover flank operations, the Cabinet met for a full discussion of
the Ashanti War. Bright argued against the Kumasi expedition.[2]
Gladstone made his first real attempt to direct policy. He drafted a
despatch warning Wolseley that the Government would be most
reluctant to sanction an expedition by British battalions. His main
object was to clear the protectorate and to make an honourable peace.[3]
    Gladstone's intervention came a month too late. Wolseley wrote
requesting British troops on 9 October 1873.[4] He had only been on
the coast for a week and could not have made any systematic attempt
to train and assess his African recruits: indeed, he had not even seen
his first operations. But Wolseley was a desperately ambitious man,
spurred on by a staff of young protégés who were all eager for action.
Wolseley also had a very poor view of Africans.[5] He had been planning his expedition to Kumasi since the spring and it is quite clear that
he did not seriously consider any other alternative when he reached
the Gold Coast.[6] It was a classic case of the home Government being
led by the man on the spot.
    A sober military appreciation of the situation would have shown

[1] Cardwell to Gladstone 20 Sept. 1873. *Gladstone Papers*, 44120/140.
[2] P. Bright (ed.), *The Diary of John Bright*, London, 1930, p. 357.
[3] Gladstone's rough drafts in Cabinet Mins. 3 and 4 Oct. 1873, *Gladstone
Papers*, 44641/193–6. Kimberley's draft (based on Gladstone's) in C.O.
96/108; Gladstone to Queen Victoria 3 and 4 Oct. 1873. *Royal Archives*,
A.46/78.
[4] Wolseley to Kimberley 9 Oct. 1873. C.O. Confidential Print: Gold
Coast, no. 36, p. 269.
[5] See J. H. Lehmann, *All Sir Garnet. A Life of Field-Marshal Lord
Wolseley, 1833–1913*, London, 1964, for his character and early career; for
his attitude to Africans, Arthur, *The Letters of Lord and Lady Wolseley*, p. 10;
Wolseley, *A Soldier's Life*, ii, p. 276.
[6] Wolseley told Winwood Reade on the voyage that he was sure he would
need British troops. *Ashantee Campaign*, p. 163.

Wolseley that he might be cheated out of his march to Kumasi. By the time he reached the Gold Coast the Ashanti retreat was about to begin and there were no more alarms for the British forts. By the end of November the main invading army had left the protectorate. On the other hand, British influence throughout the protectorate had collapsed under the impact of the invasion. In the west the Government was reduced to holding the forts of Secondi, Dixcove and Axim with naval help; a projected drive up the River Pra had been frustrated, and in the Volta region Glover was delayed by the revival of hostility from the east-bank states. The protectorate was certainly in a bad way — but the real danger from Ashanti had passed.

Yet Wolseley demanded his expeditionary force. On 17 November 1873 Gladstone's Cabinet met to consider the general's call for the British troops.[1] It sanctioned the despatch of three battalions, which sailed on the nineteenth and twenty-first. A few days later, Bright made a final, futile attempt to stop the expedition, and then contemplated resigning.[2] Gladstone now requested Wolseley to strike a blow at Ashanti as far short of Kumasi as possible and reminded the general that if the Ashanti were crushed he might reach the capital and find no one to negotiate with[3] — which is precisely what happened. This was Gladstone's last serious interference in the conduct of the Ashanti War. By the time the news of the entry into Kumasi reached home his Government had been defeated in a general election.

In the Colonial Office, Kimberley, having progressively buried the Cardwell policy, contemplated the future pessimistically. As he learnt that Glover was getting involved in the rivalries of the Volta states, and was preparing to attack Awuna to protect his flank — probably because he could not get any recruits from Accra until he did so — Kimberley began to wonder if the Volta expedition had not been a

---

[1] The Cabinet met on 10 Nov. 1873 and agreed to make preparations for sending Wolseley's reinforcements, the official request for which was expected to arrive on 15 Nov. Gladstone wrote to Queen Victoria that Wolseley 'has already expressed an opinion that they will be required'. Letter to queen 10 Nov. 1873. *Royal Archives*, A.46/88; Cabinet Min. Nov. 1873. *Gladstone Papers*, 44641/218; Gladstone to Queen Victoria 17 Nov. 1873. *Royal Archives*, A.46/93.

[2] Bright, *Diary*, p. 358.

[3] Cabinet Min. 21 Nov. 1873. *Gladstone Papers*, 44641/223.

mistake. Most of the journalists who reported the expedition (even
Glover's greatest admirers) agreed.[1] Kimberley was certain of one
thing: 'how utterly without authority we are in the protectorate and
that we are defending little more than a shadow'.[2] He seemed now
to have no constructive ideas about what to do with the Gold Coast
after the war. Ironically enough, in view of his rejection of the
Cardwell policy, he did not rule out the possibility of withdrawal.[3] He
realized that great changes were really necessary, yet he doubted if the
settlements could ever be governed satisfactorily. It was perhaps
extremely appropriate that the hard-working, but now quite weary,
Kimberley should remain in office until the eve of victory, but that
the younger, more imaginative, Carnarvon should be left with the
peace settlement.

Perhaps it was also appropriate that on 15 January 1874, the very day
on which Wolseley's main campaign in Ashanti began, Sir Andrew
Clarke opened the Pangkor conference, which laid the foundations for
the 'Resident system' in Malaya. Clarke might well have been in
Wolseley's place on the banks of the Pra, but his war plan had been
rejected. He went instead to Singapore, to face the civil wars of the
Malay Peninsula. There, so he was rightly told in London, 'matters
were much more critical and the situation more difficult than on the
African coast'.[4]

Sir Andrew Clarke was an ambitious soldier. Since 1864, when as
a forty-year-old captain he impressed Cardwell with his forthright
views on the West African Settlements, he had advanced considerably.
Nine years as Director of Works at the Admiralty brought him a
brevet colonelcy, the K.C.M.G. and valuable personal contacts in the
Government and the services. But when he went to Singapore in
1873 he was embarking on a new career. He was determined to

----

[1] Min. by Kimberley 25 Dec., on Wolseley to Cardwell 2 Nov. 1873.
C.O. 96/107. Reade, op. cit., pp. 378–81; J. F. Maurice, *The Ashantee
War. A Popular Narrative*, London, 1874, p. 390; G. A. Henty, *The
March to Coomassie*, London, 1874, p. 218.

[2] Min. by Kimberley 25 Dec. 1873. C.O. 96/107.

[3] Kimberley to Granville 17 Dec. 1873. *Granville Papers*, P.R.O.
30/29/55, p. 333.

[4] Vetch, *Life of Clarke*, p. 115.

succeed. His ideas for the West African Settlements had been twice rejected by the Government. During the Ashanti War his advice had been cast aside to make way for the plans of an upstart officer, fourteen years his junior. As governor of the Straits Settlements, Clarke would have his chance.

5. *Relations with the Malay States, 1867–71*

In Malaya,[1] Sir Andrew Clarke's impact was immediate and lasting. Before Wolseley's Kumasi expedition had even reached its objective, Clarke appointed the first British Residents in the Malay States. His action marked a completely new departure in British policy in South-East Asia. The Residents were intended as advisers to the Malay sultans. In subsequent years they became the instruments of British political control in the Malay States. Clarke's governorship is still regarded as one of the watersheds in Malayan history.

Why did Britain intervene, in this way, in Malaya? The answer may be found in a searching reappraisal of British policy in the Malay Peninsula which Lord Kimberley conducted in the period 1870–3, the same years in which he had to reconsider Britain's role in West Africa. The traditional function of the small colony of the Straits Settlements was that of a strategic seaport and trading centre, which stood as a guardian on the trade route to China. Kimberley decided it was the base for something more. Britain was 'paramount power' in the Malay Peninsula, and he instructed Clarke to find a way of consolidating the position.

THE STRAITS SETTLEMENTS AND THE MALAY STATES BEFORE 1867

The Straits Settlements had not plagued and perplexed the Colonial Office for decades like the West African Settlements. If Kimberley's reappraisal of Britain's role in West Africa stemmed from his failure to follow the Cardwell policy, in Malaya he was searching for a policy

---

[1] 'Malaya' was not officially used to describe the British colony of the Straits Settlements and the protected states of the Malay Peninsula until the late nineteenth century. During the 1860's and 1870's the normal usage was 'Malay States' or 'Malay Peninsula'. However, there is a letter to the prime minister in the *Disraeli Papers*, dated 28 Dec. 1875, in which Carnarvon used the word 'Malaya'. B/xx/He/52.

to follow. The Straits Settlements were formerly an outpost of the East India Company. The Colonial Office did not take them over

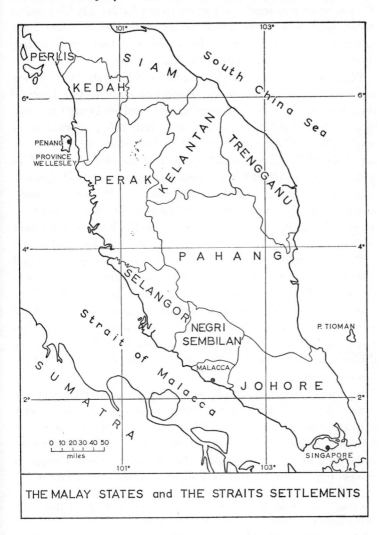

THE MALAY STATES and THE STRAITS SETTLEMENTS

from the India Office until 1867. They then became responsible for a colony consisting of three settlements. The island of Penang had been ceded by the Sultan of Kedah in 1786, and Province Wellesley on the mainland opposite was added in 1800. The island of Singapore was acquired by Stamford Raffles in 1819. The Dutch had handed over the oldest European colony on the mainland, Malacca, in 1824. They were all very small. Whatever visions Raffles may have had of British supremacy in the whole Malay archipelago, the East India Company and its successor, the Government of India, tried to keep aloof from the internal affairs of the Malay States.

When the Colonial Office became responsible for the Straits Settlements they inherited the policy of non-intervention. The Duke of Buckingham, the Colonial Secretary, instructed Sir Harry Ord, who became the first colonial governor on 1 April 1867, to establish the normal Crown Colony administration and to economize. The heading 'Political Relations', which appeared in the original draft of his instructions, was deleted.[1] The Malay Peninsula was virtually ignored. The Colonial Office treated the new colony as if it were a purely administrative problem like the West Indies or Gibraltar. They were wrong. By failing to consider the relationship between the Straits Settlements and the Malay Peninsula they committed a major blunder.

By 1867 Britain was already bound up in a complex web of political involvement in the Malay States. British sovereignty was confined to Penang, Malacca and Singapore, but British influence embraced the whole Peninsula. The last of the Indian governors had even suggested in 1861 that with the exception of 'one or two petty Independent states, the possession of the Malay Peninsula is divided between the British and the Siamese'.[2] Was his view correct? What did the 'division' mean?

Siam was recognized formally as the suzerain of the three northern states of Kedah, Kelantan and Trengganu, until the boundary treaty of 1909. But the precise status of her 'vassal' or 'tributary' states was difficult to define. In 1826, the southern border of Kedah was fixed as the limit of Siamese suzerainty, but in Kelantan and Trengganu Siamese influence was often very slight.[3] The independence of the

---

[1] Draft instructions for Ord 6 Feb., after Treas. to C.O. 26 Jan. 1867. Straits Settlements correspondence, C.O. 273/16.

[2] Cavenagh to Govt. of India 19 July 1861. *Accounts and Papers* (1863), xliii, p. 306.

[3] See Burney's Treaty 20 June 1826 in W. G. Maxwell and W. S. Gibson, *Treaties and Engagements affecting the Malay States and Borneo*, London, 1924, p. 80, Art. xi: 'Siam shall not go and obstruct or interrupt trade in the

large tin-bearing states of Perak and Selangor on the west coast had been guaranteed by the East India Company.[1] The two large, sparsely populated states of Pahang in the east and Johore in the south were by-products of Anglo-Dutch rivalry for the former Johore empire.[2] Johore itself was virtually a British creation — 'in many respects a British dependency'[3] — and its ruler lived in Singapore. The Dutch had undertaken in 1824 not to interfere in the Peninsula. A Siamese bid for power in Pahang was scotched by British intervention in 1862.[4] The Malay States had, in fact, been saved from Siamese

States of Tringano and Calantan . . . and the English shall not go and molest, attack, or disturb those States upon any pretence whatever.'

[1] Perak treaties, Maxwell and Gibson, pp. 20–26; Selangor treaties, pp. 30–35. The best account of early relations between the British settlements and the Malay States is L. A. Mills, 'British Malaya, 1824–1867', *J.M.B.R.A.S.* (1925), 1 (2), pp. 128–69.

[2] During the period of intense Anglo-Dutch rivalry stirred up by Raffles in South-East Asia after the Napoleonic Wars, the Sultan of Johore (present Johore, Pahang, Singapore and Riouw–Lingga archipelago) was living at Lingga, a puppet of the ruler of Riouw. His dominions on the Malay Peninsula were ruled by great officers of State who became virtually independent, the Temenggong of Johore and the Bendahara of Pahang. Raffles's method of securing Singapore, the Anglo-Dutch treaty of 1824 and the Pahang Civil War of 1857–63 all served to give permanence to this arrangement and to 'partition' the old Johore empire. (See Mills, 'British Malaya', pp. 19–81; W. Linehan, 'A History of Pahang', *J.M.B.R.A.S.* (May 1936), 14 (2), pp. 56–67; Cowan, *Nineteenth Century Malaya*, pp. 5–9; R. O. Winstedt, 'A History of Johore', *J.M.B.R.A.S.* (Dec. 1932), 10 (3), p. 98; and for the British treaties with Johore see Maxwell and Gibson, pp. 115–32.)   [3] Cowan, op. cit., p. 13.

[4] The Pahang Civil War really included two conflicts: a fight for the succession, between his sons Tun Mutahir and Wan Ahmad, in Pahang following Bendahara 'Ali's death in 1857; and a final attempt by a successor of the 'Riouw half' of the Johore empire to recover a mainland province. The latter was Mahmud (deposed Sultan of Lingga), who assisted Wan Ahmad. Siam saw opportunities of extending her influence and backed Mahmud, Wan Ahmad and their ally the Sultan of Trengganu. Mutahir was supported by the Temenggong of Johore. In 1862 Mahmud went to Siam and married the sister of the king and returned to Trengganu (Wan Ahmad's base) with Siamese troops. Wan Ahmad's third invasion was successful and in 1863 he became the ruler of Pahang, and he tried to cultivate good relations with the British.

or Dutch domination only by British influence. In the view of a distinguished authority, the East India Company had become 'paramount power' in Malaya by the middle of the nineteenth century.[1]

It is true that the Company did not interfere with the internal affairs of the Malay States. But the policy of non-intervention did not go unchallenged. British merchants in the Straits Settlements urged the Government to annex the Peninsula in 1844. They frequently complained of the 'utter neglect' of the Malay States.[2] One of the chief arguments in favour of the transfer of the Straits Settlements from Indian control had been that the Colonial Office would listen to the wishes of the Straits merchants. Thus, although British sovereignty was confined to Penang, Malacca and Singapore, the frontiers of British trade and political influence had already moved beyond. There had even been talk of annexation.

During the first six years of its rule over the Straits Settlements, the Colonial Office gradually came to realize that they were not a static administrative problem. They presented the problem of a frontier bordering on potentially rich, but politically unstable, states. The peculiar internal condition of the Malay States soon forced the Colonial Office to review the traditional policy of non-intervention.

BUCKINGHAM'S POLICY IN THE MALAY STATES 1867–71

How did the Colonial Office formulate its policy in Malaya? It approached the problem without preparation or experience. It reacted to circumstances. It did not think ahead. The governor was given no instructions. When problems concerning the Peninsula first appeared, they were treated as a subject for leisurely study. The

Contemporary accounts in *Accounts and Papers* (1863), xliii, pp. 303–87, and O. Cavenagh, *Reminiscences of an Indian Official*, London, 1884, pp. 303–7. See also Linehan, 'Pahang', pp. 66–89; Winstedt, 'Johore', pp. 94–96; M. C. ff. Sheppard, 'A Short History of Trengganu', *J.M.B.R.A.S.* (June 1949), 22 (3), pp. 31–34; Mills, 'British Malaya', pp. 165–6; Cowan, op. cit., pp. 15–17.

[1] Cowan, op. cit., p. 17.

[2] C. B. Buckley, *An Anecdotal History of Old Times in Singapore, from 1819 to 1867*, Singapore, 1902, ii, pp. 421–5, 575 and 584.

Colonial Office was so preoccupied by fears that the new colony would run up a deficit that it failed to perceive some of the dilemmas it would face in Malaya.

The Colonial Office was first introduced to some of the unsolved problems of the Peninsula in June 1867. A pile of documents unearthed from some cupboards in the India Office were sent across to Downing Street. They included details of some minor issues concerning relations between the colony and the states of Kedah and Kelantan, and a boundary dispute between Pahang and Johore. The papers were sent out to Governor Ord, who was asked to inquire and report.[1] No further action was thought necessary.

Charles Cox, the head of the Eastern Department of the Colonial Office, studied the India Office papers and found the task rewarding. He found them 'interesting and instructive as regards our relations and difficulties with Native Chiefs'.[2] He discovered that there had been a tendency for Straits officials to 'push British interference' in the Malay States further than was 'either necessary or desirable'.[3] The last of the Indian governors had, for this reason, tried to formulate a consistent policy. He advocated intervening only in cases of piracy or the murder of British subjects. Cox suggested to Buckingham, the Colonial Secretary, that this might be regarded as the basis for 'standing instructions' to governors faced with requests for intervention in Malaya.[4]

Here, in fact, was an established policy of non-intervention. After its first brief consideration of the Peninsula, the Colonial Office assumed that the policy of non-intervention, with certain exceptions, would be maintained. But their view was never published. Governor Ord was not told. In 1868, the Colonial Office found itself forced to modify its policy on three occasions.

The first modification was a direct result of the Colonial Office's failure to instruct Governor Ord about the Peninsula. They asked him to report on some outstanding problems in the states. They did

[1] I.O. to C.O. 6 June 1867 (with enclosures relating to the Straits Settlements, Malaya and Sumatra); Buckingham to Ord 19 and 20 July 1867. C.O. 273/15.   [2] Ibid. Min. by Cox 1 July 1867.

[3] Ibid. Govt. of India to Cavenagh 15 Feb. 1866 (extract) 'Exactions on British subjects by Chiefs of Laroot'.

[4] Ibid. Min. by Cox 1 July 1867 on papers relating to Larut.

not offer him any guidance. When Ord announced a series of completely unauthorized negotiations with Malay rulers, the Colonial Office received a rude shock. They were forced, for the first time, to consider Britain's role in South-East Asia seriously.

The irascible personality of Sir Harry Ord was the outstanding feature of the first colonial administration in the Straits. He was now forty-seven, and had had considerable, if rather narrow, experience. A somewhat inactive career in the Royal Engineers, and some rather routine posts as governor of Dominica and Bermuda, had been enlivened by his three visits to West Africa, several diplomatic missions to Paris and The Hague, and the major part he had played in the Select Committee on West Africa in 1865. He had become a rather brusque, impatient man, who was ready to act while others faltered. As the Colonial Office's 'expert adviser' on the Gold Coast, he had formed a high opinion of his own ability to 'get on with chiefs'.[1] But he had never governed a Crown Colony. He was used to solving his problems, not to reporting on them and awaiting orders. When in 1867 the Colonial Office asked him to inquire and report on outstanding questions concerning the colony's relations with Kedah and Kelantan, it was quite in character for Ord to decide he would settle the matter of dispute himself.

The Colonial Office learnt, at the end of January 1868,[2] of Ord's negotiations. They realized immediately that the governor's action raised an important question of principle: 'namely our mode of dealing with the Native Chiefs — a point on which Sir H[arry] O[rd] has had no instructions'.[3] Buckingham thought the problem was simple enough — 'Col. Ord himself is to govern the settlements not to diplomatise which may be left to the F.O.'.[4] But Rogers pointed out that the issue raised the whole question of departmental responsibility

[1] See above, pp. 98–99, for Ord's previous career.

[2] On 27 Jan. 1868 an account of the first session of the Legislative Council was received (Ord to Buckingham 18 Dec. 1867. C.O. 273/13) which included a very brief mention of Ord's negotiations with Kedah. Full details did not arrive until 12 Feb. 1868.

[3] Min. by Cox 17 Feb. 1868 on Ord to Buckingham 31 Dec. 1867. C.O. 273/13.

[4] Min. by Buckingham 17 Feb., on Ord to Buckingham 3 Jan. 1868. C.O. 273/13.

in South-East Asia, rather as the annexation of Lagos had done in the Niger region. The Colonial Office wisely considered this question of principle before going into the details of Ord's relations with Kedah and Kelantan.

In negotiating with two of the Siamese 'tributaries' Ord had stepped into the sphere of the Foreign Office. But the governor produced a weighty argument in support of his action. Under the Indian régime in the Straits, relations with the states on the Peninsula, and with the Dutch in the archipelago, had been subject to the veto of the Government of India. Straits residents had often demanded greater powers for their governor. Ord supported their view. He warned the Colonial Office that any diminution of the governor's authority would lower the prestige of the Colonial Government and encourage piracy.[1]

In the Colonial Office, Rogers understood Ord's concern. Looking at the problem in the widest context, he compared the position in the Malay States with frontier situations in South Africa, China, West Africa and Central America, where similar problems of departmental responsibility occurred. He proposed that South-East Asia should be divided into three spheres of responsibility. The governor should deal with the independent Malay States, under the supervision of the Colonial Office. He should be allowed to deal directly with the Siamese tributary states, with Foreign Office approval. Relations with the Dutch should be handled by the Foreign Office, advised by the Colonial Office. Rogers agreed with Ord that the man best placed for gaining information about the Peninsula was the governor and that his prestige was important. At the same time Rogers recognized that the governor might embark on a Siamese policy, enter into relations with the Dutch, or engage in local politics in a way which might conflict with the wider aims of British foreign policy.[2] The Foreign Office, for its part, accepted Rogers's scheme. It saw no objection to the governor having direct communication with the Siamese tributaries. 'Let the Colonial Office adopt its own rules,' said Edmund Hammond,

[1] Ord to Buckingham 31 Dec. 1867. C.O. 273/13.

[2] Ibid. Min. by Rogers 19 Feb. 1868. A large portion of the text of this min. is published in my article, 'Britain's Intervention in Malaya: The Origin of Lord Kimberley's Instructions to Sir Andrew Clarke in 1873'. *J.S.E.A.H.* (1961), 2 (3), pp. 50–51

the permanent under-secretary.[1]   He insisted only that formal negotiations should be concluded by the British consul in Bangkok.

With this agreement secured, Rogers drafted some instructions for Governor Ord.   He was told to leave relations with the Dutch in the hands of the Foreign Office, like the governors of the Gold Coast and British Guiana.   In the Malay States, however, he was granted 'a larger authority'.

> But you will remember, [Rogers warned him] that the relations of the settlements with those powers are matters which may at any time become of serious importance. . . . Although therefore circumstances may not infrequently arise in which you may be called to act absolutely on your own judgment, yet it is generally undesirable that you should enter into formal negotiations with native princes . . . except in pursuance of an object or a policy approved of by HM's Government.[2]

Here was the first modification to the policy of non-intervention in Malaya.   The governor was authorized to act on his own initiative in the Peninsula when he felt it was absolutely necessary.

The second modification to the policy of non-intervention was made for very different reasons.   This time the Colonial Office was called upon to intervene in Malaya, not by the governor, but by British businessmen with interests in the Peninsula.   In May 1868 two different enterprises made overtures to the Colonial Office.

William H. M. Read, doyen of the Singapore merchants,[3] visited London in 1868 to promote certain commercial ventures with the help of his brother-in-law, Mr Seymour Clarke, who was general

---

[1] Notes by Lord Stanley and Hammond on C.O. to F.O. 17 Mar. 1868. F.O. MSS., Siam consular correspondence, F.O. 37/47.   On the permanent under-secretary of the F.O. see M. A. Anderson, 'Edmund Hammond, Permanent Under-Secretary of State for Foreign Affairs, 1854–1875', unpublished Ph.D. thesis, London, 1956.

[2] Buckingham to Ord 22 Apr. 1868 (draft).   C.O. 273/23.

[3] William Henry McLeod Read had been in Singapore since 1841.   He was consul-general for the Netherlands, a friend of the King of Siam, and he had the ear of the Straits authorities at some crucial moments.   He was a promoter of telegraphs in Siam, Malaya and the Dutch East Indies.   He was also interested in gold-mining in Siam and planting in Borneo.   He assisted in quelling the Singapore riots of 1854 and 1863, and he was later the Municipal President.   His memoirs, *Play and Politics — Recollections of Malaya by an Old Resident*, were published in London in 1901.

manager of the Great Northern Railway. On 9 May 1868, Read
sent the Colonial Office a bitter indictment of the policy of allowing
'matters to follow their own course' in the Malay States. He suggested that new treaty relations should be opened with the Malay
rulers, who would welcome the chance to improve their revenues and
govern their states with 'good counsel and advice'.[1]

The Duke of Buckingham was somewhat alarmed by Read's
proposal. He was afraid that such ideas might encourage Ord to
meddle with the Malay, States which was 'an evil to be avoided'.
Charles Adderley, the parliamentary under-secretary, who remembered
Ord from the 1865 Committee, pointed out that 'the danger of new
friendly overtures with Natives is that they always take them to mean
more than they do'. He felt Ord could not be trusted in such matters.
Rogers argued that if the Straits residents would be prepared to pay for
an ambitious policy in the Peninsula it might be quite possible to
'undertake the duty of saying in such of these states who should govern
and how he should govern'. But he reminded his colleagues that
ambitious policies of this kind usually led to further involvement and
to territorial expansion. The consensus of opinion in the Colonial
Office was that Read's suggestions should be passed on to Singapore
but that Ord should be reminded of the policy of non-intervention.[2]

However, the issue was not closed. Another suggestion for intervention had been made at the same time. It came from the London
agents of Paterson, Simons and Company of Singapore, who had once
attempted tin-mining at Kuantan in Pahang.[3] Some of the Company's property had been confiscated during the Pahang Civil War in
1863 and the new rulers had not restored it. Appeals to the Government of India had failed to evoke a response; now the Colonial Office
was asked to intervene. As he read this further request for intervention in Malaya, Rogers sensed that another serious point of principle
was involved.

[1] Read to Buckingham, London, 9 May 1868, with a memo. on the Malay
States. C.O. 273/25.
[2] Ibid. Mins. by Adderley 13 May, Buckingham 15 May, and Rogers
(undated) 1868; Buckingham to Ord 20 May 1868 (draft).
[3] Paterson, Simons & Co. to Buckingham 8 May 1868. C.O. 273/24.
The Company's concession of 1862 is printed in *Accounts and Papers* (1863),
xliii, pp. 331–2.

Rogers was convinced that the Colonial Office should disassociate itself completely from commercial ventures in the Malay States.[1] The answer to Paterson and Simons followed the same lines as that given to Read and, indeed, to similar promoters in places like New Guinea and West Africa: merchants venturing into 'un-civilized' lands did so at their own risk; the Government would not intervene to help them when 'the state of the Country, and the disputes of rival claimants to power cause embarrassment and loss'.[2] Here, then, is another repetition of the policy of non-interference. The final phrase, however, is most significant. It represents a modification of the view propounded by Rogers. It was in fact added by Buckingham, the Secretary of State, on 4 June 1868, because he thought 'there may be cases in which it might be right and proper to take strong measures'.[3] This private admission represents the second modification of the policy of non-intervention in the Malay States.

In what cases would Buckingham permit intervention ? He provided an answer on the very same day in a despatch to Ord on the subject of Kelantan. Ord had been asked in 1867 to investigate a report that the Sultan of Kelantan had granted monopolies of the export and import of certain commodities in his state. The governor tried, without success, to persuade the sultan to permit free trade. The approach was unauthorized and the Colonial Office cautioned Ord on 27 February 1868.[4]

[1] Min. by Rogers 25 May, on Paterson, Simons & Co. to Buckingham 8 May 1868. C.O. 273/25.

[2] C.O. to Paterson, Simons & Co. 8 June 1868 (draft). Ibid. The same attitude was shown over W. Africa: 'persons who trade at remote places must understand that they are to settle their own quarrels and that they are not to expect the intervention of British forces'. (Min. by Elliot 11 July, on Blackall to Carnarvon 20 June 1866. C.O. 96/71.) Cf. the reply to the New Guinea Co. of Sydney: 'any persons who embark in it [the New Guinea expedition] must not look for aid and protection from the national forces, nor for the confirmation of HM Government of their titles to any acquisitions of land which they may make from the natives'. (Buckingham to Young 14 Sept. 1867 (draft). C.O. 201/542.)

[3] Buckingham first saw the papers on 26 May, but on 4 June he corrected the draft and added this 'escape-clause' for the benefit of the Office.

[4] Ord to Buckingham 3 Jan. 1868; mins. by Rogers 13 Feb., Buckingham 17 Feb., and Buckingham to Ord 22 Feb. 1868 (draft). C.O. 273/17.

But Sir Harry Ord refused to be deterred. In March 1868, Siamese envoys visited Singapore and signed agreements with the governor over Kedah and Kelantan.[1] When Ord acknowledged his caution on 8 April 1868 he boldly reopened the whole question of British policy in Malaya. He admitted that the precise relationship of the northern states to Siam was obscure. But he had come to the conclusion that the domination of the Malay States by 'Powers greater and more civilized than themselves' would be 'an advantage to themselves and to all who have relation with them'. He claimed that apart from Johore the whole of the southern part of the Peninsula was a dangerous political vacuum.

> Nothing can be more unsatisfactory than the condition of the Native States which are not dependent upon any superior power, in most of them there is, as a rule, neither order, peace, nor regular government.

Insecurity discouraged the development of their resources. Although tin-mining flourished in a few places, tolls levied by minor Malay rulers hampered enterprise. Ord believed that the only state which had evolved a satisfactory relationship with the colony was Perak. The sultan usually sent an officer to settle disputes, but the other states had no such system. Therefore Ord concluded by declaring:

> I feel that it would be greatly to the advantage of the Settlement if our influence could be thus extended over the Peninsula and I shall not fail to avail myself of any opening that may present itself for doing so.[2]

After a year in the Straits, Ord was firmly convinced that Britain should expand her influence in the Malay Peninsula.

At home, in Whitehall, Ord's superiors did not share his outlook. Rogers rejected Ord's proposal. In the Foreign Office, Hammond hoped that Ord would not be 'too active with the petty states'.[3] Consequently, Ord was once again reminded that the Government's policy remained one of non-intervention. He was ordered to keep clear of disorders in the Malay States — 'which do not directly affect or threaten the peace of the Settlements themselves'.[4] Here was

---

[1] The Kedah treaty is discussed separately below, pp. 164–7.

[2] Ord to Buckingham 8 Apr. 1868. C.O. 273/18.

[3] Note by Hammond 16 May, on C.O. to F.O. 15 May 1868. F.O. 69/47.

[4] See min. by Rogers 20 May, on Ord to Buckingham 8 Apr. 1868; Buckingham to Ord 4 June 1868. C.O. 273/18.

Buckingham's sole ground for local discretion. Having admitted privately to the department on the same day that some sort of intervention *might* become necessary, he permitted Ord to take action if the security of the colony was involved. Buckingham's qualification was the third, and, for a few years, the final modification to the policy of non-intervention in Malaya. His policy may be compared with Cardwell's policy in West Africa. British policy was based on the doctrine of qualified restraint.

By the end of 1868, when Gladstone came to power, with Granville at the Colonial Office, Ord's diplomacy embraced nearly the whole field of British policy in South-East Asia. Rogers briefed the incoming Secretary of State on the problems of Malaya, by warning Granville that

> Experience seems to show the great necessity of maintaining a very clear line indeed between the function of the officers of the Colonial Office and those of the F.O. Else they will certainly quarrel and probably draw us in.[1]

The history of Ord's negotiations vividly illustrated Rogers's view.

SIR HARRY ORD'S NEGOTIATIONS WITH MALAY RULERS, 1868-71

Sir Harry Ord may have forced the Colonial Office to take an interest in the Malay States. He was even partly responsible for Buckingham's modification of the policy of non-intervention. But his ideas of British expansion in Malaya had been completely rejected. A closer look at some of Ord's relations with Malay rulers will tell us why. His acts were unauthorized, his methods were precipitate; he neglected regular channels of communication and, when cautioned, refused to be restrained.

The negotiation of the Kedah treaty did more than any other single issue to damage Ord's reputation. It caused confusion in Whitehall. Throughout 1868 the issue dragged on and on — first in Penang and Singapore, then in London and Bangkok. The repercussions of Ord's action were out of all proportion to their practical significance.

The issue was a minor one. The Sultan of Kedah was raising

---

[1] Min. by Rogers 21 Jan., on F.O. to C.O. 8 Jan. 1869. C.O. 273/34.

revenue by taxing food exports to Penang. He also took advantage of a very irregular, winding boundary between Kedah and Province Wellesley to erect gambling-houses for the benefit of Chinese from the colony, where such places were illegal. The Government of India had been unable to dissuade the sultan and in 1867 Ord was asked to comment.

Sir Harry decided to settle the issue himself. Through the good offices of Tan Kim Ching,[1] a wealthy Straits merchant who was Siamese consul-general in Penang, the basis for a new treaty with Kedah was drawn up in Singapore in August 1867. The sultan agreed to reduce his customs duties, and to allow the Kedah–Province Wellesley boundary to be straightened out. On either side of the new line two miles of jungle would be cleared and no gambling-houses would be built. Ord arranged to travel to Penang for the signing of the treaty at the end of December 1867. At the close of the session of the Legislative Council he confidently announced that the colony's differences with Kedah had been 'satisfactorily adjusted'.[2] The new governor appeared to have made a bold and successful excursion into the realms of diplomacy.

Unfortunately for Ord his success was illusory. Kedah was a Siamese 'tributary'. The sultan had only accepted a 'memorandum of agreement'. When the governor appeared in Penang to sign the treaty, the sultan flatly refused. The formal treaty was differently worded than the memorandum, and the sultan would not sign without Siamese approval. Ord was furious. He not only broke off diplomatic relations with Kedah, but he stopped the pension which had been paid to the rulers of Kedah since the cession of Penang.

After taking the initiative, Ord had failed. He decided to appeal to the King of Siam and to the British consul-general in Bangkok. He also in-

---

[1] Tan Kim Ching (1829–92) was given this title by the King of Siam. He was a Straits Chinese with wide interests in the East. He had rice mills in Saigon, and influence among the Chinese in the Siamese tributaries of Kelantan and Patani; his Singapore house was known as 'Siam House'. (Song Ong Siang, *One Hundred Years' History of the Chinese in Singapore*, London, 1923, pp. 92–93, 115, 156; see also Cowan, *Nineteenth Century Malaya*, p. 56, who calls him 'a perfect example of the cosmopolitan Straits Merchant'.)

[2] Ord to Buckingham 18 Dec. 1867. C.O. 273/13.

formed the Colonial Office of his actions.¹ In London, as we have seen,
the Colonial Office and the Foreign Office concentrated on the general
principles of British policy in South-East Asia, and not the merits of the
Kedah treaty, which was sent to the Law Officers for their comments.

Meanwhile, the Siamese Government took over the negotiations
on behalf of Kedah. Envoys were appointed to visit the Straits and
negotiate with Governor Ord. They accepted Ord's terms during a
brief meeting at Penang on 13 February 1868, but requested a short
delay while they completed some urgent duties in the northern states.
It was a legitimate request. But Ord's patience collapsed. In another
fit of temper he ended the negotiations with the Siamese and hinted
that he would demand more favourable terms. Fortunately, the
Siamese ignored the governor's wrath, and in March 1868 they
visited Singapore to settle the Kedah and Kelantan issues. On 21
March 1868 the new Kedah treaty was finally signed.²

Who gained from the negotiations ? Certainly not the Sultan of
Kedah. The Siamese, however, had nothing to lose; the incident
reaffirmed their suzerainty over Kedah. Governor Ord on his part
had narrowly avoided creating a dangerous precedent. Before reporting his 'success' to the Colonial Office, he received a sobering letter
from Mr Harry Alabaster, the acting British consul in Bangkok.
Alabaster reminded Ord that an important object of British foreign
policy in South-East Asia was the maintenance of Siamese integrity
and the support of Siamese influence in the tributary states. Alabaster
pointed out that dealing with these states through the Government in
Bangkok was convenient for Britain and useful to Siam. If direct
relations were opened up with the Malay States to the south, what of
the Laos States to the north? Here the French, who had already
secured a protectorate over Cambodia in 1867, were pressing their
influence. Diplomacy in Siam was in a state of delicate balance.
Thus Alabaster objected to Ord writing direct to the king instead of
through the normal consular channels.³ Ord believed his success

¹ Ibid. Ord to Buckingham 31 Dec. 1867. For the view of the British
consul in Bangkok, see Alabaster to Stanley 18 Mar. 1868. F.O. 69/46.
² Encl. in Ord to Buckingham 26 Mar. 1868. C.O. 273/17.
³ Alabaster to Ord 10 Mar., copy in F.O. to C.O. 7 May 1868. C.O.
273/23. This letter may have reached Singapore before Ord signed the
treaty and may well have encouraged Ord to welcome Siamese envoys.

justified his means, and when he sent the treaty home he defended his correspondence with King Mongkut.

The new treaty reached London on 4 May 1868, where Ord's methods caused consternation on all sides. 'Sir H[arry] Ord has not managed this matter well,' wrote Sir Frederic Rogers.[1] He informed the Foreign Office, where Edmund Hammond exclaimed, 'The matter and the questions involved in it are in such a state of muddle that I hardly know what to advise'. Although he had accepted the general principle that the governor of the Straits Settlements could communicate with the Siamese tributaries, the Kedah affair indicated some of the dangers involved. He believed that if two different authorities, governor and consul, were allowed to negotiate with 'Eastern rulers' it would give 'the Oriental a sure opportunity of playing off one British authority against the other'.[2]

For the rest of 1868 confusion reigned in Whitehall. Adderley, who was something of an expert on the West African Settlements, could not understand the ways of 'all these Rajas' in Malaya.[3] Rogers finally suggested that they should interpret their original division of responsibility in South-East Asia in the light of circumstances.

> I am inclined to think that when a tributary can settle a question without any communication between our authorities and the Siamese authorities, the Governor sh[oul]d negotiate, but that if it is necessary that the Siamese authorities should intervene visibly it is better that whole matter should pass through the hands of the Consul . . . and the King of Siam.[4]

He decided that the Kedah issue belonged to the second category and should be left to the Foreign Office. The treaty was finally signed in Bangkok by the consul on 6 March 1869.[5] The whole matter had been taken out of the governor's hands.

Sir Harry Ord continued to play the part of a pro-consul in South-East Asia. While Whitehall tried to untangle his Siamese negotiations,

[1] Min. by Rogers 7 May, on Ord to Buckingham 26 Mar. 1868.
[2] Note by Hammond 31 May, on C.O. to F.O. 25 May 1868. F.O. 69/47.
[3] Min. by Adderley 26 June, on F.O. to C.O. 17 June 1868. C.O. 273/23.
[4] Ibid. Min. by Rogers 22 Oct., on F.O. to C.O. 17 July 1868.
[5] Knox to Clarendon 19 May 1869. C.O. 69/48. Text of new treaty in Maxwell and Gibson, pp. 82–85. It closely resembles Ord's draft of 1868.

Sir Harry went on to meet King Mongkut in person. In August 1868 the governor travelled to Whae Whan in Patani to represent Great Britain at a unique diplomatic occasion — a conference to view an eclipse of the sun.

The solar kingdom was not normally the subject of diplomacy in the Victorian Age. But in 1868 King Mongkut found himself in a dilemma. In the previous year he had been forced by France to renounce his suzerainty over Cambodia.[1] Ever since then he remained suspicious of the French. Sometimes they gave him good cause unwittingly. On one occasion, when some French scientists wished to view an eclipse of the sun from Siamese territory and travelled in a gunboat to select a good site, he doubted whether the French were actuated by scientific curiosity alone. But he conceded the point when the British sent a gunboat to follow the French.[2] Making the best of a bad situation, Mongkut turned the eclipse-viewing into an 'international event' and, with more subtlety than the foreigners gave him credit for, played off the British against the French.

Royal invitations were sent to the European and American community in Bangkok to attend the heliocentric celebrations. Governor Ord too was invited and the whole affair was like 'a picnic'.[3] The French were distinctly unhappy, especially when Mongkut, stopwatch in hand, gave the firing orders for a seven-gun salute to the British consul. He then posed for photographs with Sir Harry Ord and entertained the governor in the royal apartments. King Mongkut's return visit to Ord's quarters had, so the governor claimed, 'no parallel in history'.[4] The whole affair must have been quite a triumph for Ord's self-esteem; possibly it even improved Anglo-Siamese relations.

[1] See J. F. Cady, *The Roots of French Imperialism in South-East Asia*, Ithaca, N.Y., 1954, pp. 227–80.

[2] Alabaster to Stanley 13 June 1868. F.O. 69/46.

[3] Ibid. Alabaster to Stanley 24 Aug. 1868. The acting consul's report is even more exuberant than Ord's and includes a water-colour sketch of the scene by himself. Hammond commented drily: 'a very curious account'.

[4] Ord to Buckingham 27 Aug. 1868. C.O. 273/21. A booklet about the affair and a set of photographs arrived on 16 Nov. 1868 (in C.O. 273/22). See N. Snidvongs, 'King Mongkut's Relations with the West', unpublished Ph.D. thesis, London, 1959. Mongkut contracted a fatal illess at Whae Whan. Dr. Snidvongs regards the conference as 'a fitting finale to his reign'.

Ord's diplomatic activity did not end with the eclipse of the sun. Returning to Singapore, the governor visited the rulers of the eastern states of the Malay Peninsula on his way. The Sultan of Trengganu, the most independent of the Siamese tributaries, presented his 'friendly compliments' to the Straits Government. The Maharaja of Johore and the Bendahara of Pahang accepted Ord's mediation in their boundary dispute.[1] Finally, after getting back to Singapore he successfully persuaded the Colonial Office to send him to Netherlands India to assist in Anglo-Dutch negotiations over Sumatra and the Gold Coast. He went to Batavia in June 1869 to visit the Dutch governor-general.[2] The Colonial Office approved of Ord's actions in all these matters. They were pleasantly surprised that Ord did not exceed his instructions and make some rash commitment.

Granville only found it necessary to remind Ord of the policy of non-intervention on one occasion. In 1869 Ord tried to revive a British claim to a small coastal district known as the Dindings in Perak. Looking for new ways of suppressing piracy off the Perak coast, he discovered that according to the treaty between Perak and the East India Company, signed in 1826, the sultan had offered to cede to Britain the coastal region of 'the Pulo Dinding and the islands of Pangkor'.[3] The district was not defined and was never occupied. Negotiations which were in progress when Ord became governor had been unsuccessful. In the spring of 1869 Ord tried to reopen the question.

Unfortunately for the governor, the first news of his action to reach London was a newspaper account which caught the eye of the Hon. Henry Stanley (Stanley of Alderley). Stanley, a former diplomat, was a well-known eccentric, who had lived for a number of years in

[1] The boundary arranged in 1862, when Mutahir was Bendahara of Pahang, was the line of the Endau river, but the islands off its mouth went to Johore. Wan Ahmad rejected this agreement, but in 1867 Sultan Omar of Trengganu persuaded him to accept Ord's mediation. Ord persuaded Abu-Bakar of Johore to return the islands to Pahang which were north of the mouth of the Endau. Linehan, 'Pahang', p. 91. Cowan, *Nineteenth Century Malaya*, pp. 34–40, 60; Ord to Buckingham 20 Jan. 1869. C.O. 273/26.

[2] These negotiations are discussed in my article, 'Disraeli's Election Blunder', pp. 83–91.

[3] Perak treaty, no. 1, 1826. Maxwell and Gibson, p. 23.

Singapore; and he demanded an explanation of Ord's action from the unsuspecting Colonial Office. When Granville called for a report from the governor, Ord insisted that he had never intended to occupy any new territory without authority. But Granville decided to remind Ord that he would 'not be disposed to approve any proceedings which would extend the responsibility of H.M. Government in the neighbourhood of the Straits Settlements'.[1]

After this warning there was a lull in Ord's attempts to intervene in Malaya. He had now been cautioned no less than four times. He told his Legislative Council at the end of 1869 'my hands are tied'.[2] He refused to intervene in a civil war in Selangor when the sultan called for his aid in 1870. As Ord was sick with malaria, he went home on leave in March 1871.

In five years Sir Harry Ord ranged over virtually the whole field of British policy in South-East Asia. Within Rogers's three spheres of responsibility he made some useful contributions. He upheld Siamese power by negotiations over Kedah and Kelantan through the Siamese envoys and by attending Mongkut's scientific festival at Whae Whan. He convinced the Colonial Office that the governor should be permitted some discretion in relations with the independent Malay rulers. He visited the Sultan of Trengganu and mediated in the Johore-Pahang dispute in the east of the Peninsula, and he also visited Perak and Selangor on the west coast. In the negotiations with the Dutch over Sumatra, his Gold Coast experience and missions to The Hague gave him a special interest.

Yet in one vital issue Ord failed completely. Further British intervention in the Malay Peninsula was forbidden — except in emergencies. The Colonial Office would only permit intervention if the security of the colony itself was threatened. While he was at home on leave Ord once more tried, unsuccessfully, to persuade the Colonial Office to reconsider Britain's position in the Peninsula. Why did he fail? One of the reasons was that the Colonial Office had serious misgivings about his ability. The attitude of the policy-makers to

[1] Granville to Ord 10 Sept. 1869 (draft). C.O. 273/30. For a fuller discussion of the Dindings issue see Cowan, op. cit., pp. 54–55.

[2] Legislative Council mins. 20 Oct. 1869, received in C.O. 7 Feb. 1870. C.O. 273/43.

Ord's expansionism needs to be seen in the light of their opinion of him as a colonial governor.

ORD'S ADMINISTRATION OF THE STRAITS SETTLEMENTS, 1867–71

The first colonial Government of the Straits Settlements was a very stormy one. On the one hand, Straits residents who had longed to be rid of control from Calcutta now found they had a more vigilant master in Whitehall; on the other, the Colonial Office discovered that Ord did not know how to run a Crown Colony. At the ceremonies in Singapore to mark the transfer from Indian control, Ord immediately offended local society by his brusque manner.[1] He set the tone for an administration which managed, in turn, to cause irritation in Whitehall, the City and Singapore itself.

The Colonial Office soon discovered Sir Harry Ord's limitations. Rogers realized, as early as January 1868, that service in places like Bermuda and the West Indies, with their ancient representative institutions, was not a good training for the routine of Crown Colonies under close supervision from home. Ord's negotiations with Malay rulers, for instance, were reported home tardily, only after he had got into difficulties. Proposals for new expenditure on Government buildings and steamers led to acrimonious debates. Ord rendered his accounts and estimates in the wrong form. The governor even hinted to the Legislative Council that in view of the need for more revenue they might have to consider import duties, which led to an uproar in Singapore and the City of London where the free-port status of the Straits was regarded as a sacred principle. 'I cannot help thinking that relations between Sir H[arry] O[rd] and this office are becoming unsatisfactory,'[2] lamented Rogers, who later decided to instruct the governor in Crown Colony procedure.[3] Soon demands for special consideration over an A.D.C., and his later career, made Rogers feel that Ord was 'most unduly pertinacious'.[4]

[1] Buckley, *Anecdotal History of Old Times in Singapore*, ii, p. 786.
[2] Min. by Rogers 16 Jan. 1868 on Ord to Buckingham 7 Dec. 1867. C.O. 273/13.
[3] Buckingham to Ord 31 July 1868, confidential (draft). C.O. 273/18.
[4] Min. by Rogers (undated) on Ord to Granville 25 Jan.1869. C.O. 273/26.

If criticism came from outside the department, however, the Colonial Office rallied to the support of the governor. The opposition first centred in London. In January 1868 the Straits Settlements Association was founded 'to guard against any legislation that might prejudicially affect the interests of the Straits Settlements'.[1] With the veteran ex-governor, John Crawfurd, as president, this influential pressure group took the initiative in the attack on Ord. Month by month its members badgered the Colonial Office. They secured two interviews with Granville and at least one with Kimberley. But Ord, on the whole, emerged victorious.[2] By 1870 Herbert decided that 'the time has arrived when the Association may be relieved of the supervision of the Col[onial] Office'.[3]

Yet, just as Ord began to hold his own in London, opposition to him came to a head in Singapore. Here his internal administration and external policies led to the growth of something akin to an opposition party led by Sir Benson Maxwell, the Chief Justice and leader of the unofficial members of the Legislative Council. W. H. M. Read, the notable merchant, resigned from the Bench after a row with Ord. The governor also managed to quarrel with his official subordinates, the lieutenant-governors of Penang and Malacca.[4] In fact, Ord's growing unpopularity left people reluctant to serve on the Council, and it may also have caused some of his official colleagues to withhold important advice. Herbert's minute in 1870 was probably a fair summary of the impasse Ord had reached in his personal dealings:

I am rather inclined to think that Gov[ernor] Ord's unfortunate temper and disposition to act harshly & imperiously towards those who do not

---

[1] William Napier (secretary) to Granville 7 Feb. 1868. C.O. 273/24. See also C. N. Parkinson, *British Intervention in Malaya, 1867–77*, Singapore, 1960, pp. 20–21.

[2] Granville, always sensitive to political pressure, was fairly indulgent to the Assoc., and its letters were often the only Straits documents he endorsed. He received a deputation on 4 May 1869 but, since a reply by Ord to his attackers was received on 1 May, Granville conceded nothing. In Dec. 1868 a 'Singapore Merchant' wrote three vicious letters to *The Star*, which soon appeared as a pamphlet, *The Straits Settlements, or How to Govern a Colony*. Ord's reply was contained in a series of reasoned annotations to this, in Ord to Granville 29 Mar. 1869. C.O. 273/31.

[3] Min. by Herbert on S.S. Assoc. to Granville 31 Jan. 1870. C.O. 273/30.

[4] Anson, *About Others and Myself*, pp. 293–4.

humbly obey his will has led a party of officials to combine in giving him
trouble & putting him in the wrong. Any symptoms of this should be
repressed — but one cannot help feeling that if he is uncomfortable he
made the bed on which he lies.[1]

In the light of this assessment of his personality the failure of Ord's
Malayan policies can more easily be understood.

Yet credit must be given to Ord's achievements. He faced his
opponents courageously. He managed to produce a surplus revenue
in years of trade depression.[2] The building of Singapore's grandiose
Government House was completed in his time; and, as an officer of
the Royal Engineers, Ord was a highly suitable person to introduce
Crown Colony rule, with its much resented, but essential, ordinances
to provide more sanitary conditions in the growing city of Singapore.
Frank Swettenham, best-known of the British Malayans of a later
age, who was only twenty when he arrived as a cadet, was the governor's Malay interpreter. He remembered Ord as a 'big and very
masterful Governor, of great ability and strong character', who as well
as being a good financier was also very kindly towards the cadets.[3]
Ord's opponents came, in the main, from the European mercantile
community, never a class much trusted by aristocratic Victorians like
Buckingham, Granville, Kimberley or Carnarvon. Thus, when Ord
went on leave, Herbert was anxious to give him his due:

> We have had to find fault with him about administrative details, but he
> should have credit for conciliating and keeping in good order the Asiatic
> population.[4]

And whatever it thought of Ord, the Colonial Office was soon completely disenchanted with his *locum tenens*, Colonel Anson, the
lieutenant-governor of Penang, who not only began 'meddling'
with the question of the Malay States, but who also ordered an armed
intervention in the Peninsula.

It is worth remembering, however, that Anson only acted upon
advice which Ord had already tendered. Sir Harry had, after considering the problems of the Peninsula, recommended an expansion

[1] Min. by Herbert 22 Aug., on Ord to Granville 29 June 1870. C.O.273/38.
[2] Ord to Kimberley 19 Sept. 1870. C.O. 273/41. The surplus shown on
the estimates for 1871 was $71,192.
[3] F. A. Swettenham, *Footprints in Malaya*, London, 1942, pp. 16–17.
[4] Min. by Herbert 12 Apr., on Ord to Kimberley 3 Mar. 1871. C.O. 273/45.

of British power. He had been restrained. Anson came to the same conclusions as Ord. But he felt there was now greater urgency. To appreciate his position the situation in the Malay States at the time of Ord's leave in 1871 must be briefly reviewed.

THE MALAY STATES IN THE 1870'S

Most of the Malay States were woefully weak. Only in Johore and Kedah was there anything like effective government.[1] They were the states which adjoined the British settlements, and both their rulers received payments from Britain. Kedah has already been noted, along with Kelantan and Trengganu, as a 'tributary' of Siam, with which Ord had maintained good relations.[2] Johore had been ruled since 1862 by Temenggong Abu-Bakar, who had recently started styling himself 'Maharaja'. His family owed its position to British influence[3] and his home was in Singapore. He had visited Europe in 1866, and received a knighthood from Queen Victoria. Ord regarded him as the one Malay ruler whom Britain could trust.[4] To the east of the Peninsula, Trengganu was ruled peaceably, and firmly, by the remarkable Sultan Omar, who had built up the power of the sultanate and resisted Siamese influence.[5] By the 1870's the development of Trengganu really lay outside of the main stream of Malayan politics as it was viewed from Singapore. Pahang, the large state of the east coast, was war-sick and depopulated after the civil war in 1862 by which Bendahara Wan Ahmad had established his rule. Throughout the nineteenth century Pahang remained something of a backwater in Malaya.[6]

[1] Report of the 'Committee on Native States' in Anson to Kimberley 25 Apr. 1861. C.O. 273/47.   [2] See above, pp.155, 169.

[3] See agreement between Sultan and Temenggong of Johore, 1855. Maxwell and Gibson, pp. 127–9.

[4] See Winstedt, 'Johore', pp. 100–20. In England Abu-Bakar was created a Knight of the Star of India — the first Malay ruler to be so honoured. His special position in Singapore did not prevent him causing anxiety to the Straits Govt. on a number of occasions. W. H. Read was a frequent critic. For some of Abu-Bakar's economic interests, see Cowan, *Nineteenth Century Malaya*, pp. 36–39.

[5] M. C. ff. Sheppard, 'Trengganu', pp. 34–35.

[6] H. Clifford, *East Coast Etchings*, London, 1896, p. 11.

The real focus of interest was the west coast. Here Colonel Anson found his main challenge. The states which lay between the British settlements of Penang and Malacca, namely Perak, Selangor and Sungei Ujong, contained rich tin-bearing regions. Through them many rivers flowed into the Strait of Malacca. Along these rivers the Malay rulers raised their revenues from tolls, and the value of the tolls depended largely on the increasing traffic in tin.

There were two outstanding problems in the west-coast states. In the first place, Chinese tin-miners, attracted by the possibility of great wealth, brought into Malaya their clan rivalries from China, which led to open fighting.[1] Secondly, the decline of the Malay royal houses led to dynastic rivalries and civil wars among the Malayan population. Since the Malay rajas depended for much of their revenue on the river tolls, and the size of the revenue increased with the development of the tin trade, there was intense rivalry for jurisdiction over the mouths of the main rivers.[2] Two sorts of rivalry existed, then: among the Chinese secret societies in the mining areas, and among the Malay rulers. But they both became interwoven. When a Malay

[1] See V. Purcell, *The Chinese in Malaya*, Oxford, 1948, ch. 8; Mills, 'British Malaya', pp. 203–8, and Cowan, op. cit., pp. 46–49, for the Chinese secret societies. 'They were originally religious or benevolent "self-help" associations which assumed a political and anti-dynastic character at the time of the Manchu conquest of China and later degenerated into criminal organisations'. (Purcell, p. 155.) In Malaya they usually provided the only community organization in the early mining areas. By the 1850's two main groups had emerged in Penang: (1) the *Ghee Hin*, which was a branch of the ancient Triad Soc. of China and was composed mainly of Cantonese; and (2) the *Hai San*, which had been formed in Penang, and was composed mainly of Hakkas. In the Penang riots of 1867 the two parties (about 30,000 Chinese with some Malay allies) were involved in a regular series of street battles for ten days (Anson, *About Others and Myself*, pp. 278–83). These divisions and rivalries were projected into the Malay States, where the societies exercised a harsh control over the poor immigrant miners.

[2] See R. J. Wilkinson's chapters in R. O. Winstedt, 'A History of Perak', *J.M.B.R.A.S.* (1934), 12 (1), pp. 134–58, for an account of the various officers of State and what they were, in theory, entitled to in the way of revenue. J. M. Gullick, *The Indigenous Political Systems of Western Malaya*, London, 1958, pp. 11–14 and 42–64, analyses the Malay system of authority. Mills, 'British Malaya', pp. 170–3, says the Malay States at this time were committing political *hara-kiri* among themselves.

raja allied himself with a Chinese headman the result was the type of confused warfare which halted trade, endangered the whole region and even threatened the Straits Settlements. Here lay the significance in the situation from the British point of view. The Chinese in the tin mines raised their capital in the colony, their secret society head-quarters were located in the Straits, some of the miners were British subjects. The Malayan wars threatened the Straits Settlements. By doing so they provided the one legitimate reason for intervention in the eyes of the Colonial Office.

Turning now to the three states in question, it must be emphasized that each had its own particular problems. In Perak, for example, there was tension among the Malay leaders because there were three rival candidates for the sultanate. The reason for this was that only two months before Governor Ord went back to England, Sultan Ali had died, on 25 May 1871, and certain irregularities in the election of his successor caused the Perak aristocracy to split into rival factions.[1]

The normal constitutional processes of Perak were upset because the authority of the sultanate had been declining for twenty years.[2] The decay set in during the reign of Sultan 'Abdu'llah Muhammad Shah (1851–7), when many chiefs were in open rebellion. After the death of his successor, Sultan Ja'afar, in 1865, the influence of the royal house was so reduced that the new sultan, Ali, reigned until 1871 with very little power, while the ageing Bendahara Ismail (in theory 'chief minister') lived in isolation in the Kinta Valley. By 1871 the dominant personalities in Perak were neither the sultan nor the bendahara, but three other rivals: the Raja Muda 'Abdu'llah ('heir apparent'), a chief styled 'the Mantri of Larut', and the Raja Yusuf, who was the son of Sultan 'Abdu'llah Muhammad Shah.

[1] Wilkinson in Winstedt, 'Perak', p. 93, gives the date as 26 May. Cowan, op. cit., p. 77, gives 25 May, following the Irving Report, 24 July 1872. C.O. 809/1, p. 152.

[2] The best short survey of Perak history in this period is the introd. to C. D. Cowan, 'Sir Frank Swettenham's Perak Journals, 1874–1876', *J.M.B.R.A.S.* (Dec. 1951), 24 (4), pp. 12–20. The Constitution of Perak was described by C. J. Irving in 1872 (C.O. 809/1, p. 151), and by Wilkinson in Winstedt's, 'Perak', pp. 134–58. Usually, the heir presumptive (raja muda) was accepted as the new sultan in an election. The chief minister (bendahara) then often became raja muda, and a new bendahara was elected.

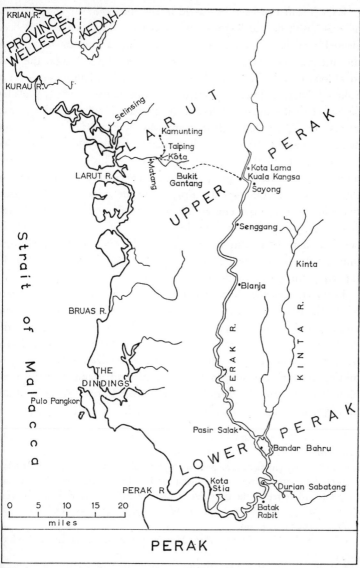

PERAK

These were the aspirants for power after 1871. Their names occur
again and again in the discussion of British intervention in Perak, and
their antecedents are worth discussing.[1]

[1] See Cowan, *Nineteenth Century Malaya*, pp. 78–79.

Raja Yusuf had been by-passed in the succession in 1857 because he was disliked, and a non-royal favourite, Raja Ismail, had been elected bendahara. Yusuf, however, continued to claim his right to the sultanate, and Swettenham later regarded him as 'by far the most royal looking man in Perak'.[1] Raja Muda 'Abdu'llah was the son of Sultan Ja'afar, and was appointed the Raja Muda in 1865, probably because Ismail's non-royal descent precluded adherence to the normal succession. 'Abdu'llah's great enemy was the Mantri of Larut, whom he antagonized by trying to collect taxes in Larut, which he regarded as a perquisite of the Raja Muda's office. This particular quarrel serves to introduce the most significant personality in the whole of Perak politics in this period. For, while the sultanate had progressively lost power, a parvenu family had carved out an almost independent principality for itself in the province of Larut. It owed its position there to wealth from taxes on the tin, mined by Chinese immigrants, who were said to number 40,000 by 1871 and to be exporting tin worth a million dollars a year.[2]

Forty years earlier, Larut had been a marshy tract on the periphery of Perak, under the nominal jurisdiction of a minor chief. About 1840, this chief employed a lowly relative, Long Ja'afar, to collect the local taxes.[3] It is said that there were only three Chinese in Larut when he first went there; but Long Ja'afar realized the possibility of mining for tin, encouraged immigration, and gradually gained for himself a nearly independent jurisdiction over Larut. After his death in 1857, his son, Ngah Ibrahim, then in his twenties, accumulated

[1] Cowan, 'Swettenham's Journals', pp. 54–56. Swettenham was told by a high officer of State: 'By rights Yusuf ought to be Sultan of Perak, but he is so severe the chiefs cannot bear his harshness.' In Feb. 1869 Yusuf had presented his case to the Straits Govt. and Col. Macpherson, the Colonial Secretary, regretted at the time that it was not possible for Britain to govern Perak 'through a nominee'. R. J. Wilkinson, 'Notes on Perak History', *P.M.S.* (1908), 4, p. 99.

[2] F. J. A. McNair, *Perak and the Malays, Sarong and Kris*, London, 1878, p. 351.

[3] Wilkinson in Winstedt, 'Perak', p. 78, calls Larut a 'no man's land' and describes the authority, such as it did exist, of the one interested Malay ruler, the Panglima Bukit Gantang (Keeper of the pass between Larut and the Perak river), whose brother married a daughter of Long Ja'afar.

greater privileges.[1] Yet if he secured nominal jurisdiction over Larut, he did not squander his wealth on providing administration. He left the Chinese miners at Taiping and Kamunting to rule themselves through their secret societies. And these societies brought trouble to Larut. After a dispute in 1861 they took up arms and the Hai San members of Taiping drove the Ghee Hins from Kamunting out of Larut, helped, it should be noted, by Ngah Ibrahim. This was only the first of a series of bloody conflicts which disrupted Perak for fifteen years, and endangered the British colony of Penang. They eventually provided the major motive for Britain's political intervention.

The incident vividly illustrated both the basis of Ngah Ibrahim's wealth and his method of gaining greater powers. By paying off the claims which were made against the sultan (who could not pay) Ngah Ibrahim was rewarded in 1862 with further rights of jurisdiction in Larut. He was appointed Orang Kaya Mantri ('Secretary of State'), one of the four great chiefs of Perak. Henceforth he was known as the 'Mantri of Larut'. If his exact constitutional position is still somewhat obscure, he was certainly by the late 1860's the *de facto* ruler of Larut. With a revenue from tin estimated at 200,000 dollars a year, he could maintain a police force of forty, a European-style house, and forts commanding both seaward and landward approaches to the tin mines of Larut.[2]

By 1871, then, there were three major contenders for power in Perak. When the sultan died, 'Abdu'llah expected to be elected to succeed. But he was afraid to attend the sultan's funeral and the

[1] The grants of jurisdiction over the Larut to Long Ja'afar and Ngah Ibrahim are best presented by Wilkinson in Winstedt, 'Perak', pp. 78–79, where he says of Long Ja'afar: 'Beginning as a mere representative of the Sultan he bought from his master one after another the various sources of revenue in the province'. Translations, made by Swettenham in 1873, of the documents said to be the grants, are quoted by Wilkinson, 'Notes on Perak History', pp. 102–5.

[2] The dispossessed Ghee Hin members made claims against the titular authority in Perak, Sultan Ja'afar. Gov. Cavenagh blockaded the Larut river to enforce the payment of $17,477. Ngah Ibrahim settled this debt (see Cowan, *Nineteenth Century Malaya*, p. 49; McNair, op. cit., p. 351; Wilkinson in Winstedt, 'Perak', p. 81; and Cavenagh, *Reminiscences*, pp. 323–4).

subsequent electoral conference. The weak, old, Bendahara Ismail
was chosen instead. This, of course, suited the ambitious mantri,
who wanted to maintain his independence in Larut, and who even

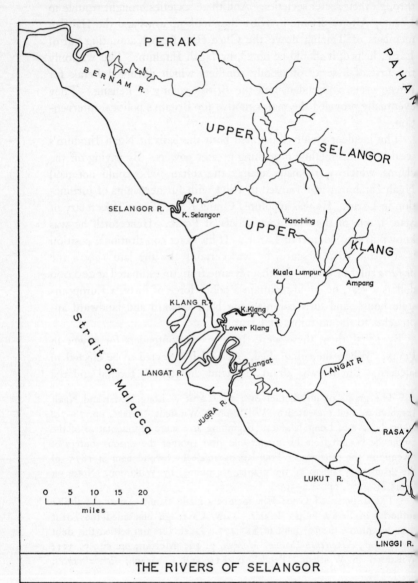

THE RIVERS OF SELANGOR

perhaps aspired to the sultanate himself. Henceforth, the Perak Malays were divided between the 'up-river' chiefs in the north, particularly the mantri, who became Ismail's chief supporter, and the 'down-river' chiefs in the south, who supported 'Abdu'llah. Raja Yusuf too, by-passed for the third time, still hovered in the background.

In Selangor a civil war, which started before Ord even went to the Straits, was reaching a more critical phase when the governor went on leave. The Sultan of Selangor actually requested Ord's help in July 1870, but the governor felt bound to refuse. Although Selangor's problems differed significantly from Perak's, some similar elements — Chinese miners' societies and rival rajas — played their part.

Selangor's decline began during the long reign of Sultan Muhammad (1826–57), who allowed the kingdom to split into what were virtually five principalities along the main waterways — the Bernam, Selangor, Klang, Langat and Lukut rivers.[1] The most powerful of these rulers by the time of the sultan's death in 1857 was Raja Juma'at of Lukut.

Like the Mantri of Larut, he became wealthy by encouraging Chinese tin-miners, whom he introduced into Selangor in the 1840's. He was soon emulated by Raja 'Abdu'l-Samad, ruler of the Selangor river, who opened up the Kanching Hills mines about 1844, and by Raja 'Abdu'llah of Klang, who started the Ampang mines on the upper Klang in the 1850's. When 'Abdul'-Samad was elected Sultan of Selangor in 1859 he gave up business and settled down to a life of indolence and semi-retirement at Langat.

It was not rivalry for the sultanate, therefore, but ambition for possession of the rivers carrying the tin trade, which caused the Selangor Civil War. The years between 1860 and 1867 were particularly disastrous. Selangor then became, to quote Swettenham's words, 'the war playground of a number of Malay Rajas whose pastime was fighting and intriguing to gain control of the rich districts in Selangor where Chinese, and a few others, were mining tin'.[2]

[1] R. J. Wilkinson, 'A History of the Peninsula Malays', *P.M.S.* (1923), 7, p. 142, calls them 'five petty states'; see also Gullick, *Indigenous Political Systems*, pp. 14–15; Cowan, *Nineteenth Century Malaya*, pp. 66–72.

[2] Swettenham, *Footprints in Malaya*, p. 20.

Most persistent and ambitious of these warring Malays was Raja
Mahdi (a grandson of Sultan Muhammad), who managed to com-
mandeer the lower Klang district in 1866. At first the sultan,
'Abdul'-Samad, did not object to the *coup*. He told Ismail, heir of the
dispossessed ruler of Klang, that as they were both young men they
should fight it out. But when Raja Mahdi stopped paying his $500
a month into the royal revenue, the sultan's equanimity faded, and he
refused to permit Raja Mahdi to marry his daughter, Arfar.

The sultan gave the hand of his daughter instead to the Tengku
Zia'u'd-din, brother of the Sultan of Kedah, who henceforth for
a decade was to be the leading figure in Selangor politics. As the
sultan had no territory to offer his son-in-law, he made him a sort of
'governor' of the Langat region to enable him to collect some tolls as
an income. Somewhat vaguely the sultan announced that he would
'give up the country with its districts to our son . . . to govern and
develop for Us and Our sons'.[1] Whatever was really intended by this
grant, the tengku was styled Wakil Yam Tuan (agent of the sultan)
and Straits officers came to regard him as 'Viceroy'.

The tengku first entered the maelstrom of Selangor politics in
March 1870 by assisting Raja Ismail to oust Raja Mahdi from the
mouth of the River Klang. Before many months passed, however,
Mahdi found a new prize. In July 1870 he drove Raja Muda Musa
from the mouth of the Selangor river. The motive for each of these
skirmishes was rivalry for the control of river mouths where tolls could
be levied on the tin traffic.

In the tin-mining areas, which lay nearer the headwaters of the
rivers, rivalries of a different kind existed. As in Perak, the Chinese
secret societies were ranged against each other. Around Kuala
Lumpur, on the upper Klang, the miners were Hai San members,
while in rival mines nearby the Kah Yeng Chew clan were Ghee
Hins. Moreover, when the Hai San headman, Liu Ngim Kong, died
in 1868, his own protégé, Yap Ah Loy, succeeded.[2] Disappointed

---

[1] Written authority dated 26 June 1868. Wilkinson, 'History of the
Peninsula Malays', pp. 144–5; 'Report on Selangor' by Thomas Braddell,
18 Feb. 1874. C.O. 809/1, p. 216.

[2] Kuala Lumpur grew up in the late 1850's at the confluence of the
Klang and Gombok rivers. Liu Ngim Kong took charge in 1861 and he
was soon elected headman, or *Capitan China*. In 1862 he called upon a more

relatives of Liu, led by Chong Chong, soon descended on Kuala Lumpur and constituted a threat to the peace of the area. Nothing happened for a while after they arrived in February 1869. But Chong Chong became the leader of the Kah Yeng Chew clan, who were planning to attack Yap Ah Loy and his supporters.

It was this situation — the inflammable clan rivalries among the miners — which caused the Malay and Chinese disputes to become interwoven in Selangor. At first, when Raja Mahdi was trying to hold on to the forts at the mouth of the Klang in 1868, Yap Ah Loy did not commit himself in the Malay dispute; he wanted to see who would gain control of the mouth of the river along which his tin was sent for sale. But in November 1869 he went to Langat to see the sultan. There he also met Tengku Zia'u'd-din and came away, so it is suggested, a 'nominal associate' of his party. Therefore, when Kuala Lumpur was attacked in the autumn of 1870 by Chong Chong and his clan aided by a Bornean soldier of fortune, Sayid Mashor, Yap Ah Loy looked to Zia'u'd-din for help. Chong Chong, who failed in his first attack, fell back to Raja Mahdi's new stronghold at the mouth of the Selangor river.[1]

This was the situation in Selangor when Governor Ord went on leave in 1871: on one side stood the tengku at Klang and Yap Ah Loy at Kuala Lumpur; ranged against them were Raja Mahdi at the mouth of the Selangor and his ally, Chong Chong, and Mashor, who did not give up hope of capturing the mines at Kuala Lumpur.

On the southern border of Selangor lay Sungei Ujong, a leading state of the Negri Sembilan, or 'Nine States'. Here a similar pattern of rivalries was repeated on the Linggi river. The river had long been a focal point for dispute. It was the main highway to the tin mines at Rasa, where Chinese miners had started workings about 1828.[2] Illegal toll-collecting often interrupted the trade of the Linggi. The

remarkable Chinese, Yap Ah Loy, to be his agent, and this man, who achieved great wealth and power, succeeded to the Capitancy in 1868.

[1] S. M. Middlebrook, 'Yap Ah Loy', *J.M.B.R.A.S.* (1951), 24 (2), pp. 23–83, provides the best account of the 'inland' sector of the war. Cf. Cowan, *Nineteenth Century Malaya*, pp. 72–77.

[2] J. M. Gullick, 'Sungei Ujong', *J.M.B.R.A.S.* (1949), 22 (2), pp. 18–19; Purcell, *The Chinese in Malaya*, p. 101.

problem here was complicated because near to its mouth the Linggi marked the boundary between Selangor and the British settlement of Malacca. Moreover, the territory which lay north of the fork between the Rembau river and the Linggi proper was disputed by the rulers of the Sungei Ujong and Rembau. Further up-stream the authority of the Dato'Klana ('territorial ruler') of Sungei Ujong was challenged by the Dato'Bandar, whose wealth, derived from tin revenues, gave him the position of a virtually independent ruler.[1] In 1849 the paramount ruler of the Negri Sembilan had imposed a settlement by which the Linggi revenues were to be divided between Dato'Klana and Dato'Bandar and they were to be recognized as politically equal. But it failed to resolve the conflict.[2] Dato'Bandar-Tunggal (1849–74) not only asserted his equality, but regarded himself as the real ruler of the middle reaches of the Linggi.

This dispute attracted a good deal of attention in the Straits Settlements, not only because of Malacca's interest in the tin trade, but because the Linggi river also provided a back door into Selangor. During the Selangor Civil War, for example, the Dato'Klana tended to support the Tengku Zia'u'd-din, while Dato'Bandar-Tunggal, a better fighter, assisted Raja Mahdi, Selangor's chief trouble-maker.

The internal disputes of the Malay States presented a daunting prospect to British officers in the Straits. Even today many aspects of the picture are still obscure. Modern writers who try to unravel the complex issues derive a good deal of their material from reports which were made by British officials in 1872 and 1874.[3] But it should be emphasized that very little of this information was available to Colonel Anson when he took over from Ord in 1871. Still less was known in London. Although conditions on the west coast were about to cause intervention by the man on the spot, the Colonial Office was still largely ignorant about Malaya.

[1] R. J. Wilkinson, 'Sungei Ujong', *J.M.B.R.A.S.* (1921), 83, p. 129.
[2] Gullick, op. cit., p. 19.
[3] Charles Irving, 'Memorandum concerning his visit to Perak and Selangor', dated 24 July 1872. C.O. 809/1, pp. 148 ff.; Allan Skinner, 'Précis of Events in Perak', dated 10 Jan. 1874. C.O. 809/1, pp. 136 ff.; Thomas Braddell, 'Report on Selangor', dated 18 Feb. 1874. C.O. 809/1, pp. 210 ff.

6. *Intervention in the Malay States, 1871–3*

SIR HARRY ORD'S sick-leave was Colonel Archibald Anson's opportunity. Ever since he had arrived in June 1867, Anson had been dissatisfied. He found Penang 'a very forsaken place', his offices 'dismal', and the governor overbearing. For a man of Anson's sociable and rather pompous character the lieutenant-governorship must have been a galling position.[1] When he went to Singapore to administer the Government, in February 1871, he was determined to make the best of it.

The colonel's first duties were splendid and picturesque. King Chulalongkorn of Siam paid a State Visit to Singapore in March 1871. Anson's self-esteem was enormously gratified. The Siamese monarch even invested him with the Order of Siam and presented Singapore with a bronze elephant. The Colonial Office allowed Anson to spend $10,000 on entertaining the guests.[2] But when Anson began to suggest modifications in Ord's policies the Colonial Office was adamant. 'A very strong check is required', wrote Kimberley, 'on the foolish tendencies of acting Governors to fussy meddling with the policy of their superiors.'[3] It was hardly surprising that, when Anson announced in June 1871 the findings of a committee which he had appointed to review the whole question of relations with the Malay

[1] See Anson, *About Others and Myself*, pp. 274–7. Anson was born in 1826, graduated from Woolwich in 1844, and served as a gunner officer in Manchester, Malta and Scotland. He saw action in the Crimean War, but was invalided out because of illness. In 1858 while serving in Mauritius he volunteered to become Police Supt. and was seconded to the Colonial Service. He organized the British mission which attended the coronation of Radama II of Madagascar in 1862. One of his first problems at Penang was the Chinese riots of 1867. A good deal of his autobiography is taken up with social pretensions.
[2] Ibid. pp. 299–303; Anson to Kimberley 14 Mar. and 25 Mar. 1871. C.O. 273/45.
[3] Min. by Kimberley 6 June, on Anson to Kimberley 25 Apr. 1871. C.O. 273/46.

States, he received a hostile reception.   Anson, it was generally agreed, was 'somewhat *over* zealous'.[1]

Kimberley would discuss Malaya with the governor alone.   He ordered Anson not to interfere.   It is therefore highly ironical that while Ord failed to shake Kimberley's faith in the policy of non-intervention, Anson not only intervened with force in Selangor, but he led Kimberley to admit, like Buckingham, that further intervention might be necessary.

ANSON'S COMMITTEE, 1871

Anson's Committee warned the Colonial Office of the potential danger of the Peninsula, and made a modest proposal.   Colonel Anson appointed the Committee because he was aware of growing tension in Perak, Selangor and the Malacca hinterland.   He was particularly concerned for the safety of the colony's trade.   There seemed to be good grounds for attempting to improve relations with the west-coast states which lay between Penang and Malacca.

It is true that the members of the Committee were probably already predisposed towards the idea of intervention in the Peninsula.   Major McNair, the colonial engineer, had served in British India; Commander Robinson, the senior naval officer, was the local disposer of Britain's armed power, and Arthur Birch (acting for Anson in Penang) was a home civil servant lent by the Colonial Office, who entered into closer relations with the Peninsula states than his department at home desired.   Later events were to prove that many of the Committee's findings were valid.

The Committee pointed out, for example, that while Straits officials remained ignorant about the Malay States,[2] certain disreputable British subjects sometimes took office under Malay rulers and caused trouble.   As a remedy the Committee proposed that carefully selected, well-qualified Europeans should be appointed to reside in the Malay States

[1] Min. by Knatchbull-Hugessen 11 Aug., on Anson to Kimberley 3 June 1871.   C.O. 273/47.

[2] Cf. Swettenham, *Footprints in Malaya*, p. 25: 'There did not exist a book of reference which supplied any information whatever in regard to the Malay States'.

on the application of the sultans.¹ They would advise the rulers on economic development, and form the channel of communication with the colony. The Committee pointed out that the Maharaja of Johore had already virtually adopted such a system. The Committee's suggestion foreshadowed the role of the later Residents. But Anson himself did not go quite so far. He wanted only a 'Political Agent' to *visit* the states² — by no means an outrageous idea in view of Ord's itinerations. Yet when the Colonial Office read his proposal they were very annoyed with Anson. Kimberley refused to discuss the matter with anyone other than Sir Harry Ord.³

Ord later claimed that he tried hard while on leave in 1871 to convince Kimberley that Britain's policy should be changed if 'we hoped to hold our own on the Peninsula'.⁴ But although Kimberley did not try to deter Ord from keeping on friendly terms with the Malay rulers, he would not widen the governor's authority. Kimberley deprecated any measures which might lead to increases of territory or clashes with the states — excepting, always, in a case of self-defence.⁵

¹ Cowan, *Nineteenth Century Malaya*, p. 87, suggests this idea came from F. J. A. McNair, who was familiar with the Indian Residents at the Courts of the Princes. McNair was a graduate of the Royal School of Mines and became an R.A. cadet in 1845. He served with his battery in India until 1850 and in the Straits and Labuan 1853–7. He was Adj. of the R.A. in the Straits, and in 1857 was made private secretary to the gov. Later he became Executive Engineer and Supt. of Convicts. He returned to Europe in 1865 and was promoted Maj. in the Madras Artillery, but in 1867 he was appointed Chief Engineer in the Straits, where he was responsible for the building of military works. Thus his Indian experience was not great. He figured prominently in the beginning of British intervention in Malaya 1874–6.

² Anson to Kimberley 3 June 1871. C.O. 273/47.

³ Kimberley saw Ord on 8 Aug. 1871. Kimberley's Desk Diary, in *Kimberley Papers*.

⁴ In Ord to Carnarvon 18 Nov. 1874. C.O. 273/78.

⁵ Ord's account of his interview with Kimberley was written after Sir Andrew Clarke's actions were made public in 1874. Ord claimed that he had tried to do the same thing in 1871 but had been forbidden. Kimberley's Desk Diary noted interviews with Ord on 21 Apr., 24 May, 7 July, 8 Aug. and 12 Dec. 1871 and 23 Jan. 1872. No doubt Ord spoke to Herbert and Knatchbull-Hugessen and Kimberley as soon as he got home. Possibly he was again consulted on the Anson Committee, and final words were no doubt exchanged in Jan. 1872. Ord does not indicate which meeting it was in his

All proposals from Anson, from the Committee, and from Ord failed to shake Kimberley's determination to follow the policy of non-intervention.

THE SELANGOR INCIDENT, 1871

Kimberley was soon obliged to modify his view. Before he even received Anson's report, the notorious 'Selangor Incident' occurred, which cost British lives, and, in a sense, vindicated the Committee. It led to political intervention in Selangor greater than Ord ever attempted. And it was approved by the home Government. What began as the pursuit of some pirates ended with the coercing of the Sultan of Selangor, and, more significantly, with the Straits Government in effect taking sides in the Selangor Civil War.

The incident received a good deal of publicity in Britain and has been fully described by a number of writers.[1] It began at the end of June 1871 with the murder, by some Chinese, of the crew of a Penang junk, which was then towed to the Selangor river. Anson despatched a search-party, which found the junk after three days; and with the permission of Raja Muda Musa, nominal ruler of the territory around the mouth of the Selangor, they landed to recover the stolen cargo. Musa, it will be remembered, however, was no longer really in control, having been ousted by Raja Mahdi in 1870; so when a Singapore police officer tried to round up the Chinese pirates, an angry crowd forced him to retire. As the police steamer took the junk in tow, shots were fired from Raja Mahdi's stockades.

Anson should have turned the matter over to the Sultan of Selangor (or to Tengku Zia'u'd-din) under the terms of the treaty of 1825 by which the sultan undertook not to harbour pirates.[2] Alternatively, since British officers had been resisted and fired upon, Anson could

---

letter. There are no records in the C.O. files of any report to Kimberley on the Malay States submitted by Ord while he was on leave.

[1] Cowan, *Nineteenth Century Malaya*, pp. 85–98; Parkinson, *British Intervention*, pp. 47–61; R. O. Windstedt, 'History of Selangor', *J.M.B.R.A.S.* (1934), 12, pp. 24–25; Wilkinson, 'History of the Peninsula Malays', pp. 145–9; the main despatches relating to the incident were published in *Accounts and Papers* (1872), lxx.

[2] Maxwell and Gibson, p. 33, see articles iv and v.

have telegraphed home for instructions.[1]   Instead he authorized a search for the remaining pirates, and a rather confusing incident ensued.   A landing-party from H.M.S. *Rinaldo* met a raja — either Mahdi or his ally, Mahmud — who refused to go on board a British steamer.   A skirmish followed in which a sailor was killed, and the upshot was that on 4 July 1871 *Rinaldo* shelled the Selangor forts and next day over 400 troops were landed to finish off the destruction.

Anson believed he was acting in a case of piracy and self-defence. He found himself interfering in the Selangor Civil War.   He claimed later that he did not know the political situation in Selangor when he ordered in the search.[2]   He had stumbled unwittingly into the complex of Selangor politics.   It was left for Charles Irving, the colonial auditor-general, who was one of the very few Straits officials who had studied the Malay political and social systems and who had already visited Selangor in 1870, to clarify the issues for Anson.   On the advice of Irving, who believed that Tengku Zia'u'd-din was the most promising candidate for power in Selangor, Anson decided to support him.   The Tengku, so Irving argued, had

> what might be called European ideas about his Government, and I am inclined to think that, if circumstances gave him the chief command in Salangore, he would prove a good ruler and a good neighbour to the Colony.[3]

On the basis of Irving's advice the Langat settlement was imposed upon the reluctant Sultan Abdul-Samad.

It was another classic case of British expansion by 'taking sides' unwittingly in a local dispute.   Anson sent James Wheeler Woodford Birch, the Colonial Secretary of the Straits Government, to make a settlement with the sultan, and a British warship was ordered to Selangor to keep Raja Mahdi away.   The ostensible purpose of Birch's mission was to deliver a letter from Anson requesting the sultan's aid in tracing the pirates, who seemed to have been aided by

---

[1] The Singapore telegraph was completed on 1 Jan. 1871.   Telegram 2 Jan. 1871.   C.O. 273/44.

[2] Anson to Kimberley 19 Oct. 1871.   C.O. 273/50.

[3] C. J. Irving, 'Memo. on Selangor disturbances' (n.d.) in Anson to Kimberley 14 July 1871.   *Accounts and Papers* (1872), lxx, p. 679.

Mahdi and Mahmud. But Anson also suggested that the sultan should appoint a 'governor' to administer the country.

The sultan knew that his son-in-law, Tengku Zia'u'd-din, was unpopular and was by no means certain to prevail in the civil war. But the sultan had little choice but to accept. When he hesitated, Birch ordered British troops to land. The tengku was appointed. The sultan in fact reiterated the old grant of 1868 with its ambiguous clause about giving up 'the country with its districts to our son . . . to govern and develop for Us and Our sons'. Henceforth the Straits Government regarded the tengku as 'Viceroy' of Selangor, and Raja Mahdi, his troublesome rival, was outlawed.[1] Whether Birch specifically promised British support was not recorded. Certainly the impression was gained locally, as the tengku toured the Selangor estuaries in the company of Royal Navy gunboats, that Britain was committed to him. Irving suggested that the Langat settlement simply brought Selangor into line with Johore: the most promising ruler would now be supported with 'advice' and 'influence'.

What did Kimberley and the Colonial Office make of the Selangor incident when news reached home? They received reports of the *Rinaldo* bombardment on 21 August 1871, while they were still considering Anson's proposal for a travelling 'Political Agent' in the Malay States. When Kimberley read of the Selangor affair on 26 August he took no exception to it, noting only that Anson had taken unnecessary risks in exposing his police.[2] In a reply to Anson, on the very same day, about the plan for the travelling agents, Kimberley reaffirmed that there could be no question of political intervention — except in emergencies.[3] Presumably, in view of Kimberley's reaction, the Selangor incident was such an emergency.

Kimberley found the report of the Langat settlement (received at

[1] Wilkinson, 'History of the Peninsula Malays', p. 149, pictures the tengku sitting 'through the interviews with impassivity, showing neither pleasure nor disappointment at the turn affairs were taking'. Cowan, op. cit., p. 91, says the affair 'is remarkable in the first instance for the great irresponsibility of the men on the spot'.

[2] Min. by Kimberley 26 Aug., on Anson to Kimberley 14 July 1871. C.O. 273/48.

[3] Kimberley to Anson 26 Aug. (draft), after Anson to Kimberley 3 June 1871 (received 31 July). C.O. 273/47.

home on 4 September 1871) 'thoroughly satisfactory'. He only hoped Birch had not really committed Britain to support Tengku Zia'u'd-din. Yet for the benefit of his colleagues in the Colonial Office Kimberley added a most significant qualification: 'I use the word "pledge" because it might become adviseable to give him [the tengku] support, but this is very different from *promising* it.'¹ Here, in fact, Kimberley provided another private statement of the frontier doctrine of qualified restraint, and he even hinted that further support for certain Malay rulers might have to follow. The Colonial Office, then, treated the Selangor incident as a matter of piracy. They obviously did not realize its full political implications.

But the affair did not go unnoticed in Britain. Sir Benson Maxwell, the retired Chief Justice of Singapore, wrote an angry letter to *The Times* on 13 September 1871 calling the incident an 'act of War'. This attracted the attention of Gladstone, who remembered the public outcry after Raja Brooke's slaughter of Dyak pirates in 1852. The prime minister's secretary asked Kimberley what had happened. Kimberley, therefore, held up his reply to Anson. On 19 September he sent all the relevant reports to the prime minister, adding somewhat melodramatically, 'The Malay pirates are desperate men, and the murders committed on this occasion were most atrocious'.² Although Gladstone was, as usual, prepared to accept Kimberley's judgement, he went to the heart of the matter and questioned whether 'on principle as well as for want of sufficient force' the governor should not have dealt with the matter through the Sultan of Selangor.³ Kimberley therefore modified his approval of Anson's action. In future incidents involving the Malay States he would instruct the governor to ensure that 'all means of obtaining redress by peaceful means are exhausted before measures of coercion are employed'.⁴ Clearly the Selangor incident was regarded by the Colonial Office as exceptional.

During Anson's administration, then, the policy of non-intervention was officially reaffirmed. The Selangor incident was treated as a case where local initiative was permissible in an emergency. But, like

¹ Min. by Kimberley 10 Sept., on Anson to Kimberley 28 July 1871 (received 4 Sept.). C.O. 273/48.
² Kimberley to Gladstone 19 Sept. 1871. *Gladstone Papers*, 44224/203.
³ Gladstone to Kimberley 21 Sept. 1871. *Kimberley Papers*, A/86.
⁴ Kimberley to Gladstone 23 Sept. 1871. *Gladstone Papers*, 44224/207.

Buckingham earlier,[1] Kimberley admitted privately that further intervention might become necessary.

ORD AND THE WEST-COAST STATES, 1872–3

The likelihood of intervention increased considerably during Ord's second tour of duty in the Straits which began in March 1872. On the west coast the situation had become so critical that Ord could not remain aloof in Singapore. But because the Straits Government had such a sketchy knowledge of Malay affairs the first thing which Ord did on his return was to make a serious attempt to find out what was really happening in the Peninsula. He sent Charles Irving to report on the west coast in April 1872. The governor himself visited Selangor and Sungei Ujong in October and November 1872. He went to Penang to deal with the Larut problem personally in 1873. Although his actions were circumscribed by the official policy of non-intervention, Ord did not hesitate to use his influence where he could. By August 1873 he finally decided to commit his Government to 'taking sides' in Perak, much as Anson had done in Selangor in 1871.

During this period a new personality made his mark in the Straits. It proved to be of the greatest significance that, up until May 1873, Ord had the benefit of someone else in place of Anson at Penang. Anson went on leave, and a temporary lieutenant-governor was found from outside the Straits service. The choice fell on G. W. R. Campbell (later Sir George). At the time, Campbell was the inspector-general of police in Ceylon, but he had had ten years' previous experience in India.[2] Just as the Colonial Office had brought to bear on Malayan problems its experience of the frontiers of empire elsewhere, so Campbell took to Penang his knowledge of Britain's role in

[1] See above, p. 162.

[2] G. W. R. Campbell was born 1835; ensign in the Argyll and Bute Rifles in 1855; went to India in 1856, where he was appointed Assist.-Supt. in the revenue survey. During the Mutiny he was Adj. of the Ahmedabad Koli Corps, Assist-Supt. of Police and Assist.-Magistrate. In Dec. 1859 he was appointed Supt. of Police and Commandant of the Rutnagherry Rangers. Promoted in 1863, he was sent to reorganize the Canara police. Transferred in 1866 to the Belgaum police, and selected to reorganize the police in Ceylon. He then transferred to the Colonial Service. Qualified in three Indian languages.

India. He began to make some frank proposals for a completely new
departure in British relations with Malaya. He seems to have impressed the Secretary of State. In fact, Kimberley's first hint that he
might consider intervention in Malaya was made after reading one
of Campbell's reports.

Campbell was important because he was something of an impartial
judge from outside, and the Colonial Office seemed to place a good
deal of reliance on his views. On the other hand, they lost all confidence in Governor Ord. For some reason Sir Harry progressively
alienated the Colonial Office in the vital years 1872–3. He was slow
in forwarding his reports. When they did reach home they created an
unfavourable impression. Some important reports by Ord's subordinates were not even sent back to England until after his successor
reached Singapore.[1] If it is true that Ord managed to convince the
Colonial Office that something needed to be done in the Malay
States, he did this by his mistakes rather than the force of his advocacy.
By the end of 1872 the Colonial Office certainly began to understand
at last the parlous state of the west-coast states and the vulnerability
of the colony. They had no confidence in Ord's ability to contain it.

There were, by now, five serious problems in the Malay Peninsula:
a disputed sultanate in Perak; war among the Chinese miners in
Larut, in which the succession dispute was becoming entangled; civil
war in Selangor; the possibility that this war might spread into Sungei
Ujong; and the repercussions all these troubles had upon the colony,
whose trade was upset and security threatened. Sir Harry Ord was as
energetic as ever and tried hard to find a solution for all the problems.

In Perak the dispute over the sultanate had become interwoven with
the war among the Chinese miners in Larut. After the members of
the Ghee Hin society forcibly ejected the Hai Sans from the mines in
February 1872, the mantri made terms with the victors, as was his
custom. The defeated clan fell back on to British territory in Penang,
there to prepare for taking their revenge. Raja Muda 'Abdu'llah
approached them in his efforts to curb the mantri.

[1] Irving's memo. on Perak and Selangor dated 24 July 1872 was not sent
home until Clarke to Kimberley 24 Feb. 1874. (C.O. Confidential Print:
Eastern 11, C.O. 809/1, p. 148.) Ord to Kimberley 6 Nov. 1872 includes
only a summary. C.O. 273/61.

Governor Ord did not learn of the cleavage over the Perak sultanate until Irving's mission in April 1872, which was nearly a year after Ismail's election. Irving pointed out that 'Abdu'llah — now openly styling himself 'Sultan' — seemed to have a better claim on the succession, although Irving regarded him as personally disreputable. Ismail had undoubtedly been elected sultan in 1871, and had considerable qualifications of character. But Irving believed he was really a pawn in the hands of the mantri. Ord sent Irving back to Perak in May 1872 in an effort to persuade 'Abdu'llah and Ismail to settle their differences, but nothing came of this overture.[1]

In the autumn of 1872 fighting flared up again in Larut. The dispossessed Hai Sans sallied forth from Penang in October to reoccupy the mines, and the turncoat mantri naturally reverted to his alliance with them. The Ghee Hins retaliated once again in December 1872, but gained no decisive victory. The two Chinese factions consequently settled down to a prolonged war, and 'Abdu'llah now offered to help the Ghee Hins against the mantri and his allies. Ord suspected, in fact, that 'Abdu'llah was preparing to attack Sultan Ismail.[2] Perak appeared to be on the verge of a full-scale civil war.

The governor had less reliable information concerning Selangor. Irving's mission revealed that Tengku Zia'u'd-din still controlled the mouths of the Klang and Selangor rivers, but that the 'rebel rajas' still commanded the headwaters and that fighting was continuing in the interior. It was still by no means certain that Zia'u'd-din would prevail, although Irving probably did not know this. After the Langat settlement in 1871 the tengku had attempted to modernize his Government and had appointed European officers to command garrisons at Kuala Lumpur and Kuala Selangor. But his position remained precarious. Neither he nor his Chinese ally, Yap Ah Loy, had removed the threat of Sayid Mashor, who held a strategic strongpoint in upper Selangor.[3] Of this 'interior sector' of the war, Ord was almost completely ignorant.

The governor was only too aware of another threat to the tengku —

[1] Irving's memo. 24 July 1872. See Cowan, *Nineteenth Century Malaya*, pp. 99–101.   [2] Ord to Kimberley 6 Nov. 1873. C.O. 273/61.
[3] The best account of the inland campaign is in S. M. Middlebrook, 'Yap Ah Loy', pp. 63–67.

this time from Raja Mahdi. After his defeat in 1871, Mahdi had taken refuge first in Sumatra and then in Johore. Ord was placed in an awkward dilemma. Charles Irving, his Malayan expert, insisted that Mahdi at large anywhere constituted a source of danger, but Thomas Braddell, the Straits Attorney-General, pointed out that the colonial Government had no legal grounds for interfering with the raja. Confronted with this conflicting advice from his officials, Ord leaned towards Braddell. He allowed Raja Mahdi to stay in Johore, and attempted to persuade him to accept a pension from Tengku Zia'u'd-din in return for an undertaking not to return to Selangor.[1] But the adventurous fugitive refused. In June or July 1872 he made his way back to Selangor via the Linggi river, and joined up with Sayid Mashor, who was preparing to launch a fourth attack on Kuala Lumpur. The tengku's cause indeed suffered several set-backs in the summer of 1872. Yap Ah Loy abandoned Kuala Lumpur, Sayid Mashor captured Kuala Selangor, and the tengku found himself reduced to the region at the mouth of the River Klang.[2]

Ord, on his part, could not ignore these developments in the Malay States because they affected the colony. Straits merchants complained when the flow of tin from the Klang mines was disrupted; some Malacca traders claimed that the Government was failing to live up to its pledge of support to the tengku. It is rather ironical that Birch, who had made the pledge in 1871, had to reply to these traders by reaffirming the policy of non-intervention. This answer did not satisfy W. H. M. Read, chairman of the Singapore Chamber of Commerce. He argued that Ord's equivocation when Raja Mahdi was in Johore had contributed to the trouble. Although the Chamber of Commerce deprecated the use of coercive measures, Read called for

> some straight forward and well defined policy in dealing with the rulers of the various States of the Malay Peninsula, for the purpose of promoting and protecting commercial relations . . . as there is every reason to believe that they would readily accept the impartial views and friendly advice of the British authorities.[3]

---

[1] Ord to Kimberley 24 Oct. 1872. C.O. 273/60.
[2] For Raja Mahdi's movements, see Wilkinson, 'History of the Peninsula Malays', pp. 151–3; Middlebrook, 'Yap Ah Loy', pp. 64–65, 110.
[3] W. H. M. Read to Colonial Secretary Straits Settlements 17 Sept., encl. in Ord to Kimberley 6 Nov. 1872. C.O. 273/61.

There can be little doubt that Ord fully agreed with this view, but he knew it was unacceptable in London. Nevertheless, he made a last attempt to intervene personally in Selangor. On 1 November 1872 he travelled to Langat with an escort of British troops. The tengku's position seemed so hopeless that Ord urged him to give up the fight.[1] But the tengku would not compromise. He held on precariously for another year. Then he made an alliance with Pahang, which brought sufficient military assistance to turn the scales decisively in Selangor.[2]

If Ord could do little for Selangor, he prevented the war from spreading into Sungei Ujong. This small state lay on the tengku's southern flank, and provided the route by which Raja Mahdi had returned to Selangor. To prevent such contingencies, Zia'u'd-din made an agreement in 1870 with the ruler of Rembau adjusting the boundary of Selangor and Rembau at Sempang in such a manner that he could build a fort and guard the River Linggi at this point.[3] After Raja Mahdi slipped through in 1872, the tengku tried to get the ruler of Rembau to revive his claim to land on the right bank of the Linggi in the tengku's interest, but the neighbouring chiefs of Sungei Ujong prepared to resist. In fact, the Dato'Klana's nephew, who was acting for him, ordered arms from Europe to resist Rembau. Thus, when Ord was asked to intervene here in September 1872, he decided that he might yet be able to avert another Malay war.[4] The ruler of Rembau, however, failed to meet Ord at Sempang to present his case, and the governor persuaded the Tengku Zia'u'd-din to drop the

[1] Winstedt, 'Selangor', p. 29.

[2] The tengku first approached Wan Ahmad in Dec. 1871, but the latter would not assist without Ord's permission. In Apr. 1872 the tengku went to Singapore to discuss the alliance (Middlebrook, 'Yap Ah Loy', p. 76). Sometime between May and Aug. 1872 Ord went to Pekan to make arrangements with the bendahara. (Cowan, op. cit., p. 106.) The first Pahang expedition crossed into Selangor in Aug. 1872, but failed to relieve Kuala Lumpur, which was not recaptured until Mar. 1873. (Linehan, 'Pahang', p. 96.)

[3] R. O. Winstedt, 'Negri Sembilan', *J.M.B.R.A.S.* (Oct. 1934), 12, (3), p. 69. 'Report on the State of the Country' in Ord to Kimberley 6 Nov. 1872. C.O. 273/61.

[4] Memo. by Thomas Braddell, C.O. 809/5, p. 52.

matter on the condition that the Dato'Klana of Sungei Ujong promised not to help the tengku's enemies.[1]

It would be fair to say, then, that in 1872 Governor Ord struggled valiantly with the problems of the Malay States. Unfortunately, the Colonial Office was unimpressed by his performances. Its first news of Ord's attempt to get the Raja Mahdi to accept a pension if he would keep out of Selangor came from a newspaper report, which made it appear that the Maharaja of Johore was harbouring Mahdi with Ord's collusion, so it naturally asked for an explanation.[2] Ord took this as a personal slight. 'I think I might have been credited with more common sense,' he wrote in a private letter, which ended with a somewhat hysterical general account of the state of the Peninsula: 'murder, plundering and burning are the order of the day and the *bad ones* are beginning to believe the popular cry that "nothing will induce the Govt. to interfere".'[3]

The Colonial Office's response to this rather desperate plea was most unfavourable. Herbert, when he read the words, minuted 'most certainly the present Governor cannot be trusted to interfere wisely', and Ord was censured for his policy over Mahdi and Johore. It is not very surprising, therefore, that the Colonial Office were likewise unimpressed by Ord's visits to Sungei Ujong and Selangor. The governor had concluded a general report on the 'state of the Country' with the words:

> I trust it will satisfy Your Lordship that I have been neither so ignorant nor so unmindful, as has been alleged, of the bearing which the internal condition of these states has upon certain important interests in the Settlements, and that notwithstanding the little actual power I am able to exercise I have done what I could to protect those interests.

[1] Ord to Kimberley 6 Nov. 1872. C.O. 273/61. Cowan, *Nineteenth Century Malaya*, pp. 109–11.

[2] The occasion of Kimberley's demand clearly illustrates the way Ord kept London in the dark. Abu-Bakar requested some rifles for his police and Ord sent a request home on 10 July 1872 (C.O. 273/58). Before asking the W.O. to supply them, Kimberley (having seen about Raja Mahdi in the *London and China Telegraph*, 26 Aug. 1872) asked for an explanation, on 2 Sept. 1872. This was not answered by Ord until 24 Oct. 1872 and was received in London on 25 Nov. Thus the newspaper had anticipated the gov. by two months.

[3] Ord to Herbert (private) 24 Oct. 1872. C.O. 273/60.

But Kimberley decided the Malayan problem was 'A tangled web which I fear Sir H. Ord is not the man to unravel'.[1] In some respects he was unfair to Ord. Within the limits of the policy of non-intervention the governor had contributed a good deal, and was to contribute more, to finding a settlement in the west-coast states. But from the Colonial Office viewpoint, Ord's only role was to provide information which enabled them to appreciate for the first time the true complexity of the Malayan problem.

The most significant advice came from Lieutenant-Governor George Campbell of Penang. On discovering that Penang was obviously the supply base of the Chinese factions warring in Larut, Campbell visited the Larut river on 16–18 October 1872 in an attempt to halt the arms traffic. He failed to achieve anything. But his first-hand report provided another indication to Singapore and Whitehall of the seriousness of the Larut War. Campbell, furthermore, also advocated a significant new departure in British policy.

Campbell had been told that the Chinese miners in Larut would be thankful if the British flag were to fly over Perak. Drawing, therefore, on his Indian experience, he advocated the extension of the Indian 'Resident system'. He called for the appointment of 'a Resident or Political Officer for certain of the Malay States'.[2] He had already mooted this idea in September 1872, and the source of his idea is abundantly clear:

I speak with diffidence, being so new to this portion of the East, but I think it worth consideration whether the appointment under the British Government of a British Resident or Political Agent for certain of the Malay States would not, as in India, have a markedly beneficial effect. Such a Resident or Political Agent would need to be an officer of some position and standing and a man of good judgment and good personal manner, and he should, of course have a thorough knowledge of the Malay language . . . In India, in many a native-ruled State, it is

[1] Min. by Kimberley 22 Dec., on Ord to Kimberley 6 Nov. 1872. C.O. 273/61.
[2] Campbell to Colonial Secretary Straits Settlements 24 Oct., encl. in Ord to Kimberley 11 Nov. 1872. C.O. 273/61. Campbell referred in his despatch to a similar suggestion he had made on 6 Sept. 1872.

marvellous what work a single well-selected British officer has effected . . .[1]

When his report reached London early in 1873, Campbell's idea appealed to Edward Knatchbull-Hugessen, the parliamentary under-secretary.

Knatchbull-Hugessen had recently launched his attack on the anomalous policies being followed in West Africa. Now he pointed out that British annexation of Larut 'would be most beneficial to Penang and contribute to the tranquility and prosperity of the Settlements in no slight degree'. But Kimberley did not agree 'that further extension of British territory is the proper remedy for these evils . . .'. If Britain annexed every part of Asia where there was misgovernment she would end in dividing the continent with Russia.[2] Campbell's suggestion of the Residents, therefore, like those of the Anson Committee in 1871, and Knatchbull-Hugessen's ideas about annexation, fell on deaf ears in January 1873. Eight months later Kimberley changed his mind.

THE DECISION TO INTERVENE IN THE MALAY STATES, 1873

Why did Kimberley decide to intervene in Malaya? There appear to have been three reasons for his crucial *volte-face* in the summer of 1873. He realized the growing seriousness of the Larut War. He was subjected to skilful pressure from companies with interests in Selangor. Finally, there was a threat of foreign intervention in Selangor.

Larut was by this time dominated by the warring Chinese societies. Although the Hai Sans managed to retain a few mines inland, the Ghee Hin invasion in December 1872 gave them control of the mouth of the Larut river. Malay authority in this part of Perak was non-existent by the early part of 1873.[3] Governor Ord tried to prohibit

---

[1] Quoted (undated) in Wilkinson, 'Notes on Perak History', *P.M.S.* (1908), 4, pp. 99–100. This may be the document of 6 Sept. referred to by Campbell on 24 Oct. 1872.

[2] Mins. by Knatchbull-Hugessen 6 Jan., and Kimberley 8 Jan. 1873, on Ord to Kimberley 11 Nov. 1872. C.O. 273/61.

[3] Cowan, *Nineteenth Century Malaya*, pp. 112–14; Wilkinson in Windstedt, 'Perak', pp. 85–86; J. M. Gullick, 'Captain Speedy of Larut', *J.M.B.R.A.S.* (Nov. 1953), 26 (3), pp. 30–31.

arms exports from the colony and sent H.M.S. *Hornet* to enforce the blockade.[1]   But, as this cut off the Chinese from their supplies, they were driven to piracy and so they became an even bigger menace to the Straits Settlements.

Here was the sort of emergency which threatened the colony. Thus, in July 1873, Kimberley said something would have to be done about Perak.   And at this very time Kimberley had an opportunity to talk over the situation with George Campbell, who was at home on leave. Campbell evidently impressed the Secretary of State.   He concluded an account of the Larut situation, which Kimberley regarded as 'an excellent report', by repeating his proposal for appointing resident officers:

> It is possible that friendly intervention on our part would end the condition of things described and it is more than probable that a resident political officer, a carefully chosen discreet man with a good knowledge of the people and their language would prevent its recurrence.   Most native ruled States in and around India have such officers and the value of their influence is unquestionable . . . I have found all the Malay potentates most amenable to reason, most courteous and most anxious to please.[2]

It seems likely that Campbell was the man who finally persuaded Kimberley to take some action, because at roughly the same time as their discussion (possibly the same day)[3] Kimberley made a note that Sir Andrew Clarke, the next governor, would have to attend to the Larut problem:

> I think we must endeavour to put a stop to these disturbances.   It is evident that Penang is a base for these contentious Chinese.   The difficulty is how to do anything without direct interference with Perak which is very undesirable.[4]

---

[1] The first news of this reached the C.O. from the Ad. in Ad. to C.O. 29 Apr. 1873.   C.O. 273/72.

[2] Campbell to Kimberley, London, 28 June, encl. 'Report on Penang', dated Suez, 5 June, and min. by Kimberley 7 July 1873.   C.O. 273/74.

[3] Campbell sent his request to Kimberley dated London, 28 June, and Kimberley minuted that they should do something on 7 July.   The following day, 8 July, he noted that he had had a conversation with Campbell; see min. on Ad. to C.O. 27 June 1873.   C.O. 273/72.

[4] Min. by Kimberley 7 July 1873 on Campbell's report cited above.

Kimberley admitted, then, that the troubles in Larut should be stopped, but he still clung to the policy of non-intervention. He was undecided what action he should take. At the end of July, however, further demands for intervention reached him. They came from an English tin company interested in Malaya, and represent the second influence which helped Kimberley to make up his mind.

The success of the Chinese miners attracted a few Englishmen to the Malay States,[1] but they wanted the Government to guarantee their security. One of the more ambitious firms was the Selangor Tin Company. The group was destined to influence British policy in an unexpected fashion. The Company included James Guthrie Davidson and William Henry Read, both prominent Straits merchants, who had long been interested in the Peninsula. Read had been joint tax-farmer in Klang briefly in 1866. Davidson's loans to Tengku Zia'u'd-din gave him a vested interest in the Selangor War. In March 1873 he secured from the tengku a ten-year concession of certain tin-mining rights, which the Selangor Tin Company was formed to exploit.[2]

The Company wanted to convince investors that operations in Selangor would be safe. Thus, Davidson's London solicitors asked the Colonial Office, on 25 June 1873, if the Company could recruit a private military force in Selangor. The request was firmly refused, so the Company tried another line of approach.[3] They turned to Read's brother-in-law, Mr Seymour Clarke, who was an important figure in the London business world. His was a strange background from which to influence the course of Malayan history.

As a young man Seymour Clarke had been chief clerk to the great

---

[1] In the 1850's some Americans worked a mine at Ricko in Selangor (Swettenham 8 Apr. 1875. C.O. 809/5, p. 138). Paterson and Simons operated in Pahang for a time (see above, p. 161). Henry Velge of Malacca promoted a Sungei Ujong Tin Co. (Braddell, 'Memo. on Sungei Ujong', in Clarke to Carnarvon 29 Dec. 1874. C.O. 809/5, p. 56.)

[2] Swettenham, *Footprints in Malaya*, p. 20; Middlebrook, 'Yap Ah Loy', p. 84; P. B. Maxwell, *Our Malay Conquests*, London, 1878, p. 36; Windstedt, 'Selangor', p. 20; the Co. was finally registered, 6 July 1874, as Malayan Peninsula (East India) Tin Mining Co. Ltd. *Accounts and Papers* (1875), lxxi, p. 500.

[3] Lambert, Burgin, Petch & Co. to Kimberley 25 June, and C.O. reply 5 July 1873. C.O. 273/74.

engineer Brunel during the construction of the Great Western Rail-way. While he was still in his twenties, as traffic superintendent of the London division, Clarke demonstrated early telegraph equipment to the Duke of Wellington. In 1842 he was responsible for arranging the first Royal Train. He rose to become the general manager of the Great Northern Railway in 1850, and he reigned at King's Cross until he retired in July 1870. He is said to have been influential with Gladstone when the latter arbitrated in railway pooling arrangements. His knowledge of telegraphs gave him an interest in some schemes for telegraph extensions in South-East Asia which Read was pro-moting.[1]

In 1873 Seymour Clarke was given the job of finding some way of persuading the Colonial Office to grant some security to the operations of the Selangor Tin Company. First of all he secured an interview with Robert Herbert. But his most striking move was to send the Colonial Office, on 18 July 1873, a copy of a letter in which the Tengku Zia'u'd-din had asked a member of the Company 'to ascertain if the English, or any other Government, would interfere in any disturbance that might arise in the territory of Salangore'. This was a rather vague, and by no means unusual, request from the ruler of a small state on the fringes of the British Empire in the mid-Victorian Age. But the tengku's letter was accompanied by suggestions of a very different kind.

Clarke added that a Singapore resident (Cowan suggests it was Read) had recently expressed the view that 'the independent sovereigns of the smaller states, in the Malay Peninsula, would put themselves under the Protectorate of some European Power and Germany is mentioned as most likely to be approached failing England'.[2] As a letter in *The Times* only a week earlier had warned against German

---

[1] Seymour Clarke (1816–76). See E. T. MacDermot, *History of the Great Western Railway*, London, 1927–31, pp. 57, 230, 661, 667; C. H. Grinling, *History of the Great Northern Railway, 1845–1902*, London, 1903, pp. 153, 246; *Great Northern Railway Minute Books*, 1/36, pp. 148, 236 (by courtesy of the Archivist, the British Transport Commission); *Herapath's Journal* (1876), xxxviii, p. 339, for his obituary; Cowan, *Nineteenth Century Malaya*, p. 167, for his telegraph interests.

[2] Seymour Clarke to Herbert 18 July 1873. C.O. 273/74. Cowan, op. cit., p. 167.

intervention in the Straits of Malacca,[1] Seymour Clarke's letter brought the third factor into play which influenced Kimberley.

Seymour Clarke had in fact touched Kimberley at a sensitive spot. There were a number of indications at this time that he appreciated the danger of foreign intervention in South-East Asia. He supported the Dutch invasion of Atjeh in northern Sumatra in 1873 because he realized that unsettled parts of Sumatra might invite foreign intervention. After the incident of the American settlement in North Borneo in 1865, the French protectorate in Cambodia in 1867, and the Italian search for a penal colony in 1870, the possibility of foreign intervention could not be ruled out.[2] When, in February 1873, the Foreign Office became aware of a Dutch rumour that Italy or the United States contemplated treaties with Atjeh, careful investigations were made in Singapore, Washington and Rome, before the story was disbelieved.[3]

Clarke's letter was not the first hint of German interest in Malaya. The Dutch had circulated a rumour in 1870 that the Maharaja of Johore intended to lease Pulo Tioman to the North German Confederation as a naval station. Sir Frederic Rogers had then said, 'if Prussia likes to have an island there — let her by all means'.[4] Most of the Colonial Office staff viewed Clarke's warning in 1873 in a similar way: 'the probability of a German Protectorate seems small'.[5]

[1] Letter by Rear-Ad. Osborn to *The Times*, 12 July 1873, in which he criticized the Govt. for allowing the Dutch to gain Atjeh, the 'keys to the Straits of Malacca', and said 'for "Holland" read "Germany"', and then weigh the consequences'.

[2] K. C. Tregonning, 'American Activity in North Borneo 1865–1881', *P.H.R.* (1954), p. 365; Cady, *Roots of French Imperialism*, pp. 279–86; F.O. to C.O. 16 Sept. 1872. Labuan correspondence, C.O. 144/39.

[3] Memo. by Vivian 25 Feb. 1873. Netherlands correspondence, F.O. 37/534; F.O. to C.O. 22 Mar. 1873. C.O. 273/73. Herbert started a min. — 'It is hardly supposed that the U.S. would interfere in the affairs of Acheen' — but he crossed it out.

[4] Min. by Rogers 20 July, on F.O. to C.O. 14 July 1870. C.O. 273/42. Cf. his min. 3 Aug., 'I believe a German colony in New Guinea would be a very good thing for the Australians. Why should it hurt them?', on Young to Buckingham 31 May 1867. (New South Wales correspondence, C.O. 201/542.)

[5] Min. by MacDonald 19 July, on Clarke to Herbert 18 July 1873. C.O. 273/74.

The senior members of the Office took Malaya more seriously.
Herbert suggested that Sir Andrew Clarke might consider extending
British influence to some parts of the Peninsula beyond the colony.
Knatchbull-Hugessen said this would be easy; but after the rebuffs
he had recently had from Kimberley over West African questions, he
doubted whether Herbert's idea would fit in with the accepted policy:

> I do not understand that to be the policy of H.M. Government, but
> rather to keep ourselves to ourselves as much as we can & to avoid these
> complications which may follow extensions of 'influence' which entails
> as a rule extensions of responsibility.[1]

He can hardly have believed in this doctrine; one senses in the phrase
'keep ourselves to ourselves' a contempt for the attitude. In fact, in
the previous year, Knatchbull-Hugessen had condemned 'the sur-
passing love of Economy', and 'dread of incurring responsibilities'
which prevented Gladstone from annexing the Fiji Islands. He wrote
bluntly, '*Serve us right* if Germany annexes Fiji'. Early in 1873 he
thought annexation was the ideal solution for the Malay States, and he
also urged the annexation of Fiji again.[2] He certainly would have
been quite prepared to adopt Herbert's new suggestion.

What is really important is that Seymour Clarke's letter alarmed
Kimberley. He saw the Malayan question in an entirely new light.
'It would be impossible for us to consent to any European Power
assuming the Protectorate of any state in the Malay Peninsula'.[3] He
immediately consulted the Foreign Secretary and the Secretary of
State for India. He considered, at first, sending instructions to Sir
Andrew Clarke empowering him to make new treaties by which the
Malay rulers would agree not to cede their territories without British
consent. Kimberley himself studied all the existing treaties carefully.

In order to gain time, Kimberley sent Seymour Clarke a formal
answer saying that the correspondence about the Selangor Tin Company would have to be dealt with by the governor.[4] At the same time
he instituted a thorough study of the Malay treaties. Meanwhile,
during the early part of August 1873, he was preoccupied with West

[1] Ibid. Mins. by Herbert 21 July, and Knatchbull-Hugessen 22 July 1873.
[2] See below, pp. 254–5.
[3] Min. by Kimberley 22 July, on Clarke to Herbert 18 July 1873. C.O.
273/74.
[4] Ibid. Kimberley to Seymour Clarke 5 Aug. 1873 (draft).

Africa, making preparations for the Ashanti expedition, for which, it will be remembered, he had originally selected Sir Andrew Clarke as commander.[1]   Before making up his mind as to future Malayan policy, Kimberley gave the department two weeks to prepare a comprehensive summary of Britain's past relations with the Malay States. After sending the formal reply to Seymour Clarke on 5 August 1873 — which reiterated the policy of non-intervention — Kimberley announced to his department that he would deal with the matter when he wrote the instructions for the new governor.

The pattern of Kimberley's decision about Malaya now seems clear: the Larut War caused him to decide early in July 1873 that Sir Andrew Clarke would have to look into the Malayan problem; the possibility of German rivalry raised by Seymour Clarke added some urgency later in July; he made the final step when he drafted Sir Andrew Clarke's instructions.   Charles Cox, head of the Eastern Department, warned his colleagues on 28 August 1873 that 'Lord Kimberley is about to consider how far it may be desirable for the British government, that is the Government of the Straits Settlements, to interfere actively in an endeavour to stop the dissension in the Malay States'.[2]   Kimberley wrote his famous draft for Clarke on 31 August. He sent it to Gladstone on 10 September 1873 — the very day on which Wolseley's instructions for the Ashanti expedition were finalized — with this rather skilful précis of the issue:

> The condition of the Malay Peninsula is becoming very serious.   It is the old story of misgovernment of Asiatic States.   This might go on without any very serious consequences except the stoppage of trade were it not that European and Chinese capitalists stimulated by the great riches in tin mines which exist in some of the Malay States are suggesting to the native Princes that they should seek the aid of Europeans . . . We are the paramount power in the Peninsula up to the limit of the states tributary to Siam, and looking to the vicinity of India & our whole position in the East I apprehend that it would be a serious matter if any other European Power were to obtain a footing on the Peninsula.[3]

---

[1] See above, pp. 145–6.

[2] Min. by Cox 28 Aug., on Ord to Kimberley 10 July 1873.   C.O. 273/67.   Kimberley's draft 31 Aug. 1873.

[3] Kimberley to Gladstone 10 Sept. 1873.   *Gladstone Papers*, 44225/103.

Just as with Wolseley's instructions, Kimberley assured the prime
minister that there was still an escape-clause; the instructions did not
'actually pledge us to anything, but they imply that some attempt is to
be made to produce a better state of things'. The instructions were
despatched on 20 September 1873, after Clarke had sailed for the East.

Ord went out in 1867 with no instructions about the Malay States.
Clarke was now told that relations with the States would be an important part of his duties. In 1867 Buckingham had insisted that diplomacy should be left to the Foreign Office. In 1873 Kimberley
decided for strategic reasons that 'we are the paramount power in the
Peninsula'. A major change of attitude had occurred in Whitehall.
It was now up to the man on the spot to work out a new policy and
advise the home Government.

ORD TAKES SIDES IN PERAK, 1873

Once again, however, the man on the spot was far ahead of the
Colonial Office. Intervention did not have to await Sir Andrew
Clarke's arrival. Before the new governor reached Singapore the main
crisis had passed, partly through the work of Sir Harry Ord. In
Selangor, for example, Tengku Zia'u'd-din recovered Kuala Lumpur
in March 1873 with the help of troops from Pahang, which had been
secured with Ord's help. By November 1873 the tengku had recovered Kuala Selangor, the Raja Mahdi's stronghold.[1]

In Perak, the governor finally decided to commit himself to one of
the sides in the dispute. The Larut War was definitely endangering
Penang and the whole coast of Perak. The Chinese factions, cut off
from their supplies by the blockade of the Royal Navy, began to prey
upon coastal shipping and brought fishing and trade to a halt. Even
more significant was the success of the Mantri of Larut, who persuaded Captain Speedy, the police superintendent of Penang, to enter
his service and raise a sepoy force in India.[2] Now an Englishman, a
favourite of Queen Victoria, was involved in the Larut War. It
seemed that a final trial of strength was about to follow. Therefore,
at the very moment when Kimberley was making his crucial decisions

[1] Linehan, 'Pahang', pp. 95–100.
[2] Cowan, *Nineteenth Century Malaya*, p. 119; Gullick, 'Speedy', pp.
32–33.

in London during August 1873, the man on the spot faced an awkward dilemma.

What could Ord do in Perak? There had been a period, early in 1873, when Larut had been virtually abandoned to the Chinese, and the Malays seemed to have found a solution to their difficulties. The Mantri apparently agreed to recognize 'Abdu'llah as sultan in return for a confirmation of his position in Larut. 'Abdu'llah also appointed Raja Yusuf his Raja Muda ('heir apparent') to secure his adherence. But the *rapprochement* was short-lived. 'Abdu'llah and the mantri soon fell out, and they lined up again with the Ghee Hins and Hai Sans respectively.

In August 1873 Colonel Anson, the lieutenant-governor of Penang, summoned a conference of all the parties in an attempt to mediate. It was soon evident that he had failed, and since Anson feared that the War was bound to spread into Penang itself he decided to commit himself to the mantri's support. An urgent telegram to Singapore brought Sir Harry Ord to the scene on 25 August 1873. 'Abdu'llah found an excuse for not attending another conference. Ord decided to accept Anson's advice. The governor finally recognized the mantri as an independent ruler in Larut. He lifted the embargo on arms for the mantri's allies. To check the spread of piracy, he organized the available resources of the Royal Navy into a flotilla of small boats to police the shores of Larut.[1] In reality, Ord had taken sides in the Perak War, just as Anson had done in Selangor two years earlier. As so frequently happened, Britain had been committed in a local dispute by the man on the spot.

Surprisingly enough, the Colonial Office did not object, even though Ord was soon driven to use force. On 16 September 1873, two officers were seriously wounded when one of H.M.S. *Midge*'s boats was fired upon from the Ghee Hin stockade at Selinsing. The bluejackets of Ord's flotilla, who were attempting to police these waters, were having a most frustrating task and rarely managed to capture a pirate boat.[2] After this attack, the Navy was eager for revenge. On 20 September 1873 H.M.S. *Thalia* destroyed 2 stockades,

---

[1] Cowan, op. cit., pp. 122–3; Gullick, op. cit., p. 34; Wilkinson in Windstedt, 'Perak', p. 87; Wilkinson, 'History of the Peninsula Malays', p. 112.
[2] Ord to Kimberley (telegram) 17 Sept. 1873. C.O. 273/69; Swettenham, *Footprints in Malaya*, pp. 28–30.

captured 3 junks, 50 guns and a large number of Ghee Hins. Like a good number of Ord's acts, news of the action first reached the Colonial Office from a London evening newspaper! When the official reports came in, one of the clerks pointed out that 'we are getting somewhat actively mixed up in Perak politics'. But, as the decision to intervene in some form had now been made, Herbert said 'I do not see that we can avoid interfering'. Kimberley approved the action.[1]

He was also prepared to sanction Speedy's recruitment of sepoys. Ord had asked the Colonial Office for their views on Speedy's action before the Straits Government recognized the mantri. But Ord did not wait for a reply. After recognizing the mantri he went ahead and gave Speedy his moral support. In London, Herbert insisted that the mantri had as much right to employ English officers as the Khedive of Egypt. Kimberley was rather annoyed that Ord did not await a reply, but he did not disapprove of Ord's decision.[2]

Speedy's private army reached Larut on 29 September 1873. Although he did not completely clear Larut of the Ghee Hins, he enabled the mantri and the Hai Sans to reopen the mines.[3] Ord's support for Speedy was, of course, quite consistent with his support for the mantri. It was also in line with his whole attitude to the Malay States. When he said his farewells to the Legislative Council of the Straits Settlements on 31 October 1873, Sir Harry took a final tilt at the policy of non-intervention,[4] which had frustrated him for so long, and which, in the last resort he had helped to end.

Sir Andrew Clarke took over the government of the colony on 3 November 1873. His instructions, unlike Ord's in 1867, emphasized

[1] *Pall Mall Gazette*, 26 Sept. 1873; mins. by MacDonald and Herbert 11 Oct. 1873. C.O. 273/69.

[2] Min. by Herbert 20 Sept., on Ord to Kimberley 14 Aug. 1873. C.O. 273/69; min. by Kimberley 16 Oct., on I.O. to C.O. 14 Oct. 1873. C.O. 273/72.

[3] For Speedy's progress see Cowan, *Nineteenth Century Malaya*, pp. 124–5. Maj. McNair was not impressed by Speedy's force, but he confirms that 'moral support' was given to it by the Straits Govt. (McNair, *Perak and the Malays*, pp. 353–4). When Anson visited Larut in Dec. 1873 he found the mantri more interested in opening the mines, his source of revenue, than clearing out his enemies.

[4] Ord to Kimberley 1 Nov. 1873. C.O. 273/71.

the problem of relations with the Malay States. Although Kimberley still insisted that the Government did not wish to interfere in the affairs of the Peninsula, he nevertheless instructed Clarke to inquire into the conditions of each state and to report any steps which the Straits Government might take to restore peace and protect trade. Kimberley added the well-known words:

> I should wish you especially to consider whether it would be advisable to appoint a British officer to reside in any of the [Malay] States. Such an appointment could of course only be made with the full consent of the native Government. . . .[1]

Kimberley was convinced that something had to be done in Malaya. He put forward tentatively the suggestion of the Residents, which had been mooted by the Anson Committee in 1871, and strongly advocated by George Campbell in 1872 and 1873. But, as with Wolseley in the Gold Coast and Commodore Goodenough in Fiji, Kimberley told Gladstone that the Government was not really committing itself. Clarke was to inquire and report.

In reality Kimberley was wrong. The Colonial Office did not know their man. Clarke later recorded his own feelings about those instructions:

> My instructions were simple. The Colonial Office was thoroughly dis-satisfied with the state of affairs in the Peninsula. I was to make it the subject of careful inquiry, and report my views as soon as possible. I fear that in some quarters there lurks a belief in the efficacy of reports. . . . It was necessary to act in the first place and to report afterwards. . . . The principles on which I acted were very simple. Personal influence has always great effect upon natives of the type of the Perak chiefs, and this influence I endeavoured to apply. . . . In place of anarchy and irregular revenues, I held out the prospects of peace and plenty. I found them in cotton; I told them that, if they would trust me, I would clothe them in silk . . . and since, I have often wondered how many of our useless, expensive, and demoralising small wars might have been avoided by similar modes of procedure . . . and I imagine that the secret of Imperial as of commercial success lies in knowing where to adventure.[2]

---

[1] Kimberley to Sir Andrew Clarke 20 Sept. 1873 (draft). C.O. 273/67.
[2] A. Clarke, 'The Straits Settlements'. A lecture delivered at South Place Institute, Finsbury, and printed in *The British Empire Series*, i, London, 1899, pp. 450–5.

His adventure began on the island of Pangkor on 14 January 1874, when he started to use his influence with the Perak chiefs.

On the same day in West Africa, Wolseley stood poised for his invasion of Ashanti.   In the Fiji Islands a conference similar to Clarke's was also beginning.   Here Goodenough and Layard were opening their formal inquiries into the question of annexing Fiji, where, as in Malaya, the situation was most urgent.   On the very day that Clarke began the Pangkor conference, in fact, one of Britain's representatives in Fiji addressed these words to the Foreign Office: 'for God's sake let there be no delay after our report is sent in, or I shall not be able to restrain these folks, they will, one side or the other, draw blood'.[1]

[1] Edgar Layard to W. H. Wylde (private) 14 Jan. 1874.   Pacific islands, consular correspondence, F.O. 58/139, p. 30.

7. Evolving a Policy in the South Pacific, 1855-71

W HILE Kimberley was reviewing Britain's role in West Africa and Malaya he faced similar dilemmas in the South Pacific. Should he annex the Fiji Islands? Should he extend British influence over a large part of Melanesia and Polynesia? In the case of Fiji he stated a clear preference for annexation in February 1873. But his reappraisal of Britain's role in the South Pacific generally followed a pattern which may be closely compared with his policy in West Africa and Malaya.

There was one major difference. Gladstone took more interest in the Fiji question than in any other part of the frontier in the tropics. The prime minister was most reluctant to annex the islands. Therefore Kimberley had to fall back on the time-honoured practice of sending someone to inquire and report. Two newly appointed British officers in the region were chosen for the inquiry. Commodore Goodenough, who was going to command the Australasian squadron of the Royal Navy, and Edgar Layard, the new consul in Fiji, were appointed to investigate the question of annexing the Fiji Islands.

Their recommendations were probably a foregone conclusion,[1] but their methods were quite unexpected. Kimberley left little doubt about his own predilections in favour of annexation in their instructions, but he did not authorize the cession of the islands which they negotiated on 20 March 1874. 'I thought Layard and Goodenough were to inquire and report', wrote a shocked member of the Foreign Office, 'not to invite a plebiscite for annexation.'[2] Just as Wolseley's immediate demand for English troops made it difficult for the Government

---

[1] Knatchbull-Hugessen believed Goodenough and Layard 'paved the way' for annexation, and he felt the Liberal Govt. would have annexed the islands. *Brabourne Diary*, v, p. 732.

[2] Min. by Tenterden 10 Mar., on Goodenough's published correspondence with the Fiji Govt. 12 Jan. 1874. F.O. archives: Pacific islands, consular correspondence, F.O. 58/139, p. 33.

to avoid the Ashanti expedition, and Clarke's Pangkor settlement was reported home after the event, so Goodenough and Layard also acted first and reported afterwards.

Fiji was only a part of the problem. A firm decision in favour of annexing Fiji could not solve the wider question of Britain's role in the South Pacific. As in West Africa and Malaya, the frontiers of British trade, investment, settlement and political influence in the Pacific had moved beyond the British colonies in Australasia. On top of this, the Pacific island labour traffic, like the earlier West African slave-trade, generated a good deal of humanitarian clamour, which became an important factor behind the decision to annex Fiji.

The formulation of British policy in the South Pacific can only be seen through the interaction of three closely related themes: Britain's response to a succession of changes within the Fiji Islands after the year 1855, her attempt to regulate the labour traffic, and a gradual awakening, in certain quarters, to the possibility of international rivalry for the Pacific. 'The waste places of the earth were being filled up . . .', said Carnarvon, 'and there were few outlying properties left.'[1] Whitehall's debate on the Pacific followed a course remarkably close to the debates over West Africa and Malaya.

BRITISH RELATIONS WITH FIJI UP TO 1863

In the mid-Victorian Age, when the frontiers of British interest began to move beyond the Australasian colonies, Britain, France and the United States had firm, though limited, stakes in the Pacific. In the south, Britain, after reluctantly gaining the finest prize, New Zealand, in 1841, had resisted requests for protection or annexation from Tahiti, Hawaii, Tonga and Samoa. In the north, the United States was assured after 1843 that the Hawaiian Islands would not become a Pacific Bermuda, and her citizens quietly consolidated their hold on the economic life of the kingdom. France was the leading Power of the eastern Pacific, having secured the Marquesas and Tahiti in 1842. In annexing New Caledonia in 1853 she had also demonstrated that the islands in the region of the British colonies were

[1] Carnarvon to a deputation of the Fiji Committee 3 July 1874; newspaper clipping in C.O. archives: Fiji correspondence, C.O. 83/5.

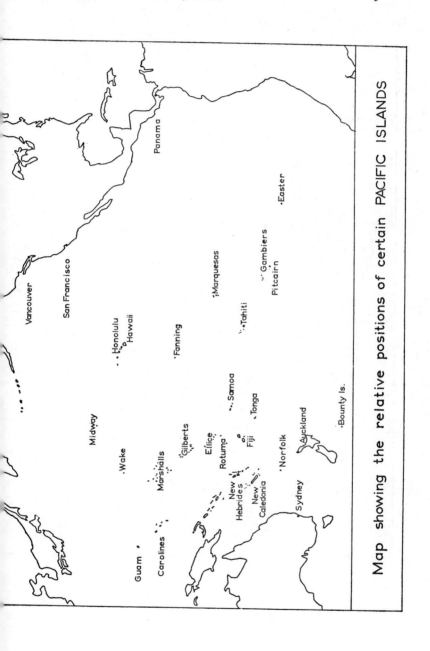

Map showing the relative positions of certain PACIFIC ISLANDS

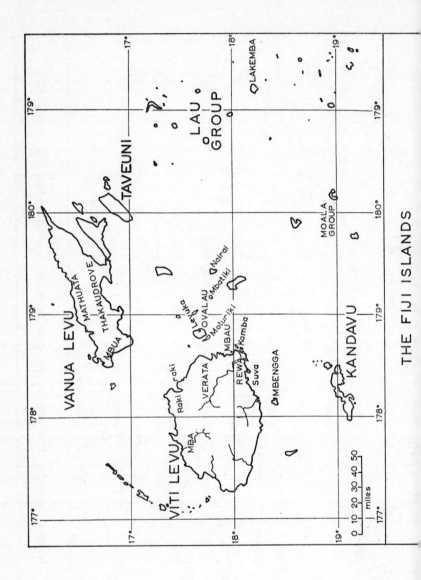

THE FIJI ISLANDS

not automatically a British preserve.¹   In the Fiji Islands, however, British influence predominated.

The group consists of over 300 islands, lying about 1,400 miles north of New Zealand.   Viti Levu, the largest island, has an area of 4,000 square miles.   In the early years of the nineteenth century, ships from India, Australia and New England sought sandalwood and bêche-de-mer for the markets of the South China Sea, and from the trading-boats and shipwrecks came many of the 'beachcombers', who gave the Fijians their first taste of Western civilization in the shape of new diseases, alcohol and fire-arms.²

The first real European impact was made by Wesleyan missionaries. They came to the islands in 1835, and their early experiences were disillusioning.³   But by 1860, with 16 missionaries in the field, aided by 200 local preachers, they claimed 60,000 church-goers and over 9,000 members.⁴   And missionary influence was not confined to religious and social life.   Ministers provided interpreters for political contacts between Fijian chiefs and visiting naval officers.   The Rev. James Calvert, head of the Ovalau circuit in the period 1861–6, tried to encourage the cession of the islands to Britain, by influencing both the Fijian chiefs and Methodist leaders in England and Australia.

In New South Wales there were, at one time, 7 Methodists in the Assembly.⁵   In 1859 one of their number, Alexander McArthur, moved a resolution calling for the annexation of Fiji.   In London, supporters of annexation were also briefed by the Methodists.   Admiral J. E. Erskine, a Member of Parliament who had once visited Fiji,

¹ For general accounts of the growth of European expansion in the Pacific, see G. H. Scholefield, *The Pacific; its Past and Future*, London, 1919; Brookes, *International Rivalry*; J. M. Ward, *British Policy in the South Pacific 1786 to 1893*, Sydney, 1948; W. P. Morrell, *Britain in the Pacific Islands*, Oxford, 1960; A. Ross, *New Zealand Aspirations in the Pacific in the Nineteenth Century*, Oxford, 1964.

² For early contacts with Fiji see G. C. Henderson, *Fiji and the Fijians, 1835–56*, Sydney, 1931, pp. 16–25; R. A. Derrick, *A History of Fiji*, Suva, 1946, i, pp. 28–40.

³ G. G. Findlay and W. W. Holdsworth, *The History of the Wesleyan Methodist Missionary Society*, London, 1921, iii, pp. 371–80.

⁴ Rev. W. Wilson to Dr Hoole May 1860. *Meth. Miss. Soc.*: various Fiji papers, file for 1858–60.

⁵ Notebook B, Calvert Papers in *Meth. Miss. Soc.*

I.F.T.——H

corresponded with Calvert. Above all, Alderman William McArthur, the Member of Parliament for Lambeth, was a leading Methodist and brother of the Sydney politician. By leading the agitation for annexation in the House of Commons he became known as the 'patron saint' of the Fiji islanders.[1]

Fijian, to the Victorian Englishman, stood for Cannibal. Yet the early discoverers and traders were often hospitably received, and they found no large units of political organization among the islanders until the late eighteenth century, when the chief 'kingdoms' to emerge were Rewa, Verata and Mbau (on Viti Levu), Thakaudrove, Mathuata and Mbua (on Vanua Levu), and Lakemba in the Lau Islands. A struggle for power in Viti Levu, which occurred during the first half of the nineteenth century, turned the land between Rewa and Mbau into 'the cockpit of Fiji'.[2] The kingdom of Mbau emerged victorious. By continual fighting the chiefs of Mbau so raised their power that by the 1850's Thakombau began to style himself 'Tui Viti', 'king of all Fiji'. The year 1855 may, in fact, be seen as the watershed of Fijian history.

In the first place, Thakombau prevailed over his rivals at the Battle of Kamba. Ironically, this frustrated his ambition to be in reality the 'king of all Fiji'. The victory was only possible with the help of King George Tupou of Tonga, whose relative, Ma'afu, had been established in the Lau group since 1848.[3] After Kamba, Ma'afu and the Tongans played an increasingly important part in the history of Fiji, and eventually Ma'afu united most of the eastern and northern islands of Fiji into a dominion to rival Thakombau's power.

Secondly, the first annexation proposals were considered in Britain in 1855. Charles St. Julian, a journalist, who was consul-general for Hawaii in Sydney, proposed that Samoa and Fiji should be taken under Britain's 'protective supremacy' on the precedent of the Gold Coast protectorate.[4] Mr G. Oliver of Bradford had much grander imperial

[1] Sir Wilfred Lawson in the House of Commons, 4 Aug. 1874. 3 *Hansard*, 221, col. 1296.

[2] Derrick, op. cit., p. 54. Phonetic spelling will be used for Fijian names. Fijian *b* is pronounced *mb*, *c–th*, *d–nd*, *g–ng*, *q–nqq*.

[3] Early Tongan contacts are discussed by Derrick, op. cit., pp. 118–28.

[4] Memo. dated 31 July 1854 in F.O. 58/82, p. 306.

visions. He suggested Britain should annex Fiji, Tonga, New Guinea, the New Hebrides and Celebes.[1] Both suggestions were evidently given careful attention in the Foreign Office. They were not accepted, but the Treasury was persuaded to sanction expenditure on the appointment of two new consuls for the Pacific, one in Fiji.[2] In the same year in July, Calvert, the Wesleyan missionary, engineered the first of Thakombau's fruitless requests for British protection — 'lest the French and Popery should gain in these islands'.[3]

Finally, an American action in 1855 set off a chain of events which dramatically influenced British policy. American traders and settlers began to enter Fiji in the 1840's, and some incurred losses through damages and thefts committed by Fijians. Their claims for redress were presented to American naval officers by the United States commercial agent, John Brown Williams, who was also an interested party. The State Department finally ordered an investigation, but Commander Boutwell, the officer selected to make it, was a 'Papist and a Southerner',[4] and not very sympathetic to Fijian Methodists. He proved high-handed in his methods. He accepted Williams's figures, although the Rev. Calvert pointed out that they were grossly inflated by 'interest' charges. But Boutwell ignored an order by a more senior American naval officer to make an impartial

[1] Oliver made his proposal in a letter to Clarendon in 1854 which has not been found. This was sent to Capt. Fremantle, senior naval officer in Australia, who reported that a protectorate over Fiji could be gained with little trouble. Oliver's suggestion was known in July 1855 to Calvert who was under the impression that the British Govt. favoured it. Circumstances seemed ripe for gaining Fiji, but no action was in fact taken. However, in 1883, Augustus Gregory, the Australian explorer, said he had received confidential instructions in 1855 to annex New Guinea, should the Crimean War continue. (Information from J. H. I. Cumpston, 'Augustus Gregory and the Inland Sea', unpublished MS., used by courtesy of the late author's daughter, Dr I. M. Cumpston, pp. 41–43.) See also Calvert to general secretary 24 July 1855. *Meth. Miss. Soc.*: Fiji incoming file 1855; and memo. on the Oliver proposal dated 5 Jan. 1855. F.O. 58/82, p. 308.

[2] Brookes, *International Rivalry*, pp. 230–1.

[3] The chief of Levuka, who was in conflict with Thakombau, had tried to get help from Roman Catholic missionaries. Calvert to general secretary 13 Aug. 1855. *Meth. Miss. Soc.*: Fiji incoming file for 1855.

[4] Ibid. Rev. J. Waterhouse to general secretary 13 Nov. 1855.

assessment, and in 1855 forced Thakombau to accept liability for $45,000.[1]

Thakombau's debt led to Britain's intervention. Another American officer arrived in 1858 to collect the money. By threatening Thakombau he secured a promise of payment in a year. Thakombau had no means of paying and turned to the newly arrived British consul, William Thomas Pritchard, who suggested ceding the islands to Britain in return for the payment of the debt. In a document signed on 12 October 1858, Pritchard recognized Thakombau's pretensions to be Tui Viti, 'having full and exclusive sovereignty and domain in and over the islands', and agreed to receive on behalf of the Crown title to 200,000 acres of land. With this agreement secured, Pritchard immediately set sail for England.[2]

Would Britain annex Fiji? Carnarvon, then a youthful parliamentary under-secretary in the Colonial Office during the short Tory ministry, defined the Government's dilemma: 'it is painful to refuse, but there must be a limit somewhere to our protecting and governing duties especially when we gain nothing by the acquisition'. He nevertheless felt it would be selfish to refuse to protect 'unfortunate islanders who are terrified by the licence of French sailors and the annexation ideas of the U.S. Government'.[3]

There was a good deal of support for annexation. The New South Wales Assembly voted an address to the Crown favouring the cession. A wealthy Australian offered to pay Thakombau's $45,000. The Admiralty's hydrographer pointed out that Britain possessed neither 'an islet nor a rock' between Sydney and Vancouver.[4] The Manchester Cotton Supply Association reported favourably on the quality of Fijian cotton. The general secretary of the Wesleyan Missionary

[1] The American claims are printed in *Treaties and other International Acts of the United States of America*, ed. by H. Miller, Dept. of State, Washington, 1942, vii (1855–8), pp. 286–93. See also my article, 'Anglo-American Rivalry in the Pacific: The British Annexation of the Fiji Islands in 1874', *P.H.R.* (1960), 29 (4), pp. 362–4.

[2] W. T. Pritchard, *Polynesian Reminiscences, or Life in the Pacific Islands*, London, 1866; a copy of the cession document printed in B. Seemann, *Viti: an account of a Government Mission to the Vitian or Fijian Islands in the years 1860–61*, London, 1862, pp. 124–8.

[3] Quoted in Brookes, *International Rivalry*, pp. 244–5.

[4] Quoted in Seemann, op. cit., p. 421.

Society raised the ogre of French intervention advancing Catholicism. But in 1859 there was a general election in Britain and the decision on Fiji had to await the outcome. Pritchard was sent back to Fiji to inform the chiefs that the offer of cession was being considered.

On his return the consul found Thakombau hard-pressed by his rivals. Ma'afu had prevailed on Vanua Levu, and now found allies on Viti Levu at Mbengga and Rakiraki who surrounded Mbau. Thakombau appealed to Pritchard for help once more. At the same time Ma'afu claimed that, as he would soon be master, the consul should recognize him instead. While the Government dallied at home, the consul faced a new dilemma.

Pritchard's instructions from the Foreign Office had been rather vague, but his actions were decisive. He decided to support Thakombau, check Ma'afu, and maintain the *status quo* at the time of the cession. He called a conference of the leading chiefs in December 1859 and obtained their signatures on a remarkable group of documents. The cession was ratified by twenty chiefs, including Thakombau. Ma'afu was persuaded to renounce his pretensions. The consul himself was granted (with the approval of the American agent) 'full unreserved entire and supreme authority to govern Fiji and to make what laws he pleased'. He later wrote in his memoirs, 'I secured the controlling power in the group in my own hands'.[1] It was the sort of act frequently committed by the man on the spot.

Unfortunately for Pritchard, Palmerston's Government had not yet decided whether it wanted Fiji. The Colonial Office, to whom the problem was passed, sent out Colonel W. Smythe, Royal Artillery, to investigate.[2] Smythe reached Fiji on 5 July 1860 to discover that Thakombau had never had authority to make the cession. He advised the Government against the cession.[3] Rejecting the various strategic and economic arguments in favour of annexation, he suggested that the group should be allowed to develop gradually under Western influences like the Hawaiian kingdom. Smythe's only really

[1] Pritchard, op. cit., pp. 225–34.
[2] Derrick (*History*, p. 144) suggests Smythe was appointed at the end of 1859, but the F.O. was not officially informed until C.O. to F.O. 31 July 1860 (draft). C.O. 83/1.
[3] Ibid. Smythe to Newcastle 9 Aug. 1860 and 9 Nov. 1861.

positive proposal was that the consul should be given jurisdiction over the British subjects in Fiji.[1]

After studying Smythe's report, the Colonial Office decided against annexation on 7 September 1861, although there was a later hint that Palmerston, the prime minister, might have welcomed the cession.[2] Rogers took the view that, after the recent outbreak of war with the Maoris in New Zealand, the 'present juncture certainly is not one in which it would be convenient to become responsible for the Government of more warlike savages than we already have on our hands'.[3] Offers of Samoa in 1862 and Rarotonga in 1866 were rejected in the same way. Until 1870 the Colonial Office endeavoured to keep clear of responsibilities in the Pacific outside Australia and New Zealand.

The Foreign Office was not able to do this. Consul Pritchard's unauthorized intervention in Fiji had briefly given him a position of power and influence. He attracted settlers from Australia. He drew up rules governing land purchases and persuaded settlers and chiefs to support a 'Mercantile Court of Fiji' consisting of British and American consuls and other assessors. He required British ships to register at the consulate before he would grant them protection. He tried to arrange more amicable relations between Fiji and Tonga. Although Smythe

[1] Report in *Accounts and Papers* (1862), xxxvi, pp. 734–42. Smythe's qualifications and his conduct of the inquiry are severely criticized by Derrick, *History*, pp. 146–7. In 1873 Smythe changed his mind over Fiji, and Knatchbull-Hugessen wrote: 'The fact is that his report in 1861 was all wrong in many of its most essential particulars'. (Min. 1 Apr., in F.O. to C.O. 26 Mar. 1873. C.O. 83/3.) This did not prevent Kimberley, who got to know Smythe in Ireland, from suggesting sending him as the Commissioner in 1873. (Kimberley to Gladstone 30 Apr. 1873. *Gladstone Papers*, 44225/29.)

[2] C.O. to F.O. 7 Sept. 1861 (draft). C.O. 83/1. Russell, the Foreign Secretary, agreed. Ten years later Kinnaird told the Commons that when he had tried to persuade Palmerston to annex Fiji the prime minister had looked at the map and recited all the depths of the harbours in Fiji, but Gladstone replied that Newcastle was the only member of the Cabinet who favoured annexation. 3 *Hansard*, 212, cols. 213–17. See also C. C. Eldridge, 'The Colonial Policy of the Fifth Duke of Newcastle, 1859–1864', unpublished PhD. thesis, Nottingham, 1966, pp. 347–52.

[3] Min. by Rogers 19 June, on Denison to Newcastle 10 Apr. 1860. C.O. 83/1. Legge suggests fears of another outbreak like the Maori Wars 'were decisive' in causing the C.O. to accept Smythe's view. J. D. Legge, *Britain in Fiji, 1858–1880*, London, 1958, p. 34.

advised that Pritchard should be dismissed, the consul had his ardent supporters.[1] But certain accusations against Pritchard could not lightly be dismissed, and the Foreign Office asked the governor of New South Wales to examine them. He found that the consul's finances were unsatisfactory, and Pritchard was suspended.[2] Britain's formal refusal of the cession was announced in Fiji in July 1862.

The Pritchard cession was a failure. It is, however, of considerable interest in our discussion of the frontier in the tropics, because during his five-year consulate Pritchard raised most of the problems which were to puzzle Whitehall for the next decade. Who was the lawful authority in Fiji? How were the British settlers to be governed? What was the strategic and commercial value of Fiji? The naval officer who delivered the Government's decision to refuse the cession was handed a paper by Robert Swanston, one of the ablest of the settlers, who stressed the economic potential and racial harmony of the islands. But he insisted that one thing was urgently needed. The British consul ought to have some jurisdiction over the British settlers. Colonel Smythe had, of course, made the same proposal. The Foreign Office agreed.[3] For the next seven years, therefore, British policy towards Fiji amounted to an attempt to give the consul some jurisdiction over British subjects in the islands.

THE FOREIGN OFFICE AND CONSULAR JURISDICTION, 1863–70

The seven-year debate in London over the question of consular jurisdiction in Fiji well illustrated the dangers of ill-defined responsibilities. In peripheral areas, like the frontier in the South Pacific, the formulation of policy was incredibly slow and muddled.[4]

[1] Commodore Seymour, the senior naval officer, Australian station (Ad. to C.O. 22 Nov. 1861. C.O. 83/1). Seemann, the botanist: his book, *Viti*, was in many ways a contradiction of Smythe. Seemann also edited Pritchard's *Reminiscences*.

[2] Commission of Inquiry report. F.O. 58/108, p. 535.

[3] Min. by Vivian 11 Mar., on C.O. to F.O. 5 Mar. 1863 enclosing Swanston's paper, dated 24 July 1862. F.O. 58/124.

[4] When Pritchard was working in the F.O. before returning to Fiji he found a parcel of forms in a corner, addressed to him at Levuka. It had been there for sixteen months. *Reminiscences*, p. 225.

The problems of Fiji were rarely discussed by the Cabinet. The Foreign Office was responsible for the conduct of Britain's relations with the islands, but it frequently consulted the Government's Law Officers before making a decision. The Colonial Office tried to remain aloof but found itself increasingly involved in Fijian issues. Many Australians were interested in Fiji. The Royal Navy's Australian squadron was based on colonial ports. Plans for jurisdiction in Fiji involved appeals to the Supreme Court in New South Wales. It was therefore impossible for the Colonial Office to keep out of the discussions. The Treasury's influence on the formulation of policy was also of great significance. So many departments were involved that it took a long time to reach decisions on the South Pacific.

Whitehall approached the question of the South Sea island labour traffic in the same way. Kidnapping-ships often sailed from colonial ports, but evidence against them was usually gathered by the consul in Fiji. Any measure of regulation depended on the Treasury's approval of the expense and on enforcement by the Navy. It was not surprising that Whitehall managed to prevaricate for ten years over providing extra-territorial jurisdiction, which had long been taken for granted elsewhere. As Herbert commented bitterly, 'a vast quantity of Polynesian business has been done twice over'.[1]

Admittedly, Fiji presented unique difficulties. Consular jurisdiction normally depended not only on the Foreign Jurisdiction Acts,[2] but on treaties with ruling sovereigns. But when the consul in Fiji was asked in 1863 if there was an authority with whom a treaty could be made, he replied that there had 'never been any law and order in Fiji'. In 1860, however, Congress had passed a law which gave United States consuls, in countries without 'civilized government', the same powers as had been obtained by treaty in Siam, China and Japan.[3] This was sufficient precedent for Clarendon, the Foreign Secretary, who approached the Treasury in 1866 about applying the Foreign Jurisdiction Acts to 'certain islands in the Pacific'.[4]

[1] Min. by Herbert 30 June, on Belmore to Kimberley 8 Apr. 1871. New South Wales correspondence, C.O. 201/563.
[2] See below, pp. 360–2.
[3] F.O. to Jones 14 Sept. 1863 (draft); Jones to F.O. 6 Oct. 1866. F.O. 58/124, pp. 30–31, 35, 43.
[4] Ibid. p. 69. F.O. to Treas. 6 Nov. 1866 (draft).

The Treasury took no less than fourteen months to reply. Finally, in January 1868, they produced the draft of an Order in Council authorizing a scheme similar to that operating in Siam, China and Japan. The consul would exercise civil and criminal jurisdiction equivalent to that of an English county court. Prisoners, serious cases, and appeals would go to New South Wales.[1] But the Law Officers decided that consular jurisdiction could not be based simply on 'sufferance'. If there was no sovereign with which to make a treaty, legislation would be necessary. Accordingly, a Bill was drafted, and only when the matter had progressed thus far did the Treasury discover the true nature of the Fijian anomaly. The Bill created a precedent.

Under the terms of the Bill the Crown would receive jurisdiction in circumstances hitherto unknown. There was a chance that British subjects might lead the Crown into exercising powers in territory which was not British and which another Power might acquire. Moreover, the scheme might lead to unforeseen expense, so the Treasury decided to halt it.

> If jurisdiction is created it may be presumed that Courts must be estab-
> lished to administer it. These cannot exist without a Government to
> protect them, nor a Government without taxes — nor taxes without
> some sort of police; and all things being created under British law they
> must . . . in the too probable case of default, be supported from imperial
> resources.

They suggested instead that Fiji should be placed under the jurisdiction of an Australian colony.[2]

Granville, the Colonial Secretary, objected to the Treasury's alternative. He believed that to make crimes committed in Fiji punishable in Australia, without colonial consent, would be '*pro tanto* a revival of transportation'.[3] He suggested a voluntary scheme of law enforcement among the settlers, or a joint Anglo-American scheme. The Americans, however, had found that their 1860 Act was ineffective. The British Law Officers could not suggest a satisfactory method of

[1] Ibid. p. 91. Treas. to F.O. 25 Jan. 1868.
[2] Treas. to F.O. 1 Jan. 1869. F.O. 58/124, p. 223. The F.O. noted that the Treas. did not realize that consular jurisdiction usually paid for itself out of fees.
[3] C.O. to F.O. 26 Feb. 1869. F.O. 58/116, p. 123.

applying the Foreign Jurisdiction Acts to Fiji. Clarendon dropped the
Bill in May 1869.[1] After eight years, the idea of consular jurisdiction
was abandoned. The Foreign Office could only rely on the 'prudence
and discretion' of the consul in Fiji.

While Whitehall dabbled with Fiji in this leisurely fashion in the
1860's, events occurred in the islands which demanded more urgent
attention. Publicity stirred up by the Pritchard cession, and high
cotton prices induced by the American Civil War caused an influx of
settlers and an increase in the value of trade.[2] Yet the rivalry of
Thakombau and Ma'afu remained. A strange series of experiments
in government followed.

The first was the work of Pritchard's successor, Henry Michael
Jones, V.C. He reached Fiji in 1864 to find no recognized, unified
authority with which to negotiate, so he tried to create one. At a
meeting on 8 May 1865 he launched the 'Confederation' in which the
seven chiefs of Mbau, Rewa, Lakemba, Mbua, Thakaudrove, Mathuata and Nanduri agreed to constitute an annual assembly which
would legislate for all Fiji. Local autonomy and taxes would remain,
but wars would have to be sanctioned by all. A national flag was
adopted. Thakombau was elected the first president. The system was
short-lived. Disputes over territory and suspicions of Thakombau
were rife. Early in 1867 Mbua, Lakemba and Thakaudrove seceded
and gave their allegiance to Ma'afu.[3]

Thakombau was not to be outdone. Encouraged by some of the
settlers, he styled himself 'King of Mbau and its dominions'. His
secretary, Samuel St. John, a Californian, drew up a constitution based
on Hawaii's. This second experiment, known as the 'Mbau Con-

[1] F.O. to C.O. 20 May 1869 (draft). F.O. 58/124, p. 274.

[2] Numbers of settlers in 1865 (Jones to F.O. 24 Nov. 58/124, p. 49):
British, 230; American, 70; German and Scandinavian, 30; others, 20.
Trade, from consuls' reports:
Value of exports:

1862	*1863*	*1864*	*1865*	*1866*	*1867*	*1868*	*1869*	*1870*
£13,030	13,085	19,764	24,225	30,970	39,960	45,167	57,020	98,735

Imports, occasionally estimated by the consul:

1865	*1866*	*1867*	*1870*
£20,000	25,000	29,000	71,000

[3] Jones to F.O. 18 July 1867. F.O. 58/124, p. 80.

stitution', launched on 2 May 1867, was as ineffective as Jones's.[1] Fiji remained basically divided into two rival camps — Thakombau in the west, Ma'afu in the east. The chief change was that now each had his settler advisers and 'ministers'. Thakombau's domain compared unfavourably with Ma'afu's.

John Bates Thurston, the British acting consul 1867–9, tried another experiment. He attempted to make the Mbau monarchy work by forcing it to live up to its responsibilities. Thurston was one of the makers of modern Fiji. He had started life in the Merchant Navy and then attempted sheep-farming in Australia. After being shipwrecked on a voyage in the South Seas in 1865, he reached Levuka in the Wesleyan mission ship. He was to devote the rest of his life to Fiji. Instead of becoming just another planter he mastered the language and land tenure system. He became an expert botanist and shipwright. Striking a close friendship with Captain Jones, he explored Viti Levu with the consul.[2] In 1867 Thurston took over the consulate. Although he had no illusions about Thakombau's pretensions, Thurston persisted with Jones's policy of encouraging the evolution of a single Fijian polity. He believed the Fijians were well disposed towards settlers, and he sought to preserve the harmony.

Two examples of Thurston's methods may be given. When a missionary was murdered by mountain tribes in the interior of Viti Levu in 1867 and Thakombau tried to disclaim responsibility, Thurston insisted that the king should assert his authority. He persuaded a British naval officer not to intervene, and he even organized several abortive Fijian expeditions against the trouble-makers. His most important action was his attempt to save Thakombau from a group of Australian speculators, who tried to erect a miniature copy of the East India Company in Fiji.

---

[1] Derrick, *History*, pp. 163–4.

[2] They discovered that they had both been together before on a ship bound for India. A. B. Brewster, *King of the Cannibal Isles*, London, 1937, p. 241; for Thurston's early career see J. Millington, 'The Career of Sir John Thurston, Governor of Fiji 1888–97', unpublished M.A. thesis, London, 1957, pp. 22–26; Derrick, op. cit., p. 160; and his introd. to 'Journal de bord d'une journée de recrutement aux Nouvelles-Hébrides en 1871, sur la Goëlette "Strathnever"' by J. B. Thurston, *Journal de la Société des Océanistes* (1957), 13, p. 69.

Thakombau remained vulnerable because of the American debt. Very little had been paid, and a United States naval officer, who visited Fiji in 1867, forced Thakombau to agree to pay the balance, in island produce, in four yearly instalments, and also 'mortgage' three islands as security. Thakombau was naturally still unable to pay and a group of Melbourne businessmen saw an opportunity for easy profit. A Polynesia Company was formed, which offered to pay off the debts and grant Thakombau £1,000 a year, in return for 200,000 acres of land with judicial and legislative rights, and a commercial and banking monopoly in the islands; Thurston managed to get the Company's first charter cancelled by issuing an injunction restraining the British directors, while he called in the senior naval officer to investigate the matter. But a new charter was granted by Thakombau on 23 July 1868. The Company did, in fact, pay off the American debts, and started introducing settlers at Suva in 1870. Thurston continued to oppose it, and the Company was never a success.[1]

In 1869 yet another experiment was launched in Fiji known as the 'Amended Mbau Constitution'. It was a scheme of constitutional monarchy drawn up by W. H. Drew, Thakombau's new secretary, who proved no more successful than his predecessor. When Edward March took over the British consulate in 1869, he found the Government so ineffective that disputes were often being referred to the British and American consuls.[2]

The position of the British consul became increasingly difficult after 1870. March was instructed by the Foreign Office to remain neutral in Fijian disputes, and try to smooth out matters involving British subjects. But events moved rapidly. 1870 was the year of the 'Great Fiji Rush'. Over 1,000 new immigrants brought the white population up to nearly 4,000. Cotton exports fetched over £90,000.[3] Rumours of annexation were rife. In a tumbledown consulate on the beach at Levuka, a place rapidly taking on the character of a rowdy frontier boom town, March's 'tact and judgement' were hard pressed. In despair he wrote:

[1] McIntyre, 'Anglo-American Rivalry in the Pacific', pp. 366–8.
[2] Derrick, op. cit., p. 189.
[3] Value of cotton exports from the consul's reports:

1862	1863	1864	1865	1866	1867	1868	1869	1870
£360	900	3,000	6,000	19,000	34,004	30,975	45,000	92,700

I am in the midst of low adventurers, absconders from the Colonies, and a class of men who are in a chronic state of excitement caused by continual indulgence in alcoholic drinks. I am at the mercy of any ruffian who chooses to walk into the office, abuse me and walk out again.[1]

He had no jurisdiction over the British settlers. In fact, he became alienated from them. In 1870 Whitehall was forced to think of Fiji again.

NEW ANNEXATION PROJECTS AND THE ROLE OF THE COLONIAL OFFICE, 1870–1

While the pace of change in Fiji quickened in the 1860's, and the Treasury and Foreign Office continued to haggle over the question of consular jurisdiction, a number of strange rumours and suggestions reached the Colonial Office. That is why Kimberley, when he took office in 1870, was forced to take the lead in what was normally a Foreign Office preserve.

Fiji suddenly appeared as a potential focus for diplomatic rivalry. A Melbourne newspaper *The Age* suggested in December 1869 that the colony of Victoria should govern Fiji through an officer like the Indian Residents, to prevent annexation by another Power.[2] A group of German settlers applied for annexation by the North German Confederation. Bismarck refused, in October 1869, but agreed to appoint a consul and to send a gunboat.[3] The idea of protection by the United States, or another European Power, was mooted at a public meeting in Levuka on 14 June 1869. If Britain would not annex Fiji, the settlers sought protection for twenty years to enable the islands to evolve a Government like Hawaii's.

A group of Americans signed a petition requesting annexation by the United States; but the United States consul refused to forward it to Washington.[4] The State Department also made it clear that it had

[1] March to T. V. Lister (private) 2 July 1870. F.O. 58/118, p. 306.

[2] *The Age*, 11 Dec. 1869, encl. in Canterbury to Granville 2 Jan. 1870. C.O. 309/93.

[3] Copy of Bismarck's letter of 16 Oct. 1869 encl. in March's 'Report on Fiji', 27 Mar. 1870. F.O. 58/118, pp. 181–96.

[4] March to Clarendon 31 Mar. 1870. F.O. 58/118, p. 175. Copy of American petition, acknowledged by U.S. consul, 31 Aug., encl. in Sutton to Granville 8 Nov. 1869. C.O. 309/71.

no intention of interfering in Fiji.¹   It was rumoured that Napoleon
III had recognized Thakombau's Government.   But it transpired
that a convention, supposed to have been signed on 8 July 1858, had
merely recognized Thakombau as 'King of Mbau' and provided
safeguards for Roman Catholics.²   The British consul sent home
memorials from Thakombau, Maʻafu and the British settlers in March
1870, purporting to request British protection.   This was never even
answered by the Government, and evidence found in 1874 indicated
that it was not a *bona fide* request.³   The cumulative effects of these
rumours and suggestions certainly gave rise to the possibility, about
1870, that some Power might take Fiji.   Admiral Erskine paid a visit
to the Foreign Office and found Clarendon and his staff 'well up and
deeply interested in the island'.⁴

What attitude did the Colonial Office take to all the alarming
rumours?   The simple answer is that it was not opposed to foreign
annexation of Fiji at this time.   Granville said he would prefer to risk
the possibility of American annexation than see Britain take the
islands.   Herbert wondered whether 'it might save the credit of
England and be of general advantage, if any diplomatic communication
could result in the establishment of a friendly European Government
over these islands'.⁵   When one of the directors of the Polynesia
Company, Lavington Evans, appeared in London claiming that he
was authorized by the Fijian settlers to seek British or German
protection, Herbert wrote:

> I do not of course at all regret the decision of this Government to have
> nothing to do with a country which is too likely to be involved very
> shortly in native difficulties.   But it is by no means unimportant to
> England that it should pass into the hands of a power likely to contribute
> to the maintainance of a fair balance of naval power in the Pacific.
> France, Holland, Russia and America have their fleets in or handy to

¹ F.O. to C.O. 16 Mar. 1870.   C.O. 201/561.
² March's 'Report'.   F.O. 58/118, pp. 181–219.
³ Ibid. p. 215.   March to Clarendon 31 Mar. 1870;   Goodenough's
Journal, iii, 12 Jan. 1874.
⁴ Rev. Calvert to Rev. Hoole 17 Mar. 1870. *Meth. Miss. Soc.*: home
letter file for 1867–70.
⁵ Min. by Herbert 11 June 1870 on Dr L. Fison to W. Fison 27 Aug. 1869
(copy) in C.O. 201/562.

the seas surrounding Australia, and as Prussia has now a somewhat considerable steam fleet, I venture to suggest that it is well worth while for
this Govt. to make some exertion with the view of causing the Fijis to
be constituted a North German Colony. . . .

If North Germany will not come forward, then possibly Belgium
might do so. About ten years ago a Belgian Commission . . . visited
Australia and the neighbouring countries with the view of reporting
upon the practicability of founding a Belgian colony in these Seas. . . .

It is really very necessary that some Government (which should not
be French or American) should be established in these islands.[1]

Herbert's opinion, which accompanied Kimberley's first brief on Fiji,
indicated that the department did not fear certain foreign Powers close
to Australia. Rogers thought that 'if Prussia w[oul]d adopt the task
of reducing these savages to Berlin order it w[oul]d be useful and
very curious to look at'.[2] He welcomed Germany into the colonial
field. He thought a German colony in New Guinea would be a good
thing for Australia, and in July 1870 he said he would be happy to let
the Germans have a base in Malaya.

Yet the idea of creating a German or Belgian 'buffer zone' to
check the United States of America and France was a trifle academic.
The much more concrete proposal arrived, in July 1870, that the
colony of Victoria should annex Fiji. The governor of Victoria
reported that an Australasian Inter-Colonial Conference, which was
about to meet in Melbourne to discuss the question of reciprocal
tariffs, would also urge the creation of a British protectorate in Fiji.
The governor of New South Wales also supported the proposal.[3]
Kimberley knew that 'feeling here is strongly against extension of
territory' but he agreed to consider the proposal.[4] When Sir John
McCulloch, the premier of Victoria, demanded a decision in
August 1870, the Colonial Office could not avoid serious study of the
issue.

Since Kimberley wished to consider the Australian request seriously,
Rogers set out the possible alternatives in an important minute:

[1] Ibid. Memo. by Herbert 10 May 1870.
[2] Ibid. Min. by Rogers.
[3] Canterbury to Granville 20 May 1870 (confidential). C.O. 309/93;
Belmore to Granville 13 July 1870. C.O. 201/558.
[4] Min. by Kimberley 14 July, on Canterbury to Granville 20 May 1870.
C.O. 309/93.

Without any dog in the manger feeling I should have thought it desirable
to encourage the occupation of these islands from Australia with British
prepossessions rather than from the US with American prepossessions.
In fact the course of events is forcing us in that direction.

He believed recent events indicated that Fiji would soon be dominated
by a European minority, which he hoped would prefer connection with
Britain rather than any other nation. The settlers needed some form
of jurisdiction among themselves; but they should be responsible for
the cost of this, and for their relations with the Fijians; 'If this is not
so, they will be arrogant & quarrelous believing that whatever they do
they will be pulled through'. There appeared, to Rogers, to be six
possible courses: an international agreement that no Power should
annex the place unless requested by the white population, a treaty with
the chiefs binding them not to cede their lands to anyone but Britain
and granting Britain extra-territorial jurisdiction, the creation of a
Crown Colony, annexation by Victoria, a protectorate, or an independent settler republic. Rogers favoured a treaty at once, and the creation
of a Crown Colony eventually.[1] Miss Drus has inferred that Rogers
really had nothing to suggest.[2] Yet his lengthy and exhaustive minute
is a classic summary of the complex of attitudes which the Colonial
Office brought to the discussion. His personal preference foretold
what followed later. Granville very shortly revived the idea of consular jurisdiction. Fiji was eventually made a Crown Colony.

What did Kimberley decide about the Australian demand for Fiji?
He considered Rogers's opinion on 22 October 1870. He had certainly not entered the Colonial Office with plans for annexation in the
Pacific. He greeted New Zealand's annexation of the Bounty Islands
with characteristic cynicism ('a valuable acquisition!').[3] He reminded
his department in December 1870 that Fiji was 'not under the
Colonial Office'.[4] He rightly maintained that relations with the
islands should be conducted by the Foreign Office. Why, then,

[1] Min. by Rogers 19 Oct., on Canterbury to Granville 12 Aug. 1870.
C.O. 309/94.
[2] Drus, 'The Colonial Office and the Annexation of Fiji', p. 95.
[3] Min. by Kimberley on Bowen to Kimberley 21 Aug. 1870. C.O.
209/559.
[4] Min. by Kimberley 7 Dec., on Belmore to Kimberley 29 Sept. 1870.
C.O. 201/559.

did he increasingly take charge of the formulation of Britain's policy ?

The answer lay in Kimberley's earnest desire to retain the goodwill of the Australian colonies. He was the one man in the Cabinet to give serious thought to the Fiji question, not so much because it was his responsibility, but because the question was frequently raised by Australians. He treated their views sympathetically partly because, although he expected that the self-governing colonies would one day become independent, he feared that their separation in anger would adversely affect Britain's prestige. 'It will be a gain for both us and them', he wrote, 'if we can keep up the connexion till they become stronger.'[1]

Moreover, in 1870, Kimberley was involved in delicate negotiations with the Australians over the question of their right to make reciprocal inter-colonial tariff agreements. There were also demands from Victoria for the federation and for the neutrality of the Australian colonies. In these discussions Kimberley became a supporter of the colonial viewpoint against the rather doctrinaire objections of Gladstone. In fact, until the passage of the Australian Colonies Customs Duties Act in 1873, Kimberley found himself caught between the views of the prime minister and the aspirations of the colonists.[2] This may well account for his willingness to consider several schemes for a new policy in Fiji in the same period. The Australian proposal for a protectorate could not be dismissed lightly. Kimberley's reply was scrutinized by Granville and Gladstone. Queen Victoria expressed some fear of American annexation.[3]

The reply was finally sent to the governor of Victoria on 16 March 1871. Kimberley was unable to alter the previous decision against annexation. He pointed out that a protectorate was too vague. The Maori Wars in New Zealand provided a warning that occupation of Fiji might require force. He said the Government's policy in Fiji was now

[1] Kimberley's *Journal*, May 1870, p. 13.
[2] See Allin, *Australasian Preferential Tariffs*; Knaplund, *Gladstone and Britain's Imperial Policy*, pp. 103–17; H. L. Hall, *Australia and England. A Study in Imperial Relations*, London, 1934, pp. 196–201.
[3] Kimberley to Gladstone 8 Mar. (copy), and Gladstone to Kimberley 10 Mar. 1871. (*Kimberley Papers* A/43 and A/86.) Gen. Ponsonby to Kimberley 12 and 14 Mar. 1871. A/40.

to give such aid as may be in their power through the Consul for the maintainance of order until the European community can establish a regular Government, and they are considering measures with a view to increase the authority of the Consul over British subjects by conferring upon him magisterial powers.[1]

After making his decision, Kimberley tried to absolve the Colonial Office from further responsibility for the Fijian question.

What did the Foreign Office propose ? It reverted to the idea of consular jurisdiction. This time an Order in Council was actually prepared for the Royal Assent, but it was never published. What is not clear is whether Kimberley pressed Granville into this action on the lines of Herbert's and Rogers's suggestions, or whether Granville acted independently because of Consul March's reports, and that his knowledge of Granville's initiative enabled Kimberley to answer the Victorian Government as he did.

The proposed Order in Council, drafted in February 1871, was designed to apply the Foreign Jurisdiction Acts to Fiji. Now it was the turn of the Colonial Office to raise objections. It reminded Granville of the view he held when Colonial Secretary that the Australasian colonies must be consulted first.[2] But the Foreign Office had decided that the Fiji problem was most urgent. The delay of an exchange of correspondence with the colonies was avoided by adding to the Bill the words 'provided that New South Wales agrees'. Treasury objections were forestalled by skilful tactics. Consular jurisdiction was known to involve expenditure on clerks, a prison and jailer. To gain the Treasury's sanction, W. H. Wylde suggested the following subterfuge:

> Let us get the Order in Council issued and a Gaoler & Constable appointed in the first instance, and let the Consul himself represent the impossibility of carrying on the Duties that will devolve upon him without further assistance. The assistance must follow and when once the machinery is started, the Treasury cannot refuse to sanction the necessary expenditure. Whereas if we frighten them now we shall come to a deadlock at once.[3]

The Treasury was merely told that the system would be the same as in the Ottoman Empire and China. They did not reply. When their memories

[1] Kimberley to Canterbury 16 Mar. 1871 (draft). C.O. 309/94.
[2] Holland to Vivian 5 Apr. 1871. F.O. 58/124, p. 314.
[3] Ibid. p. 321. Min. by Wylde on Treas. to F.O. 6 May 1871.

were jogged in July 1871 they said decision was being postponed because some new proposals for annexation were before Kimberley.

Although the Order in Council was ready to receive the Royal Assent in September 1871, Granville never authorized the consul to assume any judicial powers.[1] After ten years Colonel Smythe's suggestion was fulfilled — but only on paper! In Fiji, yet another experiment in Government had begun and, in response, British policy became one of *de facto* recognition.

DE FACTO RECOGNITION OF THAKOMBAU'S GOVERNMENT, 1871

During the final stages of the consular jurisdiction muddle in 1871, Kimberley received yet another annexation proposal from Australia. This, indeed, was the Treasury's excuse for delaying a decision. The new proposal came from New South Wales. Lord Belmore, the governor, was deluged with Fiji projects at the end of April 1871. Dr John Dunmore Lang headed a deputation from a public meeting in Sydney on 25 April.[2] Next day, a Mr Leefe from Fiji told the

[1] What happened is still rather obscure. The draft Order was sent to the Lord President of the Council on 24 Aug. 1871 (F.O. 58/122, p. 42). On the twenty-sixth the Treas. suggested postponing the matter as Kimberley was considering a new policy in view of the new situation in Fiji. (Ibid. p. 44.) But on 19 Sept. the F.O. told the C.O. that the Order had received the Royal Assent, though March would not be authorized to act. This seems to have been a mistake, as Henry Holland, the legal adviser, was told that the Order was not signed (min. by Holland 22 Sept. on F.O. to C.O. 19 Sept. 1871. C.O. 201/567). When the Niger Delta Order in Council was planned in 1872 (below, p. 362) Wylde said that the Fiji Order went to the Council, then the Treas. intervened and stopped it on the ground of expense (min. by Wylde 26 Apr. on C.O. to F.O. 25 Apr. 1872. F.O. 84/1360).

[2] Lang called for the annexation of Fiji in Sept. 1870 in a petition to the Legislative Council. Although long prominent in the political and religious life of N.S.W., he commanded little respect in Whitehall. Rogers called him a 'tiresome old demagogue', and Kimberley said, 'His last book which I have read is excessively tiresome'. In July 1870 Lang published *The Coming Event, Or Freedom and Independence for the Seven United Provinces of Australia*, in which he gave as one of the main reasons for separation the 'absolute necessity for the erection of a Sovereign and Independent Power in the Pacific, in view of the actual state of things in the Fiji Islands'.

governor that the settlers needed protection. Two days later, Charles
St Julian suggested a protectorate by Hawaii. For the second time,
then, the Fiji question was thrust into Kimberley's lap by an Australian colony.

Now significant new arguments were used. Fiji became related to
the much wider problem of the Pacific labour traffic, which will be
discussed later. It was also compared with the frontier in South Africa,
which presented the same 'spectacle of an English population without
law'.[1] The new arguments awakened Herbert and Knatchbull-
Hugessen to the possible dangers of the Fijian situation. They also
rekindled Kimberley's interest. When the proposals reached London
in July 1871, Kimberley dismissed the possibility of a protectorate by
Hawaii as a 'perfect farce'. But he did not see why New South Wales
should not govern Fiji.[2] Here was a convenient device to enable
Britain to avoid taking the responsibility. Thus Kimberley was still
open to suggestions from Australia. After rejecting the Victorian
request in March 1871, he allowed the idea of annexation to an
Australian colony to be revived in July.

Kimberley informed Granville and Gladstone that Charles Cooper,
the agent-general for New South Wales, supported the scheme, as did
Robert Lowe, Gladstone's Chancellor of the Exchequer, who had
formerly lived in Sydney.[3] Kimberley knew that Julius Vogel, the
ambitious New Zealand politician, also had his eyes on Fiji.[4] Granville,
who feared that the Fijians would suffer under a colonial régime,
suggested the Cabinet should discuss the question.

[1] Clipping of 15 Feb., encl. in Belmore to Kimberley 22 Feb. 1871.
C.O. 201/563.

[2] Ibid. Min. by Kimberley 20 July, on Belmore to Kimberley 28 Apr.1871.

[3] Kimberley to Granville 26 July 1871 (copy). *Gladstone Papers*,
44224/193. Charles Cooper was five times premier of N.S.W. from 1856
to 1870, when he became agent-general in London.

[4] Vogel was then Treasurer of N.Z., and had come to London in Apr.
1871 to make arrangements for the ill-fated mail-steamer line between Auckland and San Francisco and his first public works loans. He met Kimberley
on 27 Mar. (mins. by Dealtry and Herbert on G.P.O. to C.O. 27 Mar.
1871. C.O. 209/225). Herbert later wrote: 'If NSW hangs back New
Zealand will perhaps be glad to undertake the Fijis. Mr. Vogel seemed to
think so' (min. 18 July, on Belmore to Kimberley 28 Apr. 1871. C.O.
201/563).

But Kimberley was eager to follow up the New South Wales plan. He reminded Gladstone that it was consistent with Liberal colonial policy elsewhere:

> we have not hesitated to place all the Indian tribes in British N. America under the Canadian Gov[ernmen]t, and, if responsible government is established at the Cape, & the troops are withdrawn from the frontier, the native tribes in that colony will be left to the control of the local authorities. Of course it may be answered that these are not conclusive reasons for assuming new responsibilities; but what is the alternative? If we could leave the British settlers in the Fijis entirely to themselves, the case would be different, but no one I believe proposes total abstinence from all interference. On the contrary we are about to give our Consul magisterial powers, which will involve us in responsibility & expense without attaining the end of providing a settled government.

If New South Wales was willing to annex Fiji, Kimberley could see 'no better solution to the problem'.[1] The Cabinet agreed.[2] Kimberley drafted a despatch to the governor of New South Wales on 29 July 1871, indicating that if the colony would undertake the government of Fiji the British Government would not object. Yet this clear declaration did not, in fact, appear in the despatch which was actually sent on 10 August.[3] An entirely new complexion had been put on the issue by news of a *coup d'état* in Fiji.

A small group of settlers at Levuka had proclaimed a constitutional monarchy in Fiji on 5 June 1871. The new régime contrived to rule the islands until 1874. Thakombau was made king; Ma'afu's support was won by leaving him as governor of Lau with the style of 'Viceroy'. A Cabinet of five Europeans, with Thakombau's brother and son, was led initially by Sydney Charles Burt as premier. The dominant personality, however, appears to have been the Minister of Interior Affairs, George Austin Woods, a retired naval officer, who took over the premiership at the end of 1871.[4] A new constitution,

[1] Kimberley to Gladstone 26 July 1871. *Gladstone Papers*, 44224/187.
[2] Cabinet mins. 29 July 1871. *Gladstone Papers*, 44639/85.
[3] Kimberley to Belmore 10 Aug. (draft crossed out), after Belmore to Kimberley 28 Apr. 1871. C.O. 201/563.
[4] Burt, an auctioneer in Sydney, went to Fiji as an absconding debtor; but G. C. Henderson ('History of Government in Fiji, 1760–1875', 2 vols. in typescript, 1941, microfilm copy in the School of Oriental and African Studies,

with plenty of high-sounding phrases from the Declaration of Independence, was approved on 18 August 1871 by a new Legislative Assembly.[1] Hawaii was obviously the model for this attempt at constitutional monarchy. The United States immediately recognized the new régime.[2] Several Australian newspapers were favourable. But Edward March, the British consul, soon became one of the chief enemies of Thakombau's Government.

News of the June *coup* upset Kimberley's plan for annexation by New South Wales. Should he now recognize the new Government ? Both the Foreign Office and the Government's Law Officers saw no reason for refusing.[3] In the Colonial Office, however, Herbert adhered to the New South Wales plan. Knatchbull-Hugessen supported him. 'It is *most undesirable*', he insisted, 'that the Future of Fiji should be complicated by indiscreet recognitions of the authority of native chiefs who have not an admitted authority of any extent.'

Once again the ill-defined lines of responsibility in Whitehall hampered the formulation of policy. The various Departments of State were unable to agree over Thakombau's Government.

This is rather a puzzling matter [said Kimberley] but I do not think the Colonial Office should take the responsibility of deciding it. If the Fiji's were annexed . . . it will devolve on the Col: Off: to deal with them,

---

London, ii, p. 199) says he was an able man who went to Fiji to retrieve his fortunes and pay his creditors. Woods came from a naval family, but after creditable service he was only Lieut. when he retired aged 40. He then did marine survey work in the colonies; Brewster (*King of the Cannibal Isles*, pp. 149-50) says in Victoria, Scholefield (*The Pacific*, p. 87) says N.Z., perhaps both. Brewster says he was known in the navy as 'Magnificent George' and that Thakombau was so impressed that he made him a member of the Mbau Royal House. Woods told Goodenough (*Journal*, ii, 28 Dec. 1873) that while he was at Auckland he heard that the Germans had designs on Fiji, and he made up his mind to save the islands for Britain. A short while after this at Sydney an agent from Fiji offered him £1,000 to survey the Nanuku passage in Fiji, but when he arrived on 9 Apr. 1871 he found that the authorities could not pay him. He was about to return to Sydney when Thakombau asked him to assist in the Govt. because the whites said Woods was 'unconnected with Fiji'.

[1] Printed copy of Constitution in F.O. 58/122, p. 81.

[2] Brookes, *International Rivalry*, p. 373.

[3] F.O. to C.O. 31 July 1871 (encl. C.O. report). C.O. 201/567.

but at present they are foreign, and to be dealt with by the Foreign Office.[1]

Kimberley was also hesitant because he had no proof that New South Wales wanted Fiji. He had only the private word of the agent-general in London, Charles Cooper. Knatchbull-Hugessen made up his mind quickly and, as usual, was impatient for action. 'Our ancestors would have accepted the cession of the islands and laid the foundations of a thriving European Colony. We prefer the drifting system . . .'[2] But Kimberley would never be rushed. He took two months to make up his mind. Finally he recommended, in October 1871, against the advice of his department, that Thakombau's Government should be recognized as the *de facto* authority.

Once again, the reason for Kimberley's decision can be found in his respect for Australian opinion. While he was still drafting his New South Wales plan in Whitehall, the premier of New South Wales had informed the governor in Sydney that such a scheme was impossible. The premier's outburst was occasioned by Kimberley's reply to Victoria of 16 March 1871 conveying the Cabinet's decision not to annex and to support the creation of a stable Government in Fiji. Martin declared that there was no precedent for what was virtually an invitation to the settlers to form a Government. New South Wales, he continued, would never annex Fiji. It was a field of colonization for Europeans rather than Australians. It was an imperial question, he declared, and Britain should annex Fiji.[3]

The Colonial Office took Martin's assertions calmly. Cooper, the agent-general, who had been Martin's predecessor as premier, said Martin's views were personal.[4] Herbert, who opposed the recognition of Thakombau's Government, continued to advocate the New South Wales plan, as it would conveniently avoid either a foreign or independent Government in Fiji. He compared the New South Wales plan to the Government policy in Basutoland, which, he said, 'on the

[1] Ibid. Mins. by Herbert 5 Aug., Knatchbull-Hugessen 6 Aug., and Kimberley 7 Aug. 1871.

[2] Min. by Knatchbull-Hugessen 7 Sept., on Canterbury to Kimberley 14 July 1871. C.O. 309/100.

[3] Decision of N.S.W. Cabinet 8 Aug., in Belmore to Kimberley 9 Aug. 1871. C.O. 201/564.

[4] Ibid. Min. by Herbert 21 Oct. 1871.

application of the legislature of the Cape of Good Hope has recently
been annexed to the Colony'. Actually, it was a most unfortunate
analogy. The annexation of Basutoland had taken place in 1868,
before Herbert joined the Colonial Office. The Government had
intended the Cape to annex Basutoland, but the governor had, in fact,
annexed it to the Crown.[1]

Kimberley's second decision on Fiji was really a compromise. He
did not abandon the New South Wales plan altogether, nor did he
adopt the proposal of outright recognition. He preferred a more
flexible policy. The possibility of annexation to New South Wales was
left open. Thakombau's Government was afforded *de facto* recognition. Although not a clean-cut decision to satisfy people like Knatchbull-Hugessen, in an uncertain situation it did not commit the Government to any rigid course. Professor Legge's stricture that it was a
'precipitate decision', taken after 'lack of serious consideration', is
surely unjust.[2]

Kimberley brought the matter before the Cabinet. The moment
was ripe for announcing a new policy. The agent-general was plead-
ing that the New South Wales plan should be kept open,[3] and the
Victorian Government clamoured for directions as to its attitude to
Thakombau's Government.[4] The Cabinet accepted Kimberley's proposal on 27 October 1871, and the draft of his despatch was approved
on the 31st.[5] The Australian governors were all informed by a
circular despatch of 3 November 1871 that they should treat Thakombau's ministry as the Government *de facto*. New South Wales was
also informed that it was still open for the colony to consider annexation.[6] Kimberley had tried hard to keep the Fiji question out of the

---

[1] de Kiewiet, *British Colonial Policy*, pp. 222–4.

[2] Legge, *Britain in Fiji*, p. 122.

[3] Kimberley to Granville 25 Oct. 1871 (copy). *Kimberley Papers*, A/43.

[4] Canterbury to Kimberley 1 Aug. 1871. C.O. 309/100.

[5] Cabinet Min. 27 Oct. 1871. *Gladstone Papers*, 44639/111; and min.
by Kimberley, 'for the Cabinet Tues' (the 31st), 29 Oct., on Canterbury to
Kimberley 1 Aug. 1871. C.O. 309/100.

[6] Kimberley to Belmore 3 Nov. 1871 (draft approved by Cabinet). C.O.
201/564. Some idea of the limited status accorded to Fiji by the policy of
de facto recognition can be gathered by a note made by the legal adviser to
the C.O. when the F.O. considered receiving a plenipotentiary from the
Orange Free State. 'The O[range] River Government is no doubt indepen-

Colonial Office and failed.   For the second time, he took the initiative
in recommending Britain's policy.

---

dent of the Crown, but so is Thakombau's [Govt.] and we should not recognise a Plenipotentiary from that great potentate though we have sent him a
Consul.'   F.O. 84/1347.

8. *Decisions about the South Pacific, 1872-3*

BRITAIN's new policy in Fiji was short-lived. *De facto* recognition could only be a stopgap. The New South Wales plan remained open, but formal recognition of Thakombau's régime was possible if his Government succeeded. Kimberley's policy was intended to give the British Government plenty of room for manœuvre. But its freedom of action proved to be illusory. In 1871 and 1872 a new clamour for annexation arose because the Fiji question became linked with the wider problem of kidnapping in the Pacific.

Britain tried to regulate the transport of labourers in British ships by the passage of the Pacific Islanders Protection Act in June 1872. But Fiji lay outside British jurisdiction. Having encouraged Thakombau's Government, Britain could hardly interfere with the labour traffic within the Fiji Islands. Therefore, on account of the labour traffic, fresh proposals for the annexation of Fiji were made in 1871.

A tragedy brought matters dramatically to a head. In December 1871 the news reached London that Bishop Patteson of Melanesia had been murdered. The saintly missionary, a man much admired by Gladstone, had been clubbed to death on 20 September 1871 at Nukapu in the Santa Cruz Islands, in an act of retaliation following a visit by kidnappers.[1] The incident focused a blaze of publicity on to something Whitehall had long been aware of. Over the past decade many volumes of kidnapping case-histories had been carefully collected by the Foreign Office.[2] The Colonial Office had also been studying the operation of regulations made by the Queensland Government in 1868 covering the work of islanders on colonial plantations.[3] But the regulation of the traffic in British ships had been prevented by the Treasury for the same reasons as it prevented consular jurisdiction in Fiji. Notorious kidnapping cases now received mounting publicity,

[1] Eye-witness account in Ad. to C.O. 14 June 1872. C.O. 309/107.
[2] The correspondence is gathered together in F.O. 58, vols. 125–9.
[3] See Parnaby, *Britain and the Labor Trade*, ch. 3.

240

until the flood of indignation in 1872 made action imperative. Patteson's murder in 1871 did for Polynesia and Melanesia what Livingstone's death was to do for Central Africa in 1873.

THE KIDNAPPING PROBLEM, 1860–72

Indentured immigration, Indian coolie emigration and the recruiting of Pacific Island workers are familiar enough features in colonial history. The introduction of Indians into Fiji after 1879 may now be regarded as the most notable by-product of British rule. But 'blackbirding' in the Pacific had become a notorious trade by the 1860's. It arose because of a sharp rise in the demand for labour in the early 1860's, when guano from Peru's off-shore islands became a valuable fertilizer in the development of scientific farming, and when the cotton shortage induced by the American Civil War caused optimistic planting in Queensland and Fiji. For collecting guano and cultivating cotton, Pacific Islanders were recruited by fair means or foul, and shipped off to Peru, Queensland, or Fiji.

From all accounts the Peruvian traffic was the cruellest. A British naval officer called it 'as revolting a description of slave dealing as ever was practiced on the West Coast of Africa'.[1] Many outrageous incidents were reported before British and French pressure caused the Peruvian Government to prohibit the traffic in 1863. But Whitehall had also to consider urgently British law in relation to kidnapping by British subjects. After four Samoans had been kidnapped in 1859, the Attorney-General of New South Wales, who tried to prosecute the shipowner in the Supreme Court of the colony, found there were no powers to subpoena witnesses from outside the colony. A Bill, drafted in England in 1862, to empower governors to do this had to be dropped because the Treasury refused to sanction expenditure on prosecutions.[2]

Yet the problem could not be evaded. Islanders were introduced into Queensland from 1862. In five years Captain Robert Towns imported 382 New Hebrideans, on one- to three-year contracts to work on his cotton plantations, all of whom went back when their contracts expired. Importations into Fiji started about 1864 and, by

[1] Richards to Synge May 1863 (copy). C.O. 58/98, p. 217.
[2] Parnaby, op. cit., pp. 7–15.

the end of 1869, 1,649 immigrants were recorded.[1] The British
Government was constantly reminded of this growing traffic by the
French Government, by Scottish Presbyterian missionaries in the New
Hebrides, who feared retaliations on the missionaries, and by the
Aborigines Protection Society at home.

Gradually the pattern of 'blackbirding' became evident. Labour
recruiters from Fiji and Queensland and some from New Zealand
operated chiefly in the New Hebrides, Solomons and Santa Cruz
Islands. Queensland's laws of 1868 did not prevent kidnapping. Yet
measures to solve the problem were deferred because of the obscurity
in Whitehall as to who was really responsible. The Treasury frustrated the Colonial Office initiative in 1862. The Colonial Office
usually referred kidnapping allegations to the Foreign Office, since
kidnapping was put in the 'slave-trade' category in which the Foreign
Office had a wealth of experience.

Three particular cases became public in 1869 which added urgency
to the problem. The significant feature of them all was the failure of
the authorities to sustain a case against the perpetrators. One accusa-
tion, in the *Latona* case, was not substantiated. But as it was trans-
mitted by one of the colonial zealots, Gladstone's friend, Arthur
Kinnaird, Liberal Member of Parliament for Perth, it caused the
Colonial Office to resurrect the Bill of 1862. In the *Young Australia*
case, in Sydney, the defence secured a remission of sentence because a
witness had sworn on a translation of the New Testament and not the
whole Bible. In the case of the *Daphne* prosecution, also in Sydney,
a charge of slaving was dismissed in the Vice-Admiralty Court, and
Commander Palmer of the Royal Navy was made to pay costs.[2] This
matter was later raised in Parliament, and Palmer had his costs refunded
and was promoted in the service.[3] The lesson of all these cases was
clear: the existing laws were completely inadequate.

In 1870 the Colonial Office reopened the question of imperial
legislation. It did not try to abolish recruiting outright. The system
in Queensland showed that labour immigration could be regulated.

[1] Memo. by Buckley. F.O. 58/125, pp. 97–112.
[2] Parnaby, op. cit., pp. 16–22; T. Dunbabin, *Slavers of the South Seas*,
Sydney, 1935, pp. 164–7.
[3] 3 *Hansard*, 200, col. 1427; G. Palmer, *Kidnapping in the South Seas*,
Edinburgh, 1871, pp. 104–51.

Bishop Patteson himself had said, 'I do not advocate the suppression
but the regulation of this traffic'. The real bar to action was the
Treasury's refusal to sanction the cost of prosecutions. Kimberley
reminded the Treasury of the 1862 Bill. But, after the lapse of eight
years, the Treasury presumed the matter was not urgent, and suggested
that a better solution was the extension of the jurisdiction of the New
South Wales Supreme Court. When the Colonial Office insisted that
prosecutions should be an imperial charge, the Treasury refused.

The Treasury's decision brought the controversy in London to a
head. Kimberley informed the Foreign Office in December 1870
that the Treasury decision rendered action impossible. Yet at the
very same time, H. C. Rothery, the Treasury's adviser on the slave-
trade, admitted that kidnapping was 'slave trading in the largest sense
of the term'.[1] Millions of pounds had been spent suppressing the
West African slave-trade, but funds were apparently not available for
prosecutions in the Pacific. In a Samoan kidnapping allegation involving a British ship commanded by 'Bully' Hayes, the most notorious
freebooter in the Pacific,[2] the Treasury tried to pass the cost of the
prosecution to the Australian colonies. Rogers was outraged by their
attitude:

> This is the kind of letter which makes me think that England is ceasing
> to deserve the rank of a first class power, and had better abandon it.
> Here is a great duty attaching to her, if it attaches to anyone, as the
> great maritime power of the world, and as the centre from which these

[1] Report by Rothery, 15 Oct., in F.O. to C.O. 7 Dec. 1870. C.O.
201/560.
[2] William Henry Hayes became a legendary figure and appears as the
most dashing of the Pacific pirates. The legend reads as follows: He came
from Cleveland, Ohio. He was tall, powerful, and took to shooting people
when in a temper. He liked poodles and had many wives. Between 1858
and 1876 he turned up in most of the main ports of the Pacific, Australasia
and South-East Asia, and he was a continual embarrassment to the F.O.,
who feared he might be a British subject. He was killed in 1876 by the cook
on his ship. (See Dunbabin, op. cit., pp. 223–34; H. Stonehewer-
Cooper, *Coral Lands*, London, 1880, ii, pp. 59–65.)
In Dec. 1869 Chief Mauga of Pago Pago in Samoa seized Hayes and
handed him to Williams, the British consul. But there was no jail to keep
him until a British warship arrived, and on 1 Apr. he slipped away. Williams
to F.O. 3 Oct. 1870. F.O. 58/118, p. 454.

obnoxious proceedings directly or indirectly proceed, and the Treasury refuse to aid putting down all these abuses for fear of risking a few hundred or thousand pounds.

This seems to me governing an Empire in the spirit of a subordinate department of the Inland Revenue Office.[1]

Monsell, the parliamentary under-secretary, appealed to Kimberley to persuade the Cabinet to reverse the Treasury decision. Thus, on 14 January 1871, Kimberley ordered a case to be prepared.

On the very same day Knatchbull-Hugessen was 'installed as Under-Secretary'[2] and soon he, a former junior Lord, joined in the denunciation of the Treasury. He pointed out that a Treasury decision could not be final:

> the matter must have been fully considered by the Cabinet, as the *whole Government — and not the Treasury alone —* will have to bear the responsibility of having refused to defray from Imperial funds any portion of the expenses incurred in bringing to punishment persons guilty of an offence peculiarly repugnant to the public opinion of this country.[3]

Miss Brookes has claimed that the Cabinet had in fact decided already on imperial legislation,[4] but there is no record of a Cabinet discussion at this stage. The Treasury, indeed, still held firm. When the draft of a Bill making kidnapping a felony was sent for consideration by the Australian governors on 20 April 1871, the colonies were asked, at the express wish of the Treasury, if they would pay for prosecutions. British consuls were warned, at the same time, that the Treasury would not defray the costs of any prosecutions they brought. Knatchbull-Hugessen was so distressed by the Treasury's attitude that he wanted to tell Their Lordships what 'everybody outside their office' thought of them.[5]

---

[1] Min. by Rogers 2 Jan. 1871 on Treas. to C.O. 30 Dec. 1870. C.O. 201/560.   [2] *Brabourne Diary*, iv, p. 519.

[3] Min. by Knatchbull-Hugessen 27 Mar., on F.O. to C.O. 25 Mar. 1871. C.O. 201/567.

[4] Brookes, *International Rivalry*, p. 369.   Kimberley noted that Granville agreed to circulars to the Australian govs., but did not mention the Cabinet.

[5] Min. by Knatchbull-Hugessen on Board of Trade to C.O. 27 July 1871.   C.O. 201/565.

Kimberley once more took the initiative. The departments were all at loggerheads. The Treasury wanted to foist the responsibility on the colonies. The Law Officers pointed out that imperial legislation alone would not prevent the growing slave-trade in the Pacific. New South Wales, Queensland and New Zealand were the only colonies to offer to pay certain costs. The Foreign Office tried to get the Colonial Office to complete the matter; the Colonial Office sent the Bill back to the Foreign Office. The real focus of responsibility seemed to be as blurred as ever. But as in the Fiji case, so now with the Kidnapping Bill, it was Kimberley who took over. Came the news of Patteson's murder in December 1871, and Herbert felt that the rest of Whitehall was looking to the Colonial Office for a lead.[1]

The kidnapping problem led Kimberley back to the Fiji question. 'The real difficulty is Fiji,' he said.[2] Both questions should be looked at as one, insisted Herbert. He thought the Government of Fiji should be encouraged to adopt the Queensland regulations as a condition of formal recognition by Britain. He agreed that the Treasury made it very difficult to act. But some of the Australian colonies had agreed to co-operate. Herbert suggested that the home Government should pass the Bill, agree to bear certain costs, instruct the Admiralty to enforce the Act, then invite Thakombau's Government to do the same.[3] Kimberley took over the sponsorship of a measure which was a Foreign Office responsibility. He presented the Pacific Islanders Protection Bill to the Cabinet on 22 June 1872.[4] The Government accepted it and the Treasury was finally forced to sanction the expenses of seizing offenders. Knatchbull-Hugessen was chosen to shepherd the Bill in the House of Commons.[5]

The only opposition likely was from advocates of complete abolition.

[1] Ibid. Min by Herbert 12 Dec. 1871—'public attention has now been called to the matter by the death of Bishop Patteson'.

[2] Kimberley to Granville 16 Dec. 1871 (enclosing memo. by Herbert 15 Dec.) *Granville Papers*, P.R.O. 30/29/55, p. 247.

[3] Memo. by Herbert 15 Dec. 1871 in F.O. 58/122, p. 230.

[4] Cabinet Min. 22 Jan. 1872. *Gladstone Papers*, 44640/6. The E. African slave-trade was also discussed.

[5] Kimberley to Knatchbull-Hugessen 26 June 1872. *Brabourne Diary*, iv, p. 588.

There was widespread support for the Bill both in Britain and Australia.[1] Most poignant of all was Patteson's own appeal for imperial
legislation, published a year after his death: 'The African Slave Trade
was put down as a thing evil in itself, a disgrace to humanity and a
practical repudiation of Christianity. People did not stop to enquire
further'.[2] It was also learnt that the United States had a similar Bill
before Congress. The anti-kidnapping agitation reached its fulfilment
on 27 June 1872 when Kimberley despatched the Pacific Islanders
Protection Act to the Australasian governors. Regulations which had
been first mooted a decade before had at last been made.

THE DEMAND FOR A PROTECTORATE IN FIJI, 1872

Gladstone's Government was not allowed to sit back and wait for the
Kidnapping Act to produce results. Others beside Herbert and Kimberley realized that the unsolved Fiji question was inextricably bound
up with the kidnapping problem. It was logical that the idea of
annexation would be revived. *The Age* of Melbourne criticized the
Act, in November 1871, and scorned a Colonial Office led by 'titled
statesmen of the Carnarvon, Buckingham and Kimberley stamp'. It
demanded the annexation of a number of islands.[3] Alderman McArthur
gave notice on 6 March 1872 of a resolution in Parliament proposing
the establishment of a protectorate in Fiji.

McArthur forced the Colonial Office to consider the question of
expansion in the Pacific seriously. His proposition caused a definite
split in the political leadership of the Colonial Office similar to that
which followed Glover's dismissal in West Africa. Knatchbull-

[1] From the reformed Presbyterian Church of Scotland, the Mayor of
Leeds, the people of Falmouth, the Australian Methodist Conference, the
Glasgow and Edinburgh Synods of the United Presbyterian Church of
Scotland, the Edinburgh Ladies Emancipation Society, and from Anthony
Trollope. The latter was in Australia, and in his book, *Australia and New
Zealand*, London, 1873, there is a long defence of the Queensland traffic
(i, pp. 132-48), but he admits there was kidnapping in the Fiji traffic.
Trollope to Kimberley 12 Dec. 1871. *Kimberley Papers*, A/27^t.
[2] Memo. by Patteson 11 Jan. 1871. *Accounts and Papers* (1872), xliii,
p. 830.
[3] *The Age*, 4 Nov., clipping in Canterbury to Kimberley 23 Nov. 1871.
C.O. 309/101.

Hugessen criticized the ambiguity of Britain's attitude to Fiji: 'We have done all we can do by legislation, at home and in the colonies to suppress this traffic. . . . Even then, Fiji will be an obstacle and stumbling block in our way . . . Fiji is drifting on and on'.[1] Lord Enfield, parliamentary under-secretary for foreign affairs, wanted a British protectorate in Fiji. Knatchbull-Hugessen favoured annexation. Three days before the debate on McArthur's motion he wrote:

> The truth is that from the surpassing love of Economy which rules English statesmen now-a-days, and from the dread of incurring responsibilities which (fortunately for our English colonies today) our forefathers did not entertain, we have, wisely or unwisely, let slip the opportunity of acquiring a new Colony — or group of colonies — which would probably have cost less than we imagined . . . this matter will perhaps be judged with greater accuracy some twenty years hence.

Kimberley reminded his forthright under-secretary that the New South Wales plan was still open, and that *de facto* recognition had been granted to Thakombau's Government.[2] Unfortunately Granville had not yet instructed the consul to announce *de facto* recognition. Kimberley had to remind Granville in June 1872 to do what had been decided seven months before.[3]

The Fiji debate took place in the House of Commons on 25 June 1872 — the day after Disraeli's Crystal Palace speech. McArthur endorsed the new emphasis which the Conservative leader had placed on the Empire, and claimed that Fiji was the 'key to Polynesia'. In the interests of Christianity, commerce and liberty, he called for a protectorate like that on the Gold Coast. Admiral Erskine, seconding the resolution, also referred to the Gold Coast Protectorate.[4] One

[1] Min. by Knatchbull-Hugessen 13 June, on Ad. to C.O. 10 June 1872. C.O. 201/571.

[2] Mins. by Knatchbull-Hugessen and Kimberley 22 June, on administrator, N.S.W., to Kimberley 19 Apr. 1872. C.O. 201/569.

[3] Min. by Herbert 21 June, on administrator, N.S.W., to Kimberley 19 Apr. 1872. C.O. 201/569. Brookes, *International Rivalry*, p. 375, suggests March heard of the 1871 decision second-hand from a naval officer in June 1872.

[4] 3 *Hansard*, 212, cols. 192–219. Admiral Erskine had been in touch with the Wesleyans in 1870. He had also visited the Fiji Islands in 1849, where he had met Calvert and Thakombau. He had impressed the latter with the fire-power of a British warship, and he had, himself, greatly approved

I.F.T.—I

Member mentioned the 'annexation' of Samoa by the United States.

This last point, strictly inaccurate though it was, was not lost on Knatchbull-Hugessen. That very day, before the debate, Mr Dealtry, head of the Australasian Department, had shown him some despatches from Washington and Samoa about the 'cession' of Pago Pago harbour to an American naval officer on 17 February 1872, and the arrival shortly afterwards of a German warship on a similar mission. The truth of these reports will be discussed later,[1] but the possibility of German or American intervention in Samoa had long been dreaded by the New Zealanders.

The Colonial Office had recently rejected a proposal that New Zealand should assume a protectorate over Samoa. In fact, in his private minutes, Kimberley had not completely closed the door to New Zealand ambitions. He adhered to the doctrine of qualified restraint. Just as he had left New South Wales free to act in Fiji, so on Samoa, he said, 'we *might* wish to change our mind hereafter (perhaps in the form of allowing New Zealand to annex some of the islands in the name of the Crown)'.[2] Information about German activities had also been received from elsewhere. Viscount Canterbury, the governor of Victoria, commenting on the recognition of Thakombau's Government, expressed his fear that Germany might assume a protectorate in Fiji. Moreover, before sealing his despatch on 31 December 1871, he saw the German warship *Nymphe* enter Melbourne, bound for the South Seas.[3]

Knatchbull-Hugessen was aware of these facts when he heard the news about Pago Pago. He had supported the refusal to let New Zealand take Samoa. But on the day of the Fiji debate he wrote:

---

of the work of the Wesleyans. See J. E. Erskine, *Journal of a Cruise among the Islands of the West Pacific including the Feejees*, London, 1853, pp. 165-279. [1] See below, pp. 260-1.

[2] Note by Kimberley 22 Feb., on F.O. to C.O. 16 Feb. 1872. C.O. 209/228. S. Masterman, *The Origins of International Rivalry in Samoa, 1845-1884*, London, 1934, pp. 92-93, suggests that the C.O. did not consider the matter seriously. This neglects Kimberley's wider, private, view. He crossed out Herbert's draft reply to N.Z. giving good reasons for non-intervention in Samoa, because he thought that if they later changed their minds such opinions on record might be an embarrassment.

[3] Canterbury to Kimberley 30 Dec. 1871. C.O. 309/101.

The Americans are alive to the advantage to a naval power of having an 'advance post in the Pacific'. They could hardly object, after this, to our annexation of Fiji, did our Policy tend that way.[1]

In the light of these facts his strange speech in the Fiji debate is understandable.

In many ways it was a skilful speech. He could not let his side down, but he obviously sympathized with McArthur. So he appeared to sit on the fence, and made some general comments on colonial policy. The African analogies were inadmissible, he said. In South Africa, the Government did not want new territories and felt that annexation of new territory to the Cape was the best solution. On the Gold Coast he pointed out that the Elmina cession in 1872 had been intended to remove the source of trouble caused by the proximity of British and Dutch forts. This was all quite correct, but it begged the question. Previous speakers had referred to the Gold Coast protectorate, the wide, ill-defined area where British officers had exercised some jurisdiction since the 1830's. In the light of Earl Grey's ideas,[2] quoted by Erskine in the debate, a plausible case might have been made for this system in Fiji, although the Colonial Office was, of course, becoming acutely aware of the limitations of the Gold Coast system. Yet Knatchbull-Hugessen did not say this. It would have supported the Government's case, which he disagreed with. This part of the speech was a masterpiece of evasion.

Turning finally to Fiji he summed up the arguments for and against annexation. There was British settlement and investment in Fiji, the islands would provide a base for commerce and for the Pacific fleet; but the inhabitants had not expressed a wish for annexation, which might be costly, as the Maori Wars had cost £20 million. As for a protectorate, he had 'never been able to find out exactly what a protectorate meant'. Finally, he wished to make his own position on colonial policy clear. He did not advocate a policy which made it a rule that whenever annexation would benefit a place Britain should annex it. But he did not undervalue colonies and believed that the person who ever laid down a doctrine of non-extension would 'sound the first note of their country's retrogression in the scale of nations'.[3]

[1] Min. by Knatchbull-Hugessen 25 June, on F.O. to C.O. 22 June 1872. C.O. 309/107.   [2] See above, p. 86.

[3] 3 *Hansard*, 212, cols. 205–11.

For all his evasion, his real feelings on the Fiji resolution were not lost on the House. *The Times* commented: 'officially bound to curse he ended up by nearly blessing it altogether'. One is also tempted to believe that Knatchbull-Hugessen was trying to exonerate himself from Disraeli's strictures at the Crystal Place on the previous day. It was, therefore, left to the prime minister to state the Government's view.

Gladstone scored points off McArthur, and he deplored the idea of a protectorate — 'it might be anything or nothing; it was the most shadowy of all relations'. Annexation might be beneficial to Fiji, but he pointed out that in New Zealand the Maori population had declined by about 80,000 in 30 years. Above all, the Government had no real evidence that the Fijians wanted British rule. Gladstone then made one of his most important statements of colonial policy. He promised that

> So far as it was possible to lay down an abstract and general rule with regard to annexation, he was prepared to say that HMG would not annex any territory, great or small, without the well-understood and expressed wish of the people to be annexed, freely and generously expressed, and authenticated by the best means the case would afford.[1]

He felt Fiji did not meet these conditions, and the House agreed by a majority of fifty-one. The prime minister's statement was consistent with Kimberley's 1870 policy; the door was not closed, but a decision was postponed. The Government appeared to be taking one thing at a time, and were awaiting the results of the Kidnapping Act.[2]

On the day after the Fiji debate, the Colonial Office reminded the Foreign Office that it was time Consul March had some instructions as to his relations with Thakombau's Government. Herbert suggested that the consul should stop opposing the Fijian Government, but withhold full recognition until satisfied that it could regulate the labour traffic.[3]

THE DECISION TO SEND GOODENOUGH AND LAYARD TO FIJI, 1873

In Fiji British prestige declined rapidly. March's relations with Thakombau's ministers were so bad that they complained to the

[1] 3 *Hansard* 212, col. 217. Division: Ayes 84, Noes 135.
[2] Ibid. cols. 81–91. Speeches by Kimberley and Granville in House of Lords, 24 June 1872.
[3] C.O. to F.O. 26 June 1872. F.O. 58/133, p. 278.

Foreign Office.[1]   The consul found his position desperate.   Certain British subjects, who swore allegiance to the Fijian Government, considered themselves beyond British law.   Others found Thakombau's role inadequate and formed self-protection organizations.   A 'Constitutional Party' had formed by October 1871, to secure the release of a man arrested by the Government.   Resentful Fijians, on the other hand, drove some of the settlers from their lands.[2]   On one occasion the consul was ordered off a labour ship at pistol point by the owner — none other than Woods, the premier.   'I shall be compelled in sheer despair to quit Fiji,' he wrote in December 1871.[3]   The Foreign Office was preoccupied with the Kidnapping Bill at this time, and did not give March any help.

In 1872, the Woods Government met with growing opposition in Fiji.   With expenditure rising to £20,000, various financial devices were tried to get revenue.   But a settler group called the British Subjects Mutual Protection Association refused to pay taxes, being particularly incensed by the Government's decision to raise a Fijian army.   Some settlers quit, and trade declined, as tension mounted.[4] Crisis was only avoided because, in the absence of Woods, who went to Australia to raise a loan, John Bates Thurston, the former consul, and Swanston, Ma'afu's adviser, were persuaded to join the Government.   Thurston had been absent during the 1871 *coup d'état*, and his assumption of office in May 1872 as chief secretary gave Thakombau's Government a temporary boost.

Thurston soon became the dominant member of the Government, and thenceforth played a considerable, if highly controversial, part in the background of annexation.[5]   He was able to lull the British

---

[1] Burt to Granville 10 July 1871.   F.O. 58/121, p. 190.

[2] March to F.O. 27 Aug., 11 Oct., 30 Oct. 1871.   F.O. 58/120, pp. 179, 201, 226.

[3] Ibid. p. 255.   March to F.O. 14 Dec. 1871.

[4] March to F.O. 26 Jan. and 20 Mar. 1872.   F.O. 58/131, pp. 34, 82.

[5] Woods told Goodenough (*Journal*, ii, 28 Dec. 1873) what happened when he returned from Australia to find Thurston a minister.   He said Thurston insisted that two members of the Cabinet be dropped and that Swanston and Clarkson be elected instead.   When Woods offered to resign too, Thurston refused.   A favourable account of Thurston's role is given by D. Scarr, 'John Bates Thurston, Commodore Goodenough and the Rampant Anglo-Saxons in Fiji', *H.S.A.N.Z.* (1964), 11 (43), pp. 361–82.

Government's fears about Fiji by writing to inform Knatchbull-Hugessen, in September 1872, that Thakombau's Government was preparing legislation based upon the British Kidnapping Act of 1872.[1] It appeared, indeed, in London, that the policy of *de facto* recognition, combined with the Kidnapping Act, had solved the Fiji problem. Kimberley thought that the time had come for granting formal recognition to the Fiji Government.

For political reasons, this easy solution was not possible. Gladstone's statement in the House of Commons in June 1872 only succeeded in suppressing Fiji as a political issue for seven months. While the Admiralty attended to the enforcement of the Kidnapping Act, Granville decided to replace Consul March by someone who, coming fresh, might assist Thakombau's Government in its efforts against kidnapping. But neither the operation of the British Act, nor the progress of Thurston's ministry, gave cause for satisfaction. Kimberley began to wonder whether the labour traffic in British ships would not have to be abolished. There was also a growing conviction at home that the Fiji Government could not be relied on. It is true that the issue did not become public again in England until February 1873, but during the intervening months Knatchbull-Hugessen and Kimberley debated the matter behind the scenes as they did on West Africa and Malaya.

Their discussions focused on two particular problems. In the first place, there now appeared to be a distinct possibility of international conflict in the Pacific. Knatchbull-Hugessen was worried about German and American intentions. Bismarck had sent out the gunboat *Nymphe*, which had aroused suspicion in Australia. Although the captain had assured Vogel, now the premier of New Zealand, that Germany had no designs on Samoa, when Knatchbull-Hugessen read of this ship's arrival in Fiji, he wrote, '*Serve us right* if Germany annexes Fiji'. 'Why?' asked Kimberley, non-committal in face of such frankness. 'Because', Knatchbull-Hugessen retorted, 'we should have a foreign power in a position in the Pacific whence great annoyance might be inflicted upon the Australasian colonies, which position we might have occupied ourselves if we had so inclined.' Kimberley

---

[1] Thurston to Knatchbull-Hugessen 11 Sept. 1872.   C.O. 83/2.

did not subscribe to what he termed this 'Monro[e] Doctrine in the Pacific'.[1]

When Vogel voiced New Zealand's fears of German or American expansion, or the alternative possibility of the rise of a great independent Polynesian confederacy comprising Fiji, Tonga and Samoa, Kimberley wrote, 'I don't see how we are to interfere unless we are to lay down and enforce the doctrine that no European or American Power is to interfere in any part of the South Pacific but ourselves'.[2] Although Kimberley disliked the exclusiveness of the American Pago Pago treaty, Herbert was not, at this stage, alarmed at the possibility of American expansion:

> Probably they hope to be masters of the Pacific presently but both Canada and Australia may be ahead of them a hundred years hence. In the mean time the old dog England and her colonial puppies of course growl when any of the mangers which they cannot make use of is approached.[3]

In view of the recent decision of the *Alabama* tribunal, Knatchbull-Hugessen was cynical about the possible outcome of an Anglo-American clash. It would only end, he said, in arbitration favourable to the United States. This part of the Colonial Office discussion was remarkably unrealistic.

On the topic of Fiji itself, Knatchbull-Hugessen was more emphatic. He warned Kimberley in August 1872 that McArthur would try to get another debate on annexation in the coming parliamentary session. Kimberley tried for several months to 'postpone', to 'put by', to evade the issue. But final warning was given in February 1873 that the question would be made public. McArthur tabled a motion on 7 February. On the eighteenth he asked in the House of Commons if the (unanswered) memorial from Fiji in 1870 requesting protection had been received.[4] Finally, on the twenty-fourth, a telegram arrived

[1] Mins. on 23, 24 and 25 July, on F.O. to C.O. 22 July 1872. C.O. 201/571.

[2] Min. by Kimberley 4 Sept., on memo. by Vogel 9 June encl. in Bowen to Kimberley 26 June 1872. C.O. 209/225.

[3] Min. by Herbert 29 Oct., on Canterbury to Kimberley 7 Sept. 1872. C.O. 309/105.

[4] 3 *Hansard*, 214, col. 597. See above, p. 228. The F.O. did not send the C.O. a copy of the 1870 memorial until 6 Mar. 1873.

from Sir Hercules Robinson, the governor of New South Wales, indicating that a letter had been sent by Thurston asking the British Government, in Thakombau's name, if it would entertain an offer of the Fiji Islands.[1] A decision on Fiji now seemed unavoidable.

The respite gained by Gladstone's 1872 speech had expired. The Government would have to make up its mind by the time Thurston's letter arrived and McArthur's motion was debated. Kimberley immediately consulted the prime minister. It would seem, moreover, that Knatchbull-Hugessen's persistence had not been lost on his seemingly inert chief. Kimberley's non-committal replies to his forthright under-secretary in the latter part of 1872 probably hid a growing agreement with his views, for Kimberley now definitely advised Gladstone to annex Fiji.

Knatchbull-Hugessen, taking Robinson's telegram to be an outright offer of cession, used the same arguments as he used over West Africa. He warned Kimberley that refusal of the offer would probably lead to a hostile vote in Parliament. Although Herbert still preferred the New South Wales plan on grounds of economy,[2] Kimberley urged the prime minister to accept the cession. His argument could not be lightly dismissed by Gladstone. Kimberley reminded the prime minister that

> We are and shall be at great expense in attempting to put down kidnapping in the South Sea Islands. If Fiji were under British rule, we should cut away the root of this evil which would disappear if we had control over the European settlers in Fiji.[3]

Gladstone admitted that Fiji was a formidable question.[4] After talking over the telegram with Kimberley and Granville he decided they need not reply immediately, but should await Thurston's letter.[5]

[1] Robinson to Kimberley (telegram) 20 Feb. 1873. C.O. 201/573. Derrick, *History*, p. 222, suggests that the letter was prompted by the receipt in Fiji (14 Dec. 1872) of news of McArthur's intended motion. Henderson, 'Government in Fiji', ii, pp. 344–7, was sure the letter was sent in the expectation that the offer would be rejected; that it was part of a plot by Thurston and Woods to confound the opposition and create a despotic régime.

[2] Mins. by Knatchbull-Hugessen and Herbert 24 Feb. 1873 on Robinson's telegram.

[3] Kimberley to Gladstone 24 Feb. 1873. *Gladstone Papers*, 44225/10.

[4] Gladstone to Kimberley 25 Feb. 1873. *Kimberley Papers*, A/8c.

[5] Note by Kimberley 27 Feb. 1873. Ibid. A/43.

Gladstone's chief fear was that after Fiji they might be led on to further annexations. He could 'give no promise to be party to any arrangement for adding Fiji and all that lies beyond it to the care of this overdone and overburdened Government and Empire'.[1]

At least the political leaders of the Colonial Office were, for once, united. Although Herbert was still averse, and questioned whether Thurston's letter really represented Fijian wishes, Knatchbull-Hugessen turned to the weighty argument which he also emphasized in the West African discussions: 'I do not think we ought to reject the offer, *nor that a rejection would be sustained by the House of Commons or by Public Opinion in this Country*'[2]. There was some fear in the Foreign Office that if Fiji were taken the United States might annex Hawaii, where an American general had recently investigated the possibility of building a naval base. But Kimberley's cousin, Major James Wodehouse, H.M. consul-general in Honolulu, belittled these rumours,[3] and Lord Enfield advised Granville to support annexation.[4]

What should Kimberley advise? Thurston's letter would have to be answered. McArthur's motion was to be debated on 13 May 1873. Kimberley was convinced of the case for annexation, but he knew Gladstone's reluctance. Therefore he provided the prime minister with yet another method of postponement. He turned to the well-tried Victorian method of delay tactics. He suggested sending a commissioner to 'inquire and report' — possibly General Smythe, who went in 1860, or Sir Andrew Clarke, recently a useful adviser over the Ashanti War.[5]

Gladstone realized that Fiji was fast becoming a dangerous political issue. He was 'much exercised in mind about Fiji'. He knew that some of the Cabinet, and the 'world without', wanted to go further than he did.[6] He studied all the Fijian papers in May 1873. He

---

[1] Gladstone to Kimberley 26 Feb. 1873. Ibid. A/8c.

[2] Min. by Knatchbull-Hugessen 24 Apr., on Robinson to Kimberley 20 Mar. 1873. C.O. 201/573.

[3] Wodehouse to Granville 30 Aug. 1872. F.O. 58/132, p. 111; Gen. Schofield's report on Pearl Harbor, 8 May 1873, printed in *A.H.R.* (1925), 30, pp. 561–5.

[4] Mins. 30 Apr. and 1 May 1873. F.O. 58/139, pp. 295–6.

[5] Kimberley to Gladstone 30 Apr. 1873. *Gladstone Papers*, 44255/29.

[6] Gladstone to Kimberley 8 May 1873. *Kimberley Papers*, A/8c.

learnt that a deputation from the Aborigines Protection Society asked Kimberley on 12 May why, in view of Sir Bartle Frere's mission to get a slave-trade treaty from the Sultan of Zanzibar in 1872,[1] was no one sent to Fiji? There the inhabitants seemed about to suffer the fate of the Maoris.[2] The Cabinet also studied memoranda prepared by Consul March, now back in London, which supported the argument that another Power might step in if Britain did not annex. March suggested that Fiji would be easier to rule than New Zealand — a revenue of £12,000 might be expected, government would cost only £7,000, and four companies of marines, along with the ships of the squadron, would be sufficient for defence.[3]

The Cabinet was to have discussed Fiji on 24 May 1873.[4] But Gladstone made a last-minute attempt to avert a decision. He tried to get Kimberley to consider an idea of March's that the fiction of a united Fiji should be abandoned and the rival chiefs be left to govern their own people, with the British consul exercising jurisdiction over British subjects.[5] But Kimberley refused to retract. The Cabinet finally accepted his proposal for a commission on 7 June 1873.[6] Although for Gladstone this was only a postponement of decision, one suspects that for Kimberley the result was now a foregone conclusion. He had handled both the Fijian question, and the prime minister, skilfully.

    [1] After carefully collecting information about the E. African slave-trade in the 1860's the Church Missionary Soc. called in 1869 for a Select Committee, which met in 1871. Sir Bartle Frere was appointed Special Commissioner to the Sultan of Zanzibar in 1872 to get a treaty abolishing the slave-trade by sea. After Britain threatened to blockade his kingdom, the sultan signed a treaty on 5 June 1873. See R. Oliver, *The Missionary Factor in East Africa*, London, 1952, pp. 18–19; R. Coupland, *The Exploitation of East Africa, 1856–1890*, London, 1939, pp. 165–97.
    [2] Deputation described in *Australia and New Zealand Gazette*, 17 May 1873, in C.O. 83/4.
    [3] March's memos.: 'The State of Fiji', 7 May 1873; 'The American claims', 14 May 1873; 'Annexation of Fiji', 19 May 1873. F.O. 58/135, pp. 123, 176, 184.
    [4] Cabinet Min. 24 May 1873. *Gladstone Papers*, 44641/126.
    [5] Gladstone to Kimberley 29 May 1873. *Kimberley Papers*, A/8c.
    [6] Cabinet Min. 44641/128. Commodore Goodenough heard that Fiji 'was on' next day. Goodenough's *Journal*, 8 June 1873.

Actually the expense and publicity of a special commission of inquiry was avoided. The Government appointed Commodore Good-enough, who was about to take up the command of the Australasian Squadron, and Edgar Layard, March's successor as consul, to conduct the investigation. Gladstone was greatly impressed by Goodenough, a good churchman like himself, when they met on 10 June 1873. After the interview, the commodore recorded this impression of his task:

> The real question *therefore* is at once removed to *recognition* or *annexation* & Mr. Gladstone even more than Lord Kimberley said that I must report what wd. be most conducive to law & order and the best interests of the people black and white who inhabited, or are to inhabit these islands.
> Mr. Gladstone spoke seriously of the great disadvantage attending the acquisition of new colonies, the great difficulties of governing a country at the other end of the world . . .[1]

Now a decision had been taken, Kimberley tried to persuade McArthur to drop his motion, but he failed. Kimberley urged Gladstone to make the Cabinet's action clear to the House of Commons.[2]

McArthur rose in the House of Commons to recite the well-known arguments for annexation on 13 June 1873. It had been unworthy, he said, to expect New South Wales to take over Fiji. *De facto* recognition had been a very dangerous precedent. Referring to Glad-stone's statement in 1872, he hoped now to show a well-authenticated desire for annexation. With the help of liberal quotations from the *Fiji Times*, Thurston's letters and the kidnapping cases, and the per-tinent reminder that over a quarter of a million pounds had been spent in the past five years in attempting to suppress the East African slave-trade, McArthur came to his final entreaty. It was not only a matter of national interests. The Fiji question involved the cause of 'liberty, civilisation and Christianity' throughout the Pacific. He appealed to Gladstone to accept either the sovereignty or a protectorate of the Fiji Islands.

[1] Ibid. 10 June 1873. The full extract describing Goodenough's discus-sion with Gladstone and Kimberley is printed in my article, 'New Light on Commodore Goodenough's Mission to Fiji, 1873–74', *H.S.A.N.Z.* (1962), 10 (39), p. 273.

[2] Kimberley to Gladstone 24 May 1873. *Gladstone Papers*, 44641/126.

Gladstone replied frankly. Annexation seemed to him to be becoming a favourite topic with the House. It might be the 'chill of age' but he confessed that accessions of territory did not excite him. Since British trade with Fiji was small he was unconvinced by economic arguments. Conceding that the philanthropic arguments were important, he pointed out, nevertheless, that if McArthur's figures for Fijian church-going were correct the islands had the highest proportion of devout believers in Christendom. Gladstone also stressed the cost of the Maori Wars and said he could not permit the same errors in Fiji. Above all he wanted more information; therefore a commission would inquire and report. This was all the Government would do at the moment. A Government amendment to McArthur's resolution gained a majority of thirty-six.[1] But Gladstone admitted to the queen that it was a narrow escape.[2]

What had really happened was that Kimberley had provided another excuse for postponing the real decision on Fiji. As the Gladstone Government fell before Goodenough reported, it was never called upon to decide. But Kimberley had clearly travelled further than the prime minister on Fiji,[3] as he would do shortly over the Malay States and the Gold Coast. He had advised the annexation of Fiji as early as February 1873. Immediately after the Cabinet meeting of 7 June, he put to Gladstone four possible lines of action: consular jurisdiction, formal recognition of Thakombau's régime, protectorate, or annexation.[4] Goodenough's instructions were based on these choices, but in reality they eliminated three of them, leaving a fair impression of Kimberley's preference. He said consular jurisdiction would be difficult to justify unless the local Government was really incompetent. No arrangement that failed to regulate the labour traffic would be satisfactory. The Fiji Government could only be recognized *de jure* if it was fully accepted by the inhabitants, and if its labour laws were at

[1] 3 *Hansard*, 216, cols. 934–58. On Govt. amendment: Ayes 86, Noes 50.
[2] Gladstone to Queen Victoria 13 June 1873. *Royal Archives*, A.46/5.
[3] After the annexation in 1874 Kimberley wrote to Gladstone: 'As I expected the government have taken possession of Fiji . . . I think it would have been difficult to avoid taking Fiji' (4 Nov. 1874. *Gladstone Papers*, 44225/154). Knatchbull-Hugessen also wrote: 'it is tolerably certain that we would have annexed the islands'. *Brabourne Diary*, v, p. 733.
[4] Kimberley to Gladstone 10 June 1873. *Gladstone Papers*, 44225/54.

least as effective as Queensland's. Objections to a protectorate were 'obvious', as it would involve 'undefined responsibilities' with limited power of discharging them.

The final possibility was annexation. Here Kimberley offered no comment, other than to ask a series of practical questions: was cession desired by the inhabitants; what form of government would be most suitable; how would the Fijians be represented; what was the state of revenue and expenditure; what was the system of land tenure? Final phrases denying any British desire for annexation were really face-savers to satisfy Gladstone in case the instructions were later published.[1] The Foreign Office, on its part, instructed Layard, the new consul, to accord *de facto* recognition to the Thakombau Government, to avoid controversy, and to encourage the suppression of kidnapping.[2]

THE PROJECT FOR A CHARTERED COMPANY, 1873–4

Although Kimberley made up his mind about Fiji, on the wider question of the frontier in the South Pacific he was undecided. He certainly recognized the problem. He had put the question frankly to the Aborigines Protection Society deputation in May: Where was the process of annexation to end? Both he and Gladstone warned Goodenough that 'taking Fiji might result in our annexing all Polynesia'. Kimberley later admitted to Gladstone that 'we shall have further pressure for annexations in the Pacific'.[3]

Kimberley had, in fact, to face a number of further projects for expansion in the Pacific in his last days of office. A request for annexation was received from Rotuma. Australians became interested in New Guinea. New Zealand had its eyes on Samoa. But Kimberley took no final decisions about the Pacific. New Guinea, Rotuma and Samoa were left, along with Fiji, for the Conservatives in 1874. Beside Fiji, the most serious frontier problem was New Zealand's design on Samoa. The restraint of Julius Vogel, the premier, was one of the last acts of Gladstone's Government.

The Samoan Islands lie roughly 600 miles north-east of Fiji.

[1] Draft, after F.O. to C.O. 5 Aug. 1873.   C.O. 83/4.
[2] Granville to Layard 29 Sept. 1873 (draft seen and modified by Kimberley).   F.O. 58/135, p. 53.
[3] Kimberley to Gladstone 4 Sept. 1874.   *Gladstone Papers*, 44225/154.

British influence had predominated from the arrival of John Williams of the London Missionary Society in 1830 until the 1850's. Then the Hamburg firm of J. C. Godeffroy established its copra agency at Apia in 1857. By the 1860's Theodore Weber, the company's agent and consul for Hamburg (later for the North German Confederation), had consolidated a great commercial empire in the Pacific. He also, it seems, began purchasing land in Samoa with the idea of planting a

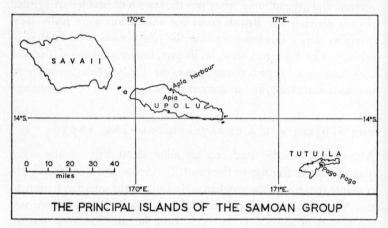

THE PRINCIPAL ISLANDS OF THE SAMOAN GROUP

German colony. The senior partner of Godeffroy's had been a friend of Bismarck's and official support was said to be forthcoming. But, although German gunboats appeared in the Pacific, Bismarck held back from colonial ventures. Weber was ordered to cultivate good relations with the Americans in Samoa.[1]

American interest in Samoa came from three sources. Henry Peirce, the United States minister-resident in Honolulu, advocated the acquisition of naval bases in the Pacific. W. H. Webb, the New York shipping-magnate, wanted coaling-stations for his Pacific steamer line. Some Californian land speculators invested in Samoa. Interest quickened in 1871 when one of Webb's agents reported that Pago Pago was 'the most perfectly land-locked harbour in the Pacific', and that Weber had plans in Samoa. Webb warned both the State Department and the New Zealand Government, which had subsidized

[1] Masterman, *International Rivalry in Samoa*, pp. 29–44, 56–59; Townshend, *Origins of Modern German Colonialism*, pp. 40–41; Morrell, *Britain in the Pacific Islands*; Stonehewer-Cooper, *Coral Lands*, ii, pp. 55–58.

Webb's short-lived mail steamer line between Auckland and San Francisco.[1]

In the early 1870's three different lines of national aspiration converged on Samoa. The New Zealand Government proposed in 1871 that the islands should be placed under the colony, on the precedent of the territories in South Africa adjoining the Cape. They hoped to forestall the Americans and Germans.[2] Commander Meade of the U.S.S. *Narragansett*, without authority from Washington, negotiated a treaty with Chief Mauga, in February 1872, securing exclusive rights to Pago Pago harbour as a naval base and coaling-station. Two weeks later Weber arrived at Pago Pago in a German gunboat and protested against Meade's treaty.[3] All these attempts came to nothing. The Senate did not ratify Meade's treaty, Kimberley refused Vogel's suggestions and Weber was not supported by Bismarck. But the American interest persisted.

A representative of the Central Polynesian Land and Commercial Company of San Francisco purchased 300,000 acres of land in Samoa for cotton-growing. He was entrusted with a petition to the United States Government requesting annexation. Although President Grant refused the request he appointed a friend, Colonel Steinberger, as special commissioner of the President to Samoa in March 1873. After visiting the islands, Steinberger returned to tell Grant in December 1873 that the Samoans wanted American protection.[4] The American mission to Samoa caused great consternation in New Zealand. Vogel, the premier, once more called upon the British Government to forestall the Germans and Americans in Samoa. Goodenough found that both Vogel and Sir James Fergusson, the governor, were preoccupied with schemes for acquiring Fiji and Samoa. There were rumours of gold discoveries.[5]

[1] G. H. Ryden, *The Foreign Policy of the United States in Relation to Samoa*, Yale, 1933, pp. 49–62.

[2] Vogel memo. 23 Dec. 1871 in Bowen to Kimberley 5 Jan. 1872. C.O. 209/226.

[3] This was the news Knatchbull-Hugessen read on the day of the 1872 Fiji debate. Clipping from *Sunday Morning Chronicle*, Washington, 2 June, in F.O. to C.O. 22 June 1872. C.O. 309/107.

[4] Masterman, op. cit., pp. 114–15; Ryden, op. cit., pp. 83–147.

[5] Goodenough's *Journal*, i, 29 Sept. 1873. Fergusson to Kimberley 1 Aug. 1873. C.O. 209/230.

The Colonial Office was by no means united over Samoa. Henry Holland, the legal adviser, hinted that after the New South Wales plan for Fiji, the New Zealand plan for Samoa was perfectly reasonable. But Herbert argued that Samoa was much further from New Zealand than Fiji from Sydney. There were no British settlers in Samoa. 'Mr. Vogel is everything just now', said Herbert, 'and this is one of his wild schemes.' Kimberley, having refused only a few months before New Zealand's proposals for Fiji, completely rejected Vogel's plan. Knatchbull-Hugessen preferred Fiji to Samoa. But he too pointed out that a flat rejection of New Zealand's plan was hardly consistent with the New South Wales plan for Fiji. Kimberley nevertheless sent his refusal by telegram on 14 October 1873.[1]

The New Zealanders were not deterred. On 22 December 1873 two far-reaching proposals reached the Colonial Office, both supported by Governor Fergusson. In the first, Vogel claimed that New Zealand should be considered as an instrument of British expansion in the South Pacific. A decision on Fiji in isolation was inadequate, Vogel insisted. A policy was needed for Polynesia as a whole. If expansion was to take place it should be comprehensive, not in an impromptu international scramble. There should either be a joint protectorate with Germany, the United States, France and Holland, or Britain should take everything. In the latter case Vogel pleaded that 'local efforts to maintain peaceful relations with an uncivilized race are far more successful than those directed by a distant Power.'[2]

Sir James Fergusson, the governor, who supported Vogel's ideas, pointed out that in Fiji a clash between Thakombau's Government and the settlers was only prevented by the 'anomalous interference' of the Royal Navy. He suggested that the imperial Government should consider annexing Tonga and Samoa as well as Fiji. Britain might govern them through a Resident as in the Indian states, or make them a province of New Zealand. The second proposal, from Mr Coleman Phillips, was for a chartered company on the lines

[1] Ibid. Mins. by Holland 2 Oct., Herbert 3 Oct., Kimberley 5 Oct., and Knatchbull-Hugessen 10 Oct. 1873.

[2] Vogel memo., 17 Oct., in Fergusson to Kimberley 22 Oct. 1873. C.O. 209/230. Cf. Ross, *New Zealand Aspirations*, pp. 106–14.

of the East India Company, to secure dominion over the South Pacific.[1]

The Colonial Office viewed the new schemes with disfavour. Kimberley agreed with Herbert that Vogel's projects were 'foolish' and 'impudent'. Herbert conceded that the idea of the company was more useful, but Kimberley did not like the look of it. He decided that New Zealand's expansionism was a question for the Cabinet to consider.[2] Kimberley sent the New Zealand proposals to Gladstone on 24 January 1874, commenting that they were 'most extravagant'.[3]

On the day before the Cabinet met to consider them, much fuller details of the chartered company plan arrived, again supported by Governor Fergusson. A South Pacific Trading Company was envisaged which would be guaranteed in New Zealand. 'The ultimate object which I have in view', said Vogel, 'is the establishment of the Polynesian Islands as one Dominion, with New Zealand the centre of Government: the Dominion like Canada, to be a British Dependency'. After receiving this, Herbert changed his mind about the Company. He said Vogel was 'the most audacious adventurer that perhaps has ever held power in a British Colony', and he regretted that the governor supported him.[4] But Fergusson did not enjoy being a governor. An ex-Tory Member of Parliament, who had held Government office, he missed parliamentary life, and doubtless his visionary premier added spice to his exile.

The Cabinet met to discuss the New Zealand projects on 27 January 1874.[5] Their views were not truly represented in the short negative despatch which was sent to the governor on 10 February. For in view of the political crisis at home a decision about the scheme was postponed until after a general election. Only a week later

[1] Fergusson to Kimberley 23 Oct. 1873. C.O. 209/230. For the Polynesia Co. see Ross, op. cit., pp. 115–24.
[2] Mins. by Herbert 24 Dec., and Kimberley 28 Dec., and Herbert 22 Dec., and Kimberley 23 Dec., on Fergusson 23 Oct. 1873. C.O. 209/230.
[3] Kimberley to Gladstone 24 Jan. 1874. *Gladstone Papers*, 44225/138.
[4] Min. by Herbert 26 Jan. 1874 on Vogel memo., 23 Nov., in Fergusson to Kimberley 24 Nov. 1873. C.O. 209/230.
[5] Cabinet Min. 27 Jan. 1874. *Gladstone Papers*, 44641/255.

Gladstone announced the dissolution of Parliament. Vogel's plan and the chartered company, like the annexation of Fiji, was left to Disraeli's Government.

The New Zealand plans were, however, remarkably consistent with Gladstone's colonial policy. For this reason they were favourably received by the prime minister. His real views were reflected in a draft reply which was never sent to New Zealand. Herbert and Kimberley were no doubt exhausted by the long debates over Fiji and other tropical regions. In reacting violently to the proposals from Vogel, who cast doubts on the adequacy of their new Fiji policy, they failed to recognize the distinct advantages of the New Zealand schemes. Gladstone conceded Vogel's claim that local efforts in relation with indigenous inhabitants were likely to be more successful than metropolitan control from afar. This was consistent with his words to Goodenough about the difficulty of governing at a distance.

Gladstone agreed that Vogel's memorandum was 'extremely crude' but he felt that the idea about local expertise was 'one piece of sound doctrine'. Moreover, he seemed to appreciate New Zealand's willingness to shoulder the burden as compared with New South Wales's attitude to Fiji:

> singular to say the memorandum seems to partake of the nature of a retraction as to New Zealand of the contemptuous answer received from (I think) New South Wales to our observation that they might if they pleased frame for consideration a plan for annexing or governing Fiji.

Therefore the original draft of the reply to New Zealand announced that the British Government was 'quite ready to consider any plan which may be framed in New Zealand for the purpose of directing such local efforts to the establishment of closer relations with the uncivilized races of Polynesia beyond the limits of the colony'.[1] Possibly the chartered company would have been acceptable. Even Herbert was slightly favourable at first. Gladstone showed no hostility. He simply noted after the Cabinet meeting 'the proposal is more

---

[1] *Gladstone Papers*, 44543/55. Gladstone to Kimberley 24 Jun 1874 (copy). Kimberley altered his despatch to N.Z. and incorporated Gladstone's ideas. Filed after Fergusson to Kimberley 22 Oct. 1873. C.O. 209/230.

enlarged — a joint stock company'.[1] The unsent draft has prompted Professor Ross to surmise that if Gladstone had not been defeated in 1874, Vogel's schemes for the Pacific might have been successful.[2]

It might appear surprising that Gladstone, not Kimberley, should favour Vogel's projects. Perhaps Kimberley was unduly influenced by Herbert's distrust of Vogel. Maybe, having won his way in the lengthy battle over Fiji, Kimberley gave up on the wider problem of the Pacific, just at the moment when Gladstone really became aware of it. Knatchbull-Hugessen had seemed to capitulate over Ashanti and Fiji just as Kimberley took his stand. Pioneering advocates often give up the cause, only after inspiring others to go further than they would.

Yet Gladstone's stillborn policy for the Pacific islands was quite consistent with Liberal colonial policy elsewhere. Since Cardwell's Colonial Secretaryship there had been an effort to withdraw the 'imperial factor' from various parts of the Empire. The Government tried to pass responsibility for administration, internal security, and frontier questions to the self-governing colonies. If new annexations were demanded, they were to be made by the 'colonial imperialists' who wanted them, not by the home Government. Gladstone's ministry approved Canadian expansion into Rupert's Land and the Cape's expansion into Basutoland and Griqualand West. It suggested New South Wales's expansion into Fiji and New Guinea. A policy of support for New Zealand expansion into Polynesia would have been perfectly logical. Vogel's scheme presented a way of avoiding a costly 'imperial factor' in the South Pacific. But Gladstone was defeated at the polls. The frontier question in the Pacific was another matter which was left for Carnarvon's decision in 1874.

The three interrelated themes — Fiji, kidnapping and expansion — had given increasing trouble to Gladstone's Government. In each case a policy was all but formulated by the beginning of 1874: the

---

[1] Cabinet Min. 27 Jan. 1874. *Gladstone Papers*, 44641/255. Gladstone noted that the Cabinet considered 'Kimberley's draft respecting NZ proposal to extend in Polynesia to be prepared (the proposal is more enlarged — a joint stock Co.)'.

[2] Ross, *New Zealand Aspirations*, p. 114. In treating the Vogel project and the Polynesia Co. separately Ross neglects the fact that Gladstone evidently treated the questions as part of one problem.

way was paved for the annexation of Fiji, the results of the Kidnapping Act were being studied, expansion by Britain was deprecated, but the door was not closed to local expansion. The Government had clearly moved away from the non-interventionist position of the 1860's. The final decisions, however, had not been taken. They were left for Disraeli's Government.

PART THREE

The New Experiments

DECISIONS were still awaited about the frontier in the tropics when the Conservatives triumphed in the general election of 1874. Disraeli went to Windsor to receive his commission from Queen Victoria to form a Government on 18 February; at the age of seventy he had finally come to power. Lord Carnarvon, who agreed to serve once again as Secretary of State for the Colonies, took over the office on 21 February. There, within a few days, he encountered the crises on the frontier in the tropics, for which Kimberley had mooted new policies, but had not made final decisions.

Carnarvon immediately discovered that, in Fiji, Commodore Goodenough was endeavouring to secure annexation. On 23 February he therefore warned the commodore by cable not to prejudge the issue. Two days later, Carnarvon read of Vogel's visionary schemes of expansion in the Pacific, and of the suspicious activities of an American agent in Samoa. Next day, 26 February, a telegram announcing Wolseley's entry into Kumasi arrived. That same day, Seymour Clarke, London director of the Selangor Tin Company, having heard about Sir Andrew Clarke's Pankgor conference in Malaya, tried to get a word of approval from Carnarvon for his Company. After only a week in office, Carnarvon was only too vividly aware of the unsolved problems which confronted him concerning the frontier in West Africa, Malaya and the South Pacific.

In many ways, Carnarvon was better prepared for the Colonial Office than his predecessor. Carnarvon's early Government experience had been in colonial affairs. More significantly, he had already encountered some of the problems of the three tropical regions on which he was now called to decide as parliamentary under-secretary in Derby's Government, 1858–9, and as Secretary of State from June

1866 to March 1867. His memorandum on the Gold Coast in 1858, for example, had been a landmark in the evolution of West African policy. He had sympathized on similar moral grounds with the request for annexation from Fiji in 1859. He had even contemplated creating a British South-East Asian union of the Straits Settlements and the 'Borneo Settlements' (a premature project for 'Malaysia') which, with its centre at Singapore, would have provided a link between the Indian and Australasian empires.[1] He had been party to some of the preliminary discussions which led to the transfer of the Straits Settlements from India Office to Colonial Office control in 1867. Carnarvon was, therefore, familiar with the office, and familiar with the problems of the frontier in the tropics. Now the Colonial Office was made particularly congenial for him by the presence of Robert Herbert, his cousin and Eton and Oxford contemporary, as permanent under-secretary.

Carnarvon reached most of his important decisions about the frontier in the tropics by August 1874. His policies won enthusiastic approval from the Press. It must, however, be admitted that he did not give equal attention to each region. In the same period he was already meditating upon the intractable problems of South Africa, which were to dog the later years of his administration. The future of the Gold Coast, which the Ashanti War had brought very much into the public eye, received urgent consideration and, with the vigorous co-operation of the governor, new policies had been successfully inaugurated by October. Commodore Goodenough's report on Fiji did not arrive until 10 June, but the islands had been annexed (without a Cabinet discussion) before the end of October. Beyond Fiji, however, Carnarvon remained cautious in the Pacific. Making it clear that the new colony was an experiment in Polynesian government, he decided to meet the other problems which Britain faced in the region by the creation of the Western Pacific High Commission. The idea of the High Commission was evolved over a period of several years. Its significance lies in the fact that it fell short of the assumption of sovereignty. Malaya was regarded by Carnarvon as the least urgent frontier problem. Sir Andrew Clarke's recommendations after the Pangkor conference were not acted upon quickly. When even-

[1] In 1858, after James Brook tried to persuade the Govt. to annex Sarawak. Memo. by A. S. Green 22 Sept. 1874. F.O. 58/145, p. 268.

tually the appointment of Residents to advise two of the Malay rulers was approved in September 1874, Carnarvon made it clear that this scheme was also to be treated as an experiment. At first the experiment was not a happy one. It was not until the first Resident in Perak was murdered in 1875 that Carnarvon treated Malaya with the same urgency as he accorded to the Gold Coast and Fiji. In any case, it should be emphasized that Carnarvon's policies in all these questions were not original.

The experiments which the Conservatives launched in the Gold Coast, Malaya and Fiji were those which Kimberley, the Liberal Colonial Secretary, had already considered. In some cases Kimberley had definitely recommended the new policies to Gladstone, but final decisions had been postponed while Government envoys went to 'inquire and report'. The implication is therefore clear that the accession of the Conservatives was not the signal for a 'forward movement' on the frontier in the tropics. Carnarvon was deeply interested in empire, but he did not come to office as an expansionist. He wanted to strengthen the Empire by promoting co-operation between the self-governing colonies, particularly through regional federations. If Carnarvon believed that colonial policy was 'the greatest of all political questions',[1] Kimberley, it should be remembered, had confessed to Gladstone that he took 'a more sanguine view of the power and influence of this country than you do'.[2]

The difference between Kimberley's and Carnarvon's approach to colonial issues was a subtle one, which cannot be judged solely in terms of a preference for or against expansion. Kimberley's preoccupation was with strategy and prestige and Britain's role in the world. Carnarvon was more interested in colonial problems for their own sake, and he could be more imaginative. But when it came to the question of the frontier in the tropics the difference was largely one of circumstance. During Kimberley's period of office the frontier problems became increasingly urgent; therefore various possible courses of action were studied. Carnarvon took over when the immediate dangers had been faced, and the spade-work had been done. Moreover, he was not worn out by four strenuous years of office like his

[1] Carnarvon to Knatchbull-Hugessen 18 Aug. 1874 (copy). *Carnarvon Papers*, P.R.O. 30/6/44, p. 145.
[2] Kimberley to Gladstone 26 Nov. 1873. *Gladstone Papers*, 44225/10.

predecessor.[1]   Coming fresh upon the scene, Carnarvon could give thought to the future before finally committing himself to the new experiments.

[1] In the years 1871–3 Kimberley's family life was overshadowed by the suffering of his son Armine from typhoid fever (Kimberley's *Journal*, pp. 22, 44).   During Carnarvon's years of office he was shaken by his wife's death, during childbirth, on 25 Jan. 1875.   (Hardinge, *Life of Carnarvon*, p. 78.)

9. West Africa after the Ashanti War, 1874–6

THE Ashanti War was the most dramatic predicament on the imperial frontier in the tropics which Disraeli's Government inherited. Uncertainty as to the outcome of Wolseley's march on Kumasi added an element of suspense to the general election of 1874. An editorial in *The Times*, when Parliament dissolved on 26 January 1874, speculated on the unfortunate, and irrelevant, influence the war might have on the election. News of the capture of Kumasi, it felt, 'would be worth many seats to the Government, while anything so untoward as a disaster would be ruinous to the Government'.

The uncertainty was the result of a prolonged poll. The election period spread over the last week of January and the first week of February.[1] *The Times* was still regretting, only a day before Disraeli's victory became certain, that 'the news of a victory or a defeat coming at the crisis of a General Election would turn to one side or the other thousands of votes'.[2] The publication on the following day, 6 February, of a telegram from Wolseley, indicating that the Ashanti ruler had agreed to accept terms, was seen as a 'welcome gleam for the government'. But it was too late. Disraeli's secretary reported that very day that the Liberals were conceding defeat.[3]

The anxieties of the editor of *The Times* were really unnecessary. As an election issue, the Ashanti War had degenerated into a comedy turn. This was because Disraeli blundered into accusing Gladstone of causing the war by making a bargain with the Dutch over the Gold Coast and Sumatra. By receiving the cession of Elmina in 1872 in return for permitting the Dutch to invade Atjeh in northern Sumatra, Disraeli claimed that Britain had not only incurred Ashanti hostility, but also relinquished command of the Straits of Malacca — the main trade route to Singapore and the Far East. The issue was a highly technical one, which Disraeli obviously did not fully understand.

[1] Buckle, ii, pp. 618–19.
[2] *The Times*, 5 Feb. 1874, ed., p. 9.
[3] Corry to Disraeli 6 Feb. 1874. Buckle, ii, p. 619.

It did, in fact, contain material for a legitimate case against the Liberals, but Disraeli's handling of the issue proved to be a blunder.[1] After providing the subject for a series of oratorical exchanges by the party leaders as to the precise location of the Straits of Malacca, the issue was quietly dropped when *The Times* suggested it was more suitable as the subject for a question in the civil service examinations. Since the final outcome of Wolseley's expedition was still unknown by the time Gladstone resigned, the war can hardly have affected Disraeli's triumph.

WOLSELEY'S SUCCESS AND FAILURE

The news of the occupation of Kumasi reached London five days after Carnarvon took over the Colonial Office.[2] The post-war settlement on the Gold Coast became the most urgent frontier problem confronting the new Government. Carnarvon's first decision was to dissuade Disraeli from making political capital out of the war. Although he produced for the prime minister, confidentially, a list of Liberal mistakes, and suggested that they had 'run the expedition too fine in time and men',[3] Carnarvon warned Disraeli that it would be unwise to try to discredit Gladstone publicly for becoming involved in the war.

> There is no question to my mind [wrote Carnarvon] that the Ashantees have been for a considerable time preparing to invade us and that it has been an invasion of the British territory quite as much as of the protectorate. I should ... prefer to accept the fact of the war, and unless we are attacked (which is most unlikely) treat it as a transaction for which we are not responsible but which, ... we are determined to make the best of.[4]

As for the conduct of the military operations, Carnarvon found 'more to praise than to blame'.

Carnarvon realized that Wolseley's march to Kumasi was a popular military success. His expedition appeared neat, effective, and a fitting advertisement for Cardwell's reorganized Army. Wolseley's staff proved that English troops could fight effectively in tropical Africa. The campaign was also an important stage in the building of the

[1] See my article, 'Disraeli's Election Blunder', pp. 77–105.
[2] Wolseley to Kimberley (telegram) 5 Feb., received 26 Feb. 1874. Printed in C.O., Confidential Print; African, C.O. 806/4, p. 14.
[3] Undated memo. *Carnarvon Papers*, P.R.O. 30/6/85.
[4] Carnarvon to Disraeli 6 Mar. 1874 (copy). P.R.O. 30/6/11, p. 3.

'Wolseley gang' or 'Ashanti ring', one of the more progressive cliques of the later Victorian Army. Administratively, especially in medical services, the campaign seemed a model; a field telegraph operated from the front.

The build-up of British strength had progressed smoothly. The troops from Britain were kept at sea in their ships until January 1874, when three battalions and naval units began their march to the River Pra. Sleeping overnight in well-prepared camps, they were still fresh when they entered Ashanti territory on 15 January. Flank movements were made to east and west by African forces under British officers. From the mouth of the Volta, Captain Glover disengaged himself from the war on the east bank. He crossed the Pra on 15 January, and headed for Juaben, second town of Ashanti, which lay to the north-east of Kumasi. Wolseley entered the Ashanti capital on 4 February, and began his return march to the coast two days later after setting fire to the town. Glover passed through the smouldering ruins from the north-east on 12 February and followed Wolseley to the coast. By 23 February the last man had sailed for home. In less than two months, the second brisk colonial foray in the career of Gilbert's 'modern major-general' was complete.

Newspapers at home eagerly published despatches from Ashanti. The campaign was covered by famous travellers such as Winwood Reade for *The Times*, and Henry Morton Stanley for the *New York Herald*; the *Illustrated London News* produced numerous lithograph prints. A spate of campaign histories were quickly published, one of them by Frederick Maurice, who had received his baptism under fire. The story of the campaign is one of the better-known episodes of Victorian military history.[1] Wolseley became a popular hero. He

---

[1] See W. W. Reade, *Ashantee Campaign*; H. M. Stanley, *Coomassie and Magdala: The Story of Two British Campaigns in Africa*, London, 1874; J. F. Maurice, *The Ashantee War*; G. A. Henty, *The March to Coomassie*; H. Brackenbury, *The Ashanti War*, London, 1874; W. W. Claridge, *History of the Gold Coast and Ashanti*, ii, chs. i–ix; Ward, *History of the Gold Coast*, pp. 261–81; A. Lloyd, *The Drums of Kumasi. The Story of the Ashanti Wars*, London, 1964; Lehmann, *All Sir Garnet*, chs. 7 and 8; McIntyre, 'British Policy in West Africa: The Ashanti Expedition of 1873–74', *H.J.* (1962), 5 (1), pp. 37–46; F. Wolfson, 'British Relations with the Gold Coast', ch. 6, 'The Imperial War'.

was invited to Windsor by the queen, and congratulated before both
Houses of Parliament. Even Glover got a knighthood. As the first
of the returning troopships anchored at Spithead on 19 March 1874
they were in time to be welcomed in the Address from the Throne
during the opening of a new Parliament.

Yet Wolseley had really failed. Members of both Houses did not
realize, as they listened to hints of imperial glory, that the Ashanti
expedition had been a continual conflict between the instructions and
inclinations of their heroic general. Winwood Reade produced a
theory that Wolseley wanted to build up a reputation as a diplomatist.
Thus he hoped he could bring the Ashanti to terms without having to
fight for Kumasi.[1] The course of his diplomacy must therefore be
considered.

Wolseley had been instructed to drive the Ashanti from the Gold
Coast protectorate, and negotiate a new treaty with Ashanti. His
inclination, however, was to enter Kumasi, without fighting if possible,
and dictate a new treaty to Kofi Karikari, the asantehene, in his own
capital, leaving the Ashanti kingdom intact, but submissive.[2] The
first aim was achieved painlessly since the Ashanti army left the
protectorate even before the British battalions arrived. But the asantehene did not reply, at first, to Wolseley's proposals for a new treaty.

Wolseley imagined that the invasion of Ashanti would be 'child's
play'. A few battles inside Ashanti territory, he thought, would soon
bring Kofi Karikari suing for peace.[3] It looked, indeed, as if
Wolseley was right. Just as the British advance party crossed the
Pra, Wolseley's terms were accepted by the Ashanti ruler, who begged
the general to call off his invasion. It therefore seemed that the
second part of Wolseley's instructions would be achieved with his
inclinations unfulfilled. Possibly for this reason Wolseley now demanded terms so humiliating that it was impossible for the asantehene
to accept.[4] Winwood Reade considered that Kofi Karikari out-

[1] Reade, op. cit., p. 288.

[2] Wolseley to Gen. Biddulph 26 Oct. 1873 (extract) in *Kimberley Papers*,
A/22.

[3] Ibid. Wolseley to Cardwell 11 Dec. 1873, private (copy).

[4] Wolseley to Kofi Karikari 2 Jan. 1874. C.O. 806/2, p. 97; Kofi to
Wolseley 9 Jan. 1874; Wolseley to Kofi 13 Jan. 1874. C.O. 806/4,
pp. 6–7. Wolseley demanded not only the handing over of prisoners from

witted Wolseley in diplomacy, and forced the general to fight for Kumasi in order to save his reputation at home.[1]

After the battle of Amoafu on 31 January 1874 five days of hard fighting followed before Kumasi was occupied. Wolseley then entered the Ashanti capital in triumph and called for three cheers for the queen. But having satisfied his inclination, he had still not achieved his aim. Although the asantehene had already agreed to make peace, he had fled from the capital when it was obvious that Wolseley would not be deterred. Thus Kumasi became deserted; no one came forward to sign a treaty, and Wolseley had to set off back to the coast with his aim unaccomplished. Ashanti envoys did not reach him until 13 February at Fomana, a place which gave its name to the new treaty, the draft of which was handed over by Wolseley. This was not signed formally until 14 March 1874, when Wolseley had already left for England.[2]

For all the display of British armed might, the new treaty was not very different from Maclean's 1831 treaty which it displaced. The asantehene renounced his claim to Elmina and for rent payments from the British forts. Both sides pledged themselves to keep open trade routes and to maintain the primitive road to Kumasi. Kofi Karikari promised to try and stop human sacrifices in his dominions and agreed to pay an indemnity of 50,000 ounces of gold. The treaty finally secured Elmina for Britain, therefore, and it also removed doubts about the allegiance to Ashanti of protectorate states such as Denkyera, Assin and Akim. The only new departure was the renunciation of Ashanti suzerainty over Adansi, which had requested to join the protectorate. As this was a precedent for the secession of other parts of Ashanti, Wolseley had deliberately hastened away to avoid political complications which might detract from his success. It was no part of British policy to destroy Ashanti; all she wanted was peaceful relations.

the protectorate and half the indemnity, but hostages who were to include the asantehene's heir, the queen mother and the heirs of the four leading Ashanti kings. Ward, op. cit., p. 273, suggests they were impossible conditions.

[1] Reade, op. cit., pp. 290–2.
[2] Text of new treaty in Crooks, *Records Relating to the Gold Coast*, pp. 521–3.

THE NEW GOLD COAST COLONY

Ashanti had been humiliated, a long-standing threat removed; but
what was to become of the protectorate? Here Carnarvon faced
precisely the same dilemma as Kimberley had before the Ashanti
invasion. Should Britain abandon the coast, or should she remain
and strengthen her position? Kimberley had rejected withdrawal in
February 1873 and was making plans for defining Britain's position
more firmly. How would Carnarvon resolve the dilemma?

For a while the future of the Gold Coast seemed an open question.
Rather than go ahead with Kimberley's scheme the Colonial Office
considered a number of other alternatives. Herbert suggested, for
example, in April 1874, that the time for 'half measures' in the
protectorate was past. 'Unless we directly govern, up to the Prah,
we can have no guarantee against wars and disturbances.' He viewed
the prospect of annexation 'with horror' but wondered whether it
might not be the only safe alternative to a retreat into the forts. There
is no hint that Herbert seriously considered withdrawal. James
Lowther, the parliamentary under-secretary, however, obviously
viewed possessions like the Gold Coast with great disfavour.

> Complete annexation or total abandonment are I fear the only sound
> alternatives. The former is too ghastly to contemplate, the latter too
> charming of execution. All these halting tentative half measures such
> as Protectorates etc. may do for a time & I suppose something of the
> kind will have to be attempted until the vulgar prejudice which is
> now a days dignified by the name of 'Public Opinion' veers round to a
> common sense and unsentimental view of this question.

'A very evil choice to have to make' was Carnarvon's view.[1] But he
refused to consider it in such oversimplified terms. Sketching the
alternatives for himself rather more imaginatively, he ranged over a
number of possibilities:

1. *Abandonment of Coast.*
   Consular Govt. on Coast & resid[t] at Coomassie.

---

[1] Mins. by Herbert 17 Apr., Lowther 20 Apr., and Carnarvon 21 A pr.
on Fitzgerald to Carnarvon 13 Apr. 1874. C.O. 96/114.

2. *Transference to a Company.*
   Tho' formerly done time passed for this. Practical difficulties in creating a monopoly. Abuses wd. grow up & Govt wd. be held responsible.
3. *Fanti or other Confed^n.*
   such as Ld. Grey proposed — impracticable.
4. *Direct Govt* — Anglo-Indian plan — resid^t in Coomassie.
   Coomassie burnt. It wd. increase probable obligations & connections.
5. *Actual Annex^n & Govt. of territory.*[1]

As he weighed these possible courses, Carnarvon had the benefit of plenty of advice. Sir Arthur Phayre and Colonel Yule related their experiences in Burma.[2] John Bright still pleaded for complete withdrawal and Gladstone for friendly relations with Ashanti.[3] Earl Grey (the former Colonial Secretary) suggested a return to the protectorate system. Confine British territory to the forts because of domestic slavery, said Grey; create African states in the protectorate, possibly on the lines of the Fante Confederation, and appoint a High Commissioner to supervise it all.[4] In the House of Commons a Member suggested that Britain should simply

> Act the part of policemen there, and let things take their natural course, giving the people an opportunity of learning the arts of peace, and educating them, so that the superior members of their race might administer side by side with us.[5]

The one thing which became quite clear to the Colonial Office was that the small body of opinion which was interested in West Africa would not accept withdrawal. Arthur Mills, one of the colonial enthusiasts, insisted during a long debate in Parliament on 4 May 1874 that Britain could not honourably abandon the coast. Disraeli, in reply, told the House of Commons, quite truthfully, that the Government was considering the matter most carefully.[6]

Carnarvon knew that a small but influential body of opinion felt a

[1] Undated memo. *Carnarvon Papers*, P.R.O. 30/6/85.
[2] Ibid. Undated memo. on interview.
[3] Clipping from *Daily News*, 14 Mar. 1874. P.R.O. 30/6/50, pp. 82–84.
[4] *The Times*, 14 Mar. 1874. Draft of a proposed new treaty encl. in Grey to Carnarvon 13 May 1874. P.R.O. 30/6/44, p. 30.
[5] 3 *Hansard*, 218, col. 1213.
[6] Ibid. 218, cols. 1592–1664.

sense of obligation towards the Gold Coast. Nevertheless, he was still
left asking the same questions which had puzzled Kimberley more than
a year before; above all, what should become of the protectorate?
Here his final decision was greatly influenced by the permanent
officials of the Colonial Office. In March 1874 a searching review of
the whole basis for Britain's role in the Gold Coast was undertaken by
Augustus Hemming and Edward Fairfield of the African Department.
Four clear conclusions emerged from their study. The policies of
Cardwell ten years earlier were found inadequate. The 1865 policy
was finally condemned as 'vague and inconclusive'.[1] The policy of
military disengagement was rejected, while the duty of protection was
reaffirmed. As Fairfield put it:

> The duty arises from the fact that our presence renders the protected
> tribes less able to defend themselves, whilst our peculiar policy has
> exposed them to the undying hatred of their most powerful enemies.[2]

The system of governing all the West African Settlements through a
single governor-in-chief at Freetown was found defective. The
existence of the protectorate, for example, rendered the Gold Coast
potentially the most dangerous responsibility, yet authority for local
decisions lay with the governor in Sierra Leone. Finally, domestic
slavery was recognized as the chief bar to better government. Within
British territory slavery was illegal. This was the real reason why
the Government frequently shirked new annexations in West Africa.
Yet, without annexation, effective British rule could not be developed.
Therefore, Fairfield suggested the gradual abolition of domestic
slavery.[3]

Carnarvon announced his new policy for the Gold Coast in the
House of Lords on 12 May 1874. There could be no withdrawal.
If Britain had no written obligations on the Gold Coast, she had
moral ones.

[1] Memo.: 'Gold Coast, Enquiry of 1865', by A. W. L. Hemming,
Mar. 1874. C.O. 806/12, p. 16.
[2] Memo.: 'The Origin and Extent of the British Obligation towards the
Native Tribes on the Gold Coast', by E. Fairfield, 24 Mar. 1874. C.O.
806/11, p. 18.
[3] Memo.: 'Domestic Slavery, the Jurisdiction of the Judicial Assessor and
the Legal Character and Limitation of British Power on the Gold Coast', by
Fairfield, 19 Mar. 1874. C.O. 806/9, p. 22.

A great nation like ours must be sometimes prepared to discharge disagreeable duties; she must consent to bear burdens which are inseparable from her greatness ... it is certainly not a desire of selfish interests or the ambition of larger empire which bids us remain on the West Coast of Africa; it is simply and solely a sense of obligations to be redeemed and of duties to be performed.[1]

Carnarvon had decided to treat the Gold Coast and Lagos problems as one — something Herbert had advocated three years earlier. The Gold Coast forts would be added to Lagos and its outstations at Badagry and Leckie, to form a new Crown Colony on the model of the Straits Settlements. Better-qualified officials would be sought, and a new capital built at Elmina or Accra, and possibly a hill station (a West African Simla) might be created. Armed Hausa police would prevent the Ashanti from being molested in the protectorate. On the question of domestic slavery Carnarvon could promise no sudden emancipation, but agreed that the subject would be investigated.

For all the grandeur of Carnarvon's words about the obligations of greatness, his speech must have been something of an anticlimax to expansionists. Here was no dramatic change of policy. The protectorate was retained very much as it had existed before the Ashanti War. Influence rather than edict would still be Britain's method of advancing 'Commerce, Christianity and Civilization'. But this was not all. Two additions were made to this modest programme later in 1874, which in the long run profoundly influenced the history of the Gold Coast. They caused a considerable amount of confusion both to contemporaries[2] and among historians, who have often maintained that Britain annexed the Gold Coast in 1874.[3]

The first change concerned an extension of the authority of the Crown. While British sovereignty was not extended in the Gold

---

[1] 3 *Hansard*, 219, cols. 157–68.

[2] A missionary wrote in 1875: 'The Gold Coast is now a Colony and not a Protectorate and already the more decisive measures of British Rule are making themselves felt.' W. Penrose to Boyce, Accra, 26 Apr. 1875. *Meth. Miss. Soc.*: Gold Coast file for 1875–6.

[3] J. D. Fage, *An Introduction to the History of West Africa*, Cambridge, 1955, p. 140; Ward, *History of the Gold Coast*, pp. 257–60; F. M. Bourret, *Ghana, Road to Independence 1919–57*, Oxford, 1960, p. 20; Cowan, *Nineteenth Century Malaya*, pp. 172–3, 200.

Coast, the Legislative Council of the new colony (which included both Lagos and the Gold Coast forts) was empowered to legislate for the protectorate, and the queen was proclaimed the sole authority on the Gold Coast.[1] The colonial Government, instead of confining itself to police and judicial functions, as before, would also comprehend health, education, roads, economic and social regulation. However singular the exact legal position became, it might be said that the protectorate was 'annexed administratively' to the colony.

Secondly, domestic slavery was declared illegal. There was good reason for not tampering with a complicated feature of West African society. But the Government was embarrassed by a motion in the House of Commons on 29 June 1874, when the Hon. Evelyn Ashley (son of the factory reformer) called for the abolition of all slavery. He pointed to the hypocrisy of a Government shirking annexation only because of the existence of domestic slavery. If Russia in central Asia, and Britain herself in Zanzibar could force local potentates into abolition, why should slavery be allowed to persist on the Gold Coast? Toleration of slavery in West Africa, said the Liberal Goschen, only supported the charge that the British abolished slavery only when it suited their interests. Disraeli, taking note of these views, prevented a vote being taken by assuring the House that he hoped slavery could soon be abolished.[2]

Ashley's resolution forced Disraeli's Government to tackle the question of domestic slavery. In a secret despatch on 21 August 1874 the governor was informed that, as the Fante did so little to defend themselves in the recent Ashanti War, the queen was 'entitled to require of them a greater degree of deference and conformity to the known desires of herself and her people than she has in former times exacted'.[3] The governor was ordered to request the chiefs to cease importing slaves, and to draw up regulations governing the relations between domestic slaves and their masters. Badly treated imported slaves were to be emancipated at once, on compensation to the masters, and children were to be declared free as soon as possible. Carnarvon's approach was still very tentative, and he asked the governor to inquire

[1] Order in Council 6 Aug. 1874.   C.O. 806/19, p. 6.
[2] 3 *Hansard*, 220, cols. 607–41.
[3] Carnarvon to Strahan 21 Aug. 1874 (secret). C.O. 806/19, p. 8.

and report.   Privately, he expressed the hope that compensation could be avoided to save revenue.[1]

Carnarvon did not know his man on the spot.   It was Governor George Strahan,[2] who was really responsible for the attack on domestic slavery, and who provided the Conservatives with an unexpected political windfall in 1874.   Taking only nine days to answer Carnarvon's despatch he recommended immediate prohibition of slave-trading, the emancipation of imported slaves and children, and the ending of recognition by the courts of any rights over personal liberty.[3]   In short, Strahan proposed abolishing slavery as a legal status on the Gold Coast by proclamation.   He certainly took the Colonial Office by surprise.

Strahan had not made a hasty, ill-considered proposal.   Ever since his arrival on 25 June 1874, he had boldly faced up to the slavery problem.   By making it clear to the Gold Coast kings that he did not want to hear them talk of slaves, he had, in a way, been preparing the Gold Coast for abolition.   British prestige remained high as a result of Wolseley's expedition.   Before Ashanti disintegrated and ended the external threat to the protectorate, Strahan believed that abolition was possible.   There were dangers, he admitted.   Poverty might afflict elderly domestic slaves suddenly freed from the care of their masters; force might be necessary to back up the new regulations; and if the idlest slaves demanded their freedom first, they might form dangerous marauding bands.   The governor was convinced, however, that a large number of slaves would want to stay with their masters, so that emancipation would, in fact, be gradual.   Strahan thought the gamble was worth taking and, in anticipation of Carnarvon's

---

[1] Carnarvon to Strahan 3 Sept. 1874, private and confidential (copy). *Carnarvon Papers*, P.R.O. 30/6/24, p. 12.

[2] Capt. George Strahan joined the R.A. in 1857.   He was A.D.C. to Gladstone when he was High Commissioner in the Ionian Is., 1859, and in Feb. of that year he became A.D.C. to Sir Henry Storks, Gladstone's successor, who became gov. of Malta in 1864.   Strahan went to Malta with him and became Chief Secretary of Malta, 1868–9.   He was Colonial Secretary, Bahamas, 1869, and acting gov., 1871–3.   Administrator of Lagos, 1873, until appointed gov. of the new Gold Coast Colony, June 1874.   Gov. of the Windward Is. 1876.

[1] Strahan to Carnarvon 19 Sept. 1874 (secret).   C.O. 806/23.

approval, he arranged conferences of chiefs for October and November 1874.[1]

Carnarvon, for his part, agreed the stakes were worth playing for. Two days after receiving Strahan's plan, and in the same letter in which he announced the annexation of the Fiji Islands, he sought Disraeli's permission to take some mild military precautions on the Gold Coast in case of trouble.[2] Disraeli showed complete confidence in Carnarvon's colonial policy at this stage, just as Carnarvon had a remarkable trust in Strahan. Leaving the final decision, as usual, to the man on the spot, he pleaded only that undue risks should not be taken lest Britain's newly won prestige in West Africa be lost. Armed support was promised should anything go wrong.[3] Having passed the real responsibility to Strahan, the home Government proceeded to congratulate itself on its success. 'It is a masterly, indeed admirable performance,' said Disraeli in flattering Carnarvon, 'your conduct of your office cannot be too highly praised.'[4]

No unfortunate incident marred this success. Strahan's conferences were successful. The proclamation was made without incident. If Carnarvon's mild programme of May 1874 was no panacea, his gamble of October was regarded at home as a huge success, and he was hailed as the most statesmanlike Colonial Secretary since Grey.[5] This was less than justice to Captain Strahan, whose boldness gave Disraeli's Government the credit for a major reform in Africa. Domestic slavery did not, of course, end, and remained into the twentieth century. The chief effect of Strahan's measure was to reduce the internal slave-trade, and the lot of domestic slaves was said to have improved.[6]

Beyond these two rather nebulous reforms Carnarvon refused to move. Although the protectorate was brought within the sphere of the colony's laws, and for many purposes colony and protectorate were

---

[1] Strahan to Carnarvon 20 Sept. 1874 (private). *Carnarvon Papers*, P.R.O. 30/6/24, p. 15.

[2] Ibid. Carnarvon to Disraeli 17 Oct. 1874 (copy). P.R.O. 6/11, p. 26.

[3] Ibid. Carnarvon to Strahan 22 Oct. 1874, private (copy). P.R.O. 30/6/24, p. 16.

[4] Disraeli to Carnarvon 26 Oct. 1874. Quoted in Hardinge, *Life of Carnarvon*, ii, p. 79.

[5] Clipping from *Northern Echo*, 6 Jan. 1875. P.R.O. 30/6/47, p. 174.

[6] Claridge, *History of the Gold Coast and Ashanti*, ii, pp. 183–4.

treated as one, the sovereignty of the region was not acquired. This did not take place until the protectorate was annexed after another Ashanti War in 1901. Then Ashanti was also annexed.[1] The Government's reluctance to go beyond the modest changes of 1874 meant that the best of good intentions were very slow to be implemented.

> We are now apparently, particularly on the G[old] Coast, committed to a policy of development & improvement a policy of real and earnest efforts to raise the natives of our Settlements from the slough of ignorance and barbarism. . . . The agents of this policy must be, among other things, roads and schools . . .[2]

But little was done to follow this fine-sounding ideal.[3]

The chief reason for this was lack of revenue. It was also for the same reason that the question of the Gambia exchange was revived in 1874. When the French reopened the matter in April 1874, the Foreign Office, quite willing to go ahead, said it would 'depend entirely' on Carnarvon's decision as to the future of the Gold Coast.[4] There was, consequently, a delay while Carnarvon evolved the policy which has just been outlined. But because of the fiscal problem West African policy was, for a rare moment after the Ashanti War, looked upon as a whole. Carnarvon saw the Gambia exchange as the 'desirable compliment' of the recent changes on the Gold Coast.[5]

THE FAILURE OF THE ANGLO-FRENCH ATTEMPT TO PARTITION THE COAST

France's desire to revive the Gambia exchange was welcomed in the Colonial Office. It offered them an opportunity to solve a number of outstanding problems in West Africa. The Sierra Leone Government wanted to levy duties in the rivers to the north of the colony. The Gold Coast Government wanted to prevent trade to Ashanti, particularly arms, from by-passing the British ports by using the French

[1] Order in Council 21 Sept. 1901. *London Gazette*, 1 Oct. 1901, p. 4380
[2] Min. by Hemming 14 Oct., on Manchester Chamber of Commerce to Carnarvon 13 Oct. 1875. C.O. 87/108.
[3] Wolfson, 'British Relations with the Gold Coast', p. 360.
[4] Memo. by Wylde, 20 Apr. 1874. F.O. 27/2226.
[5] Carnarvon to Ponsonby 29 July 1875. *Royal Archives*, P. 17/26.

comptoirs at Grand Bassam and Assini. At Lagos the question of the
annexation of Porto Novo had been revived. Fairfield thought it
would enable Lagos to control the Egba trade, and Herbert was
tempted by the idea.[1] Moreover, now that Lagos and the Gold Coast
were being combined into one colony, the Colonial Office thought it
would be useful to gain control of the entire seaboard in between.

Elimination of French claims north of Sierra Leone, west of the
Gold Coast and in the territory between the Gold Coast and Lagos
was therefore suggested to the Foreign Office as a 'fair equivalent'
for the Gambia.[2] A bargain with the French on these territories, said
Carnarvon, would remove any source of foreign objection to a modest
expansion of the jurisdiction of Sierra Leone and the Gold Coast for
the purpose of collecting revenues.[3] Clearly there was no desire for
expansion, as such, merely the sanction of a little 'custom-house
imperialism'. Lord Derby, the Foreign Secretary, accepted the proposal. A little anxious that the abandonment of the Gambia was not
quite consistent with the Conservative attitude to the Liberals during
the crisis of 1869–70, he satisfied his conscience by writing 'after Fiji
and the Gold Coast we are not likely to be reproached with a policy of
colonial surrender'.[4]

Negotiations began in 1875. When Gavard, the French ambassador, reopened the Gambia question,[5] the Colonial Office proposed
that the French should give up all territorial claims between the Rio
Pongo in the west to the River Benin in the east.[6] This was approved by the Cabinet on 17 April 1875 and Lord Derby explained
the position to the French ambassador on 30 April.[7] The Foreign
Office did not, however, want to appear too eager for a settlement. In
May 1875 Wylde suggested that the Niger Delta ought to be included

[1] Mins. by Fairfield and Herbert 5 Aug., on Banners to Carnarvon 20
Aug. 1874. C.O. 147/30.

[2] Min. by Carnarvon 22 Feb., on memo. by Hemming 20 Feb. 1875.
C.O. 87/108.

[3] Carnarvon to Derby 12 Dec. 1874 (copy). *Carnarvon Papers*, P.R.O.
30/6/8, p. 61.

[4] Ibid. p. 64. Derby to Carnarvon 16 Dec. 1874.

[5] Hargreaves, *Prelude to the Partition*, pp. 177–9.

[6] C.O. to F.O. 5 Mar. 1875. F.O. 27/2226.

[7] Min. by Herbert 21 Apr., on F.O. to C.O. 11 Mar. 1875. C.O.
87/108; F.O. to Gavard 30 Apr. 1875 (draft). F.O. 27/2226.

in the bargain. Although Britain had no intention of occupying this region, she did not want the French to step in.[1]

The plan was put to the French on 23 July 1875. France was to abandon all her claims between the Pongo and Gabon, while Britain would give up her territory to the north.[2] Although the French Colonial Department was disturbed by this addition, the Foreign Ministry readily accepted it in the interest of good Anglo-French relations.[3] Moreover, as the Assembly was about to end its session, the French Government went ahead and published the project. Carnarvon told Disraeli 'this clearly forces our hand'.[4] But Disraeli rejected Carnarvon's advice. Fearful of defeat after the political passions sparked off by Samuel Plimsoll during a debate on the Government's Merchant Shipping Bill on 22 July, the prime minister did not want to risk a controversial Gambia Cession Bill in the same parliamentary session. The matter was postponed.[5]

Disraeli's delay wrecked the project. It gave time for opponents of the exchange in the Gambia, in Britain and in France, to mobilize their resources. In Britain, Gambia merchants, missionaries and colonial zealots created a pressure group known as the Gambia Committee.[6] In France, some merchants in Marseilles feared that the French Government might abandon their interest in the eastern part of the Guinea coast, but they made little impact on the Foreign Ministry.[7]

The growing opposition to the exchange in Britain undoubtedly annoyed the Colonial Office. For Hemming it was all a matter of getting the priorities right. Publicity at the time of the Ashanti War had shocked public opinion into realizing that very little had been done in West Africa 'in the way of advancement of civilisation'. Now certain reforms were at last being made, especially on the Gold Coast, and

[1] F.O. to C.O. 15 May 1875. C.O. 87/108.

[2] F.O. to Gavard 23 July 1875. F.O. 27/2226.

[3] Hargreaves, op. cit., pp. 181, 191.

[4] Carnarvon to Disraeli 28 July 1875 (copy). *Carnarvon Papers*, P.R.O. 30/6/11, p. 81.

[5] Buckle, ii, pp. 721–7.

[6] Manchester Chamber of Commerce to C.O. 13 Oct. 1875. C.O. 87/108; Royal Colonial Institute to F.O. 12 Jan. 1876. F.O. 27/2227; Gambia missionaries to general secretaries 29 Jan. 1876. *Meth. Miss. Soc.*: Incoming Gambia letters 1868–76.

[7] Hargreaves, op. cit., pp. 190–4.

The interests of the few British merchants at the Gambia are hardly to be
weighed against the possibility of providing the means of carrying the
blessings of civilization and imparting the advantages of education to
thousands of British subjects.[1]

The Colonial Office was definitely committed to the plan. Carnarvon
went ahead and announced the exchange in the House of Lords on
17 February 1876, when he emphasized that Britain would be gaining
exclusive right to the Niger Delta.[2]

Unfortunately, Whitehall was in some confusion about the state
of the Anglo-French negotiations. Obviously when Carnarvon spoke
in the House of Lords he did not know that the French had already, on
11 February, asked for certain explanations of the British proposal.
This was because the draft agreement provided that the region west of
the Rio Pongo would be left to 'l'influence français', while everywhere
to the south was reserved for 'l'action de l'Angleterre'. The difference
probably arose from a translation error, but the French feared that a
large new area would be brought under British control as opposed to
'influence' or 'jurisdiction'. They therefore, wanted an explanation.[3]
Derby was sure that the original proposal was unambiguous, but for
some reason he failed to consult the Colonial Office on this. So Carnarvon's speech naturally alarmed the Marseilles merchants who were
interested in the eastern part of the coast. Regis's agent in Britain
wrote informing the Colonial Office that the French would never, for
example, give up their claims on the Dahomey coast.[4] When this
caused the Colonial Office to consult the Foreign Office as to whether
there had been a change in French policy, the latter department
finally passed on the French note of 11 February.

'A wonderful mess', was the verdict in the Colonial Office.[5] They
urged the Foreign Office to check with the French Government
immediately. As a result, the French Government formally agreed
to the exchange, in a note of 8 March 1876, but they sought an

[1] Min. by Hemming 14 Oct. 1875 on Manchester Chamber of Commerce, cited above.

[2] 3 *Hansard*, 227, cols. 374–84.

[3] French note 11 Feb. 1876.   F.O. 27/2227.

[4] Ibid. Marseilles merchants to J. F. Hutton, Manchester, 21 Feb., in
C.O. to F.O. 29 Feb. 1876.

[5] Min. by Meade 2 Mar., on F.O. to C.O. 1 Mar. 1876.   C.O. 87/109.

assurance that Marseilles merchants would not be excluded if Britain took over the whole of the coastline within her sphere.[1] This was a perfectly legitimate condition, and it is hard to read into it a rejection of the British proposal. But Fairfield thought it was 'an end to the matter'.[2] Other members of the department were less pessimistic, but Herbert came to the conclusion that they should warn the French of their intention to gain the whole coastline between the Gold Coast and Lagos. Carnarvon thought they could not ask Parliament to sanction the cession of the Gambia without some such compensation.[3]

As a result of this episode, the project failed. After two years of dilatoriness by the British Government, and a last-minute muddle, the Gambia exchange was allowed to lapse again. The best chance of developing the new Gold Coast–Lagos colony by raising revenue to improve the administration was lost. An unfortunate train of recriminations followed. Disraeli blamed Carnarvon, whose colonial policy was now coming under serious fire in South Africa and the West Indies.[4] Derby claimed that the Colonial Office was 'in a hurry to begin this negotiation, and in a hurry to break it off'.[5] Carnarvon blamed the Foreign Office for not telling him of the French note of 11 February. It was 'solely an error of the FO', he said. 'Had this paper been forwarded to the CO none of the present differences could have arisen'.[6]

A more accurate verdict would recognize that Disraeli's political fears in July 1875 gave the Gambia pressure group enough time to frighten Carnarvon into refusing to go to Parliament without a considerable bargain for the Gambia. It meant that Disraeli's Government badly muffed one of the preliminaries of the scramble for Africa. As Professor Hargreaves suggests: 'If, as seemed possible at this time,

---

[1] Text encl. in F.O. to C.O. 10 Mar. 1876. C.O. 87/109.

[2] Ibid. Min. by Fairfield 15 Mar. 1876.

[3] C.O. to F.O. 15 Mar. 1876. F.O. 27/2227.

[4] Disraeli to Lady Bradford 26 Apr. 1876. Buckle, ii, p. 815.

[5] Min. by Derby on memo. by C. B. Robertson 21 Apr. 1876. F.O. 27/2227.

[6] Min. by Carnarvon 14 May 1875 on F.O. to C.O. 8 May 1876 (C.O. 87/109), in which he continued: 'But this cannot and ought not to be stated.'

a single British administration had been permitted to control the coast, and develop the hinterlands of modern Ghana, Togo, Dahomey and Nigeria, the political geography of twentieth-century Africa would have been strikingly different.'[1]

[1] Hargreaves, *Prelude to the Partition*, p. 195.

10. *The Beginnings of British Political Control in Malaya, 1874-6*

THE wars in Malaya were not an election issue in 1874 like the Ashanti War. The Straits of Malacca question, which briefly held the political headlines during January 1874, concerned the Dutch invasion of northern Sumatra, not Britain's intervention in the Peninsula. Although a telegram announcing the appointment of the first Resident reached the Colonial Office on 24 January 1874, and a Reuter's cable indicating that Clarke had ended the war in Perak actually appeared in *The Observer* on the following day, neither of the political leaders found any political ammunition in them for their election manifestoes which were being drafted over the same week-end.[1]

Since the full details of Clarke's action did not arrive until 30 March 1874, the Colonial Office did not consider the future of Malaya until after deciding about the Gold Coast. The aftermath of the Ashanti War created a sense of urgency for a settlement in West Africa, which was not accorded to Malaya. Malay affairs received somewhat leisurely treatment in 1874. This was largely due to the methods of the man on the spot.

Sir Andrew Clarke was sent out to inquire and report. His philosophy was: 'To take responsibility, to act first and always to act, to write about it afterwards'.[2] Fully conscious that the Pangkor settlement was a *fait accompli* far in excess of his instructions, he was confident of his policy. As his Gold Coast proposals had been rejected in favour of those of a brilliant commander, fourteen years his junior, Clarke probably wanted to shine in Malaya. A sense of destiny comes through his private letters to political friends in England. He

[1] Clarke to Kimberley (telegram) 23 Jan. 1874. C.O. 273/75; *The Observer*, 25 Jan. 1874. For the election debate see my 'Disraeli's Election Blunder', *R.M.S.*, pp. 93-100.
[2] Sir G. S. Clarke in Vetch, *Life of Clarke*, pp. vii and xii.

represented his acts as the great watershed in Malayan history. 'I feel
I have done a good stroke', he wrote to Hugh Childers, '. . . all the
people here say that nothing has been done so complete and equal since
Raffles's time.'[1] To Disraeli's secretary he pointed out 'it is hard in a
few months to neutralise the neglect of close on a century'.[2]

SIR ANDREW CLARKE AND THE FIRST RESIDENTS IN PERAK AND SELANGOR

Clarke reached Singapore on 3 November 1873, and very soon realized
the urgency of his problem in Perak. Although the mantri's forces
and the Royal Navy's boats had had some success in restoring order in
Larut, piracy was growing alarmingly off the coast. Things were so
bad that Colonel Anson anxiously telegraphed Singapore on 13 December 1873.[1] That evening W. H. M. Read, one of the most prominent
of the Straits merchants, dined at Government House. The conversation turned to Perak. Clarke had had a month to plan his intervention.
Read asked if he intended to act quickly. The governor is reputed to
have replied, 'I am ready at a moment's notice if I can get the key to
the door'. 'Give me a fortnight', interjected Read, 'and I will get it
for you.'[4]

Read's 'key' came from Raja Muda 'Abdu'llah, pretender to the
Perak sultanate. 'Abdu'llah had visited Singapore in October 1873
when his fortunes were at their lowest. He brought an introduction
from his Ghee Hin allies to Tan Kim Ching, the rich Chinese merchant, who was Read's business partner. 'Abdu'llah needed help.
Read thought he should wait for the new governor. Kim Ching, who
found he was a very expensive and scandalous guest, wanted him to go
home. But, before leaving, 'Abdu'llah promised Kim Ching that in
return for help he would grant the farm of the revenues of Larut for
ten years.[5] Thus Read probably had a vested interest in 'Abdu'llah's

[1] Vetch, *Life of Clarke*, p. 154.
[2] Clarke to Corry, Singapore, 19 Nov. 1874. *Disraeli Papers*, B/xxi/C/236.
[3] A. Skinner, 'Précis on Perak Affairs', 10 Jan. 1874. C.O. 809/1, p. 147.
[4] Read, *Play and Politics*, p. 25.
[5] C. B. Plunket, 'Enquiry into the Complicity of Chiefs in the Perak
Outrages', 1 Dec. 1876, p. 3. Copy encl. in Jervois to Carnarvon 14 Dec.
1876. C.O. 273/86.

success in Perak; so after his dinner with the governor he promptly drafted a letter, in 'Abdu'llah's name, asking the governor to act as 'umpire' in the Perak succession dispute, requesting British protection, and asking for an officer to 'assist and advise' in the government of the state. A copy, duly signed by 'Abdu'llah, reached Singapore on 9 April 1874.[1]

Clarke did not rely solely on Read. The alarming growth of piracy made a settlement in Perak imperative. The governor sent William A. Pickering, the Chinese expert of the Straits Government, to try to make terms with the rival Chinese headmen in Larut.[2] Pickering met the beleaguered Ghee Hin leaders on 4 January 1874. He found them eager for peace, and persuaded them to accept the governor's mediation.[3]

Here was Clarke's 'key' to the door. He acted quickly. A telegram to Anson in Penang gave instructions for the calling of a conference at Pangkor Island on 14 January 1874. Frank Swettenham was sent to obtain a cease-fire from Captain Speedy and the mantri. Major McNair and Captain Dunlop went to Perak to call upon the pirates to surrender their boats, to seek information about the succession dispute, and to escort the Malay chiefs to the conference. Two days after 'Abdu'llah's letter (inspired by Read) arrived, Clarke left for Pangkor. Negotiations began on 15 January. Both the Chinese and Malays signed agreements five days later. While General Wolseley slowly invaded Ashanti, Clarke made quick work of Perak.

The settlement among the Chinese was straightforward and, in practice, it proved satisfactory. The Ghee Hins were heartily sick of fighting. The recently victorious Hai Sans were naturally more doubtful. But both factions had no confidence in the Malay rulers and rather hoped that Britain would take over in Perak. By an agreement signed on 20 January 1874, they undertook to disarm, destroy their stockades, and allow a free return to the mines, where British officers would settle outstanding claims. The Chinese agreed to respect the authority of the Sultan of Perak's officials. They also

[1] Read, op. cit., pp. 25–26; Plunket attributes this to Kim Ching.

[2] William Alexander Pickering lived in Formosa, 1863–70, where he helped the U.S. Govt. in negotiations with the inhabitants in the south of the island. He was appointed Chinese Interpreter to the Straits Govt. in 1871.   [3] Pickering to gov. 8 Jan. 1874. C.O. 809/1, p. 176.

accepted a British Resident in Larut to regulate such things as the water-supply to the mines.[1] Speedy, the mantri's commander, became, provisionally, Assistant Resident for Larut, and the settlement was an immediate success. The Chinese soon flocked back to the mines; a wartime population of 4,000 rose to 33,000.[2] One Chinese summed up the success of the Pangkor settlement in the Larut area of Perak in the words, 'Empress good-coolie get money: Keep it'.[3]

In Perak proper, however, settlement was not so simple. Sir Andrew Clarke was unable to grasp the essentials of the succession dispute. His emissaries could throw no more light on the disputed election of 1871 than Irving. In 1872 Irving had favoured 'Abdu'llah's case after failing to meet Ismail and hearing his case only from the mantri. But in 1873 both George Campbell and Colonel Anson at Penang had taken the opposite view. They opposed 'Abdu'llah and were pro-mantri. Their view had culminated in Sir Harry Ord's recognition of the mantri in August 1873.[4]

Clarke gained the quite erroneous impression, as he prepared for the conference, that 'Abdu'llah was sultan *de jure* while Ismail reigned *de facto*. The governor understood the former to be an opium addict and unpopular with the people, while the latter had powerful support in the mantri and the 'up-river' chiefs. McNair and Dunlop failed to clarify the matter. They could only record the mantri's independent position in Larut,[5] which Clarke realized he might have to confirm. The governor appears to have gone to Pangkor hoping to reaffirm Ismail as sultan and regularize the mantri's position in Larut. No one seems to have noticed the claims of Raja Yusuf.

Clarke completely changed his mind at Pangkor. He was surprised to find 'Abdu'llah 'a man of considerable intelligence',[6] who was supported by all the chiefs present except the mantri. Clarke was not

---

[1] C.O. 809/1, pp. 105–6; Cowan, *Nineteenth Century Malaya*, pp. 180–4.

[2] Speedy's first annual report encl. in Clarke to Carnarvon 6 Apr. 1875. C.O. 809/5, p. 97.

[3] I. L. Bird, *The Golden Chersonese and the Way Thither*, London, 1883, p. 255.

[4] Cowan, op. cit., pp. 185–6, n. 30, suggests that Clarke was aware of this action, but disagreed with it.

[5] Report of 14 Jan. 1874. C.O. 809/1, p. 99.

[6] Clarke to Kimberley 26 Jan. 1874. C.O. 273/75.

impressed by the mantri, who was reluctant to disarm his Hai San allies. He was also suspected of harbouring ambitions for the sultanate. He denied it, but was given short shrift by Clarke. 'Abdu'llah, on the other hand, was conciliatory, agreed to confirm the mantri's authority in Larut, and he won the loyalty of all the chiefs present. Only the mantri hedged. Afterwards he complained that with 'Abdu'llah and his supporters at Pangkor, and Ismail and Yusuf absent, there had been little choice.[1] The charge was quite true. Sir Andrew Clarke had taken the law into his own hands. He concluded that he could regard Ismail's election in 1871 as a temporary expedient, and he set about reversing it.[2] Subsequent events would prove this to have been a major blunder.

The 'Pangkor Engagement' of 20 January 1874 completely reversed the situation in Perak.[3] 'Abdu'llah was recognized as sultan, Ismail being permitted to retain the title of 'Sultan-Muda'. The idea of the Residents was adopted for the future government of Perak. The Residents' advice would be asked and acted upon in all matters except Malay religion and custom; an Assistant Resident would advise the mantri in Larut. Residents' salaries would be a first charge on the Perak revenues; sultan, bendahara and mantri would be provided with a civil list; and revenue collection and expenditure would be supervised by the Resident. Finally, to aid the suppression of piracy, two small portions of territory on the coast — the Dindings and Krian — were to be ceded to Britain.

Less than three weeks after Pangkor, Clarke turned to Selangor. The civil war had ended, but piracy provided the motive for intervention as it had in Perak. A notorious incident had occurred in the Jugra river in November 1873. Nine suspects in the case had been arrested in the colony at Malacca, and this gave Clarke his 'key' to Selangor.

He planned to force Sultan 'Abdul-Samad to suppress piracy under the terms of the 1826 treaty. Therefore, after stationing an impressive display of naval force at the mouth of the Langat, Clarke sailed

[1] Cowan, 'Swettenham's Journals', p. 62.
[2] Braddell's account 28 Jan. 1874. C.O. 809/1, pp. 191–8.
[3] Text in C.O. 809/1, pp. 103–4; Parkinson, *British Intervention in Malaya*, pp. 137–8, discusses a slightly variant Malay text of the Engagement. Cowan, op. cit., pp. 184–9.

upstream on 8 February 1874. The sultan was at first, reluctant to meet the governor. He probably feared that the Tengku Zia'u'd-din was about to be made sultan,[1] rather as 'Abdu'llah had been selected in Perak. But when the sultan agreed to negotiate, Clarke made sure that the sultan bore his son-in-law no ill will. He then sent for Zia'u'd-din. This was Clarke's first sight of the tengku. The governor was very impressed by the effect of the dramatic little encounter on the sultan, who, after cheerfully greeting the tengku, proceeded to explain his status in Selangor.

Clarke soon felt he had the measure of the Selangor chiefs. Sultan 'Abdul-Samad' seemed quite able to manage affairs if he wished; but, being an indolent opium-smoker, preferred to enjoy life. 'A rather careless heathen philosopher,' Braddell called him.[2] Tengku Zia'u'd-din, on the other hand, impressed Clarke's party as 'a very good fellow'.[3] The governor decided, therefore, to maintain the *status quo* in Selangor. As the Jugra pirates had murdered some British subjects the sultan must bring them to law. 'Abdu'l-Samad readily agreed, and appointed Zia'u'd-din to try them. Clarke also insisted that the sultan must prevent piracy in the future and promised British support. Piracy could no longer be brushed off as 'the affair of the boys' and the sultan told his sons (one of whom was suspect in the Jugra case) to heed the governor. With British warships in Selangor's rivers, the sultan really had no option but to comply with Clarke's demand.

Sir Andrew Clarke left Selangor on 12 February 1874 after a conference quite as swift as Pangkor. Major McNair and James Davidson remained to ensure that the pirates got a fair trial. The tengku pronounced the accused guilty on 15 February, execution followed next day, and the Jugra stockades were destroyed. To underline the new phase in his régime the Tengku Zia'u'd-din toured southern Selangor in gunboats of the Royal Navy.[4]

It is true that the Langat conference was not sealed with a document like the Pangkor Engagement. But the sultan no doubt reaffirmed Tengku Zia'u'd-din's position in some way, and he agreed to a British officer as adviser. By May 1874 it became known that

[1] Braddell's 'Report on Selangor', 18 Feb. 1874. C.O. 809/1, p. 214.
[2] Ibid. p. 219.   [3] Vetch, *Life of Clarke*, p. 160.
[4] McNair and Davidson to Colonial Secretary Straits Settlements 21 Feb. 1874. C.O. 809/1, p. 222.

James Guthrie Davidson, the tengku's Singapore banker, was to be Resident.[1] Later Frank Swettenham became Assistant Resident, with the task of advising the sultan at Langat. Thus, after less than three months at Singapore, and two quick visits to the Malay States, Sir Andrew Clarke had laid the foundations of the 'Resident System' in Malaya.

COLONIAL OFFICE CAUTION

The governor's speed was not matched by the Colonial Office. After cautiously approving the Pangkor telegram they had then sat back to await the full report.[2] Accounts of the Pangkor and Langat conferences did not reach the Colonial Office until 30 March 1874. They were accompanied by the endorsement of the leading Straits officials, of whom only Irving disapproved of the Residents. Braddell thought the 'innate superiority of the ordinary Englishman in his sense of honour and justice, is sufficient to dominate the inferior character of the Malay'.[3] Birch, the Colonial Secretary of the Straits, believed 'complete annexation' or a 'Protectorate' were the only alternatives, and he preferred the latter.[4]

These reports created no alarm in the Colonial Office. The matter was obviously not treated with any degree of urgency. Charles Cox, the head of the Eastern Department, who usually endorsed documents on the day of receipt, studied them for a week before venturing an opinion. He was impressed by Clarke's achievement, but feared that force might have to be used to uphold the agreements.

> It appears to me that Sir A[ndrew] C[larke] deserves the greatest credit for having brought all these disturbing elements to agree to the proposed arrangement & I do not see why it is not to work well. At the same time we must not keep out of sight that from some unforseen cause we may possibly be called upon to take steps to prevent some attempted violation

---

[1] Clarke did not report this home until the end of the year, but it became known in London in May. Stanley of Alderley to Carnarvon 10 May 1874. *Carnarvon Papers*, P.R.O. 30/6/21.

[2] Mins. by Cox 3 Mar., Herbert 5 Mar., and Carnarvon 6 Mar., on Clarke to Kimberley 21 Jan. 1874. C.O. 273/75.

[3] C.O. 809/1, p. 246.   [4] Ibid. p. 247.

of the Agreement, or to enforce an adherence to some of its provisions.
I do not think it is likely so long as the Residents shall act judiciously
avoiding as much as possible interference in minor matters.

Herbert, on the other hand, was much more optimistic. He did not
think they would be 'dangerously compromised in any way'.

> We are now obliged to interfere frequently on the Coast to prevent
> piracy & as English enterprise makes its way into the interior we shall
> almost certainly have to follow it to redress outrages on Englishmen
> unless we adopt Sir A[ndrew] Clarkes's preventative policy which may
> be expected to give the best prospect of avoiding complications.[1]

But not everyone at home was so satisfied. Just as Parliament forced
the Conservative Government to tackle the problem of slavery in the
Gold Coast, so a motion in the House of Lords forced Carnarvon to
come to a decision about Malaya.

Lord Stanley of Alderley, possibly briefed by Sir Benson Maxwell,
the former Singapore Chief Justice, moved a resolution of censure on
the Government's policy in Malaya on 19 May 1874. He maintained that Clarke did not understand what he was doing in Malaya.
The Straits officials had led him into 'equivocal and entangling'
engagements. Stanley predicted that the result of it all would be an
invasion, conquest of the Peninsula, possibly another campaign like the
Ashanti War. The Residents would virtually become the rulers of
the states, as experience in India indicated. Lord Stanley, in fact,
made a harsh indictment of Clarke's policy — and very shortly was
to be proved right. Unfortunately, he did not commend his case to
the House of Lords by his inaudibility, or by producing an array of
skeletons from the cupboard concerning past years, and he lost his
vote.[2]

The House of Lords debate, however, provided an important landmark in the Malayan question. It forced Carnarvon to make a preliminary decision on the Resident system. On the day after the debate
he recorded his first general approval of the Pangkor and Langat

[1] Mins. by Cox 6 Apr., and Herbert 2 May, on Clarke to Kimberley
24 Feb. 1874. C.O. 273/75.

[2] 3 *Hansard*, 219, cols. 467–73. In the C.O. it was thought that Lord
Stanley was being encouraged by Sir Benson Maxwell, former Chief Justice
of the Straits and Sir Harry Ord's great opponent.

settlements.[1]   But, at the same time, he wrote privately cautioning Clarke:

> Peace and order, the revival of trade and the suppression of piracy must conduce directly to English interests: and I certainly am not disposed to quarrel with an extension of English influence rightly and fairly developed . . . we are entering upon new ground and relations of a somewhat delicate nature. The history of Indian 'Residents' is too recent and marked not to serve to throw light upon similar appointments in the Peninsula . . . we become through them much more closely connected than heretofore with things and persons and political combinations that may easily lead us further than we now intend to go. This new phase therefore of Colonial policy needs very careful watching—and I think more by those on the spot, where is far greater power of immediate control, than by the Secretary of State in London.[2]

Carnarvon's letter reveals a good deal about the spirit of Britain's assumption of control in some of the Malay States. The man on the spot had, as so frequently happened, exceeded his instructions. Although he was given this mild caution, a wide local discretion was also re-affirmed. Carnarvon realized clearly that a major change of course had been made in Malaya. It is significant, however, that he wished it to be known that the Resident system was an experiment which still needed careful watching.[3]

THE SUNGEI UJONG EXPEDITION

While the Colonial Office proceeded cautiously, Clarke turned his attention to the territory between Selangor and Malacca. Here trouble centred on the Linggi river — the navigable highway to the tin mines of Sungei Ujong. This region became the scene of Sir Andrew Clarke's third Malayan settlement. Dato'Klana-Sayid

[1] Min. by Carnarvon 20 May, on Clarke to Carnarvon 24 Feb. 1874. C.O. 273/75.

[2] Carnarvon to Clarke 27 May 1874, private (copy). *Carnarvon Papers*, P.R.O. 30/6/40, p. 2.

[3] That the Residents were understood as an 'experiment' is clearly proved by Gen. Ponsonby's explanation of the system to Queen Victoria after the Perak War in 1875. 'Sir Andrew Clarke . . . appointed residents in Malay territory, but merely as an experiment.' 15 Dec. 1875. *Royal Archives*, P. 25/17.

'Abdu'r-Rahman of Sungei Ujong bound himself to govern on principles of justice and equality and to protect the traffic on the river. The agreement, which was signed in Singapore on 21 April 1874, also provided that 'the Station, District or Settlement of Sempang as far as Permatang Passir shall be placed under the control and direction of the British Government'. In return for this concession and surety for $50,000, Clarke promised the 'moral and material guarantee and protection' of the British Government for the maintenance of the independence of Sungei Ujong.[1]

By comparison with the Pangkor and Langat settlements, the Sungei Ujong agreement was grandiose but incredibly vague.[2] It was probably a preliminary move to get the Dato'Klana to join a general settlement of all parties interested in the Linggi. A conference on the spot was planned for the beginning of May 1874.[3] But, when Clarke duly arrived to unlock his third 'door' into the Malay States, escorted by his usual force of British warships, this time the key failed to turn smoothly. The Dato'Perba of Rembau, whose stockade at Bukit Tiga had been threatening river traffic, failed to turn up. Clarke was reduced to committing himself to one side in Sungei Ujong, as he had in Perak. His men destroyed the offending stockade. He decided to throw the weight of his Government's power to the support of the Dato'Klana as controller of the Linggi.[4] In other words, having failed to secure a third 'Pangkor', Clarke resorted to the usual practice of expanding British influence by taking sides in a local dispute.

When reports of his action reached London the Colonial Office again had no objections. They realized that the settlement was only a second best, but felt they could overlook the engagements which Clarke 'failed to secure'.[5] For the remainder of 1874 little news of any kind reached London from Malaya. Carnarvon decided, never-

[1] Windstedt, 'Negri Sembilan', p. 71; Vetch, *Life of Clarke*, p. 165. Clarke alluded vaguely to the meeting in a private letter dated 23 Apr. 1874. *Carnarvon Papers*, P.R.O. 30/6/40, p. 1.

[2] Sir Benson Maxwell called it 'a bond gone mad' (*Our Malay Conquests*, London, 1878, p. 38).

[3] Clarke to Carnarvon 8 May 1874. C.O. 809/1, p. 257.

[4] Clarke to Carnarvon 29 June 1874 (private). *Carnarvon Papers*, P.R.O. 30/6/40, p. 3.

[5] Min. by Carnarvon 20 July on Clarke to Carnarvon 8 May 1874. C.O. 273/75.

theless, to go ahead with the Resident system. As Disraeli had trusted his Colonial Secretary completely over the Gold Coast and Fiji, which both attracted more publicity in Britain in 1874, Carnarvon had no reason to hold back with the new experiment in the Malay States.

The month of August 1874 became the time for final decision on the imperial frontier in the tropics. The governor of New South Wales was authorized to annex Fiji by a telegram on 10 August. Governor Strahan of the Gold Coast was sent his secret orders to inquire and report on the possibility of abolishing domestic slavery on 21 August. One imagines, therefore, that when one of the assistant under-secretaries suggested on 29 August that they should provide Clarke with instructions as to the Malay States, Carnarvon was quite prepared to approve the new policy in what he obviously regarded as the least urgent of the three cases.[1] Authority for the appointment of Residents in Perak and Selangor was sent on 4 September 1874.[2] As Clarke himself was appointed a member of the Viceroy of India's Council early in 1875, the formal approval of the choice of Residents, and investigations into the problem of Malay debt-slavery, would be left to his successor Sir William Jervois.[3]

Clarke's last contribution to Malayan policy was to lay the foundations of the Resident system in Sungei Ujong. This time the initiative came more directly from the Malay ruler. The Dato'Klana requested support in September 1874. He wanted to fly the British flag over his house at Ampangan 'so as to be under the protection of the Great Governor'.[4] The Dato'Bandar was about to attack the Dato'Klana. The Chinese miners at Rasa were likely to take sides as in Perak and Selangor. Clarke therefore sent Pickering to the Linggi on 4 October 1874 to mediate in the Malay dispute and try to prevent a new Chinese War.

Pickering's mission to the Linggi vividly illustrates Sir Andrew Clarke's failure to realize what he was doing in Malaya. Only at this stage of his involvement in Sungei Ujong did he discover that there was

[1] Mins. by Meade 29 Aug., and Carnarvon 30 Aug., on Clarke to Carnarvon 27 June 1874. C.O. 273/76.
[2] Carnarvon to Clarke 4 Sept. 1874. C.O. 809/1, p. 266.
[3] Carnarvon to Jervois 8 Apr. 1875. C.O. 809/5, p. 89, and 25 May 1875. Ibid., p. 119.
[4] Dato'Klana to Shaw 24 Sept. 1874. C.O. 809/5, p. 64.

a long-standing constitutional relationship between Dato'Klana and Dato'Bandar. The latter claimed both a share of the Sungei Ujong revenues and a right to be consulted in affairs of State.[1] Clarke's earlier Linggi agreements, in April and May 1874, had completely

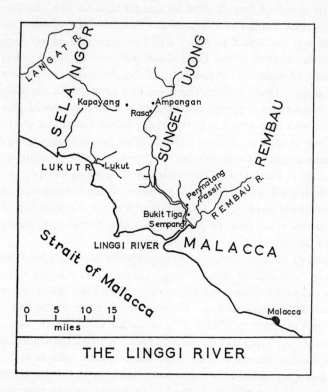

THE LINGGI RIVER

failed to take this into account. The governor, while largely ignorant of the situation in Sungei Ujong, had committed himself to a weak and unpopular ruler.

Pickering was not able to salvage very much by persuasion. Although Dato'Bandar-Tunggal at first undertook not to attack the Dato'Klana, he refused to join the Linggi agreements. Asserting his independence he fortified himself in stockades at Kapayang. The Dato'Klana tried to dislodge him by force and captured the forts at Rasa and Rahang on

[1] See above, pp. 183–4. Clarke to Carnarvon 29 Dec. 1874. C.O. 809/5, p. 32.

16 November 1874, but his men ran away before Tunggal's fort at Kapayang. The Dato'Bandar soon recovered Rasa and Rahang.

At this stage Pickering sent a desperate appeal for help to the colony: 'The Tunku Klana is a cur . . . but we don't like to leave him . . . we are surrounded here'.[1] A small detachment of British troops therefore left Malacca immediately, which enabled Pickering to recapture Rasa on 23 November. The governor rushed up from Singapore and landed 180 marines, sailors, police and infantry at Lukut. They advanced to Kapayang, to find the forts deserted on 30 November. Clarke therefore hastened on to Selangor to make sure that Sultan 'Abdu'l-Samad did not harbour Dato'Bandar-Tunggal. With Swettenham there to keep him to his word the sultan refused to help the fugitive, who finally gave himself up in Singapore in December 1874. With the chief source of trouble removed, a settlement was now possible in Sungei Ujong.

The British expedition retired in December 1874. Having lost only one sailor it had survived well in the interior. Sir Andrew Clarke was rather pleased with his little foray.[2] Captain Tatham, the commanding officer, became the first Resident in Sungei Ujong, with a detachment of 50 men to keep order. Pickering found over 10,000 Chinese around Rasa. He persuaded them to give up their arms, and sign an agreement by which leases, royalties, water-supplies and boat licences would be regulated by the Resident. Mining soon resumed and tin traffic began to flow down the Linggi. Clarke had made good the failure of the spring. But his intervention in Sungei Ujong had been rather more impromptu than the conferences at Pangkor and Langat. The rescue of the Dato'Klana represented the first use of force to uphold the new policy in Malaya.

THE PERAK WAR

In Perak force was needed on a much larger scale. Here the British Government faced a crisis which was compared with the Ashanti War. The superficiality of the Pangkor settlement led to a major disaster. Already by April 1874, when James Birch and Frank Swettenham

[1] Vetch, *Life of Clarke*, pp. 167–8.
[2] Clarke to Carnarvon 15 Dec. 1874 (private). *Carnarvon Papers*, P.R.O. 30/6/40, p. 21.

toured Perak, there were signs of tension. The Malays of Perak determined to resist British encroachment.

Birch, the Colonial Secretary of the Straits, had applied for the post of Resident. But he discovered that not only were Ismail, Yusuf and the 'up-river' chiefs — none of whom were at Pangkor — most dissatisfied with the new régime, but that even Sultan 'Abdu'llah's supporters were uneasy. The governor's intentions in appointing the Residents were obviously not understood by the Malays. It was even rumoured that Britain intended to take over the whole of the state. The general impression abroad in Perak was that Clarke had 'appointed' 'Abdu'llah as sultan. Clarke always maintained that the chiefs had elected 'Abdu'llah freely at Pangkor.[1] The regalia remained in the hands of Ismail, who refused to meet the governor in Penang.

Both the Malay factions, had, in fact, set about undermining the Pangkor Engagement. 'Abdu'llah had asked a Penang lawyer named Dukes if the Dindings cession could be rescinded. Ismail and Yusuf planned with the mantri's lawyer, Robert Woods, to send a deputation to Parliament to get the Pangkor Engagement cancelled.[2] Raja Yusuf, who had been completely ignored by Governor Clarke, impressed Swettenham both by his bearing and his intelligently expressed claims to the succession. By the time Birch became the Resident for Perak proper in November 1874 the atmosphere within the state was hardly conducive to careful experiments in government.

Moreover, if Clarke had been blind to the real situation in Perak, Birch was equally blind to Malay susceptibilities when he tried to make the Resident system work. He has been condemned by many writers for his haste, and C. N. Parkinson has even suggested there was a suicidal element in his actions.[3] After establishing his Residency at Bandar Bahru, on the lower Perak river, in 1875, he commenced his administrative reforms by brushing aside the Malays who stood in his way. He offended Ismail and the mantri's party by his determination to install 'Abdu'llah as sultan. He also treated 'Abdu'llah with con-

[1] Anson, *About Others and Myself*, p. 322; Cowan, 'Swettenham's Journals', pp. 57–62.

[2] 'Précis of Evidence', p. 4; Clarke to Carnarvon 4 Nov. 1874 (private). *Carnarvon Papers*, P.R.O. 30/6/40, p. 13.

[3] Parkinson, *British Intervention in Malaya*, pp. 219–22.

tempt and endeavoured to exclude him from the effective government of the state.

Even Sir Andrew Clarke became displeased with Birch's methods. He confessed to Colonel Anson:

> I am very much annoyed with Birch, and the head-over-heels way in which he does things; he and I will come to sorrow yet, if he does not mind. He . . . does not seem to have impressed either the Sultan or the ex-Sultan very favourably.[1]

What none of the Straits officials realized, however, was that 'Abdu'llah was secretly encouraging Ismail to retain the regalia. By the time Sir William Jervois arrived in Singapore on 8 May 1875, all the chiefs in Perak seemed bent on opposition to the new régime.

The new governor was expected to pave the way for the final settlement in Malaya. He brought instructions from Carnarvon to inquire and report so that the appointment of the Residents could be confirmed.[2] His attention was also drawn to the problem of Malay debt-slavery. As Carnarvon had made a successful gamble in starting to abolish domestic slavery in the Gold Coast, it was logical that he should desire 'the abatement of a practice so cruel and impolitic' in Malaya.[3]

Jervois began his administration, however, in somewhat unfortunate circumstances. Because of a request from the London Straits Settlements Association, Clarke was asked to stay on for two weeks to talk over Malay matters with his successor. Jervois was the senior officer. It was quite obvious that all was not going well with Clarke's plans for Perak. A deputation from 'Abdu'llah was in Singapore, complaining about Birch, when Jervois arrived. Birch soon announced his conviction that 'Abdu'llah was a 'vain little idiot', that he was quite unfit to rule, and set on breaking the Pangkor Engagement. The people of Perak seemed to prefer Ismail.[4]

As soon as Clarke was out of the way, Jervois warned Carnarvon that 'there is not that "holy calm" reigning in the Peninsula which the Pangkor treaty is generally supposed to have inaugurated'.[5] There is

[1] Anson, op. cit. p. 323.
[2] Carnarvon to Jervois 8 Apr. 1875. C.O. 809/5, p. 89.
[3] Ibid. p. 119. Carnarvon to Jervois 25 May 1875.
[4] Birch to Secretary of Native States 13 May 1875. C.O. 809/6, p. 39.
[5] Jervois to Carnarvon 29 May 1875 (private). P.R.O. 30/6/40, p. 22.

every likelihood that Jervois and Clarke disagreed during their discussions over Perak. Clarke had supported 'Abdu'llah and was not
very satisfied with Birch. Jervois decided to support Birch and to
reconsider the question of Ismail. When Clarke called to bid farewell
to Colonel Anson in Penang he hinted at a disagreement by remarking
that 'Jervois has plunged into the native states head-over-heels'.[1]

Jervois had, in fact, decided that Perak should be annexed. He
outlined his policy for Perak in a private letter to Carnarvon on 10
July 1875. 'Abdu'llah was useless, he said. The rajas were still
levying their own taxes along the Perak river, and the Straits Government had already advanced about £15,000 to Perak. On top of all
this, debt-slavery and Malay–Chinese rivalry persisted.

> It appears to me that the Residential system which implies advice as
> distinguished from control, is not calculated to meet the requirements
> either present or future of the case. The Sultan and Rajahs . . . are our
> obstacles to any just and enlightened system of government . . . we
> should, as opportunity offers, take possession of those States. . . . This
> may be done without shedding blood and without opposition from the
> people, except Sultans and Rajahs who profit by the present state of
> things.[2]

Jervois proposed pensioning off the troublesome rajas and ruling Perak
indirectly through men (presumably like Tengku 'Zia'u'd-din of
Selangor) 'who would virtually become British officers and would be
associated with the British official element only so far as necessary to
supplement the native element'. The time seemed ripe for this in
Perak; revenue would be adequate; it would benefit the state, and the
cause of humanity and freedom.

Jervois's plan for annexation came as a rude shock for Carnarvon.
Now for the first time the Malay States presented him with an urgent,
and possibly dangerous, decision. Jervois forced Carnarvon to consider
the Malay States seriously. He called for a map of the area on 1
September 1875. He studied memoranda about the states.[3] During
the previous year, when he had treated the Fiji and Gold Coast
questions urgently, and had worked hard on his new policy, he tended
to leave Malaya to the permanent officials. The Resident system was

[1] Anson, op. cit. p. 324.
[2] Jervois to Carnarvon 10 July 1875 (private). P.R.O. 30/6/40, p. 28.
[3] Min. by Carnarvon 1 Sept. 1875 in C.O. 273/80.

a matter for leisurely experiment. Now Jervois was advocating something much more akin to the Fiji annexation or the scheme of legislative control in the Gold Coast. Jervois almost seemed to be appealing
to the Gold Coast and Fiji cases. The existence of slavery in the
former and 'undefined serfdom' in the latter had moved Carnarvon
to take up a position of moral responsibility in both.

Professor Cowan has gone as far as to suggest that Carnarvon was
so shocked by Jervois's letter that he determined to 'nip such ideas in
the bud'.[1] But this opinion is based upon the answer which Carnarvon
gave to a later letter. The remarkable thing is that when he first read
Jervois's plan Carnarvon agreed in principle with the idea. He admitted
to his colleague Lord Salisbury, the Secretary of State for India, and
to Queen Victoria, that while he did not want to change influence
and protection into direct sovereignty at the moment, he thought the
'time must come for this and probably soon'. For the present, the
Government had commitments elsewhere:

> my hands are *extraordinarily* full of very heavy work now. Moreover
> I shall probably be obliged to annex Zululand ... and I am beset on all
> sides with applications to take New Guinea. I therefore much desire to
> keep the existing system in the Malay Peninsula for a time at all events:
> and I think it can be done.[2]

Salisbury, for his part, fully agreed. Annexation in Malaya might
alarm other Asian states and complicate Britain's relations with Burma,
Siam and China. Worse still it might 'raise to a fever heat the war
passions of the Anglo-Indians. It might be possible in a year's
time'.[3] Thus there was no intention at home of approving Jervois's
plans.

Yet only a week later, on 13 September 1875, Carnarvon had a
bigger shock. He had the unfortunate experience of discovering,
while in attendance on Queen Victoria at Balmoral Castle, that
Jervois was embarking on his new plans without waiting for approval.
He learnt that after a visit to the east coast of Malaya in July 1875

[1] Cowan, *Nineteenth Century Malaya*, p. 231.
[2] Carnarvon to Salisbury 3 Sept. 1875, private (copy), *Carnarvon Papers*,
P.R.O. 30/6/10, p. 20. To Queen Victoria, Carnarvon wrote: 'the time
may come when such a policy will be desirable, but he thinks that the moment
has not yet arrived'. 12 Sept. 1875. *Royal Archives*, p. 24/164.
[3] Salisbury to Carnarvon 5 Sept. 1875. P.R.O. 30/6/10, P. 21.

Jervois had failed to persuade the Bendahara of Pahang to accept a Resident,[1] but that in Perak he expected that Yusuf and Ismail would shortly ask the British Government to intervene. 'Everything seems to render it inevitable that Perak must become part of the British Dominions — and that, without costing a penny or firing a shot.'[2] On the day he read this, Carnarvon wrote an urgent reply from Balmoral. He still agreed that Jervois's policy might eventually become necessary, but he ordered the governor to stop. In view of events in Burma and China, and the fact that public opinion at home was only adjusting itself to the novelty of the new Residents, the new plan was not to be attempted.[3] This was the letter quoted by Professor Cowan. But the warning was too late. The next information to reach London was a dramatic telegram on 4 November 1875 announcing the murder of James Birch, the Resident in Perak.

Birch's murder was the major crisis of Britain's intervention in Malaya. It was the response of the Malays to the Jervois plan for Perak. The governor had made up his mind very quickly that the best solution was 'to declare Perak British territory, and govern it accordingly'. But since this would have involved British law and citizenship for the inhabitants, Jervois had decided, in practice, to adopt a cheaper system of governing Perak by British officers, ruling in the name of the sultan. Instead of advising, as stipulated in the Pangkor Engagement, the Resident would control the state. With the title now of 'Queen's Commissioner', he would co-operate with the Malay ruler and a Malay council.[4]

Jervois toured Perak with a large party of officials early in September 1875 to persuade the rulers to accept his plan. Raja Yusuf agreed, but neither Ismail nor 'Abdu'llah would answer. In view of certain important events in Peark, of which the governor was not aware, this was not surprising. A movement was, in fact, afoot to get rid of Birch and oust the British. Swettenham, for one, certainly sensed

[1] Jervois to Carnarvon 7 Aug. 1875 (confidential). C.O. 809/6, p. 9. Received in C.O. 13 Sept.

[2] Jervois to Carnarvon 7 Aug. 1875 (private). *Carnarvon Papers*, P.R.O. 30/6/40, p. 30.

[3] Carnarvon to Jervois 13 Sept. 1875, private (copy). P.R.O. 30/6/40, p. 29.

[4] Jervois to Carnarvon 16 Oct. 1875. C.O. 809/6, pp. 33–34.

a tension in the air.[1]   But no one knew that 'Abdu'llah was prepared to unite with Ismail to get rid of Birch.   All the time while Jervois was in Perak plans were going ahead in a plot to murder Birch.

Jervois made a final desperate bid for the sultan's acceptance at the end of September.   He provided Birch with two documents: one was for 'Abdu'llah to sign indicating that he accepted the Jervois plan, the other was an offer of the sultanate to Yusuf, should the first document fail.   Actually, 'Abdu'llah accepted the Jervois plan without the threat being used.   But when Birch then tried to get him to sign proclamations appointing Englishmen as judges in Perak, with powers over finance, 'Abdu'llah hesitated.   Then Birch produced the second document and forced him to give way.

It was on a trip to the lower Perak river distributing these proclamations that Birch was killed on 2 November 1875, at Pasir Salak, the home of Maharaja Lela, the chief who had volunteered to arrange the deed.[2]   A small force of British troops, summoned to the spot from Penang, tried to capture the stockade at Pasir Salak on 7 November.   They were rebuffed with the loss of Captain Innes, the commanding officer.   At this point Governor Jervois arrived on the scene.

Birch's murder, which wrecked the Jervois plan for Perak, and nearly ruined its author's career, was primarily the result of the governor's obstinacy.   After giving Birch the go-ahead in Perak, Jervois wrote a long account of his new policy for Carnarvon.[3]   Shortly after sending it he received Carnarvon's urgent letter from Balmoral.   Yet instead of restraining Birch, Jervois obstinately stuck to his guns.   He believed it was too late to go back.   He defended his action in a private letter by insisting that if the advice of the Resident was really followed he would, in practice, become the ruler of the state.   If, on the other hand, the advice was not followed, there were only two alternatives: withdrawal or the use of force.   If Britain retired, the causes which had led to intervention in the first place would be left free to operate

[1] Cowan, 'Swettenham's Journals', p. 96.
[2] See 'Précis of Evidence', pp. 21–27; Cowan, *Nineteenth Century Malaya*, pp. 228–9, 232–9; Parkinson, *British Intervention in Malaya*, pp. 238–9.
[3] Jervois to Carnarvon 16 Oct. 1875.   C.O. 809/6, p. 28.

again.   The obvious choice was therefore to take steps to enforce the Resident's advice from the start.   This was the justification of the Jervois plan.[1]

It is important to realize, however, that when Carnarvon received the news of Birch's murder, on 4 November 1875, this explanation by Jervois had not reached London.   As a major crisis in Asia loomed on the horizon, the Colonial Office was ignorant of the exact plan and its justification, let alone the precise cause of the murder.   All Carnarvon knew was that Jervois had contemplated annexation, and had been forbidden to attempt it.   When Carnarvon was asked to sanction the employment of a brigade of troops he was naturally shocked at the scale of Jervois's campaign.   The Cabinet sanctioned military support, but hoped to avoid large-scale operations.[2]

A week after the first news of the murder a series of urgent telegrams had still failed to produce an explanation from Jervois.   The governor had gone to the scene of action where there was no telegraph. No answer had arrived by 12 November 1875, when Carnarvon learnt the details of the military requirements: 750 infantry and 80 artillerymen from the Straits garrison were already in the field;   General Colborne, the commander-in-chief, was bringing 300 regulars from Hong Kong;   Jervois also wanted 2 battalions and a mountain battery from India.   He planned to march one force through Larut overland to the upper Perak, and send another up-river from the Residency.   In other words, he demanded large reinforcements from a Government which was in the dark as to their purpose.

Lord Salisbury shared Carnarvon's amazement and was reluctant to let the battalions leave India.   'A more unsatisfactory explanation of a war I never read,' he wrote.   'Perak can if need be be recaptured; a panic in India might be irreparable.'[3]   Carnarvon believed that they should not withhold reinforcements but 'prevent if possible this expedition growing into a serious war'.[4]   To cap it all the cable between

[1] Jervois to Carnarvon 18 Oct. 1875 (private).   *Carnarvon Papers*, P.R.O. 30/6/40, p. 32.

[2] Carnarvon to Ponsonby 5 Nov. 1875.   *Royal Archives*, P. 24/169.

[3] Salisbury to Carnarvon 13 Nov. and Nov. 1875.   P.R.O.   30/6/10, pp. 30–31.

[4] Carnarvon to Queen Victoria 13 Nov. 1875.   *Royal Archives*, P. 24/170.

Madras and Penang broke down. And Carnarvon still had no explanation from Jervois. As he remarked to the queen's secretary, 'The curtain has fallen at the moment when it had become most interesting'.[1] Disraeli was preoccupied at this moment with buying the Suez Canal shares.[2]

Not until 22 November, nearly three weeks after Birch's murder, did Jervois's despatches (written, of course, before the event) reach London. Members of the Cabinet were immediately informed. Carnarvon noted that Jervois understood that some of the Perak chiefs wanted Britain to govern Perak and had gone ahead with his plans. He seized on this as the 'cause of the war'.[3] He claimed that Jervois had directly announced the annexation of the province. On 23 November a cable was opened to Singapore via Siberia, and soon a telegram dated 18 November (which had, in fact, gone by ship to the cable station in Ceylon) brought the governor's long-awaited explanations. He claimed there was universal support for his action in the Straits and demanded a show of force in Perak.[4]

News arrived on 24 November that Pasir Salak had been captured, and that, although 'Abdu'llah professed his loyalty, some of his chiefs were implicated in the murder. Jervois feared a national uprising in Malaya. He now went as far as to suggest that the whole coastline from Krian to the mouth of the Perak river should be annexed and held by force.

The Perak expedition of 1875, like the Ashanti expedition of the previous year, appeared to the Cabinet in London to be a major crisis on the frontiers of empire. In contrast to the march on Kumasi, however, the Perak expedition should be described as an occupation rather than a war. As the British forces arrived in Perak, 'Abdu'llah and others professed their loyalty, but the guilty Maharaja Lela fled to join Ismail at Blanja. Jervois's military objective was the pursuit of the fugitives and the occupation of upper Perak. In order to attempt

[1] Ibid. P.25/1. Carnarvon to Ponsonby 16 Nov. 1875.
[2] Ibid. Disraeli to Queen Victoria 18 Nov. 1875. A.49/50 and 24 Nov. 1875. A.50/3.
[3] Note on Jervois to Carnarvon 18 Oct. 1875. *Carnarvon Papers*, P.R.O. 30/6/40, p. 32.
[4] Jervois to Carnarvon (telegram) 18 Nov. 1875. C.O. 809/6, p. 64.

I.F.T.—L

this, an excessive force was used, which failed in the first object, and resented the second.[1]

Major-General Colborne's 300 men from Hong Kong left Bandar Bahru, on the lower Perak, on 8 December 1875, and reached Blanja by river on 13 December. Ismail had fled to Kinta. After a difficult overland march the troops reached Kinta on 17 December, but Ismail had by then slipped away. Brigadier Ross led the troops from India up the Larut river on 29 November. Crossing the hills to Kuala Kangsa on the upper Perak, they sent a belated party down-river to link up with Colborne at Blanja. The rest of Ross's men cleared out a trouble-nest at Kota Lama on 4 January 1876, when the brigade major lost his life. A third force landed at Pangkor to subdue the coast region if necessary. None of these formidable forces succeeded in capturing the fugitives.

At home in England the Perak expedition caused a good deal of alarm. British leaders have sometimes grumbled that crises always seem to occur at the week-end. The Perak crisis disturbed Carnarvon's Christmas in the country. When he heard that the fugitives Ismail and Lela had escaped to Patani, in Siamese territory, he did not know what to to do.[2] Writing to Sir Stafford Northcote, the Chancellor of the Exchequer, on Christmas Day 1875, he regretted there was no summer palace to sack in Perak as in Elgin's Peking; there did not even seem to be anything worth confiscating in Perak.[3]

Northcote's particular concern, expressed to both Carnarvon and Disraeli, was the impact of the war on public opinion at home, and, more important, on Britain's whole reputation in the East. Britain's ultimate goals in Malaya ought, he believed, to be defined.[4] He met Carnarvon to discuss the matter at Dulverton in Devon on 27 December 1875. He told the Colonial Secretary of Disraeli's

---

[1] Brig. J. Ross, who had served in Afghanistan, hated the jungle. He said they had 'been sent out on policemen's work; that it was an insult to the service'. 'Needs Explaining', in J. G. Scott, *Cursed Luck*, London, 1908, p. 184.

[2] Jervois to Carnarvon (telegram) 23 Dec. 1875. C.O. 809/6, p. 121.

[3] Carnarvon to Northcote 25 Dec. 1875. *Iddesleigh Papers*, British Museum, Add. MS. 50022/201. Carnarvon to Disraeli 25 Dec. 1875. *Disraeli Papers*, B/xx/He/131.

[4] *Iddesleigh Papers*, 50017/146. Northcote to Disraeli 26 Dec. 1875, pressing and confidential (copy); Northcote to Carnarvon 26 Dec. 1875. *Carnarvon Papers*, P.R.O. 30/6/7, p. 109.

insistence that Jervois be checked, but that his prestige should not be impaired. The prime minister suggested that proclamations should be issued in Perak 'repudiating annexation, but announcing occupation with a view to obtaining indemnity'.[1] Carnarvon accordingly drafted a proclamation by Jervois embodying Disraeli's view. But he suggested to the prime minister that they should not commit themselves too rigidly on future policy. If the war went on he thought it would be 'extremely hard to avoid annexing'.[2] Carnarvon sent these orders to Jervois in secret telegrams on 29 December 1875.[3] In days before the telegraph existed, of course, the governor would have accomplished his objective without interference from home.

When the war was over, Carnarvon was satisfied with the conduct of the military operations. They cost less than £100,000 and were eventually paid out of the Perak revenues.[4] Yet for all the display of British power, the Army did not fulfil its aim. The final pursuit of Lela and Ismail was carried out by police and irregulars with the co-operation of the Malay rulers and the King of Siam. Ismail surrendered with the regalia in March 1876 to the Sultan of Kedah. Lela was captured by the Maharaja of Johore in July. Soon after this 'Abdu'llah's complicity in the plot was uncovered and, after much soul-searching in the legal department of the Colonial Office, Lela and the immediate murderers were hanged. 'Abdu'llah was deported to the Seychelles. Ismail lived on in exile in Johore. Britain's intervention in Perak completely disrupted the traditional aristocracy of the state.

The crisis had, of course, been predicted. Lord Stanley of Alderley prophesied in 1874 that something like the Ashanti expedition would follow in Malaya. Inevitably, the Perak expedition was compared with Wolseley's march to Kumasi. Jervois, however, maintained that there was no analogy with this or with Napier's Abyssinia campaign of 1867. The emphasis in Perak was on occupation to prevent new trouble. The former had been designed to strike a blow and

---

[1] Corry to Chancellor of Exchequer 27 Dec. 1875. *Iddesleigh Papers*, 50017/151.

[2] Carnarvon to Disraeli 28 Dec. 1875. *Disraeli Papers*, B/xx/He/52.

[3] Ibid. 13/xx/He/53 and 53a.

[4] E. Sadka, 'The Journal of Sir Hugh Low, Perak, 1877', *J.M.B.R.A.S.* (1954) 27 (4), p. 31.

retire.¹ The soldiers did not like comparisons with Wolseley's popular success. General Colborne maintained that his task had been harder than Wolseley's.² While the Ashanti victor had been covered with glory, Colborne's appointment had caused uneasiness from the start and Brigadier Ross had to be reprimanded for hanging a Malay.³

The political settlement which followed the Perak War meant a complete reversal for Jervois. But the governor continued to defend his ideas to the last and, when he received a harsh despatch of censure, he claimed it was unjust. He maintained that his plan had been the logical outcome of the Resident system which Carnarvon had approved.⁴ He almost challenged Carnarvon, in February 1876, to announce the Government's new policy. He continued to condemn the idea of withdrawal from Perak, or a return to the system of government by advice. In a full reply to Carnarvon's censure he stuck obstinately to his position, informing the Secretary of State bluntly that he had not understood either the situation in Perak or the policy which he had approved there.⁵ Carnarvon regarded this reply as a personal attack: 'I am afraid I must characterise this despatch as one of the least satisfactory that I have ever received since I have been connected with this office. It unquestionably has the merit of cleverness; but it is unscrupulous in argument, unbecoming in tone, and very disingenuous in character.' The original copy in the Colonial Office files is peppered with his indignant comments.⁶

Yet Carnarvon had also become rather obstinate. He seemed to be more intent on establishing that Jervois had started to annex Perak than in facing the real limitations of the system of government by advice. The permanent staff of the Colonial Office, who had not been personally insulted, were noticeably more indulgent towards Jervois. Moreover, Sir Andrew Clarke had sent home only seven

---

¹ Jervois to Carnarvon (telegram) 28 Dec. 1875. C.O. 809/6, p. 123.

² Anson, *About Others and Myself*, p. 332.

³ Carnarvon to Stanley 12 Nov. 1875 (private), *Carnarvon Papers*, P.R.O. 30/6/17, p. 142; Cowan, 'Swettenham's Journals', p. 127.

⁴ Jervois to Carnarvon (telegram) 15 Jan. 1876. C.O. 809/6, p. 188.

⁵ Jervois to Carnarvon 10 Feb. 1876. C.O. 273/83.

⁶ Ibid. Min. by Carnarvon 22 Mar. 1876. See Cowan, *Nineteenth Century Malaya*, pp. 239–43, for a careful discussion of the Carnarvon–Jervois controversy.

despatches on Perak between Pangkor and Jervois's arrival. These had all led the officials to believe that government by advice was working well. They ignored Lord Stanley of Alderley's warnings. Pangkor had been based on the assumption that the advice of the Resident would be readily sought. The Colonial Office had been quite ignorant of the forces which had been at work in Perak to combat this. In the aftermath of the Perak War, they seemed to be somewhat at a loss as to what to suggest. Robert Meade thought that annexation in Perak might well be 'the ultimate result' but could see no reason why it should take place 'for some time to come'.[1] Herbert partly excused Jervois's insubordination by the fact that he was an army officer not used to colonial work. The governor was simply told at the end of the war to take no further action. The final decision on the future of Perak was again not treated very urgently.

Carnarvon sent his instructions on the policy to be followed in Perak on 1 June 1876. Annexation was forbidden, troops were not to be used to impose the Residents upon unwilling populations. Carnarvon did not consider that the original Resident idea had been given a fair trial. The name 'Resident' was therefore to be retained, and the officers would confine themselves to advice. Jervois's idea of a Malay Council, however, was accepted and could be tried. The main principle behind Carnarvon's policy appeared to be some form of indirect rule:

> It should be our present policy to find and train up some Chief or Chiefs of sufficient capacity and enlightenment to appreciate the advantages of a civilized government and to render some effectual assistance in the government of the country.[2]

This was the rather vague conclusion Carnarvon had come to. The choice of the new Sultan of Perak was left to the governor. Having salvaged a few of his ideas Jervois now backed down and admitted that he had 'stepped beyond proper bounds'.[3]

There can be no doubt that Jervois was rash and wrong to persist in his plan after Carnarvon's warning. He was insubordinate in his continued advocacy. The Perak War is a classic example of the man

[1] Min. by Meade 21 Mar. 1876 on Jervois's despatch of 10 Feb. C.O. 273/83.
[2] Carnarvon to Jervois 1 June 1876. C.O. 809/7, p. 112.
[3] Jervois to Carnarvon 30 Nov. 1876 (private). *Carnarvon Papers*, P.R.O. 30/6/40, p. 33.

on the spot embarrassing the home Government. It should not be forgotten, however, that Jervois was trying to clear up the chain of trouble left by Sir Andrew Clarke's equally rash acts. And Carnarvon was not without blame. There is no evidence that he gave to Malay affairs the same urgent and detailed study which he gave to Fiji and the Gold Coast. He did not check Clarke in any way after taking over the Colonial Office in February 1874. Most of the trouble stemmed from Clarke's initiative. Carnarvon was quite ignorant of the real forces at work in Perak in 1874 to 1876. He refused to recognize that in Perak there was no Tengku Zia'u'd-din or Maharaja Abu-Bakar to rely upon. A Resident in Perak had either to govern or be superfluous.

The Jervois plan, on the other hand, was in some ways consistent with both Kimberley's and Carnarvon's basic policy of finding a way of achieving order on the frontier in the tropics by some method which fell short of the extension of British sovereignty. Fiji was only annexed after ten years of investigation into the possibility of consular jurisdiction or government by an Australian colony. The Gold Coast protectorate was deliberately excluded from the territorial dominions of the Crown, and Ashanti was neither annexed nor provided with a Resident. There were really no obstacles to annexation on the frontier in the tropics at this time, except for the deep-seated and legitimate reluctance of the British Government. Jervois's policy was consistent with the Colonial Office's in that he did himself recoil from outright annexation. His proposal for a system of indirect rule had some affinity to Carnarvon's system of dealing with the Gold Coast protectorate. The 'Queen's Commissioners' might have become rather grandly titled District Commissioners.

In Perak, personalities played a vital and unfortunate role. Birch was an inflexible instrument, 'Abdu'llah an insincere participant, and Jervois an unscrupulous advocate of the plan. Yet one cannot avoid the conviction that the Resident system of government by advice, as it was eventually evolved by men like Sir Hugh Low, bore a certain affinity to the Jervois plan.[1]

[1] See E. Sadka, introd. to 'The Journal of Sir Hugh Low, Perak, 1877', *J.M.B.R.A.S.* 1954 27(4) and 'The State Councils in Perak and Selangor, 1877–1895', *P.M.H.* (ed. by K. G. Tregonning), Singapore, 1962, pp. 89–119.

11. *The Annexation of Fiji,* *1874*

In Fiji the Conservative Government's hand was forced once again by the man on the spot. The officials who had been commissioned by the Liberals to inquire and report decided to act first and report afterwards. The Fiji question did not feature in the election of 1874 as did the Ashanti War and the Strait of Malacca issue, but the activities of Commodore Goodenough, who had been sent to Fiji to report on the question of annexation, demanded Carnarvon's attention as soon as he took over the Colonial Office. Indeed, only two days after taking office, he sent a telegram warning Goodenough not to commit the Government.

The warning was too late. Goodenough went ahead and signed what was virtually a treaty of cession. He did this because when he reached Fiji on 17 November 1873 he discovered that two significant developments had occurred since the British Government had drawn up his instructions. On the one hand, British intervention had already occurred to prevent bloodshed; on the other, John Thurston, the premier, was planning a new constitution which would give him autocratic power to rule in the interests of the Fijians. Thurston was, in fact, skilfully using British support to maintain the Fijian régime. The Governor of New South Wales had, at Thurston's request, stationed a warship from Australia in Fiji throughout 1873.[1] When Goodenough arrived to find this new situation, he believed that the intervention by the Royal Navy constituted a 'virtual protectorate',[2] and very quickly decided that annexation was necessary.

THURSTON'S GOVERNMENT AND THE ROYAL NAVY

Goodenough's most alarming discovery was that the British Government had, in a sense, been tricked into sending commissioners to

---

[1] Thurston to Robinson 20 Dec. 1872 in Robinson to Kimberley 27 Jan. 1873. C.O. 201/573; Ad. to C.O. 18 Mar. 1873. C.O. 83/3. H.M.S. *Dido* reached Levuka in Jan. 1873.

[2] Goodenough and Layard to Kimberley 13 Feb. 1874. C.O. 808/2, p. 60.

consider the annexation of Fiji. Thurston's invitation of 31 January
1873, which caused Kimberley to advise Gladstone to annex the
islands, led to serious Cabinet discussions, and ultimately to the decision
to send Goodenough and Layard, had not been the 'offer of cession'
which Knatchbull-Hugessen and Kimberley took it to be.[1] Apparently
it really meant 'Do you recognise or intend to annex us, because your
interference is a hindrance to us and if your intention were decided we
could get on'.[2] Thurston had also written to the governor of New
South Wales suggesting that Britain should either concede that Fiji
was an independent state or should annex the islands. Because the
policy of *de facto* recognition was accompanied by an announcement
that Fijian citizenship would not exempt British subjects from British
law, Thurston had requested the presence of a British warship to
control the British settlers.[3] Goodenough realized that while the
British Government dallied in 1873 Thurston had decided to 'get on'
with his plans behind the shield of a British gunboat.

British intervention had, therefore, already taken place in Fiji
before Goodenough arrived. Thurston used British naval officers to
keep order for him. His handling of the Mba river revolt of March
1873, for example, provided a good illustration of his methods. In this
case, members of the British Subjects Mutual Protection Association
decided to take revenge on Viti Levu mountain tribes who had
murdered a settler family. A clash with Fijian Government troops
was only avoided because Thurston called on Captain Chapman of
H.M.S. *Dido* to arrest the ringleaders. Thurston then agreed to drop
proceedings against them provided Chapman deported them to Australia.[4] The incident led to considerable embarrassment in Whitehall,
but Gladstone believed that Chapman acted wisely.[5]

[1] See above, pp. 253–5.

[2] Goodenough to Goschen 18 Nov. 1873, private (copy). *Carnarvon
Papers*, P.R.O. 30/6/44, p. 2. Henderson developed on this view, and
suggested ('Government in Fiji', ii, p. 347) that the letter of 31 Jan. was
part of a plot by Thurston to achieve despotic power; that the letter was
sent in the belief that it would be refused. In Jan., however, the Fiji Govt.'s
prestige was low.

[3] Thurston to Robinson 20 Dec. 1872. C.O. 201/573.

[4] Thurston to Chapman 29 Mar., in Ad. to C.O. 14 June 1873. C.O. 83/3.

[5] Ibid. Mins. on the despatch: Ad. to F.O. 14 Apr. 1873. F.O. 58/140,
p. 39; Goodenough's *Journal*, i, 10 June 1873.

The Navy had been called in again during another incident following Thurston's constitutional changes. After the 1871 constitution broke down in May 1873, because the Legislative Assembly refused to support the Government's financial policies, Thakombau dissolved the Assembly but retained his ministers.[1] The idea of a new Assembly elected by all Fijians was unacceptable to the settlers, so Thurston drew up a new constitution. The atmosphere in the islands then became so tense that the commodore of the Australasian Squadron decided to station H.M.S. *Blanche*, commanded by Captain Simpson, at Levuka, and to appoint the ship's paymaster, Lieutenant Nettleton, as acting British consul. When a German merchant forcibly withdrew goods from the bonded warehouse in September 1873 as a protest against the Government's taxes, British intervention was again necessary.

Thurston once more showed his skill. The Government first tried to arrest the offender, a clerk named Schule. This led the German consul to appeal to Captain Simpson, who, trying to be impartial, warned British subjects not to take up arms on either side. But after Thurston explained his Government's case, Simpson issued a proclamation warning British subjects not to resist Thakombau's Government. Moreover, since a Fijian armed force was standing ready, and a group of drunken Germans fortified themselves in Hedeman's store, Lieutenant Nettleton decided to take the initiative. He entered the store, arrested Schule, and prevented bloodshed. The naval officers had further committed themselves to Thurston's support. Schule was handed over to the Government. Simpson published a notice on 8 September 1873 announcing his support for the lawful arrests of Thakombau's Government.[2]

The affair of the Germans was a storm in a teacup. In Australia, however, the news caused great alarm.[3] A war between the races in Fiji was feared. Thurston might use the Fijian Army to suppress the white settlers with the support of the Royal Navy. As the news

[1] Derrick, *History*, pp. 229–30; F.O. to C.O. 10 Nov. 1873. C.O. 83/4.
[2] Nettleton to Granville 8 and 26 Sept. 1873. F.O. 58/135, pp. 253–88; Robinson to Kimberley 6 Oct. 1873. C.O. 201/574; a much fuller account, including Simpson's correspondence with Thurston, reached London in 1874. Simpson to Stirling 29 Dec. 1873. C.O. 808/2, pp. 47–58.
[3] Robinson to Kimberley (telegram) 15 Nov. 1873. C.O. 201/574.

reached London, this alarming possibility confirmed Kimberley's conviction of the necessity for annexation. But Gladstone was still most reluctant. Kimberley now tried to overcome the prime minister's scruples by suggesting, 'I take a more sanguine view I confess of the power and energy of this country than you do'.[1] But, having commissioned Goodenough to inquire and report, the Liberal Government did not take any further action.

Meanwhile in Fiji, Thurston, having won Captain Simpson's docile support, went ahead with his new constitution. A draft was circulated secretly among the chiefs at the end of September 1873. It provided for an Assembly of nominated chiefs, with a minority of elected Europeans, a Cabinet of three, and a Privy Council consisting of the Cabinet, the ministers and a chief from each province. Under this system Thurston believed he could control the settlers. For some reason he sent a copy to Simpson, who persuaded him to hold it over until the British Government's commissioners arrived.[2]

Goodenough took only a few days to make up his mind to stop Thurston's constitution.[3] It seemed to him, coming fresh upon the scene, that Thurston and a handful of supporters were proposing to rule Fiji, using a Fijian army to enforce their edicts. If only eight members of the proposed Assembly of twenty-six represented the settlers, he felt they would have a real grievance. The commodore found Thurston personally 'rather a puzzle' and 'full of the most extravagant ideas of his own position and the claims of his little government'.[4]

In the weeks before Layard, the consul, arrived, Goodenough and Thurston had several arguments over the constitution. Goodenough warned Thurston that if he used Fijian troops against the settlers he would be prosecuted in the New South Wales Supreme Court. Thurston, on his part, claimed that the old Assembly had striven for 'a Fiji for the whites instd. of a Fiji for the Fijians'. He reiterated his conviction that either a strong Fijian Government or annexation

[1] Kimberley to Gladstone 26 Nov. 1873. *Gladstone Papers*, 44225/10.

[2] Derrick, op. cit., p. 237. The proposed constitution was published in the *Sydney Morning Herald*, 4 Nov. 1873, copy in F.O. 58/153, p. 319.

[3] Goodenough's *Journal*, ii, 22 Nov. 1873.

[4] Goodenough to Goschen 2 Dec. 1873, private (copy). *Carnarvon Papers*, P.R.O. 30/6/44, p. 4.

to another powerful nation was imperative. Goodenough could not
be sure, however, that Thurston really wanted annexation, and he was
certainly not prepared to accept Thurston's word against 1,500 settlers.[1]
Therefore, only two weeks after his arrival, the commodore wrote
home that he could 'see no way out of the muddle but by annexation'.[2]
Thenceforth his activities in Fiji were designed to achieve this end.

THE GOODENOUGH CESSION, 20 MARCH 1874

If pressure in favour of annexation was no part of Goodenough's
instructions, it was fully in keeping with his character. He was not a
man to shirk a challenge. Criticisms that Goodenough and Layard
were unqualified for their task, which have been made by Professor
J. M. Ward, are unjustified. To start with, they did not really constitute a 'commission' in the formal sense. Gladstone, in announcing
the inquiry to Parliament, simply referred to 'two trustworthy and
competent men'.[3] They had already been selected for posts in the
Pacific as Commodore of the Squadron and consul in Fiji, and it
turned out that they both had valuable qualifications. Layard was a
barrister, who had had experience of New Zealand, the Cape, and the
East African slave-trade.

Goodenough was an exceptional naval officer, who in several
respects seemed well suitable for this mission. A son of the Dean of
Wells, a pious and devoted churchman, he was the sort of man who
would appeal both to Gladstone and the missionary interest. A captain
who taught teetotalism to his ship, he would not be swayed by the
rowdy 'beach' element in Levuka. He had also some experience of a

[1] For a fuller account of their argument see my article, 'New Light on
Commodore Goodenough's Mission to Fiji, 1873–74', *H.S.A.N.Z.* (1962),
10 (39), pp. 276–7. Thurston's view is upheld by Scarr, 'John Bates
Thurston, Commodore Goodenough and the Rampant Anglo-Saxons in
Fiji', *H.S.A.N.Z.* (1964), 11 (43), pp. 361–82.
[2] Goodenough to Goschen 2 Dec. 1873. P.R.O. 30/6/44, p. 4.
[3] 3 *Hansard*, 216, col. 953; 'Commodore Goodenough and myself were
never "commissioners". That office and title was withheld from us by Her
Majesty's Government. It is given us here, but we have never assumed it'
(Layard to Dupuis 29 May 1874, quoted by Henderson, 'Government in
Fiji', ii, p. 417). See also Ward, *British Policy in the South Pacific*, pp. 249–
250.

semi-diplomatic nature as a naval attaché in the United States during
the Civil War and in Europe during the aftermath of the Franco-
Prussian War. For a naval officer he was a man of wide cultural
interests, being concerned about social problems and accomplished at
languages.[1] His library on H.M.S. *Pearl* contained 400 volumes and
his leisure reading in the South Pacific was formidable.[2] Before leaving
London he visited the Wesleyan missionary headquarters, which must
have commended him to McArthur, under whose influence he may
well have come. The leading Wesleyan missionary in Fiji, who was
not an annexationist, wrote of Goodenough and Layard: 'Unquestionably they are the men for the work . . . they are gaining golden
opinions everywhere they go'.[3]

The most noticeable trait in Goodenough's character was his self-
discipline and inflexible devotion to duty. Captain Moresby admired
his 'fine scientific and sailor-like qualities, his promptitude, his iron
nerve'.[4] An Australian acquaintance remarked on his 'resolution and
fixedness of purpose'. Had it not been for his tragic death in 1875 at
the age of forty-five, Goodenough would probably have reached the
highest ranks of the Royal Navy. It is only in the light of such views
of his character that Goodenough's actions in Fiji should be judged.
Just before writing his final report he admitted that he saw annexation
as 'a positive duty'.[5]

Having decided, then, that annexation was necessary, Goodenough
set about achieving it with his usual resolution. He decided to maintain the naval intervention which had kept the peace in Fiji. He
warned the Admiralty that if a crisis occurred he would hoist the
Union Jack beside the Fijian flag 'as a Protectorate for a time'[6] and
that he would make the Fijian Government submit its Acts to the

[1] See Mrs. V. H. Goodenough, *Memoir and Journal of Commodore
Goodenough*, London, 1876.

[2] Gordon, *Fiji*, i, p. 116.

[3] Rev. F. Langham to McArthur 13 Feb. 1873 (copy) in Chesson to
Carnarvon 8 May 1874. C.O. 83/5.

[4] J. Moresby, *Discoveries and Surveys in New Guinea and Polynesia*,
London, 1876, p. 278.

[5] Mrs. Goodenough, op. cit., p. 117.

[6] Goodenough to Goschen 2 Dec. 1873, private (copy). *Carnarvon
Papers*, P.R.O. 30/6/44, p. 4.

foreign consuls for approval.   He informed Thakombau and Thurston
that, as soon as his colleague Layard arrived, a public meeting would
be called to find out if the chiefs and people wanted annexation.
Meanwhile, before Layard's arrival in January 1874, Goodenough
toured Viti Levu and talked with many settlers.

Goodenough found widespread opposition to Thurston.   'I have
consequently had the disagreeable task', he reported, 'of keeping the
contending sides asunder in this quarrelsome . . . little place which is
full of idle penniless people on the one hand and rather high-handed
government men on the other.'[1]   After listening to British and
American settlers, German and American consuls and the French
Roman Catholic missionary, who all advocated strong rule by Britain,
Goodenough decided that annexation to New South Wales or New
Zealand would be unsatisfactory.   He though Fiji should become a
Crown Colony, ruled by a politico-military officer with North-West
Frontier experience.[2]   Layard accepted the commodore's view and
did not delay in letting the Foreign Office know his preference for
annexation.[3]

The two envoys began their self-appointed task of securing annexation in January 1874 by publishing their intentions to the islanders.
They announced that they were 'two chiefs' come to inquire whether
the Fijians wanted annexation.   They proclaimed their object as the
peace and welfare of Fiji.   Their intentions were unmistakable:

> It is no new thing for England to govern islands like Fiji.   She owns
> and governs in several parts of the world a great number of similar
> islands to Fiji, and it will be very easy for her to govern Fiji also, and
> preserve its peace, and promote the welfare and prosperity of its people.
>   But England will never take Fiji by force or stealth if the King and
> Chiefs do not wish it. . . .
>   But there is one matter to be considered by the King and Chiefs of
> Fiji, they must know that the number of Foreigners in Fiji will greatly
> increase from year to year, as well as their property, and their residence
> in Fiji will cause, or create, great intricacies, and for these reasons the
> King and Chiefs must think and study well over the matter, whether

---

[1] Ibid. p. 11.   Goodenough to Milne 27 Dec. 1873, private (extract).
[2] Ibid. p. 20.   Encl. in Hunt to Carnarvon 2 May 1874.
[3] Layard to Wylde 14 Jan. 1874 (private).   F.O. 58/139, p. 30.

they will be able to conduct their Government in the future, under more difficult circumstances, or not.[1]

Like Clarke in Malaya, Goodenough had been sent to inquire and report. In the same spirit, indeed during the very same week as the Pangkor conference, Goodenough was trying to solve the problems of Fiji and would report afterwards. He set about trying to persuade the chiefs to accept annexation.

The Fijian chiefs were less tractable than Goodenough expected. He met with Thakombau on 17 and 26 January, and explained the system of government in Ceylon.[2] He informed the king that Thurston's constitution was unsatisfactory. But although he confidently expected that a request for annexation would follow, he was disappointed. Indeed, after a series of meetings during the first week of March 1874, Thakombau rejected the idea of annexation and determined to carry on his régime.

Goodenough had, by this time, reason to suspect that Thurston was working against annexation. Just before the abortive conference opened, he noted a change in Thurston: 'His manner has changed and there is an independence about it which I don't understand, unless he intends to play false'.[3] It also came to Goodenough's notice that Thurston told the leading chiefs at the meeting on 2 March 1874 'openly I have said I am in favour of annexation but you know that I am not and that I can keep the government going'.[4] Next day, so Goodenough was told, when the ministers continued to oppose annexation, Thakombau lost his temper and stormed, 'I will send for the commodore tomorrow morning, and give the country to Britain'.[5] It seems clear, in fact, that the aged Fijian ruler was confused. No decision had been reached when Goodenough and Layard attended the conference on 5 March to give further assurances about the position of the chiefs and the land under British rule. Goodenough still expected that a request for annexation would come. Sometime during

---

[1] Correspondence between Goodenough and Layard and the chiefs published by Thurston, 12 Jan. 1874. F.O. 58/139, p. 33.
[2] 1st Progress Report 13 Feb. 1874. C.O. 808/2, p. 60.
[3] Goodenough's *Journal*, iii, 1 Mar. 1874.
[4] Statement of Rev. F. Langham, ibid. iv, 29 Sept. 1874.
[5] Statement of Swanston, ibid. iii, 11 Mar. 1874.

the next twenty-four hours, however, Thakombau changed his mind. On 6 March 1874 annexation was rejected.[1]

Goodenough was not deterred and immediately tried to get the decision reversed. He rebuked the chiefs for having authorized the letter to the British Government of 31 January 1873. He warned them that if they wished to carry on their own government they must drop the new constitution, reduce expenditure, and simplify the administration. He declared that he would not tolerate the use of force against the settlers. Having thus made the continuance of the Thakombau régime very difficult, Goodenough left the scene of the conference for a few days, to assist a distressed ship in the south.

During his absence, Thakombau, apparently unshaken by the commodore's warning, requested Thurston to carry on the government. Thurston, on his part, decided to return to the 1871 constitution and call an Assembly. Goodenough, however, refused to accept this decision. He now decided to frustrate Thurston. 'I have tried to believe in Thurston's straightforwardness', he told Swanston, 'but have not been able to do so, I am convinced to the contrary now from all that he has done.'[2] Going now behind Thurston's back, Goodenough and Layard reopened the question of annexation and began secret negotiations with Thakombau. If necessary, they planned to restrain Thurston:

Speaking to various people I said ... the position is this. Mr. Thurston is one Englishman claiming to advise King Cakobau on the sole responsibility of himself towards the chiefs & in opposition to every white man here.

I & Consul are two Englishmen acting under a sense of responsibility to their own Government & most friendly to Cakobau's Govt. but wishing to see all possible conciliatory measures adopted towards either side & we forbid Mr. Thurston accepting office. Should he persist we then remove him for a while to his plantation or elsewhere till all is quiet & Govt. reorganised.

It is the only way.[3]

---

[1] 2nd Progress Report, 19 Mar. 1874, with memo. on meeting. C.O. 808/2, pp. 74–78. Thurston maintained that he stood for annexation — with conditions — and that the decision should come from the chiefs. Scarr, op. cit. pp. 379–81.

[2] Goodenough's *Journal*, iii, 11 Mar. 1874.

[3] Ibid. 12 Mar. 1874. Cf. Henderson, 'Government in Fiji'. 'The truth would appear to be that, at this stage of his career, he [Thurston] was not the

With the approval of the United States and German consuls the commodore issued an ultimatum to Thakombau.

On 17 March 1874 Goodenough announced that if Thurston's ministry was retained he would 'leave them to their fate'. If force was used against the settlers, he would intervene. Next day he personally warned the king that 'weak people are obliged to look to support from the strong'.[1] A tense interview followed with Thurston, who, although Goodenough did not believe him, agreed now to support annexation. Thus the commodore's pressure succeeded. Thakombau publicly announced on 20 March 1874 that he and the chiefs were prepared to cede Fiji to Britain, 'but it must be understood', he went on, 'that he was giving only the Government of the Country, not his men or his earth'.[2] Goodenough had got what he wanted. It should not be overlooked, however, that the document which he signed on 21 March 1874 gave rise to considerable confusion.

Thurston regarded the document as an 'Offered Cession' of the Fijian kingdom. This is how the Colonial Office received it, but the London Press reported it as the 'cession'. Goodenough, in the speech he made at the signing ceremony, was rather ambiguous:

> I receive this intimation of the wish of the kings & chiefs of Fiji to cede the Govt. of these islands to the Queen of G[reat] B[ritain]. I have heard what Mr. T[hursto]n has said & I agree to his explanations that you here cede the Govt. only. Not the land or the people. That is right & so I receive the cession. From this moment that on the part of H.M. the Queen I rec[eiv]e this offer a solemn duty rests upon the Queen's officers to take care that all here sh[oul]d prosper & that no dweller in these islands sh[oul]d suffer.[3]

Support for either interpretation can be found in Goodenough's remarks. From the Fijian point of view, however, it was probably the crucial moment of decision. Thakombau proposed Queen Vic-

---

kind of man who should have been entrusted with supreme power. The moral qualities of his nature were too liable to be overborne by vanity and vindictiveness, and also by anxiety for his own advancement and aggrandisement.'

[1] *Journal*, iii, 19 Mar. 1874.
[2] Goodenough and Layard to Carnarvon 20 Mar. 1874. C.O. 83/5.
[3] Goodenough's *Journal*, iii, 21 Mar. 1874.

toria's health and said, 'This day we give ourselves to her'.[1] Goodenough had admitted Britain's responsibility for the islands. Layard told the Foreign Office that Thakombau had 'formally ceded these Islands to the Queen of England'.[2] Goodenough felt that Thakombau and the chiefs seemed greatly relieved by the decision. He thought, 'Now I must work heart and soul to get the Government to take the islands or all will be worse than before, a great deal worse'.[3] He made arrangements for an interim Government. His official report to the British Government was accompanied by a private letter earnestly recommending annexation.

THE UNCONDITIONAL CESSION, 10 OCTOBER 1874

Goodenough's actions in Fiji greatly embarrassed the Colonial Office. His early bias in favour of annexation struck Carnarvon forcibly as soon as he took office in February 1874. After reading the commodore's correspondence with Goschen, the Liberal First Lord of the Admiralty, Carnarvon consulted Lord Derby at the Foreign Office.[4] A telegram was sent to the Governor of New South Wales instructing him to warn Goodenough that hoisting the Union Jack as 'a protectorate' would complicate matters. Nothing was to be done until the home Government had considered the case.[5]

Carnarvon's warning was too late. A progress report from the envoys, clearly indicating that they favoured a Crown Colony in Fiji, reached the Colonial Office on 7 April 1874. It was quite obvious that they were still exceeding their instructions. But even greater shocks were in store. Next day, a Reuter's telegram appeared in London newspapers announcing the cession of 20 March.[6]

[1] Ibid. iii, 21 Mar. 1874.

[2] Layard to Granville 20 Mar. 1874. F.O. 58/142, p. 69.

[3] Goodenough's *Journal*, iii, 21 Mar. 1874.

[4] Carnarvon to Derby 23 Feb. 1874, private (copy). *Carnarvon Papers*, P.R.O. 30/6/8, p. 10.

[5] Carnarvon to Robinson (telegram) 23 Feb. 1874 (copy). F.O. 58/142, p. 323.

[6] *The Times*, 9 Apr. 1874, p. 5. Reuter's telegram: 'Cession of the Fiji Islands', Melbourne, 7 Apr. 'The sovereignty of the Fiji Islands has been formally ceded by King Cacaban [*sic*] to England, and Mr. Layard, the British Consul, has accepted the cession subject to ratification by the home government.'

Considerably alarmed, Carnarvon immediately prepared the matter for the Cabinet's consideration.[1]   He warned Disraeli that the time for a decision on Fiji approached.[2]   At the same time, Queen Victoria was very surprised by the Press reports.[3]   General Ponsonby warned the Foreign Secretary that Queen Victoria was 'not very eager to count among her subjects, a population; two thirds of whom practice cannibalism, strangulation of widows, infanticide and other enormities'.[4]

The picture began, in fact, to look very much as it had under Gladstone: Colonial Secretary telling prime minister the matter was urgent; commissioners' report being used as an excuse for delay — then, true to form, the redoubtable McArthur calling the attention of the House of Commons, on 14 April 1874, to the newspaper reports of the 20 March cession.   Carnarvon could only hedge when he reported to the House of Lords on 20 April that he had received no official notification of this act, that the commissioners appeared to have disobeyed their instructions.[5]   Professor Parnaby has suggested that the prime minister was 'just as evasive as Gladstone'.   But this was not true.   Disraeli had already confessed rather grandly to the queen that she would 'feel it necessary to accept the Sovereignty of this Southern Archipelago'.[6]

The Goodenough–Layard Report did not reach the Colonial Office until 10 June 1874.   Carnarvon refused to commit himself publicly until then.   The Colonial Office seemed to be very uncertain in its mind over Fiji.   Henry Holland, the legal adviser, was hostile to Goodenough's action, and the £80,000 of liabilities owed by the Fiji Government were viewed with some alarm.[7]   Herbert, however, had

---

[1] Mins. by Holland 8 Apr., and Herbert 15 Apr., on Goodenough and Layard to Kimberley 13 Feb. 1874.   C.O. 83/5; Ad. to F.O. 8 Apr. 1874 encl. telegram.   F.O. 58/144, p. 148.

[2] Carnarvon to Disraeli 11 Apr. 1874 (private).   *Disraeli Papers*, B/xx/He/162.

[3] Ponsonby to Derby 9 Apr. 1874.   *Royal Archives*, P.24/96.

[4] Ponsonby to Derby 12 Apr. 1874.   Ibid. P.24/99.

[5] 3 *Hansard*, 218, cols. 544–5, 809–10.

[6] Parnaby, *Britain and the Labor Trade*, p. 47; Disraeli to Queen Victoria 14 Apr. 1874.   *Royal Archives*, A.47/16.

[7] Mins. by Holland 5 May, and Herbert 5 May, on Goodenough and Layard to Carnarvon 20 Mar. 1874.   C.O. 83/5.

already admitted privately that he looked upon annexation as 'one of those steps which it is impossible to avoid'.[1] Carnarvon, maintaining his silence at the beginning of May 1874, agreed it was a 'difficult question', but put off a decision until he saw the Report. The governor of New South Wales sent a telegram on 18 May 1874 stating that his Government demanded annexation.[2] With so much speculation in London Carnarvon informed Goodenough that the news of the 20 March cession left him awaiting the Report with 'increased anxiety'.[3]

When it finally arrived, the Report was accompanied by a private letter giving a clear statement of Goodenough's views. The lawlessness of the British settlers pointed to annexation, quite apart from the arguments about commerce, strategy and the suppression of kidnapping. Consular jurisdiction might, in the past, have encouraged the development of a well-ordered white community: now it was too late.[4] The Report itself, although rather unsystematic, dealt with most of the problems a colonial Government would have to meet. A short survey of the recent Government was not hostile to Thurston, and it conceded that when he came to power in 1872 he had everyone's confidence. Where the commissioners disagreed with Thurston was on the realities of Fijian politics. Thurston believed in a theoretical unity of the islands, with Thakombau governing through his ministers in the interests of all Fijians. The commissioners, although sympathetic to the theory, found that in practice all Fijians did not appreciate the efforts of the ministers.

A native Chief has been raised to supreme power by the white population. In working a constitution under him the latter have found themselves, as a matter of fact, the disposers of the interests of the natives. A ministry which at first rested upon the support of the whites, has, by raising an armed force, felt it possible to make itself independent of them, and

---

[1] Herbert to Gordon 5 June 1874. A. H. Gordon, *Mauritius. Records of Private and Public Life, 1871–1874*, Edinburgh, 1894, ii, pp. 660–1.

[2] Robinson to Carnarvon (telegram) 18 May 1874. C.O. 808/2, p. 103.

[3] Ibid. pp. 103–4. Carnarvon to Goodenough and Layard 22 May 1874.

[4] Goodenough to Carnarvon 18 Apr. 1874 (private). *Carnarvon Papers*, P.R.O. 30/6/44, p. 17.

has sought to govern the country on the theory of preserving native interests and treating whites as aliens. In the course of two years they have spent about £124,000 and are £87,000 in debt.

If Fiji was not annexed, the consul would have to be granted magisterial powers and the Royal Navy would have to be employed against the labour traffic. This would amount to a kind of protectorate, and a 'protectorate of an undefined and inconvenient character'. There was an almost unanimous demand for annexation. The commissioners recommended that Fiji should be made into a Crown Colony on the model of Ceylon or Singapore.[1]

Here was a clear conclusion — the rest of the Report dealt with the financial and administrative matters which would have to be cleared up. By the same mail came the official views of the nearby British colonies. Premier Parkes of New South Wales supported annexation because of Fiji's alleged commercial and strategic position and for fear of foreign intervention.[2] Governor Fergusson of New Zealand reminded Carnarvon that the Fiji Banking and Commercial Company, to whom the Government of Fiji was indebted, was a New Zealand concern.[3]

The moment had arrived for Carnarvon to decide on the Fiji question. Yet it is hard to say when he really made up his mind. He did not announce the Government's policy until he spoke in the House of Lords on 17 July 1874. In the meantime, one or two hints were given about his attitude. On 30 June 1874 he asked Disraeli for a Cabinet discussion.[4] He told a deputation from the 'Fiji Committee' and the Aborigines Protection Society on 4 July that the whole question of annexation in the Pacific was being considered as the 'waste places of the earth were being filled up'. He admitted that he certainly did not have a comprehensive policy on annexation; each case would be judged on its merits.[5] Undated memoranda in his

[1] Goodenough and Layard Report 13 Apr. 1874. C.O. 83/4. Later Goodenough wrote in his *Journal*, iv, 5 Sept. 1874: 'It is too staccato & does not sufficiently show my own opinion for my own justification'.
[2] Robinson to Carnarvon 10 Apr. 1874. C.O. 201/577.
[3] Fergusson to Carnarvon 13 Apr. 1874. C.O. 808/2, p. 184.
[4] Carnarvon to Disraeli 30 June 1874. *Disraeli Papers*, B/xx/He/23.
[5] The delegation included McArthur, and his brother Alexander from Sydney; other M.P.s, Dixon, Salt, Young, Jenkins, Kinnaird, Corry;

private papers indicate that it was probably in connection with this deputation that Carnarvon seriously formulated his views.[1]

Herbert told Sir Arthur Gordon in a letter on 3 July 1874 that a decision was expected in a very few days.[2] Carnarvon informed Disraeli's secretary on 6 July that a Cabinet decision on Fiji was urgent.[3] On 9 July he sent Derby, Salisbury and Disraeli the draft of a telegram, addressed to Sir Hercules Robinson, the governor of New South Wales, instructing him to visit Fiji, inform the inhabitants that the conditions of Goodenough's cession could not be accepted, and to find out if unconditional cession was possible.[4] Although the telegram was not actually sent until 10 August, it proves that by early July Carnarvon had made up his mind to annex Fiji, provided it was offered without conditions. In the course of his studies and discussions Carnarvon had drawn up a revealing list of the arguments in favour of annexation:

1. Convenient depot from wh[ich] to exercise police supervision.
2. English settlers — English capital — English crime — wanted an English Government . . . chaos in prospect.
3. Kidnapping.
4. A convenient stepping stone.
5. Objection by Australians to foreign neighbours.
6. Desire of Aust[ralia] and N[ew] Z[ealand] for them to be British.
7. [Opinion of the] H[ouse] of C[ommons.]
8. Probably ultimately paying — like other groups of islands like Bahamas . . . wh[ich] do just pay even with their Assemblies. But if governed as Crown Colony it may pay better.
9. Tolerably healthy.

Finally, although Fiji had prohibited kidnapping, Cameron knew it lay in the centre of the kidnapping region and was a place where

---

colonial representatives, and Rev. W. B. Boyce, general secretary of the Wesleyan Missionary Soc.

[1] In the *Carnarvon Papers* (P.R.O. 30/6/51) some notes about the discussion with the deputation, possibly made during the meeting, serve to date them. They were obviously used in drafting his subsequent announcement to the House of Lords.

[2] Herbert to Gordon 3 July 1874. Gordon, *Mauritius,* ii, p. 672. 'I expect Carnarvon will send you'.

[3] Carnarvon to Corry 6 July 1874. *Disraeli Papers,* B/xx/He/25.

[4] Carnarvon to Disraeli 9 July 1874. Ibid. B/xx/He/26.

kanakas were employed.[1] Yet material considerations like these were
not the only reasons which impressed the Colonial Secretary.

Carnarvon had nobler imperial visions. He scribbled a note: 'But
not a question of money. Mission of England. A spirit of adventure
to fill up waste places of the earth.'[2] He was assured, at the same time,
of the general assistance of New South Wales. New Zealand specifically offered to undertake the government of Fiji.[3] Carnarvon possibly
thought that the annexation of Fiji could be made into an act of imperial co-operation. He informed Queen Victoria on 13 July 1874
that although Goodenough's conditions were not acceptable, the offer
could not be rejected:

> looking to the opinion of New Zealand and Australia, and, as far as it
> can be gathered, of Parliament and this country, and looking also to the
> advantages which these islands possess as an intermediate station between
> America and Australia and the risks of great disorders arising unless
> some Government is constituted, it seems impossible to give a direct
> refusal to the cession.[4]

He was also careful to point out to Her Majesty that most of the
barbarous customs which she feared had been abandoned by the Fijians,
who were mostly Christians.

Carnarvon made his decision public when he presented the Goodenough–Layard Report in the House of Lords on 17 July 1874. He
announced that a genuine offer of cession to Governor Robinson would
not be declined, and suggested a Crown Colony 'of a rather severe
type' should be created. The theme of Carnarvon's speech was very
reminiscent of his announcement of the new policy on the Gold
Coast in May. Now, as he announced his Fijian policy, he declared:

> I am loathe to use words which seem too strong for the occasion and
> therefore I hardly like to say that England has a mission to extend her
> policy of colonization in this part of the world, but at all events it does
> seem to me that there is an indirect duty which lies upon us, as far as we

---

1 Memos. in *Carnarvon Papers*, P.R.O. 30/6/51, pp. 23 and 24.

2 Memo. in *Carnarvon Papers*, P.R.O. 30/6/51, on back of p. 22.

3 Robinson to Carnarvon 14 May 1874. P.R.O. 30/6/25, p. 59; Fergusson to Carnarvon 13 Apr. 1874. C.O. 209/232. Herbert wrote, 11
June, 'Yes, New Zealand might be able to govern Fiji better and more
cheaply than this country could'.

4 Carnarvon to Queen Victoria 13 July 1874. *Royal Archives*, P.24/101.

can, to take under our protection a place into which English capital has
overflowed, in which English settlers are resident, in which it must be
added, English lawlessness is going on, and in which the establishment
of English institutions has been unsuccessfully attempted. . . .[1]

Here was a touch of the grandeur of 'that greatest of all political
questions — the unity and maintainance of the Empire'.[2] Yet Carnarvon was careful to insist that the case had been judged solely on its
merits and that it should not be linked with his Gold Coast speech. In
the short debate which followed, Kimberley could hardly object to a
policy which was virtually his, but Granville feared 'a leap into the
dark at a very long distance'.[3]

Among those listening to Carnarvon's announcement was
McArthur, who immediately returned to the Commons chamber in
great excitement. On 4 August 1874 he rose to move the support of
the House for Carnarvon's decision to send Robinson to Fiji and to
congratulate the Government on carrying out the policy of the Crystal
Palace speech in the Gold Coast and Fiji. McArthur thus gave
Gladstone an opportunity to make a final onslaught on the policy of
annexation. The Goodenough–Layard Report was characterized by
Gladstone as one of the most chaotic public documents he had ever
seen. Moreover, it referred to Fijians in a relation of 'undefined
serfdom' to the chiefs — what was that but another name for slavery ?
Reminding the House that the question of Thakombau's American
debts lay at the bottom of the whole question of involvement with Fiji,
Gladstone hinted that it might bring the country to the threshold of
another *Alabama* crisis:

> I see disagreeable and distorted phantoms stalking across the stage of
> this House. I see new Votes in the Estimates — new Votes for future
> wars in Fiji — new Votes for future engagements — a reproduction in
> an aggravated form of all we have had to lament in New Zealand.[4]

McArthur, his motions, his pamphlets and his 'sadly deluded philanthropy' did not escape Gladstone's scorn. But Knatchbull-Hugessen

[1] 3 *Hansard*, 221, col. 185.
[2] Carnarvon's phrase in letter to Knatchbull-Hugessen 18 Aug. 1874
(copy). *Carnarvon Papers*, P.R.O. 30/6/44, p. 145.
[3] 3 *Hansard*, 221, col. 197.
[4] Ibid. col. 1287.

reminded the House of Kimberley's four alternatives, and suggested that as three of them had manifestly failed, annexation alone remained. Several speakers alluded to the Gold Coast policy, and one pointed to the apparent paradox that in the Gold Coast question it had been pleaded that they could not retreat from commitments on the coast, while here, where there was no commitment, they were being asked to enter one. Another member proposed leaving the 'Methodists and cannibals' to settle things among themselves.

Disraeli must have been reminded, as he noted the tone of the debate, of his difficult moments over the Gold Coast only a month earlier. Parnaby suggests that Carnarvon's announcement in the House of Lords 'precipitated a crisis'.[1] But there was no crisis over Fiji. Disraeli had already stated the view that annexation was inevitable. The Cabinet crisis concerned the opposition of its High Church members to the Public Worship Bill, which was designed to check ritualism in the Church of England. While the Commons were debating McArthur's Fiji resolution on 4 August 1874, the House of Lords was in the process of rejecting amendments to the Bill which had just passed the House of Commons with Disraeli's support. Carnarvon and Salisbury spoke and voted against the Bill.[2]

Disraeli did not want to risk a Cabinet meeting. He was also anxious about the possible expense of the new colony in Fiji. Thus, Cabinet discussion of the Fiji question was put off and, when the parliamentary session ended with the Cabinet publicly divided on the Church issue, the Fiji question was 'indefinitely postponed'. Greatly annoyed by Disraeli's pique, Carnarvon wrote a 'rather stiff letter' to the prime minister on 7 August 1874, complaining that 'after all, the matter resolves itself into one of confidence in the judgment of the minister who is responsible'. He felt that it would be impossible to go on if his policy was restricted.[3] After this thinly veiled threat of resignation, Disraeli wrote a conciliatory letter. He told Carnarvon that the split on the Public Worship Bill caused the postponement of the Cabinet, and that he would leave Fiji 'entirely in your hands'.[4]

[1] Parnaby, *Britain and the Labor Trade*, p. 47.
[2] See Buckle, ii, pp. 653–71; 3 *Hansard*, 221, cols. 1226–51.
[3] Carnarvon to Disraeli 7 Aug. 1874. *Disraeli Papers*, B/xx/He/28.
[4] Disraeli to Carnarvon 8 Aug. 1874, quoted in Hardinge, *Life of Carnarvon*, ii, p. 74.

As soon as Carnarvon received this assurance from the prime minister he sent the telegram (which he had drafted in July) to the governor of New South Wales. As with Malaya and the Gold Coast, Disraeli gave Carnarvon a free hand and he may well have been surprised by the Colonial Secretary's speed of action. By the time the prime minister was back in London for the resumption of Cabinet business in the autumn, Fiji had been annexed.

Sir Hercules Robinson reached the islands on 23 September 1874. Although he found a certain amount of opposition to the cession, he seemed to make an excellent impression on the chiefs. Where Goodenough had been rather diffident, and always asked if there were any questions, Robinson was masterly and 'chief-like'.[1] Thakombau admitted, on 25 September 1874, that 'if matters remain as they are Fiji will become like a piece of driftwood in the sea and be picked up by the first passer by'.[2] After consulting his council on 28 September, the old chief finally offered the islands unconditionally to the governor. The Deed of Cession was signed on 30 September 1874; Fiji was proclaimed a Crown Colony on 10 October. To symbolize the passing of the old régime in Fiji Thakombau presented his favourite war club as a gift to Queen Victoria.

Carnarvon was able to report the annexation of Fiji to Disraeli in the same letter as he requested permission to go ahead with the abolition of slavery on the Gold Coast.[3] The prime minister seemed to be impressed. Carnarvon 'seems very busy annexing provinces to the Empire', he told his confidants; and 'Carnarvon seems to be distinguishing himself'.[4] The Liberals made no objection to the annexation of Fiji. Indeed, Kimberley and Knatchbull-Hugessen must have felt that their own ideas had been vindicated.[5] Even Gladstone stopped

[1] Account of overheard conversation in David Wilkinson to Hutchins 22 Oct. 1874 (copy). *Carnarvon Papers*, P.R.O. 30/6/25, p. 75.

[2] Robinson to Carnarvon 3 Oct. 1874. C.O. 83/5.

[3] Carnarvon to Disraeli 6 Oct. 1874 (copy). *Carnarvon Papers*, P.R.O. 30/6/11, p. 26.

[4] Disraeli to Lady Bradford 18 Oct. 1874 and Lady Chesterfield 20 Oct. Zetland, *The Letters of Disraeli to Lady Bradford and Lady Chesterfield*, London, 1929, i, p. 161.

[5] Kimberley to Gladstone 4 Nov. 1874. *Gladstone Papers*, 44225/154; *Brabourne Diary*, v, pp. 732–3.

making trouble when he discovered that his friend and former secretary, Sir Arthur Gordon, had accepted the governorship.[1] Carnarvon
was delighted with Robinson's successful mission — 'It is like a
dream'.[2] The incident had widespread publicity. In fact, the annexation of Fiji provided one of the frills of empire which seemed to fit in
with Disraeli's ideas. He tried to flatter the queen by suggesting the
new colony should be called the Windsor Isles, but fortunately Victoria
preferred to stick to 'Fiji'.[3]

[1] Gordon to Carnarvon 1 Nov. 1874 (private). *Carnarvon Papers*,
P.R.O. 30/6/39.
[2] Carnarvon to Disraeli 27 Oct. 1874. *Disraeli Papers*, B/xx/He/3.
[3] Disraeli to Queen Victoria 30 Nov. 1874. Queen to Derby 3 Dec.
1874. *Royal Archives*, P.24/131.

12. *Informal Empire in the South Pacific, 1874–7*

THE annexation of Fiji did not solve the problem of the frontier in the South Pacific. Further expansion was demanded. A number of similar frontier questions confronted Carnarvon in 1874. The chiefs of Rotuma had requested annexation. Samoa was still coveted by New Zealanders, New Guinea attracted Australians. Vogel pressed for his chartered company and the kidnapping problem remained.

Despite his decision to annex Fiji, Carnarvon opposed further expansion in the Pacific. 'For the present at least I think we may leave Rotuma beyond the limits of the Empire', he wrote, 'The day may come when it and possibly other islands may be included: but this is hardly yet.'[1] He did not rule out further expansion completely. But, for the present, Fiji was regarded as a trial case. In order to forestall new demands for expansion Herbert proposed to Carnarvon, a few days after the decision about Rotuma, a formula which could be used in reply to ambitious projects:

> the establishment of a separate Colonial Government in Fiji will afford H.M. Govt. increased facilities of considering the requirements of this country & of British subjects in the Pacific, and for the present you are not prepared to decide in favour of or against any particular schemes for the development of British influence among the Islands.[2]

Fiji was to be an experiment in the government of a Pacific island. The decision to limit expansion to Fiji was not made hastily.

[1] Min. by Carnarvon 1 Nov. 1874 on F.O. to C.O. 21 Mar. 1873. C.O. 83/3. Rotuma lies about 400 miles north of Fiji. A letter from a Wesleyan missionary, the Rev. John Osborne, dated 5 Aug. 1872, indicating that the Rotuman chiefs feared the French and wished Britain to take possession of the island, was encl. in Ad. to C.O. 19 Feb. 1873. (C.O. 201/575.) Kimberley put off a decision until after the Fiji question was settled. He later said he would consider it along with Thurston's letter of 31 Jan. 1873, but did not do so. Herbert reminded Carnarvon in Oct. 1874.

[2] Min. by Herbert 7 Nov., on Fergusson to Carnarvon 24 June 1874. C.O. 209/232.

Carnarvon did not finally make up his mind until August 1874 after sending Robinson to Fiji. Throughout the discussions he worked in close accord with Herbert, the permanent under-secretary, who had taken a personal interest in the region since his Australian days. Moreover, although Herbert disliked Vogel and accepted the principle that further annexations should be postponed until experience had been gained in Fiji, he remained uncertain about Samoa, New Guinea and the chartered company project. The question of expansion in the South Pacific received a good deal of thoughtful attention in 1874.

SAMOA AND THE CHARTERED COMPANY SCHEME

Gladstone's qualified approval of the chartered company scheme had not been intimated to the New Zealanders.[1] This project was yet another of the questions which confronted Carnarvon on taking office. He read the papers concerning Samoa and the chartered company on 25 February 1874. He also learnt of Colonel Steinberger's return to the United States with a petition from the foreign residents in Samoa requesting American protection. Would there be a scramble for Samoa?

Commodore Goodenough, who had visited Samoa, played down the possibility of an American protectorate. The Americans were only really interested in Pago Pago harbour.[2] Herbert suggested that as Britain was unlikely to take Samoa 'we may be well satisfied to see the Americans there', although he also thought this unlikely.[3] The Colonial Office did not want to annex Samoa. But the attitude of Herbert and Carnarvon to the chartered company scheme is not easy to define.

When Herbert originally showed Carnarvon the documents containing Gladstone's views he remarked that Vogel's project was a 'very speculative and audacious policy'.[4] At other times he seemed quite attracted to the idea. Probably if Vogel had not been its advocate,

[1] See above, pp. 264–5.
[2] Goodenough's *Journal*, i, 6–8 Nov. 1873; Goodenough to Ad. 14 Nov. 1873 in Ad. to C.O. 20 Feb. 1874. C.O. 83/5.
[3] Min. by Herbert 25 Feb., on F.O. to C.O. 21 Feb. 1874. C.O. 209/233.
[4] Memo. by Herbert 25 Feb. 1874 on Fergusson to Kimberley 24 Nov. 1873. C.O. 209/230.

the scheme would have been given more serious attention. As it was, Carnarvon trod very cautiously. He thought the project was 'Visionary — dangerous — open to speculation and corruption'.[1] He sent a much more guarded expression of his views to New Zealand than Gladstone's Government had drafted. Carnarvon neither liked the ambition of the company to build a great dominion like India or Canada, nor its desire for a monopoly. His despatch of 5 March 1874 still included Gladstone's invitation to the New Zealanders to send more details, and it admitted that Britain could not resist the creation of new settlements 'within a reasonable distance' of the Australasian colonies. But Carnarvon warned the New Zealand Government that, as there were other Powers trading in the islands, great caution was needed.[2] Vogel's project, then, was not rejected outright, but it was given no encouragement. Carnarvon probably handled Vogel with more finesse than Kimberley did.

What Carnarvon was obviously trying to do at this stage was to put off having to make a firm decision over either Samoa or the chartered company until the Fiji question had been settled. Yet Samoa had the habit of demanding Colonial Office attention. As he read about the American reaction to Steinberger's visit, Herbert began to have the uneasy feeling that Samoa might turn out to be a better bargain than Fiji.[3] He suggested that if the Americans did not annex Samoa, and if Britain *did* annex Fiji, Pago Pago might be acquired as well. Lowther, the parliamentary under-secretary, suggested that the Fiji question should be used as an opportunity for declaring a general policy for the South Pacific.[4] The nearest approach to a general proposal for the region, of course, was Vogel's plan for the chartered company!

Vogel continued to advocate his project. In fact, he had already presented a Bill authorizing the scheme to the New Zealand

---

[1] Memo. by Carnarvon 26 Feb. 1874. *Carnarvon Papers*, P.R.O. 30/6/51, p. 3.

[2] Original draft by Herbert 6 Feb. 1874 on Fergusson to Kimberley 24 Nov. 1873; min. by Carnarvon 26 Feb. 1874, final draft by Herbert 5 Mar. C.O. 209/230.

[3] Min. by Herbert 12 June, on F.O. to C.O. 2 June 1874. C.O. 209/233.

[4] Ibid. Mins. by Herbert and Lowther 22 June, on F.O. to C.O. 19 June 1874.

Parliament. He frankly announced that he looked forward to the day
of a mighty federated British Empire with irresistible world-wide naval
power, in which New Zealand would be regarded as the natural
metropolis of Polynesia. As the British Government did not seem
likely to take action, even if circumstances forced them to annex Fiji,
Vogel had considered that New Zealand might do so on her own. 'It
seems to me that New Zealand may earn for reluctant Great Britain
without committing her to responsibilities she fears — a grand Island
Dominion.'¹ To this end his Government made an agreement with
Frederick Whitaker, a New Zealand financier, who was also chairman
of the Fiji Bank, to form a joint-stock company with capital of £1
million, and headquarters in Auckland, to operate as merchants, ship-
owners, planters, producers, manufacturers, brokers, insurance agents,
bankers and money-lenders in the Pacific islands and in Britain and
New Zealand. Political motives were not explicitly set out on the
Bill before the New Zealand Parliament. But, as Herbert did not
fail to note, Vogel envisaged New Zealand in a 'metropolitan position
in the Pacific'.²

Vogel withdrew his Bill, but his grandiose vision and persistent
lobbying antagonized the Colonial Office. Herbert thought 'Mr.
Vogel's unscrupulousness and Sir J[ohn] Fergusson's pliability threaten
us with a more awkward difficulty than we have in Fiji'.³ Lowther
urged that the whole project be promptly 'snuffed out'.⁴ When the
New Zealand Government answered Carnarvon's despatch of 5 March
1874 by suggesting that other colonies were allowed to subsidize
similar companies, and went on to argue that Britain should not check
New Zealand's expansion just because the colony was more enterpris-
ing than her jealous Australian neighbours, Herbert felt they were
'impertinent'.⁵

¹ Vogel memo., 5 Mar., in Fergusson to Kimberley 11 Mar. 1874.
C.O. 209/232.
² Ibid. Min. by Herbert 17 May 1874. Cf. Ross, *New Zealand Aspirations*, pp. 119–23.
³ Min. by Herbert 17 May, on Fergusson to Kimberley 12 Mar. 1874.
C.O. 209/232.
⁴ Ibid. Min. by Lowther 18 May, on Fergusson to Kimberley 11 Feb.
1874.
⁵ Ibid. Min. by Herbert 11 July, on Fergusson to Carnarvon 8 May
1874 (secret).

But by this time the cession of Fiji had been secured. Carnarvon decided that the problems of administration and finance there were complicated enough. He could not afford to meet the new set of problems which might arise over a chartered company. He privately instructed the Marquis of Normanby, who was about to become Fergusson's successor as governor of New Zealand, that Vogel was not to be encouraged. The experiment in Fiji was given as the reason for not proceeding with the chartered company.[1]

AUSTRALIA AND NEW GUINEA

While the New Zealanders were making their plans for Polynesia, many Australians cast covetous eyes on Papua. After annexing Fiji and restraining the New Zealanders, Carnarvon had to turn to yet another expansion issue and to formulate his policy in the question of the Australian frontier in the South Pacific.

New Guinea first began to attract Australian interest when the Admiralty began surveys of the Torres Strait, which was used by ships plying between New South Wales and India and China in the 1840's. Part of the south-eastern coast of New Guinea was explored and in 1846 a naval officer took formal possession of it for Great Britain.[2] In 1864 the Government of Queensland, with some financial help from the imperial and other Australian Governments, founded a settlement at Somerset, Cape York, to police Torres Strait. Optimists envisaged a new Singapore.[3] But projects for colonization in New Guinea were discouraged.

When, in 1867, a New Guinea Company of Sydney planned a 'Pioneer Expedition', the Colonial Office responded most unfavourably. Frederick Elliot threw the whole weight of his colonial experience against it:

> for the last 27 years it has fallen to my lot, in one capacity or another, to see every important question about new colonies or acquisition of Native Lands, and that this Department has always steadily resisted the

---

[1] Carnarvon to Normanby 20 Aug. 1874, private and confidential (copy). *Carnarvon Papers*, P.R.O. 30/6/25, p. 30.

[2] Memo by Capt. Frederick Evans, Ad. hydrographer, 2 July 1875. C.O. 808/11, p. 3.

[3] Moresby, *New Guinea and Polynesia*, p. 11.

monstrous doctrine that private persons can buy vast tracts of Country
from helpless Natives for a bottle or two of rum and a few coats and
trousers.[1]

Rogers thought a German colony in New Guinea would be a good
idea,[2] but Adderley, while hostile to the Sydney venture, did not
want to make a general policy ruling: 'who shall say that New
Guinea shall not be settled, or that the Australian English should not
settle it'.[3] The Duke of Buckingham gave the Australians the same
reply he gave to similar projects in West Africa and Malaya: he would
not sanction any settlements in these regions, and adventurers who
went there could expect no protection or confirmation of land titles.[4]
A scheme for settling Chinese from Hong Kong in New Guinea was
rejected in 1869.[5] Seventy young men from the Sydney New Guinea
Prospecting Association came to grief on the Great Barrier Reef in
1872.[6]

In the period 1873–5 there was something of a New Guinea fever,
following Captain Moresby's explorations and the arrival of the London
Missionary Society in Papua. The Rev. William Wyatt Gill of the
London Missionary Society reported to the Government of New South
Wales in January 1873 that some of the Society's teachers had been
located on the south-east coast, and he hoped that Britain would forestall the Germans, who were said to be interested in New Guinea.[7]
A writer named Rendall, who claimed he had once asked Palmerston
to annex New Guinea and Fiji, wrote to the Colonial Office suggesting that Moresby's explorations gave the Liberals a chance of dis-

[1] Min. by Elliot 13 Aug., on Young to Buckingham 22 June 1867.
C.O. 201/542.

[2] Ibid. Min. by Rogers 3 Aug., on Young to Buckingham 31 May 1867.

[3] Ibid. Min. by Adderley 13 Mar. 1867 on despatch of 22 June.

[4] Ibid. Buckingham to Young 14 Sept. 1867 (draft).

[5] Memo. on New Guinea encl. in F.O. to C.O. 26 June 1875. C.O.
808/10, pp. 27–28.

[6] Belmore to Kimberley 29 Dec. 1871. C.O. 201/565. Cf. D. C. Gordon,
The Australian Frontier in New Guinea 1870–1885, New York, 1951, pp.
83–87.

[7] Rev. Gill to G. A. Lloyd 28 Jan. 1873, copy encl. in Robinson to Carnarvon 7 Sept. 1874. Confidential Print, C.O. 808/10, p. 16. Cf. R.
Lovett, *History of the London Missionary Society 1795–1895*, London, 1899,
i, p. 442; Townshend, *Origins of Modern German Colonialism*, p. 41.

proving some of the charges made by Disraeli in the Crystal Palace speech.[1] Colonel James Scott, of Melbourne, sought Colonial Office confirmation for the purchase of 10,000 acres from the Papuans and the privilege of selecting 10,000 acres to be paid for by the British

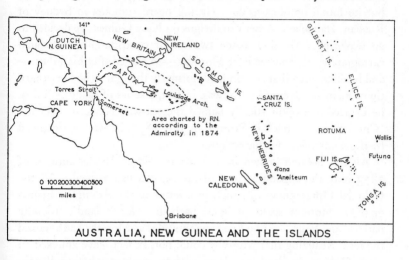

AUSTRALIA, NEW GUINEA AND THE ISLANDS

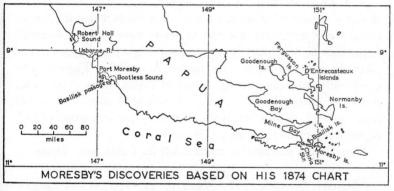

MORESBY'S DISCOVERIES BASED ON HIS 1874 CHART

Government in the territory annexed by Moresby.[2] New Guinea was suddenly in the news. Kimberley decided that the Colonial Office should find out what Captain Moresby had been doing.

[1] Rendall to Kimberley 17 Sept. 1873. C.O. 201/576.
[2] Bowen to Kimberley 12 Aug. 1873. C.O. 309/110; Scott to Kimberley 26 June 1874. C.O. 808/15, p. 26.

Moresby's discoveries were, in reality, extremely modest. But his official report did not reach the Colonial Office until April 1874. Exaggerated notions circulated freely in Australia and England. He had been sent to Torres Strait in September 1873 to check kidnapping, but he found nothing to do. Having heard rumours in Sydney of Russian, Italian and American designs on New Guinea, he decided to go exploring. He then made two minor contributions to Papuan cartography. He charted Port Moresby — so named after his father — and he discovered that certain land, formerly thought to be the eastern tip of mainland New Guinea, was, in fact, a series of islands. These he charted and optimistically named the sea-way between them the 'China Strait'.[1] Back in Sydney, in July 1873, he was reprimanded by the commodore for his actions.[2]

All this became known in London in 1874. In the autumn of 1873 only the vaguest picture of his exploits had arrived. All the Colonial Office knew was that, in a letter to the Admiralty hydrographer, Moresby spoke of 'good harbour', 'fertile land', 'friendly natives' and 'gold'.[3] The Press announced that Moresby had annexed the lot. Realizing that Moresby could not, in fact, have annexed all New Guinea, Holland, the legal adviser, doubted whether Britain should recognize what he had taken. But Herbert was the former premier of Queensland and was therefore alive to New Guinea's importance to Australia: 'another power might have stepped in and taken the part most valuable and nearest Australia'.[4] Thereafter, he consistently advocated getting control of Papua before anyone else. For the time being, however, no decision could be taken until the full report arrived. Kimberley, while advocating the annexation of Fiji, deplored any further annexations in the Pacific.

New Guinea was another problem left for Carnarvon. It was, in

[1] Moresby, *New Guinea and Polynesia*, pp. 142–230, and *Two Admirals* London, 1909, p. 264.

[2] Stirling to Ad. 13 Oct. 1873 (copy). C.O. 201/578. Received in C.O. on 20 June 1874. Comm. Goodenough, who believed Stirling 'cared nothing for hydrography', was more sympathetic to Moresby, who he thought was merely 'tactless'. He authorized Moresby to explore the north-east coast of New Guinea in 1874. Goodenough's *Journal*, i, 13 Oct. 1873.

[3] Ad. to C.O. 15 Sept. 1873. C.O. 201/575.

[4] Min. by Herbert 15 Oct., on Ad. to C.O. 14 Oct. 1873. C.O. 309/111.

fact, squarely placed before him in March 1874 by Francis Labilliere, the Australian imperialist who lived in London. He probably got hold of some inside information about Moresby's reports to the Admiralty in 1873. He realized that Gladstone would be sure to rebuff him, so he waited until after the election in 1874. He then wrote to Disraeli and Carnarvon placing New Guinea in the context of the imperial frontier in the tropics. 'Good or bad, we cannot help having to do with [the Papuans] . . . for they must henceforth affect British interests much more than the Ashantees and Fijians.' In the interest of the Papuans and the defence of the Australian colonies, he called for annexation, claiming that 'Our most prosperous Colonies never exhibited to first explorers such evidence of richness as New Guinea has displayed'.[1]

By the time Carnarvon received Labilliere's proposal, Moresby's official report was available. Herbert immediately took up the question of Australian fears about New Guinea.

> This is a much more important question to the Australian Colonies &
> to the Empire, than that of the annexation of Fiji. The great wealth
> and extent of New Guinea and its close proximity to Australia render
> the question of its ownership a somewhat pressing one. I do not think
> there is any hope of our being able to keep clear of interference with
> New Guinea. The brutalities of our traders must demand our frequent
> presence whenever they commence operations on its coasts. I do not
> at all anticipate that the occupation of New Guinea if judiciously
> entered upon need be very costly. If a settlement (which *might* in the
> first instance be a penal establishment for Australia) were made on the
> South Eastern & healthy part of the Coast, and our ships employed to
> control & regulate trading operations, we should probably spend much
> less than by letting matters drift until we have to interfere, & probably
> fight, on a large scale.[2]

On Herbert's suggestion Carnarvon agreed to sound the views of the Australasian governors.[3]

The replies were discouraging: the colonies vaguely endorsed

---

[1] Labilliere to Carnarvon 26 Mar. 1874. C.O. 808/10, pp. 1–3. He also said he sent a copy to Disraeli.

[2] Min. by Herbert 3 Apr., on Labilliere to Carnarvon 26 Mar. 1874. C.O. 234/34.

[3] Circular to Australasian govs. 17 Apr. 1874. C.O. 808/10, p. 4.

British expansion, but offered no help. New Zealand was more
interested in Polynesia. South Australia was not concerned. Western
Australia was favourable in principle, but its governor did not think
any of the colonial Governments would want to undertake the administration of Papua. Governor Bowen of Victoria pointed out that the
climate of New Guinea was unsuitable for white settlement and
suggested that Britain did not need any more 'black subjects'. He was
reminded, in fact, of the recent trouble on the Gold Coast by the
presence in western New Guinea of the Dutch, whose position might
prove to be a thorn in the side as Elmina had been. The Dutch would
then have to be induced to give up their interests, so 'New Guinea'
would prove to be as embarrassing as 'Old Guinea' — only the
Papuans would turn out to be more formidable enemies than the
Ashantis.[1]

The typical Australasian viewpoint of the question of the frontier
in the South Pacific was expressed in the reply from New South Wales.
Henry Parkes, the premier, enclosing a copy of the Rev. Gill's warning
about the Germans, claimed that no country had such attractions as
New Guinea,[2] and that its colonization by another Power would be
an embarrassment to Australia. Sir Hercules Robinson — who was
about to set sail for Fiji on his mission to secure the unconditional
cession — confirmed that annexation of New Guinea would be
popular in Australia. Pointing out that the colonies would gain an
advantage without paying for it, he reminded the Colonial Office that
since New Guinea was within 10° of the Equator it could never
be a home for European settlement; at best, it would be another
Java or Ceylon. Robinson did not think that occupation by another
Power was likely, for any nation wanting a naval base would find
a better spot, and Britain could not stop them. He presumed that
Britain did not intend to annex 'every available spot in the South
Pacific'.[3]

Queensland was also generally favourable to annexation, but showed
little specific interest at this stage. It was felt in the colony, however,
that if Britain held back, Germany, France, Italy, Russia or the

[1] Bowen to Carnarvon 1 Sept. 1874. C.O. 808/10, p. 10.

[2] See above, p. 342.

[3] Robinson to Carnarvon (confidential) 7 Sept. 1874 enclosing Parkes's
memo. 27 July 1874. C.O. 201/577.

United States might step in. In short, the colonies did not want the responsibility of annexing New Guinea themselves, but they were eager for the British Government to ward off other nations.

'This is one of the dilemmas of Empire,' declared Herbert in April 1874. He was convinced there would be an outcry in Australia if another Power established itself only eighty miles from Australia. He believed this could be prevented at little cost. He even suggested that Vogel's Polynesia Company might be developed into something in which 'all the Australian colonies should unite for colonization in Oceania generally'.[1] English taxpayers, he knew, would not approve paying for new annexations 'while the Australian taxpayer, who is much better able to pay, reaps the commercial profit of the enterprise'. What he feared, above all, was that they might merely drift into annexation.[2] This is what Carnarvon wanted to avoid. Although he could agree with the views of a Royal Colonial Institute delegation, who came to discuss New Guinea on 2 May 1875, he reminded them of the recent experiments in the Gold Coast and Fiji and pleaded for 'some breathing time'.[3]

Yet pressure for annexation in New Guinea mounted from all sides in 1875. Carnarvon could not avoid facing up to his dilemma. Derby, the Foreign Secretary, for one, confessed his dislike of 'the notion of letting foreigners come so near to us', and he added: 'We shall want New Guinea ourselves some day'.[4] Herbert suggested that the Admiralty should survey the coast directly opposite Cape York and that Britain should at least secure this territory for herself, even if large-scale annexation did not take place. Various expeditions to New Guinea were planned in London, Sydney and Melbourne. When a delegation supporting one of them called on the prime minister of New South Wales they were treated to a grandiose project for expansion throughout Polynesia.[5] Referring back to Kimberley's New South Wales plan for Fiji, Premier Robertson insisted

[1] Ibid. Min. by Herbert 4 Nov. 1874.
[2] Min. by Herbert 26 Apr. 1875 on Gov. Cairns to Carnarvon 22 Feb. 1876. C.O. 234/35.
[3] *The Times*, 3 May 1875, p. 6.
[4] Derby to Carnarvon 19 July 1875 (private). *Carnarvon Papers*. P.R.O. 30/6/8, p. 71.
[5] Account of delegation in *Sydney Morning Herald*, 20 Apr. 1875.

that, as in the case of Fiji, the New Guinea question was an imperial matter.

These were not just the effusions of a colonial politician seeking to satisfy a rather influential delegation. They were intended for the ear of the Secretary of State. Robertson advised, for example, on 31 May 1875:

> My colleagues and myself venture respectfully to offer our opinion that on many grounds it would be desirable in the highest interests of civilization that Great Britain should, with as little delay as possible, take possession not only of the magnificent Island of New Guinea, but of the Islands of New Britain, New Ireland, and the chain of islands to the north-east and east of New Guinea from Bougainville Island to San Christoval, the south eastern most island of the Solomon Group, the group of the New Hebrides, including Espiritu Santo, Mallicolo and Sandwich, with smaller adjoining islands, and the Marshall, Gilbert and Ellice Islands, to all of which the traffic from the Port of Sydney extends.
>
> It appears to us that a more extended dominion over these waters on the part of the British Empire would be not only consistent with the maritime supremacy of England but would conduce much to the tranquility and peace of these Australian colonies. . . . The question is wholly an Imperial one and it seems to us to regard it in any other light would neither conduce to the satisfaction of the colonies nor to the dignity of the Empire.[1]

This was probably more than even Herbert had bargained for, but the New South Wales proposal was soon followed by ominous threats from Melbourne. Colonel Scott now announced that he had written to Bismarck about New Guinea and would next try the French President or the Tsar. This must have sounded to the Colonial Office very much like the Selangor Tin Company's blackmail in Malaya, but Herbert thought it just possible that Scott might manage to interest another Power. He therefore suggested that a public despatch should be sent to the Australasian colonies putting it on record that

> the labours & explorations of British officers & men of science as well as other British subjects constitute a priority of claim which no friendly power could ignore; and that while the positive annexation of New

---

[1] Memo. by Robertson 31 May encl. in Robinson to Carnarvon 3 June 1875. C.O. 808/15, p. 50.

Guinea by England ... must be a question for very serious consideration ... HM Government can have no hesitation in saying that they could not recognise any pretension on the part of any other Power to assume the sovereignty of the Island.[1]

In short, Herbert wanted to announce Britain's 'paramountcy'. Carnarvon promised to consult the Cabinet.

He was finally forced to announce his policy for New Guinea in October 1875 by the plans for a quasi-military expedition drawn up by the New Guinea Colonization Association. This body intended to enlist 'New Guinea Volunteers' under the Volunteer Act, and hoped that its officers would be appointed Justices of the Peace under the Government of Fiji. The Association tried to present itself as a humanitarian venture, and claimed that both Hudson's Bay Company and the East India Company had opened up less fertile land, initially, than New Guinea.

Carnarvon refused to support the scheme. William Malcolm, newly appointed third assistant under-secretary, had made a careful study of the whole issue and his conclusions were decisive. New Guinea was, he suggested, useless for colonization; the Somerset settlement in Queensland already provided protection for Torres Strait shipping; the short route to China through Moresby's 'China Strait' was unproven; and there was no reason to expect foreign annexation. In spite of 'a varnish of piety on the prospectus' the Colonization Association was really attempting a 'land jobbing speculation',[2] and it turned out that the commander selected for the expedition was a dismissed naval officer. Carnarvon therefore rebuffed the Association. He told a Cabinet colleague that 'at present I am prepared to resist the cry for annexation and to get over the difficulty by another means'.[3]

Carnarvon now announced his policy over New Guinea to the Australian colonies. He sent a despatch to New South Wales on 8 December 1875 which was, in many ways, more skilful than Kimberley's despatch on Fiji. Carnarvon declared publicly, and the colonial

[1] Min. by Herbert 3 Oct., on Scott to Carnarvon 9 July 1875. C.O. 309/113.

[2] Min. by Malcolm 25 Oct., on New Guinea Assoc. to Carnarvon 9 Oct. 1875. C.O. 201/580; Ad. to C.O. 5 Nov. 1875.

[3] Carnarvon to New Guinea Assoc. 30 Oct. 1875. C.O. 808/15, p. 85.

Press generally accepted, what Kimberley had really wanted to say to
the Australian colonies over Fiji: It is in your interest — you pay!
He warned the Australians that

> it is simply impossible either for me to admit, or . . . to persuade the English
> people that the Australian Colonies have no special interest in the
> annexation of New Guinea, and that the responsibility of the measure
> rests exclusively with the Imperial Government.

The only ground he could see for immediate action would be foreign
intervention, but the United States seemed unlikely to step in, and the
German Government had announced it would seek no colonies. It
was anyway unlikely that any Power would take New Guinea without
consulting Britain.[1]

In this way Carnarvon successfully resisted the pressure for the
annexation of New Guinea, as he had Rotuma and Samoa. Though
Herbert was still not satisfied and still hoped for the securing of the
territory facing Cape York he had to admit that he felt 'at a loss for
any really constructive suggestion'. He, perhaps more than any one
in the Colonial Office, realized Britain's dilemma:

> If we delay annexation, the very serious risk is run of an almost immediate
> collision with Australia. If we are too hasty in annexing we stimulate a
> rush of people to an almost uninhabitable country, and saddle this
> Government with very heavy expense.[2]

Carnarvon's decision over New Guinea stood for a few years.

KIDNAPPING AND THE WESTERN PACIFIC HIGH
    COMMISSION

Although Carnarvon successfully resisted the cry for further annexations in the Pacific, he was nevertheless convinced that there was need
for some form of extended jurisdiction over British subjects. He
realized that the annexation of Fiji had increased British interest in
the region generally, which might, in turn, give a fillip to the labour
traffic. Therefore, even before the annexation of Fiji, he had begun

---

[1] Carnarvon to Robinson 8 Dec. 1875. C.O. 808/15, pp. 93–94.
[2] Min. by Herbert 24 July 1876 on F.O. to C.O. 21 July 1875. C.O.
201/582.

studying methods of solving the kidnapping problem and had later hinted about trying 'another means'.

Abuses in the labour traffic had not been purged by the Kidnapping Act of 1872. Kidnapping by British subjects had been made a felony and the transport of islanders in British ships, and their importation into the colonies, was regulated, but the importation of islanders into Fiji and their movement from island to island, where British planters hired them, was largely untouched. It was true that Consul March and Premier Thurston had tried to control it, but Whitehall was sceptical about their efforts. This had indeed been Kimberley's chief argument in favour of the annexation of Fiji. As a focus of the traffic, yet beyond British jurisdiction, the islands were the blind-spot of Britain's anti-kidnapping campaign. Yet even outside Fiji this Act had its limitations. One of the most notorious kidnapping cases, the *Carl* massacre, only received publicity in England after the 1872 Act had been passed, and, as the leading perpetrators escaped the death penalty because of legal technicalities, the whole case seemed to detract from the usefulness of the Act.[1] For this reason the London Missionary Society had demanded that the Royal Navy be given wider powers in the Pacific.

Here was yet another problem which claimed Carnarvon's attention.

[1] The exact details of this incident are not very clear, but it appears that the *Carl* sailed from Melbourne early in 1871 and by June had put into Fiji, where Dr James Murray, the owner, decided to go 'blackbirding'. He collected islanders from the New Hebrides and the Solomons, but 80 fierce men from Bougainville caused trouble in the hold and fights broke out. All efforts to calm the human cargo failed: Murray panicked, and on about 20 Sept. 1871 the 'massacre' took place. The crew fired into the hold until the islanders were subdued. About 70 were killed and their bodies thrown into the sea; 20 were wounded, but the crew of H.M.S. *Rosario* found nothing amiss when they boarded the ship on 17 Nov. However, Edward March, H.M. consul in Fiji, found some obviously unwilling islanders on board, one with a gunshot wound; and at a court of inquiry on 22 May 1872 Murray's story came out. Thus by providing Crown evidence he escaped punishment, and the master and mate, although sentenced to death, had this commuted to life imprisonment because they were following Murray's orders. (Account of the court inquiry in March to Granville 27 May 1872. *Accounts and Papers* (1873), l, pp. 278–91: report of trial in *Sydney Morning Herald*, 2 Dec. 1872; statement in House of Commons in *The Times*, 26 Feb. 1873; see also Dunbabin, *Slavers of the South Seas*, pp. 209–18.)

Indeed, during his very first week at the Colonial Office another kidnapping case achieved so much publicity that Carnarvon asked Herbert, on 26 February 1874, to talk the matter over with him.[1] It became clear that in 1874 both Foreign and Colonial Offices realized that some new policy governing the actions of British subjects in the South Pacific was desirable. Carnarvon told a large deputation from the Aborigines Protection Society, which came to discuss the Gold Coast and Fiji on 6 March 1874, that he did not think that the annexation of Fiji would solve the kidnapping problem. Even before the Goodenough–Layard Report arrived, then, Carnarvon realized that a decision was needed, whether Fiji were annexed or not.

This resolve was not only confirmed by the Goodenough–Layard Report, but the commissioners provided a definite proposal. Paragraph thirty-eight of the Report may be seen as the germ of the Western Pacific High Commission.

> We think that the Commission of the Governor of Fiji should give him authority over the persons and acts of British subjects in the New Hebrides and the Solomon Islands, or the Islands of the Pacific south of the equator and west of meridian of 168° west longitude (except New Caledonia and the Loyalty Islands, which are under the French flag). This would be very satisfactory to Englishmen living in those islands, who would then be able to refer their disputes to the Courts of Fiji and would be able to register vessels and take out licences to carry labourers in a regular way, whereas they are now doing so either by stealth or through the fiction of a French flag and registers obtained from New Caledonia. . . . The formation of a centre of law and order could not fail to have a good influence in this part of the South Seas, where the number of adventurers in various pursuits is yearly increasing.[2]

The proposal was one of great importance and was accepted in principle. It was intended, after the annexation of Fiji, to extend the Kidnapping Act to these islands. Gradually it was also accepted that someone should be given authority over British subjects throughout the South Pacific.

The idea eventually adopted was for the governor of Fiji to have consular jurisdiction in the whole area. First recorded by Herbert

[1] Min. by Herbert 26 Feb. on *Daily Telegraph* clipping of 24 Feb. 1874 in C.O. 309/112.
[2] C.O. 808/3, p. 10.

on 6 November 1874,[1] it is probable that this idea of the 'High Commissionership' came from Sir Arthur Gordon, whose appointment as governor of Fiji had been in Herbert's mind even before the annexation.[2] The son and one-time private secretary of the prime minister, Lord Aberdeen, an ex-Member of Parliament and former private secretary of Gladstone, Gordon was not prepared to endure the more humdrum side of colonial service,[3] and the idea of a wide authority in the South Pacific seemed attractive to him. Moreover, a precedent for such authority already existed, as the governor of Labuan was also consul-general for North Borneo, and the idea was also consistent with policy on the imperial frontier elsewhere. Gordon once claimed, in fact, that it had been originally suggested to him that as governor of Fiji he would have the same relations with the 'wild tribes in the vicinity but beyond his jurisdiction' as did the governors of the Gold Coast, the Cape and the Straits Settlements.[4] This, then, was the basis for the Western Pacific High Commission. It could not be inaugurated, however, until 1877 because of a lengthy battle over the details of the new jurisdiction between the Foreign Office, Colonial Office and Treasury.[5]

Whitehall was rather secretive about the plans because it feared that the new policy might arouse international suspicion. The Foreign Office was cautious about giving the governor of Fiji wider powers in case it was regarded as a prelude to more annexations. When the new Kidnapping Bill was presented to Parliament on 6 March 1875 there was no mention of the High Commission. But Carnarvon clearly regarded the new scheme as an essential part of his policy of restraint in the South Pacific. Indeed, it is highly significant that the moment he chose for the announcement of the new policy was his speech to

[1] Min. by Herbert 6 Nov., on Robinson to Carnarvon (telegram) 4 Nov. 1874. C.O. 83/5.

[2] Lady Gordon to Gordon 2 June, and Herbert to Gordon 5 June 1874. Gordon, *Mauritius*, ii, pp. 658, 660–1.

[3] See Chapman, *Arthur Hamilton Gordon*, for his earlier career.

[4] Gordon to Carnarvon 17 Feb. 1875 (private). *Carnarvon Papers*, P.R.O. 30/6/39, p. 69.

[5] See my article, 'Disraeli's Colonial Policy: the Creation of the Western Pacific High Commission, 1874–1877', *H.S.A.N.Z.* (1960), 9 (35), pp. 279–94.

the deputation on 29 April 1875 who wanted him to annex New Guinea.

Carnarvon agreed in general with the deputation's views about slavery. But he warned them that it would be 'impossible to appropriate every territory and every island'. Instead, he promised that a clause would be inserted into the Bill authorizing the governor of Fiji's appointment as High Commissioner with consular jurisdiction in the region so that he would be 'commander of these tribes'.[1] What the last phrase was really supposed to mean is rather obscure, but it would seem to be a hint that the High Commissioner would have special regard for relations with the islanders, as well as authority over British subjects. The Admiralty had assured Carnarvon that technically the eastern coasts of New Guinea were washed by the Pacific Ocean, so he was able to include the territory within the High Commissioner's jurisdiction.[2] In this way both the kidnapping and expansion problems could be conveniently met together.

The Treasury tried to make trouble, but Carnarvon brushed their quibbles aside.[3] When the new Pacific Islanders Protection Act became law on 4 August 1875, not only was the colony of Fiji included within the definition of an Australasian colony, but a new clause six provided the authority for the High Commission. The Crown was empowered to

> exercise power and jurisdiction over Her subjects within any island and places in the Pacific Ocean not being within Her Majesty's dominions, nor within the jurisdiction of any civilized power, in the same and as ample a manner as if such power and jurisdiction had been acquired by the cession or conquest of territory.[4]

The High Commissioner would receive his consular jurisdiction by an Order in Council. This was not passed until 1877 because of further complications raised by the Foreign Office in view of the growing American and German interest in Samoa.

---

[1] *The Times*, 3 May 1875.

[2] Min. by Herbert 28 Apr. (C.O. 201/580), on Ad. to C.O. 24 Apr. 1875. C.O. 808/10, p. 20.

[3] W. H. Smith to Carnarvon 1 May 1875 (private); Carnarvon to Smith 2 May 1875 (copy). *Carnarvon Papers*, P.R.O. 30/6/17, pp. 17 and 15.

[4] 38 & 39 Vict. cap. 51.

Although the evolution of the High Commission policy was not without difficulty, and its execution was not very successful, it provided Carnarvon with a very useful instrument for gaining his 'breathing time', and it enabled him to avoid making further annexations. Sovereignty was not to be acquired in the area of the High Commission. The Act did not derogate from the rights of the Pacific islanders. Yet Sir Julius Vogel, who was in London at the time (and who, indeed, dined with Carnarvon the night before the announcement of the new policy to the New Guinea deputation),[1] knew perfectly well what had been done. He saw the High Commission as 'an admirable compromise between that taking possession of the other islands which I have advocated and that leaving them to grow into lawless communities which on all sides had been admitted an evil'.[2] Like the new administration in the Gold Coast protectorate and the Residents in the Malay States, the Western Pacific High Commission was an experiment in providing order and jurisdiction without assuming sovereignty — an exercise, in fact, of informal empire.

Vogel knew what would follow. Just as Herbert once suggested that the alternatives on the Gold Coast were withdrawal or complete annexation, and Jervois realized that Residents in Malaya would only control or become ornaments, so Vogel saw the High Commission as 'the means to tentatively and gradually establish British sway in Polynesia without undertaking at the commencement responsibilities which might frighten those who look with dread upon the enlargement of her colonial possessions'.[3] As usual, Vogel sent on a few ideas to hasten the process. Herbert resisted them but he appreciated the logic of Vogel's view.

If Robert Herbert's attitude may be taken as typifying the Colonial Office view in the mid-1870's, that view is, ironically, not unlike Vogel's. Herbert believed Britain should be regarded as 'paramount power' in the South Pacific, and he wished to stave off foreign intervention in the area. Yet he felt that the time for further annexation had not come. His view of the Pacific was, in fact, very like Kimberley's explanation to Gladstone of Britain's interest in the Malay

[1] Memo. by Carnarvon 28 Apr. 1875. P.R.O. 30/6/47. This note says they talked about telegraph extensions.
[2] Vogel to Carnarvon 4 May 1875. P.R.O. 30/6/47, p. 216.
[3] Ibid. p. 216.

Peninsula. Herbert revealed his attitude frankly when he suggested
that

> Further annexation will come at the proper time, but to tell the world
> (Germany, United States, France etc.) that we *now* contemplate it would
> be to defeat the object and prevent us from quietly acquiring paramount
> influence among the islands.[1]

Carnarvon's 'other means' in the South Pacific were thoroughly
consistent with his new policies in West Africa and Malaya. What
the impatient colonial expansionists failed to realize was that the apparently obstinate Colonial Office often had the same ends in view.
The real difference was over timing. After the innovations of 1874,
Carnarvon asked for a breathing-space. He wanted a time for consolidation and appraisal to observe the working of the modest, but, in
the long run, far-reaching, experiments being made in the Gold Coast,
Malaya and the South Pacific.

[1] Min. by Herbert 5 May 1875 on Vogel's draft amendments to the
Carnarvon clause.   P.R.O. 30/6/47, p. 225.

The Frontier in Perspective

PART FOUR

The Frontier in Perspective

13. *Techniques of Informal Empire*

'I IMAGINE we shall some day have to extend — or abandon — this settlement.' 'Complete annexation or total abandonment are I fear the only alternatives.' In such stark uncompromising terms politicians were sometimes inclined to view Britain's dilemma in West Africa. As Carnarvon admitted, it was 'a very evil choice to have to make'. In the Malay Peninsula and Melanesia–Polynesia, where Britain had little territory, the choice seemed to lie between annexation or disengagement from the consequences of piecemeal intervention. Each case was, of course, different. But, as civil servants and politicians contemplated the future, they were tempted to reduce the question to simple terms: forwards or backwards? Should we expand, or should we retire to a secure, unambiguous and inexpensive position?

In reaching their decisions they rejected their own oversimplifications. They discovered that a simple *either-or* could not suffice. They eventually presented themselves with a comparatively wide range of choice. This is becoming increasingly appreciated by historians.[1] The now generally accepted concept of 'informal empire' rules out the simple choice of annexation or nothing: 'study of the formal empire alone . . . is rather like judging the size and character of icebergs solely from the parts above the water-line'.[2] But recognition of 'informal empire' leads us on to further questions. 'Refusals to annex are no proof of reluctance to control.'[3] This may be true. But willingness to control is no proof of desire. The question should be: What sort of control and to what purpose? Why were certain techniques of control tried while others were rejected? What range of possibilities really emerged, and which proved to be the most generally applicable?

[1] See the series of definitions used by Professor D. A. Lowe to distinguish between the various stages of British control in Uganda: 'Lion Rampant', *J.C.P.S.* (1964), 2 (3), pp. 248–50.
[2] J. Gallagher and R. E. Robinson, 'The Imperialism of Free Trade', *Econ. Hist. Rev.* (1953), 6 (1), p. 1.
[3] Ibid. p. 3.

The case-studies described in previous chapters show that a number of alternatives were available. By 1873 events in the three tropical regions, and the public controversies about them at home, presented what seemed at first to be a broad choice between advance or withdrawal. But these extremes were (except for one case) rejected. Both Kimberley and Carnarvon sought some way of keeping order and stability on the frontier in the tropics which fell short of the extension of British sovereignty. They were exponents of 'informal empire', but what did this mean? In the three tropical regions in the early 1870's informal empire could mean five different possibilities: extra-territorial jurisdiction, Residents, chartered companies, protectorates or a claim to be 'paramount power'.

EXTRA-TERRITORIAL JURISDICTION

The first possibility was a grant of extra-territorial jurisdiction. British subjects could be brought under the control of consular courts, complicated clashes between legal and cultural systems would be avoided, and British nationals would be placed under some protection and restraint with a minimum of interference with indigenous authority. By the middle of the nineteenth century it was a well-tried expedient, which stemmed from the European jurists' distinction between Christian and Oriental legal systems.[1] It began with the judicial rights which the Levant Company was granted over British subjects in the Ottoman Empire in the seventeenth century. A similar system was extended in the nineteenth century into Siam, China and Japan. But doubts were cast on the legality of these arrangements.

Thus, in 1843 the first Foreign Jurisdiction Act was passed. It sought to define the powers which had been acquired by the Crown outside British territory 'by Treaty, Capitulation, grant, usage, sufferance, and other lawful means'. They were deemed by the Act to be the same as powers exercised in Crown Colonies by right of cession or conquest.[2] Similar doubts about the jurisdiction exercised by George Maclean on the Gold Coast were resolved (from an English point of

[1] H. L. Jenkyns, *British Rule and Jurisdiction Beyond the Seas*, Oxford, 1902, pp. 127–42; G. Schwarzenberger, *Power Politics*, London, 1951, p. 35.
[2] 6 & 7 Vict. cap. 94.

view, at any rate) by the West Africa and Falkland Islands Act in 1843 and the Gold Coast Order in Council of the following year.[1]

During the 1860's a way of applying the system to Fiji was also sought. But Fiji presented a new problem. Who was sovereign? Non-Christian states or states outside the 'International Family' were, in the mid-Victorian period, divided into two categories. If they were 'Eastern countries', like the Chinese and Ottoman empires or Siam, China and Japan, they were, although 'non-Christian', undoubtedly regarded as sovereign states. Extra-territorial jurisdiction was secured by treaty. The rest of the world was classified as 'barbarous communities' and some jurists were inclined to take the view that it was 'impossible to regard an island in the South Seas or a kingdom in the heart of Africa as having the necessary marks of a State'.[2]

Gladstone disliked these distinctions. When he announced Goodenough and Layard's mission to Fiji in 1873 he pleaded for 'the same measure of justice for ourselves and other people'.[3] M. F. Lindley has asserted that 'there has been a persistent preponderance of juristic opinion in favour of the proposition that lands in the possession of any backward peoples who are politically organised ought not to be regarded as if they belonged to no one'.[4] The trouble in Fiji was that in the 1860's no single authority existed with which a treaty could be made. Since the Crown Law Officers decided that extra-territorial jurisdiction could not rest upon 'sufferance', a Bill was drafted to overcome the difficulty. Although the Royal Assent was about to be given to a scheme for consular jurisdiction for Fiji in 1871, this was never completed because the local circumstances changed.

A proposal was also made in 1871 for extending the extra-territorial jurisdiction of the Straits Settlements courts to British subjects caught in the colony for offences committed in the Malay States. The idea was unexceptionable and was adopted in 1874. But the Attorney-General of the Straits Government also raised the question of 'giving to the Legislature of the Colony authority . . . to legislate for matters

---

[1] 6 & 7 Vict. cap. 13; Order in Council 3 Sept. 1844.

[2] W. E. Hall, *A Treatise on the Foreign Powers and Jurisdiction of the British Crown*, Oxford, 1894, p. 130

[3] 3 *Hansard*, 216, col. 945.

[4] M. F. Lindley, *The Acquisition and Government of Backward Territory in International Law*, London, 1926, p. 20.

beyond the Colony'.[1] But he did not press the proposal. Yet a
similar idea was adopted on the Gold Coast in 1874, where the Legislative Council of the colony was empowered to legislate for the protectorate, which was not under British sovereignty.

In only two minor cases was extra-territorial jurisdiction extended
in the tropics. In the Niger Delta the Foreign Office wished to
maintain the *status quo* and it curtailed the British consul's powers of
intervention. But extra-territorial jurisdiction was adopted here for a
technical reason. British traders in the delta employed a large number
of Africans from the British colonies on the West Coast. When con-
victed for petty crimes in the merchants' informal 'Courts of Equity'
in the delta, offenders often appealed to colonial courts on the Gold
Coast, which usually overruled the Courts of Equity. To avoid these
difficulties the Foreign Office decided to reconstruct the delta courts.
In 1872 they became consular courts.[2] Here was a case where jurisdiction which had been exercised by 'sufferance' was recognized.

The second case was in Samoa and Tonga. Treaties were negotiated in 1878–9 providing for exclusive jurisdiction over British
subjects, which was exercised by Deputy Commissioners under the
Western Pacific High Commission.[3] As a technique of control, extra-
territorial jurisdiction played some part, then, in British policy on the
frontier in the tropics. But it obviously did not provide an adequate
method of securing order everywhere.

RESIDENTS

The second idea to be mooted was the appointment of Residents after
the well-known system of relations with the independent rulers in
India. A Melbourne newspaper, *The Age*, suggested in 1869 that the
Colonial Office should govern Fiji through a Resident.[4] When Julius
Vogel insisted that Samoa should become a province of New Zealand,

[1] Report by Thomas Braddell 10 Apr., in Anson to Kimberley 12 May
1871. C.O. 273/47.
[2] Order in Council 21 Feb. 1872. Hertslet's Commercial Treaties, xiii,
p. 50.
[3] Ibid. xv, pp. 334 and 396.
[4] *The Age*, 11 Dec. 1869, clipping in Canterbury to Granville 2 Jan. 1870.
C.O. 309/73.

the governor suggested that the islands might be controlled by an officer like the 'Residents at Native Courts in India'.[1] In West Africa Sir Arthur Kennedy suggested a 'Resident Agent' with somewhat different functions should be sent to Ashanti; both Kimberley and Carnarvon briefly revived this idea in 1873–4.[2] Commander Glover as governor of Lagos several times suggested 'Residents' or 'Agents' at Abeokuta and Porto Novo. There was talk of appointing a Sierra Leonian 'Political Agent' to the Mellacourie region in 1872, and Edward Blyden wanted an 'Agent in the Interior' sent to Fouta Djallon.[3] After the Ashanti War in 1874 Carnarvon considered stationing Residents in the states of the Gold Coast protectorate. Captain Brackenbury suggested that an itinerant officer should visit the Gold Coast rulers to hold periodic *durbars*.[4] Residents were, indeed, frequently proposed for the frontier in the tropics.

Only in the Malay States was the suggestion followed. First mooted in 1871 by the Anson Committee, and advocated more persistently by George Campbell, the Ceylon official who acted as lieutenant-governor of Penang in 1872–3, this suggestion appealed to Kimberley. The same week in which he decided to intervene in Perak he interviewed Campbell. However, Kimberley's suggestion of the Residents, which figured in his celebrated instructions for Sir Andrew Clarke in 1873, was almost certainly for an adviser to the Malay rulers, not for an officer who would actually run the states. Although accepted in a single case, therefore, Residents were no panacea for stabilizing the frontier.

CHARTERED COMPANIES

The third alternative was the chartered company. This had, of course, been the characteristic instrument of overseas activity in the

[1] Fergusson to Kimberley 22 Oct. 1873. C.O. 209/230.

[2] Kennedy to Kimberley 16 Dec. 1871. C.O. 96/89; Kimberley to Wolseley 10 Sept. 1873 (draft). C.O. 96/108; memo. by Carnarvon, P.R.O. 30/6/85.

[3] Mins. by Hemming 28 Sept. 1872 (on Pope-Hennessy to Kimberley 1 Sept. 1872. C.O. 267/316) and Knatchbull-Hugessen 4 Mar. 1873 (on Pope-Hennessy to Kimberley 10 Feb. 1873. C.O. 267/320); E. Blyden, 'Report on the Timbo Expedition, 1873', in Harley to Kimberley 22 May 1873. C.O. 267/320.

[4] Undated memo. in *Carnarvon Papers*, P.R.O. 30/6/85.

seventeenth century. After the British North Borneo Company
charter in 1881, large areas of Africa briefly came under the sway of
the Royal Niger, Imperial British East Africa, and British South
Africa Companies. But as the East India Company had only been
finally abolished after the Mutiny, and Hudson's Bay Company surrendered its territorial rights to the Dominion of Canada as recently
as 1869, the British Government was reluctant to allow new companies of this kind. Private ventures with ambitious semi-military
schemes in the tropics received short shrift from the Colonial Office.
The Selangor Tin Company's request to be allowed to use its own
troops in Malaya in 1873 was rejected outright. Various New Guinea
companies were given no encouragement.

Although Carnarvon briefly considered transferring the Gold Coast
to a company in 1874, he decided there were 'Practical difficulties in
creating a monopoly'. He was sure abuses would follow and the
'Govt. wd. be held responsible'.[1] The most specific and ambitious
plan for a chartered company was Vogel's South Pacific Company,
for which the East India and Hudson's Bay companies were frankly
cited as the models. It is significant that Gladstone (who in 1881 was
to approve the British North Borneo Company's charter) was faintly
interested. But Carnarvon found the scheme 'Visionary — dangerous
— open to speculation & corruption etc.',[2] and he let the matter drop.
In the 1870's, then, the chartered company was not regarded as a
suitable instrument in frontier regions.

PROTECTORATES

Most commonly advocated was the fourth alternative — the creation
of a protectorate. The meaning of this device has always been exceedingly ill-defined. Before the Berlin West African conference in
1884–5, when coastal protectorates in West Africa were recognized,
subject to certain conditions,[3] international lawyers seemed to have
ignored such protectorates as already existed in the region. Travers

---

[1] Undated memo. in *Carnarvon Papers*, P.R.O. 30/6/85.

[2] Memo. in *Carnarvon Papers* dated 26 Feb. 1874. P.R.O. 30/6/51,
p. 3.

[3] General Act of the Berlin Conference 26 Feb. 1886. *Accounts and
Papers*, xlvii, pp. 107–17 for Art. 34.

Twiss, who found the title 'Protected State' inadequate, drew a distinction in 1861 between what he called 'Protected Independent States' (such as the Ionian Islands under Britain) and 'Protected Dependent States' (like the Princely States of India).[1] He ignored the so-called Gold Coast protectorate which was the source of so much trouble. W. E. Hall admitted in 1894 that 'protectorate' had 'different meanings in different circumstances and in the mouths of different persons'.[2] Indeed, the ambiguity of 'protectorate' in international law can be illustrated by the definition in a standard modern authority, who admits that the concept 'lacks precise legal precision', but might be regarded as '*a kind of international guardianship*'.[3]

If exact legal precision has never been possible, international lawyers have none the less tended to erect their own hierarchy of protectorates. They might be termed: (1) the *true* protectorate of one European state over another (like the Ionian Islands); (2) the *Oriental* protectorate (or what Oppenheim called 'the protectorate a member of the Family of Nations exercised over such non-Christian States as are outside that family');[4] and (3) the *African* or *South Seas* protectorate, where treaties were made not with heads of sovereign states but with 'heads of tribal communities'[5] — this was sometimes called a 'colonial protectorate'.

[1] T. Twiss, *The Law of Nations*, Oxford, 1861, vol. i, pp. 26–35.

[2] Hall, *Foreign Powers and Jurisdiction*, p. 204.

[3] H. Lauterpracht, 8th ed. (1955) of L. Oppenheim, *International Law*, i, p. 192. Protectorate is defined as follows: 'A protectorate arises when a weak State surrenders itself by treaty to the protection of a strong State in such a way that it transfers the management of all its more important international affairs to the protecting State. Through such a treaty an international union is called into existence between the two States, and the relation between them is called protectorate. The protecting State is internationally superior to the protected State; and the latter has with the loss of the management of its more important international affairs lost its full sovereignty, and is henceforth only a half sovereign State. Protectorates, however, a conception which, like suzerainty, lacks exact legal precision, and its real meaning depends very much upon the special case. Generally speaking, protectorate, may, again like suzerainty, be called a *kind of international guardianship*. . . . Great Britain exercises a protectorate over a number of "protected states" in Asia, but their international status is not clear. They must be distinguished in any case from the protectorates over African tribes. . . . These "protectorates" possess no international status whatsoever.'

[4] Oppenheim, op. cit. (1905 ed.), i, p. 281. [5] Ibid.

This classification is open to many objections, but it demonstrates an important point. Victorian lawyers obviously believed that there was no authority-structure in much of Africa and Polynesia capable of making internationally valid agreements. They took the attitude that it was 'little short of ridiculous to apply the principles of European international law with prudish exactness to the savages of the Santa Cruz Islands'.[1] Such views did not go completely unchallenged, as Gladstone pleaded for equal justice for all. Moreover, after studying the legal aspects of expansion, Lindley came to the conclusion that the great Powers usually grounded their protectorates on treaties with local rulers. He felt that this could not be regarded 'otherwise than as the rule of law'.[2] On the whole, however, from the standpoint of international law, protectorates were not important in the three tropical regions in the 1870's. When they were recognized later in the nineteenth century they were regarded as 'nothing else than steps to exclude other Powers from occupying the respective territories'.[3]

However reticent international lawyers may have been about protectorates, this did not prevent either the mid-Victorians, or the rulers they came into contact with, from using the term pretty freely. 'Protectorate' on the Gold Coast referred to a large area where extra-territorial jurisdiction, and some jurisdiction over Africans, had been acquired. After the first Residents had been appointed in Malaya, the Attorney-General of the Straits Settlements approved a tin concession which stated in its text that Britain had 'assumed a protectorate over the State of Selangor'. The head of the Eastern Department of the Colonial Office agreed that Britain was the 'protecting Power' in Malaya.[4] Similarly, without providing any definition of what they meant, advocates of the annexation of Fiji always suggested that the alternative to cession was a protectorate. Chief Thakombau, who was said to prefer the latter, provided another variation of the theme.

Thakombau said in 1858: 'I do not give the land. I only want

---

[1] Hall, op. cit., p. 235.

[2] Lindley, *Government of Backward Territory*, p. 176.

[3] Oppenheim, op. cit. (1905 ed.), i, p. 281.

[4] Min. by Cox 28 Apr., on Braddell to Agent of the Malay Peninsula (E. India) Tin Mining Co. 10 Mar. in Clarke to Carnarvon 18 Mar. 1875. C.O. 273/79.

them to be here to protect me.'[1] Again in 1874, after refusing to give
up the islands, he changed his mind and agreed to 'cede the country to
England . . . but it must be understood that he was giving only the
Government of the country, not his men, or his earth'.[2] Here is a
most revealing interpretation — a concept of protectorate from one
who literally sought 'protection'. Yet another version was produced
by Commodore Goodenough. He announced that the presence of
British warships in Fiji and the intervention of naval officers constituted a 'virtual protectorate' and he determined to quell disorders by
hoisting the Union Jack 'as a Protectorate for a time'.[3] Such illustra-
tions show that in everyday usage, as well as in law, the term had very
little real meaning in the 1870's.

This ambiguity became a very useful asset during the period of the
'Scramble for Africa'. But in the early 1870's there is no doubt that
the idea of 'protectorate' was deprecated in Whitehall. Rogers gave
a very clear indication of these misgivings during the discussion about
Fiji in 1870:

> A protectorate is sometimes proposed. I do not quite know what this
> means. I suppose it is an intimation to the world—that nobody then
> must assume sovereignty over the Islands or make war on them — but
> if they have a grievance against them they must apply to us . . . I do not
> myself very much like this kind of thing.[4]

Knatchbull-Hugessen thought a protectorate was 'a very absurd as
well as a curious state of affairs' and he declared in 1872 that he had
'never been able to find out exactly what a protectorate meant'.[5]
Gladstone was even more suspicious: 'It might be anything or
nothing: it is the most shadowy of all relations; it might involve almost
all the responsibilities of government'.[6] Kimberley refused to 'adopt
a Protectorate in Fiji'. In Goodenough's instructions he dismissed

[1] Quoted in Brookes, *International Rivalry*, pp. 234–5.
[2] Goodenough's *Journal*, 20 Mar. 1874.
[3] Goodenough to Goschen 2 Dec. 1873 (private). *Carnarvon Papers*,
P.R.O. 30/6/44, p. 4.
[4] Min. by Rogers 19 Oct., on Canterbury to Granville 12 Aug. 1870.
C.O. 309/94.
[5] Min. by Knatchbull-Hugessen 17 Apr., on Kennedy to Kimberley
29 Mar. 1871. C.O. 267/310; 3 *Hansard*, 212, col. 209.
[6] Ibid. col. 215.

the idea firmly: 'it would be impossible . . . undefined responsibilities, with limited powers of discharging them'.[1]

In the 1870's fear of commitments made the policy-makers shun protectorates. Where the long-standing title of protectorate was retained, on the Gold Coast, Kimberley determined in 1873 to define 'the powers and obligations of the Protecting State and . . . the obligations of the natives towards us'.[2] Thus, while the idea that Britain was 'protecting Power' was accepted in the Gold Coast and Malaya, on the whole protectorates were regarded as an unsatisfactory way of stabilizing the frontier in the tropics.

PARAMOUNTCY

The final alternative lay in the conviction, which gained increasing currency in the 1870's, that Britain should be recognized as 'paramount power' in certain regions. It implied that 'spheres of influence' existed where her 'paramountcy' was exerted. Lawyers regarded this as 'the step preceding the establishment of Colonial Protectorate in the modern process of territorial acquisition'.[3] Thus an extremely vague concept — the least specific of the five alternatives — was the most attractive to the Colonial Office in 1873–5.

The doctrine of paramountcy raises further problems of definition. The best-known case of British paramountcy was in South Africa. When it was challenged by the declaration of the German protectorate over Angra Pequena in 1884, Edward Fairfield declared that if intervention by another Power had been expected in South Africa 'Great Britain as the paramount power, would have taken possession of it long ago'.[4] By the end of the nineteenth century the staking-out of spheres of influence came to play a large part in diplomatic activity.

---

[1] Remarks to a deputation, 12 May 1873. Clipping from *Australia and New Zealand Gazette*, 17 May 1873 in C.O. 83/4; draft of instructions in confidential memo. 10 June 1873. *Gladstone Papers*, 44225/45. Scholefield's assertion (*The Pacific*, p. 90) that 'The Colonial Office itself had expressed a preference for a protectorate' is quite wrong.

[2] Min. by Kimberley after 20 Mar., on question by McArthur 18 Mar. 1873. C.O. 96/104.

[3] Lindley, *Government of Backward Territory*, p. 207.

[4] Quoted in de Kiewiet, *Imperial Factor in South Africa*, p. 314.

But Hall admitted in 1894 that 'no very definite meaning is as yet attached'.¹ He suggested that a 'sphere of influence' represented something less than a protectorate.

> It represents an understanding which enables a state to reserve to itself a right of excluding other European powers from territories that are of importance to it politically as affording means of future expansion to its existing dominions or protectorates, or strategically as preventing civilized neighbours from occupying a dominant military position . . . the phrase 'sphere of influence' taken by itself, rather implies a moral claim rather than a true right.

The emphasis was on a general pre-emptive right rather than the commitment implied in a protectorate. Already by the 1870's the utility of such vague, flexible notions can be detected.

In the three tropical regions, the idea of Britain's 'moral' right to a sphere of influence and to be recognized as 'paramount power' was sometimes explicitly stated. After Kimberley decided to intervene in the Malay States and was spurred on by the rumour of a German protectorate, he wrote 'we are the paramount power in the Peninsula . . . it would be a serious matter if any other European power was to obtain a footing in the Peninsula'.² Similarly, annexations in the South Pacific (outside Fiji) were postponed because, as Herbert hinted in 1875,

> Further annexation will come at the proper time, but to tell the world (Germany, United States, France etc.) that we *now* contemplate it would be to defeat the object and prevent us from quietly acquiring paramount influence among the Islands.³

In West Africa the idea of paramountcy was less explicit, but it was nevertheless implied by the Government's policies. The idea of creating spheres of influence to avoid international friction lay behind the Anglo-Dutch partition of the Gold Coast in 1868 and the proposed Anglo-French dividing-line north of Sierra Leone between 1869 and 1876. The Foreign Office clearly regarded Britain as 'paramount power' in the Niger Delta and was anxious to keep out the French.⁴

¹ Hall, *Foreign Powers and Jurisdiction*, pp. 228–9.
² Kimberley to Gladstone 10 Sept. 1873. *Gladstone Papers*, 44225/103.
³ Min. by Herbert 5 May on Vogel to Carnarvon 4 May 1875. *Carnarvon Papers*: P.R.O. 30/6/47, p. 216.
⁴ F.O. to C.O. 15 May 1875. C.O. 87/108.

Although Kimberley resisted ideas of expansion into the West African interior and Carnarvon rejected the opportunity of annexing all the Gold Coast and Ashanti in 1874, British policy along the seaboard aimed at establishing British paramountcy between the Gold Coast and Lagos for fiscal reasons.

In general the idea of spheres of interest in West Africa appealed to the Colonial Office. Knatchbull-Hugessen believed that a rumoured German acquisition of Liberia in 1871 would be 'a general benefit'.[1] Kimberley attacked what he called 'a dog-in-the-manger policy' in the rivers north of Sierra Leone in 1872. 'Either we should take steps to open the trade of these rivers ourselves, or we should let the French do so'.[2] In the 1860's there had been hopes that Britain could disengage from all her territories in West Africa and maintain only trading relations. Between 1870 and 1874 the dream faded. Knatchbull-Hugessen successfully propounded the view that

> England has sown the seeds of civilization and christianity upon these coasts, and whether for the furtherance of these great objects, or for the mere development of the resources of a country evidently teeming with underdeveloped wealth, her continued presence and action is most desirable in the interests of W[est] Africa and of the world.[3]

The idea gained ground that Britain should remain in West Africa, and local events conspired to strengthen the resolve. But the Government did not wish to stay at the expense of clashes with other Powers.

Thus already, in the decade before the period of intense colonial rivalry, the idea that Britain was 'paramount power' in certain spheres of West Africa, South-East Asia and the South Pacific had taken root. Lindley argues that the treaties signed with African rulers between 1868 and 1875 'imply some kind of paramountcy'.[4] In Malaya and the South Pacific explicit claims to paramountcy were made. The concept of 'paramountcy' was the highest common factor in Britain's response to her troubles on the frontier in the tropics. It was a peaceful,

[1] Min. 27 Jan. 1871 on Kennedy to Kimberley 28 Dec. 1870. C.O. 267/307.

[2] Min. 8 Oct., on Pope-Hennessy to Kimberley 1 Sept. 1872. C.O. 267/316.

[3] Ibid. Min. 3 Oct. 1872.

[4] Lindley, *Government of Backward Territory*, p. 185.

not an aggressive form of 'imperialism', which was designed to avoid international territorial disputes.

From a wide range of choice the Colonial Office selected the vaguest of its alternatives. The phrase 'informal empire' does not, on its own, do justice to the possible techniques which were considered. No ready-made institutional formula existed for stabilizing the frontier in the tropics. The Colonial Office decided to experiment in each region. Carnarvon claimed that each issue had been judged on its merits. Our case-studies show that the experiments were also part of a wider whole.

CONCLUSION

Mid-Victorian Imperialism: a Pragmatic Approach to Empire

THE frontier developments which occurred in the years 1873–5 may now be seen in perspective. They were not the start of a 'new imperialism'. They were experiments in the administration of tropical dependencies. They were strictly limited experiments. Carnarvon refused his consent to annexations beyond Fiji, he appointed Residents in only three of the Malay States, and in West Africa the keynote of his policy was caution. The new policies represented a minimum fulfilment of responsibilities which had been unwillingly incurred.

The conventional view that there was a pattern of British colonial policy in which an age of 'anti-imperialism' gave way in the 1870's to a 'new imperialism' advocated by Disraeli, is now unacceptable. Most of the decisions which led up to the new experiments were made in 1873 by Kimberley, and the advent of the Conservatives in 1874 did nothing to speed the changes. Disraeli had less influence than Gladstone over the planning of the new experiments in the tropics.

The thesis that the changes on the frontier in the tropics signalized the start of a 'forward movement' must also be modified. To be sure, the Pangkor Engagement, the cession of Fiji and the Ashanti War were each major landmarks in regional history. But, when they are seen as part of the broad stream of colonial policy in the mid-Victorian Age, more emphasis should be placed on the Government's reluctance to move than on the fact that small extensions were made. The experiments were intended to mark the beginning of a period of deliberate restraint.

This is not to deny that the logical consequences of limited intervention were appreciated. Kimberley feared that expansion in the vicinity of Lagos might lead on to Timbuktu, and he warned Gladstone that new clamours for expansion in the Pacific were inevitable. Carnarvon

372

believed that Britain would one day have to annex the Malay States and he accepted the need for modest territorial expansion along the West African seaboard. Knatchbull-Hugessen and Herbert were both convinced that Britain would come round to an expansionist policy in the Pacific. Rogers feared that Britain would be drawn into Central Africa, the Far East and the Pacific islands. Few politicians or civil servants would deny that one day Britain *might* find herself extending widely in the tropics.

But in 1874 Carnarvon clearly wished to call a halt. After launching his three small experiments — the Gold Coast–Lagos Crown Colony, the Residents in Perak, Selangor and Sungei Ujong, and the new Crown Colony in Fiji — he drew the line. There was a marked lull before expansion was resumed in the 1880's. Then, a host of new factors, notably the colonial activities of France, Germany, the United States, Leopold II and Italy, brought this about. The changes of 1873–5 should not be taken as the beginning of the forward movement; they should be regarded as a response to individual situations and the result of a determination to pursue limited objectives.

If the old view of a 'forward movement' following an age of 'anti-imperialism' is inadequate, how far do these case-studies substantiate the recent thesis that there was a 'fundamental continuity of British expansion throughout the nineteenth century'? Gallagher and Robinson argue that when the growth of 'informal empire' is taken into account the mid-Victorian years should be regarded not as an era of indifference but as 'the decisive stage in the history of British expansion overseas'.[1] Do our case-studies lend support to this thesis? In one sense they do. Carnarvon's policy of achieving order on the frontiers of empire without resource to annexation was clearly an extension of informal empire –– although the motives were not primarily economic. Expansion in the 1880's and 1890's usually proceeded from foundations which had been laid earlier. The methods of late-Victorian expansion were, on the whole, not new; they had been pioneered in the mid-Victorian period or earlier. Thus the decision not to quit West Africa and to assert paramountcy in Malaya and the South Pacific definitely shaped the pattern of expansion later on. It is significant that the five alternatives considered by the Colonial Office in

[1] 'The Imperialism of Free Trade', *Econ. Hist. Rev.* (1953), 6 (1), pp. 5 and 11.

1873–5 covered the whole range of the techniques of control adopted in the later period of rapid territorial expansion.

Nevertheless, the 'continuity' thesis must be qualified for the tropical empire in one important respect. The continuity was one of direction rather than time. British expansion proceeded by a series of uneven thrusts, which began for particular reasons at different times and in different areas. The changes in the tropics in 1873–5 represented one such landmark and they were followed by a pause for reflexion. They were a part of the continuity of mid-Victorian expansion, but they also mark a definite break in the continuity.

The years immediately preceding 1873 were ones of ferment and disintegration in these regions. Crises on the frontier in the tropics forced the Colonial Office to examine the whole basis of Britain's involvement, and to consider the various possible lines of action which were open. The new policies adopted in 1874–5 were regarded as test cases, by which new methods of informal empire were to be tried. Thus within a general continuity of direction, movements of greater or lesser activity must still be recognized.

If the experiments may now be seen in the general context of colonial policy, what do they tell us about the motives, methods and consequences of Britain's acquisition of her tropical empire? Close study of the deliberations in Whitehall which led up to the experiments certainly reveals a good deal about the process of policy-making. What stands out most vividly is the fact that the decisions were made on the basis of incomplete and inaccurate information. The mid-Victorians were obviously caught up in a current of colonial expansion which they did not fully understand, which they sought to avoid, but which they were unable completely to check.

Why did Britain expand in the tropics in these years? This question must be approached cautiously. As Robinson and Gallagher admit, the recorded arguments of mid-Victorian ministers did not always bring out fully their 'unconscious assumptions'.[1] Politicians like Knatchbull-Hugessen, Kimberley and Carnarvon might talk of fostering 'Commerce, Christianity and Civilization', of 'obligations to be redeemed' and of 'duties to be performed' or even of a 'mission of England', but does this suggest that they were mainly actuated by

---

[1] *Africa and the Victorians*, p. 20.

some philanthropic or humanitarian motive? Could it even be that they did not really know what they were doing? Adderley declared to Disraeli in 1873: 'It looks as if the English were destined just now to open up Africa, but it's an awful destiny'.[1] And Salisbury indeed admitted in the heat of the scramble for Africa: 'I do not exactly know the cause of this sudden revolution. But there it is.'[2]

Undoubtedly there is an authentic ring to all these contemporary explanations. But, unfortunately, historians have been all too prone to isolate particular aspects of the problem and erect comprehensive theories of imperialism around them. Yet their theories usually reflect the prejudices and preoccupations of their own day. Five main theories of imperialist motive may be tested against our case-histories.

The earliest comprehensive theory of British imperialism was made on the eve of the scramble of the 1880's and it implied that expansion was unintentional. In 1883 Sir John Seeley gave birth to one of the most extraordinary clichés of all time: 'We seem, as it were, to have conquered and peopled half the world in a fit of absence of mind'. India, in particular was acquired 'blindly', nothing was done 'so unintentionally, so accidentally'.[3] This sort of explanation did not end with Seeley. After the First World War, by which time new theories of imperialism were making numerous converts, Joseph Schumpeter defined imperialism as 'the objectless disposition on the part of a state to unlimited forcible expansion'. He moved beyond Seeley, however, in his emphasis of the role of 'aggressiveness'. He envisaged 'expansion for the sake of expanding, war for the sake of fighting, victory for the sake of winning, dominion for the sake of ruling'.[4] A new stress on this 'irrational' element in imperialism has been laid by David Fieldhouse, who points to the role of 'the same social hysteria that has since given birth to other and more disastrous forms of aggressive nationalism'.[5] Emphasis has also, at various times, been given to the role of public opinion in creating an imperialism of 'prestige'. 'Basically the

[1] Adderley to Disraeli 23 Jan. 1873. *Disraeli Papers*, B/xxi/A/124.
[2] Speech in 1891, quoted in *Africa and the Victorians*, p. 17.
[3] J. R. Seeley, *The Expansion of England*, London, 1889, pp. 8 and 179.
[4] J. Schumpeter, *Imperialism* (trans. H. Norden), Cleveland, 1955, pp. 5–6.
[5] D. K. Fieldhouse '"Imperialism": An Historiographical Revision', *Econ. Hist. Rev.* (1961), 14 (2), p. 209.

new imperialism was a nationalist phenomenon,' wrote Carlton Hayes; it expressed a 'psychological reaction, an ardent desire to maintain or recover national prestige'.[1]

The second, and most influential, theory of imperialism concentrates on the profit motive. John A. Hobson, writing shortly after the hey-day of the chartered companies and Cecil Rhodes and the South African War, sought to explain an apparent paradox. He calculated that only one forty-fifth of British income came from external trade, and of this only a tiny proportion came from new tropical acquisitions. But 'although the new Imperialism has been bad business for the nation', he claimed that 'it has been good business for certain classes and certain trades within the nation'.[2] Above all, surplus capital sought new outlets and this became the 'economic taproot of imperialism'. Hobson popularized the idea of a capitalist conspiracy by 'economic parasites', later refined by Lenin, who defined imperialism as the 'monopoly stage of capitalism', which would lead inexorably to the age of 'international monopolist capitalist associations which share the world among themselves'.[3] For many people the Hobson–Lenin theory has remained the orthodox explanation of imperialism. Imperialism means economic imperialism. Even historians who reject the theory of the 'capitalist conspiracy' are still prepared to retain the economic motive as the prime element of imperialism. Thus Robinson and Gallagher, who declare, 'It would be a gullible historiography which could see such gimcrack creations as necessary functions of the balance of power or as the highest stage of capitalism', do not reject the economic motive. They remove the emphasis from investment and stress rather the influence of the expanding British industrial economy. They define imperialism as the political function necessary in 'this process of integrating new regions into the expanding economy'.[4] At its least complicated level this involved a search for raw materials.

[1] C. J. H. Hayes, *A Generation of Materialism 1871–1900*, New York, 1963, p. 220. See also G. N. Sanderson's conclusions about the Fashoda crisis in *England, Europe and the Upper Nile 1882–1899*, Edinburgh, 1965.

[2] J. A. Hobson, *Imperialism: a Study*, London, 1902, pp. 31, 51.

[3] V. I. Lenin, 'Imperialism, the Highest Stage of Capitalism' (1916), *Collected Works*, vol. 22, Moscow and London, 1964, p. 266.

[4] 'The Partition of Africa', *N.C.M.H.* xi, 1962, p. 639; 'Imperialism of Free Trade', *Econ. Hist. Rev.* (1953), 6 (1), p. 5.

While economic interpretations of imperialism continue to hold the field, a third school of thought developed during the period after the First World War when European Powers began publishing diplomatic documents going back roughly to the 1870's in an effort to lay the blame for 1914 on their rivals. Thus a new generation of diplomatic historians began detailed case-studies of imperialist acts (especially Bismarck's sudden entry into the lists). They evolved the theory of an imperialism of diplomatic calculation centred on Europe. Africa and the Pacific were seen as safe tournament grounds for European power rivalries. 'New worlds were being brought into existence in the vain hope that they would maintain or redress the balance of the old'.[1]

The diplomatic historians, by their case-studies, certainly added a new precision to the argument and a by-product of their approach has been the evolution, in recent years, of a fourth theory. It is hardly surprising that a generation dominated by problems of security and global strategy should re-examine the relevance of these concepts for the history of imperialism. Thus Robinson and Gallagher suggest that the prime influence upon the British 'official mind' during the scramble for Africa was strategic. They see Britain drawn into Africa as a response to nationalist movements in Egypt and the Transvaal. Africa was not valuable for its own sake, but as security for the routes to the existing empire in India, South-East Asia, Australasia and the Pacific. Similarly, J. A. S. Grenville implies that the guiding motive behind Lord Salisbury's diplomacy at the end of the nineteenth century was the need to defend the British Empire.[2]

From this brief survey of what contemporaries and several generations of historians have said about imperialism, we find that five motives are suggested as the explanation for expansion: humanitarian; irrational and emotional; economic; diplomatic; and strategic. Do any of these explanations fit the experiments in the tropics in 1873–5? The answer is that each of these motives played a part, but that all the general theories are inadequate.

If we look first at West Africa we have to recognize that the doctrine of furthering 'Commerce, Christianity and Civilization' was no mere hypocritical rationalization for expansion. Early Victorian

[1] Fieldhouse, op. cit., p. 206.
[2] J. A. S. Grenville, *Salisbury and Foreign Policy. The End of the Nineteenth Century*, London, 1964.

ministers tried hard to disengage from West Africa. Their aim was the extirpation of the slave-trade and, when this failed by naval action off-shore, the new policy of substituting a 'legitimate commerce' for African slave-trading came to imply the maintenance of considerable influence on the coast. The missions in the Yoruba region fitted in well with the new policy. Palm oil exports from the Niger Delta were both valuable to British industry and consistent with the official policy. Humanitarian and economic motives here went hand in hand. However, at Lagos and Abeokuta, in Glover's day, the trade motive defeated the humanitarian motive. Capitalists on the other hand who tried to promote new enterprises in West Africa normally received short shrift from the Colonial Office. But we must also remember that the small pressure group of Gambia merchants successfully stopped the Gambia cession in 1870.

Irrational and emotional motives had their place in West Africa. The eagerness of the 'Wolseley ring' to serve in the Ashanti War provides an illustration of Schumpeter's 'aggressiveness'. One officer, Colley, rushed all the way from North America to take part. Wolseley's own ambition definitely distorted the whole nature of the campaign. There was also in the Ashanti War an element of the restoring of British prestige on the Gold Coast and there was more popular interest (expressed in newspapers, magazines and histories) in this campaign than in any other aspect of the frontier in the tropics in this period. The accident of the 1874 general election coming during the campaign served to heighten this interest.

Diplomatic and strategic motives played a minor role in West Africa. The Anglo-French exchange project was designed to avoid international rivalry, although minor extensions to consolidate Britain's position in her own spheres were implied by the Anglo-French overtures. Security was always an underlying influence since even during the years of non-intervention a local discretion was always permitted if the security of the settlements was threatened. West Africa did not figure in grand strategic concepts, but Glover did believe that Lagos had a strategic role for the trade routes from the Niger region to North Africa.

If we turn next to Malaya we find that the same elements played their part, but the whole emphasis must be changed. There were no missionaries. The only possible humanitarian argument might be a

suggestion that Britain was interested in law and order and the suppression of piracy. There was little of the irrational and prestige-seeking motives, except perhaps Ord's and Clarke's personal ambition and Jervois's somewhat desperate campaign to restore British influence in 1875. But in Malaya a critical interplay between strategic and economic motives predominated. Straits Settlements merchants (mainly Chinese) were interested in the tin of western Malaya. Although British promoters like the Selangor Tin Company were usually rebuffed by the Colonial Office (like their counterparts elsewhere), when they conjured up a strategic threat they had an immediate influence. The security motive was in fact of prime importance at two levels. During the period of non-intervention, the governor (as in West Africa) was given a local discretion to act if the security of the Straits Settlements was threatened. In the wider context the Straits Settlements were seen as a strategic base on the trade routes to the Indonesian archipelago and the South China Sea. When the unlikely threat of German intervention in Selangor was raised in 1873 Kimberley acted quickly.

For the South Pacific, finally, the elements of the pattern must be rearranged once more. Here humanitarian pressures were strong. The Wesleyan Missionary Society was deeply interested in Fiji and had their spokesmen in Parliament. The London, Scottish Presbyterian and Wesleyan missionary societies and the Aborigines Protection Society were anxious about the labour traffic. There was little of the objectless, irrational and aggressive motive in these remote waters, although there is a hint in Carnarvon's talk of a 'mission of England'. Economic pressures were, as usual, normally resisted by the Colonial Office. But the Manchester Cotton Supply Association was briefly interested in Fijian cotton during the American Civil War, and some New Zealand investors in the Fiji Bank managed to interest the New Zealand Government, which in turn tried to influence the British Government. Diplomatic rivalry was deprecated in this region, as in West Africa and Malaya. The Colonial Office even toyed with the idea of allowing another Power to acquire Fiji, but gradually it came to prefer the idea of British annexation. Strategic arguments were advanced about the importance of Fiji as a possible base lying between Sydney and Vancouver; of Samoa (especially Pago Pago harbour) on a future route between Auckland and a Panama Canal; of New

Guinea's proximity to Queensland. But the strategic motive was finally harnessed to humanitarian aims. Fiji, unannexed, was seen as a flaw in British labour traffic regulations. Kimberley tried to persuade Gladstone that if they took their attempt to regulate the labour traffic seriously Fiji would have to be annexed to close the gap.

Thus, by testing the five major theories of imperialist motive against the experiments of 1873–5, we find that these motives certainly had their part but there was considerable variation of emphasis according to the region. What all five explanations neglect is the human factor. The new experiments in the tropics were on the periphery of affairs and depended largely upon the work of comparatively obscure individuals, to whom considerable attention must be paid by historians. Who, then, were the decisive individuals?

The experiments in the tropics were not the work of great and famous 'empire-builders' at home or overseas. Kimberley was painstaking and conscientious. He studied problems carefully, he did not shirk difficult decisions, but he was reluctant to advance. In each case he went through several months of great uncertainty during 1872–3 before a combination of Knatchbull-Hugessen's persistence, public opinion and the urgency of the issues forced him to come down on the side of intervention. Even then, after deciding upon action, he was still not always sure what final form it should take. Carnarvon, coming in when the ground had been prepared, showed considerable imagination and flexibility in the face of the men on the spot, who, in 1874, acted first and reported afterwards. Later, as his problems multiplied and his ill-starred attempt at South African confederation came to dominate the Colonial Office, he seemed to lose his touch. His handling of Jervois in Malaya in 1875 and the Gambia exchange question in 1876 was much less sure than his original launching of the three experiments.

With Whitehall so generally reluctant to move (with the exception of Knatchbull-Hugessen and Herbert) the main impetus for action must have come from elsewhere. Behind each experiment there was an important element of 'sub-imperialism'. In West Africa, the Lagos merchants and Government became entangled in the Yoruba region. Sierra Leonians became involved in the northern rivers and some even looked to the interior of the Soudan. In Malaya, the Straits Settlements merchants and Government were responsible for awaking the unsuspecting Colonial Office to the insecurity and dangers of the Malay States. In the South Pacific the British Government had to lend an ear to the elected colonial Governments of New Zealand, Queensland, New South Wales and Victoria.

But in the last resort we must concentrate on particular individuals, rather than groups, and notice the great significance, in each tropical region, of the men on the spot. A large responsibility for the new experiments rested on them, in spite of Robinson and Gallagher's assertion that policy was made in London.[1] In the first place, the Government's decisions were based on the information which the men on the spot selected. Whitehall's understanding was therefore always imperfect. Major decisions had to be based on political considerations or generalized guesses about where Britain's interests lay. Even more significant was the fact that the understanding of the men on the spot was also imperfect. Their decisions really involved judgements about the pattern of regional history which they were not qualified to make. Glover, Wolseley, Ord, Clarke, Jervois and Goodenough were all highly ambitious, conscientious, service officers, who were evidently often in the dark on the frontier.

As we turn to the role of the man on the spot, therefore, we must consider the methods of mid-Victorian expansion in the tropics. Britain's initial political intervention nearly always took the same form. Her representatives 'took sides' in a local dispute. British officials did not face or create a *carte blanche* as they might in an uninhabited island or wide-open prairie. They tried to 'select the winner' in the local political stakes. This is what makes the changes of 1873-5 so significant for regional history.

In West Africa Glover switched the Lagos colony's support from the Egba to Ibadan. The Fante and protectorate states in the Gold Coast were supported against Ashanti. In Malaya, Sultan 'Abdu'llah

---

[1] *Africa and the Victorians*, p. 21. The role of the man on the spot was recognized by J. S. Galbraith: 'Seldom did the London government initiate frontier policy, rather, it reacted to the policies of its governors.' See 'The Turbulent Frontier as a Factor in British Expansion', *C.S.S.H.* (1960), 2 (2), p. 168, and D. S. Landes: 'imperialism was in large measure built on the *fait accompli* ... with the state almost always ready to pull its nationals' chestnuts out of the fire', 'Some Thoughts on the Nature of Economic Imperialism', *J.E.H.* (1961), 21 (4), p. 505.

382 Conclusion

of Perak was upheld against Ismail and the Tengku Zia'u'd-din was assisted against Raja Mahdi and his cohorts in Selangor. In Fiji the pretensions of Thakombau were bolstered against Ma'afu. The choice of ally in the Gold Coast was dictated by a long history of friendly relations. In Malaya, on the other hand, the choice depended very much on the judgement of Irving and Braddell, the two men who tried to unravel the complexities of Malay politics — but who did not agree on their findings. In Fiji, the choice was partly determined by the Pritchard cession, partly by the presence of British settlers, and partly by Goodenough's decision not to take Thurston's word against those of a thousand settlers. The choices of the man on the spot were often of the utmost significance. They determined the side which Britain would support. Incredibly delicate decisions had to be made by men untrained in the history and workings of West African, Malay or Melanesian and Polynesian institutions.

The consequences were sometimes disastrous. British intervention was usually resisted. Indeed, later administrators often concluded that Britain had 'backed the wrong horse'. In the Gold Coast army officers were disgusted at the military failings of their Fante allies, and compared the 'demoralised new men' of the coast with the 'virile warriors' of Ashanti. Carnarvon lamented to Disraeli that by the Ashanti War Britain had 'either crushed or irritated to the highest degree the dominant race in that part of the world'.[1] In Perak, Jervois once contemplated installing Ismail in preference to the loose-living Sultan 'Abdu'llah. In Sungei Ujong, the recalcitrant Dato'Bandar Tunggal was regarded as a much more valiant figure than the Dato'Klana, who became the ward of the Straits Government. In Fiji, Ma'afu excited more personal admiration than Thakombau. These choices led to major turning-points in regional history. They must always have given a characteristic imprint to British intervention. An incipient opposition to government already existed because intervention was never impartial; it involved the selection and cultivation of only one strand of local political evolution.

Perhaps the most ironical result of this expansion by 'taking sides' was that Britain came to be ranged against the growth of nationalism. In Europe, it had become one of the traditions of British diplomacy

[1] Carnarvon to Disraeli 7 Mar. 1874. *Disraeli Papers*, B/xx/He/17.

to support constitutionally governed nation states, and in the days of Palmerston and Grey such a policy had been outlined for West Africa. But in the crises of 1873–5 such notions were swept aside. The Fante Confederation movement in the Gold Coast was hailed by *The African Times* in 1872 as 'the birth of a NATION'.[1] But in spite of some support from Members of Parliament, this incipient movement of Gold Coast nationalism was ignored. Similarly, Jervois suggested that Perak's resistance to Birch's encroachments was part of a 'national rising' in Malaya,[2] which ought to be resisted. In Fiji before annexation there had been an attempt to create a constitutional monarchy on the Hawaiian model, but the British Government decided it could not be trusted. The 'national' element in all these movements should not be over-emphasized. What is significant is that British intervention was as much a response to these incipient nationalist movements as a fulfilment of some metropolitan initiative. Colonial nationalism has not always grown simply as an opposition to European imperialism. Imperialism sometimes was a response to nationalism.

Even when we recognize that the men on the spot, in 'taking sides', virtually committed Britain to certain courses, one important source of difficulty remains. What were the motives of the contending parties in the local disputes which led British officers to intervene? These are notoriously difficult to understand. If the crucial moments of decision in each region are studied in the closest possible detail, it is still today extremely difficult to judge on them with any certainty.

For the Pangkor Engagement, which provided for the first Resident in Malaya, there are variant Malay and English texts. Shortly after the agreement some of the signatories tried to repudiate it. For the vital conferences of chiefs in Fiji in March 1874, when the decision to cede the islands was taken, no authoritative record appears to exist. The second-hand accounts conflict with each other. What the Fijians seemed to have in mind was giving up the responsibility for governing Fiji, but not handing over themselves or their lands. Similarly, for the reaction of the Ashanti to Wolseley's terms or the reaction of the protectorate chiefs to Strahan's terms in 1874, only the official record of the successful officers seems to exist. Yet we know that the defeated asantehene soon lost his throne.

[1] Kimble, *Political History of Ghana*, p. 249.
[2] Irving to Carnarvon 22 Nov. 1875. C.O. 808/6, p. 28.

But, although the precise motives of each party remain obscure, we can be fairly sure on one point. The local West African, Malay, Melanesian or Polynesian rulers did not play a purely passive role. As Professor Hargreaves suggests, 'often they had clear aims in view'.[1] Thus, in West Africa, Ibadan 'used' the Lagos Government in its rivalry with the Egba. Minor states of the Gold Coast had, for years, made trouble with Ashanti in their confidence (perhaps misguided) that the British would save them. Rival rajas, in Malaya, enlisted the support of Straits Settlements officials. Thakombau, the key personality in Fiji, used the British to bolster his desire to be 'King of all Fiji'.

Therefore any satisfactory explanation of expansion must not stop with the role of the British officers on the spot. It also requires a much more difficult examination of the role of those minor local rulers who managed to embroil the world's major imperial Power for their own ends. At least we can say that there were a few men in Whitehall who had no illusions on this score. Edmund Hammond, the permanent under-secretary of the Foreign Office, realized that, if British representation in South-East Asia was too diffuse, 'Eastern rulers' would have 'a sure opportunity of playing one British authority against the other'.[2] And Gladstone, ever wary and perceptive in such matters, heartily deplored 'the disposition of John Bull to put his head . . . into a noose'.[3]

In all these events vital decisions, affecting the whole course of regional history, were made. Yet it is impossible to be perfectly sure what was really in the minds of the participants. For this very reason the somewhat ambiguous solutions which were adopted by the Colonial Office in 1874–5 appear in rather better light. British colonial policy in the three tropical regions did not, as yet, seek to impose uniformity on regional development. Britain's response to the perplexing events which had been highlighted in the crises on the frontier in the tropics were, in a sense, appropriate in their modesty.

The troubles on the imperial frontier in the tropics which demanded Kimberley's attention in the years 1870 to 1873, and the policies

---

[1] *Prelude to the Partition*, p. x. See also Robinson and Gallagher, 'Partition of Africa', *N.C.M.H.*, pp. 617–20.

[2] Note by Hammond 31 May, on C.O. to F.O. 25 May 1868. F.O. 69/47.

[3] Gladstone to Kimberley 21 Aug. 1873. *Kimberley Papers*, A/52.

pursued by Carnarvon in 1874–6, undoubtedly represent an important stage in the rise of British control in West Africa, Malaya and the South Pacific. But they should not be regarded as the vital stage. The period was, rather, one when the Colonial Office began to comprehend the problem of the imperial frontier in the tropics and began seriously to weigh up the alternatives which lay open to it. The frontier in the tropics was not, after all, the central issue of British colonial policy at the time of Gladstone and Disraeli. The relations between Britain and the self-governing colonies in Canada, Australia, New Zealand and South Africa were what interested the public. Only rarely did the frontier in the tropics reach the headlines. But a conviction of British paramountcy in these regions was certainly growing. The decision, modest as it was, was clear. Before further territory could be annexed, certain experiments would be carried out. The mid-Victorians, for all their love of doctrinal controversy about empire, retained a pragmatic approach to their new commitments in the tropics.

BIBLIOGRAPHY

1. MANUSCRIPTS
   (*a*) GOVERNMENT RECORDS
   (*b*) PRIVATE PAPERS

2. GOVERNMENT PRINTED SOURCES
   (*a*) CONFIDENTIAL PRINTS
   (*b*) PARLIAMENTARY PAPERS
   (*c*) OTHER OFFICIAL PUBLICATIONS

3. CONTEMPORARY WRITINGS

4. SECONDARY BOOKS AND ARTICLES
   (*a*) COLONIAL OFFICE, BIOGRAPHY AND GENERAL
   (*b*) WEST AFRICA
   (*c*) MALAYA
   (*d*) SOUTH PACIFIC

5. UNPUBLISHED THESES

1. MANUSCRIPTS
   (*a*) GOVERNMENT MANUSCRIPTS IN THE PUBLIC RECORD
   OFFICE

Consulted for the period 1865–75, and in most cases for a longer period.

Colonial Office	*Foreign Office*
C.O. 273 Straits Settlements	F.O. 58 Pacific Islands
C.O. 96 Gold Coast	F.O. 84 Slave Trade
C.O. 267 Sierra Leone	F.O. 27 vols. 2226 and 2227
C.O. 147 Lagos	France–Gambia exchange
C.O. 87 Gambia	F.O. 37 Netherlands
C.O. 83 Fiji	F.O. 69 Siam
C.O. 309 Victoria	*War Office*
C.O. 201 New South Wales	W.O. 25/3913 Records of service,
C.O. 209 New Zealand	Royal Engineers
	W.O. 32/826 Despatches from
	Gold Coast

These materials form the main source material of this book. Where papers were printed either for Parliament or confidentially the Prints have been cited for ease of reference, but it is always necessary to go to the MSS. files for the minutes and drafts. Moreover, many of the crucial decisions were made in Cabinet or privately between ministers; to discover how policy was formed it is therefore necessary to consult available private papers.

(*b*) PRIVATE PAPERS

Royal Archives, Queen Victoria's correspondence, Windsor Castle (by gracious permission of Her Majesty the Queen).

Kimberley Papers, Wymondham Hall, Norfolk, by courtesy of the Earl of Kimberley.

Carnarvon Papers, Public Record Office (formerly Gifts and Deposits), P.R.O. 30/6.

Gladstone Papers, British Museum Add. MSS., and Cabinet Minutes, by permission of the Cabinet Office (historical section).

Disraeli Papers, Hughenden Manor, High Wycombe, Bucks., by courtesy of the National Trust.

Granville Papers, P.R.O. 30/29.

Cardwell Papers, P.R.O. 30/48.

Iddesleigh Papers (letters of Sir Stafford Northcote), British Museum Add. MSS.

Norton Papers (certain papers of Sir Charles Adderley), Birmingham Public Library.

The Political Diary of Lord Brabourne (Edward Knatchbull-Hugessen), 1858–88, 8 vols., by courtesy of Lord and Lady Brabourne. (This is an autobiographical compilation based on three sources: (1) Lord Brabourne's private diaries, (2) his political journals, and (3) his correspondence.)

Commodore Goodenough's Private Journal, 1873–5, 6 vols., by courtesy of Miss Cecilia Goodenough, M.A., the Commodore's granddaughter.

The Glover Papers, by courtesy of the Royal Commonwealth Society.

The Methodist Missionary Society Records. The Calvert Papers, and the Fiji, Gambia and Gold Coast correspondence files.

Great Northern Railway Minute Books, British Transport Commission Archives (for information about Seymour Clarke).

2. GOVERNMENT PRINTED SOURCES

(*a*) CONFIDENTIAL PRINTS

(1) *Colonial Office*
     C.O. 806 African.
     C.O. 808 Australian.
     C.O. 809 Eastern.

(2) *Foreign Office*
     Memorandum relating to the Netherlands Authorities in the Eastern Archipelago, 1824–62, by A. S. Green, 24 Aug. 1864 (copy in C.O. 273/9).
     Treaties, Conventions etc. between the Dutch and Native Princes in the Eastern Seas, 1857–64. Dec. 1866 (copy in C.O. 273/15).

Correspondence respecting the policy of the Netherlands Government in the Eastern Seas as affecting British Commerce, 1824–67. Sept. 1867 (copy in C.O. 273/14).

Papers on Ord's Mission to Batavia, June 1869. F.O. 37/488.

Memorandum upon the Sumatra and Gold Coast Treaties between England and Holland, by H. P. Anderson, 5 Jan. 1874. Printed Jan. 1874 (copy in C.O. 273/77).

Memorandum relative to the Proposals made by Raja Brooke for the annexation of Brunei to the British Dominions, by A. S. Green, 22 Sept. 1874 (copy in F.O. 58/145, p. 261).

3. *War Office*

Memorandum: *The British Possessions on the West Coast of Africa,* by Captain Andrew Clarke, R.E., June 1864. W.O. 33/13/1387.

Wolseley Papers. Confidential Prints relating to Ashanti War.

(*b*) PARLIAMENTARY PAPERS

Reports from Committees (1842), xi. Report from the Select Committee on the West Coast of Africa.

Accounts and Papers (1854–5), xxxvii, p. 375 [383] The existing Civil and Judicial Constitutions of the British Settlements on the West Coast of Africa.

Accounts and Papers (1862), xxxvi, p. 701 [2992] Correspondence relative to the Fiji Islands. (Col. Smythe's mission.)

Accounts and Papers (1863), xliii, p. 299 [541] Papers connected with the attack upon Tringanu in Nov. 1862.

Accounts and Papers (1864), xli, p. 133 [385] Ashanti War, Despatches, p. 165 [3364] Further papers relating to military operations on the Gold Coast.

Reports from Committees (1865), v [412] Report from the Select Committee on Africa (Western Coast).

Accounts and Papers (1865), xxxvii, p. 287 [170] Report of Col. Ord, Commissioner appointed to inquire into the Condition of the British Settlements on the West Coast of Africa.

Accounts and Papers (1870), l, p. 539 [444] Correspondence respecting the proposed cession of the Gambia to France.

Accounts and Papers (1872), xliii, p. 685 [C–479] Correspondence between the Governor of N.S.W. and the Earl of Kimberley respecting statements made by Capt. Palmer in his book entitled 'Kidnapping in the S. Seas'.

— p. 711 [C–496] Further correspondence respecting the deportation of S. Sea Islanders.

Accounts and Papers (1872), lxx, p. 557 [C–474] Convention between H.M. and the King of the Netherlands for the transfer to Gt. Britain of the Dutch possessions on the Coast of Guinea.

Accounts and Papers (1872), lxx, p. 565 [C–473] Convention between H.M.
and the King of the Netherlands relative to the Emigration of Labourers
from India to the Dutch Colony of Surinam.
— p. 577 [C–475] Convention between H.M. and the King of the Netherlands for the Settlement of their mutual relations in the Island of
Sumatra.
— p. 753 [C–670] Correspondence relating to the cession of the Dutch
Settlements on the West Coast of Africa.
— p. 661 [C–466] Papers relating to recent Proceedings at Salangore. (The
Selangor Incident of 1871.)
Accounts and Papers (1873), xlix, p. 121 [171] Correspondence with Pope-
Hennessy over the Fante Confederation.
— p. 451 [266] Gold Coast Despatches.
— p. 679 [266–1] Ditto pt. ii.
— p. 869 [C–819] Ashanti Invasion.
— p. 883 [C–801] Ashanti Invasion.
— p. 889 [C–802] Ashanti Invasion.
— p. 909 [C–804] Ashanti Invasion.

(c) OTHER OFFICIAL PUBLICATIONS

The London Gazette.
Hertslet's Commercial Treaties.
Hansard's Parliamentary Debates, Third Series.
The Public General Statutes.
The Colonial and Foreign Office Lists.
Treaties and Other International Acts of the United States of America, ed.
by H. Miller, Department of State Publications, Washington, 1942,
vol. vii: 1855–8.

3. CONTEMPORARY WRITINGS

Adderley, C. B. (Lord Norton), *Some Reflexions on the Speech of Lord John
Russell on Colonial Policy*, London, 1850.
— *Letter to the Right Honourable Benjamin Disraeli on the Relations of
England with the Colonies*, London, 1861.
— *Review of 'The Colonial Policy of Lord John Russell's Administration',
by Earl Grey, 1853; and of subsequent Colonial History*, London, 1869.
— *Our Relations with the Colonies and Crown Colonies*, London, 1870.
Anson, Sir A. E. H., *About Others and Myself, 1745–1920*, London, 1920.
Baillie Hamilton, W. A., 'Forty-four Years at the Colonial Office', *The
Nineteenth Century* (Apr. 1909), 65, p. 599.
Bird, I. L., *The Golden Chersonese and the Way Thither*, London, 1883.
Bowdich, T. E., *Mission from Cape Coast Castle to Ashantee*, London, 1819.
Brackenbury, H., *The Ashanti War*, 2 vols., London, 1874.

Bramston, Sir J., 'The Colonial Office from Within', *Empire Review*, Apr. 1901.

Brewster, A. B., *King of the Cannibal Isles*, London, 1937.

Bright, P. (ed.), *The Diary of John Bright*, London, 1930.

Buckle, G. E. (ed.), *Queen Victoria's Letters*, 2nd ser., London, 1926.

Butler, Sir W., *Akim-Foo: the History of a Failure*, London, 1875.

Buxton, T. F., *The African Slave Trade and Its Remedy*, London, 1840.

Cavenagh, Sir O., *Reminiscences of an Indian Official*, London, 1884.

Clarke, Sir A., 'The Straits Settlements', *British Empire Series*, i, London, 1899.

Clifford, H., *East Coast Etchings*, London, 1896.

Cruikshank, B., *Eighteen Years on the Gold Coast of Africa*, 2 vols., London, 1853.

Dilke, C. W., *Greater Britain: a Record of Travel in English-Speaking Countries during 1866 and 1867*, 2 vols., London, 1868.

Doyle, P., *Tin Mining in Larut*, London, 1879.

Ellis, A. B., *A History of the Gold Coast of West Africa*, London, 1893.

Erskine, J. E., *Journal of a Cruise among the Islands of the West Pacific including the Feejees*, London, 1853.

Escott, T. H. S., *Pillars of the Empire*, London, 1879.

Forster, W. E., *Our Colonial Empire*, London, 1875.

Godley, A. (Lord Kilbraken), *Reminiscences*, London, 1931.

Goodenough, Mrs. V. H., *Memoir and Journal of Commodore Goodenough*, London, 1876.

Gordon, A. H., *Fiji. Records of Private and Public Life, 1875–1880*, 4 vols., Edinburgh, 1897–1912.

— *Mauritius. Records of Private and Public Life, 1871–1874*, Edinburgh, 1894.

— *Story of a Little War. Letters and Notes written during the Disturbances in the Highlands of Viti Levu, Fiji, 1876*, 2 vols., Edinburgh, 1879.

Grant Duff, M. E., *Notes from a Diary, 1886–1888*, London, 1900.

Grey, Third Earl, *The Colonial Policy of Lord John Russell's Administration*, 2 vols., London, 1853.

Hall, W. E., *A Treatise on the Foreign Powers and Jurisdiction of the British Crown*, Oxford, 1894.

Hemming, A. W. L., 'The Colonial Office and the Crown Colonies', *Empire Review* (July 1906), (66).

Henty, G. A., *The March to Coomassie*, London, 1874.

Hinderer, A., *Seventeen Years in the Yoruba Country*, London, 1873.

Kimberley, 'Journal of Events during the Gladstone Ministry, 1868–1874', ed. by E. Drus, *Camden Miscellany*, 1958, xxi.

Knaplund, P. (ed.), 'Gladstone–Gordon Correspondence, 1851–1896. Selections from the private correspondence of a British Prime Minister and a Colonial Governor', *Transactions of the American Philosophical Society*, n.s. (1961), 51 (4).

Lyall, A., 'Frontiers and Protectorates', *The Nineteenth Century*, Aug. 1891.

McNair, F. J. A., *Perak and the Malays, Sarong and Kris*, London, 1878.

Maudslay, A. P., *Life in the Pacific Fifty Years Ago*, London, 1930.

Maurice, J. F., *The Ashantee War. A Popular Narrative*, London, 1874.

Maxwell, Sir P. B., *Our Malay Conquests*, London, 1878.

Merivale, H., 'The Colonial Question in 1870', *Fortnightly Review*, Feb. 1870.

Mills, A., 'Our Colonial Policy', *Contemporary Review*, June 1869.

Moresby, J., *Discoveries and Surveys in New Guinea and Polynesia*, London, 1876.

— *Two Admirals*, London, 1909.

Palmer, G., *Kidnapping in the South Seas*, Edinburgh, 1871.

Pritchard, W. T., *Polynesian Reminiscences, or Life in the Pacific Islands*, London, 1866.

Ramm, A. (ed.), 'The Political Correspondence of Mr. Gladstone and Lord Granville 1868–1876', *Camden Society*, 3rd ser., lxxxii, 1952.

Ramseyer, F. A., and Kühne, J., *Four Years in Ashantee*, ed. by Mrs Weitbrecht, London, 1875.

Read, W. H. M., *Play and Politics — Recollections of Malaya by an Old Resident*, London, 1901.

Reade, W. W., *The Story of the Ashantee Campaign*, London, 1874.

Rogers, Sir F., *Lord Blachford's Letters*, ed. by G. E. Marindin, London, 1896.

Seemann, B., *Viti: an Account of a Government Mission to the Vitian or Fijian Islands in the years 1860–61*, London, 1862.

Stanley, H. M., *Coomassie and Magdala: The Story of Two British Campaigns in Africa*, London, 1874.

Twiss, T., *The Law of Nations Considered as Independent Communities*, 2 vols., Oxford, 1861–3.

Wolseley, G. (Field-Marshal, Viscount), *The Story of a Soldier's Life*, 2 vols., London, 1903.

— *The Letters of Lord and Lady Wolseley, 1870–1911*, ed. by Sir G. Arthur, London, 1923.

Wood, E., *From Midshipman to Field Marshal*, 2 vols., London, 1906.

Zetland, Marquis of (ed.), *The Letters of Disraeli to Lady Bradford and Lady Chesterfield*, 2 vols., London, 1929.

4. SECONDARY BOOKS AND ARTICLES

(a) COLONIAL OFFICE, BIOGRAPHY AND GENERAL

Allin, C. D., *Australasian Preferential Tariffs and Imperial Free Trade*

(University of Minnesota Studies in the Social Sciences, 19), Minneapolis, 1929.

Aydelotte, W. O., *Bismarck and British Colonial Policy*, Philadelphia, 1937.

Biddulph, R., *Lord Cardwell at the War Office. A History of His Administration 1868–1874*, London, 1904.

Bodelsen, C. A., *Studies in Mid-Victorian Imperialism*, Copenhagen, 1924.

Brunschwig, H., *French Colonialism: Myths and Realities, 1871–1914*,
London, 1966.

Burt, A. L., *Imperial Architects*, London, 1913.

Cady, J. F., *The Roots of French Imperialism in South-East Asia*, Ithaca,
N.Y., 1954.

Carrington, C. E., *The British Overseas*, Cambridge, 1950.

Chapman, J. K., *The Career of Arthur Hamilton Gordon, First Lord Stanmore
1829–1912*, Toronto, 1964.

Childe-Pemberton, W. S., *The Life of Lord Norton: Rt. Hon. Sir Charles
Adderley, 1814–1905*, London, 1909.

Childers, S., *Life and Correspondence of Rt. Hon. Hugh H. C. E. Childers,
1827–1896*, London, 1901.

de Kiewiet, C. W., *British Colonial Policy and the South African Republics,
1848–1872*, London, 1929.

— *The Imperial Factor in South Africa*, Cambridge, 1937.

de Klerck, E. S., *History of the Netherlands East Indies*, 2 vols., Rotterdam,
1938.

Erickson, A. B., 'Edward Cardwell — Peelite', *Transactions of the American
Philosophical Society*, Philadelphia, 1959.

Farr, D. M. L., *The Colonial Office in Canada 1867–1887*, Toronto, 1955.

Findlay, G. G., and Holdsworth, W. W., *The History of the Wesleyan
Methodist Missionary Society*, London, 1921.

Froude, J. A., *The Earl of Beaconsfield*, London, 1905.

Gallagher, J., and Robinson, R. E., 'The Imperialism of Free Trade',
Economic History Review (1953), 6 (1).

Gathorne-Hardy, A. E., *Gathorne-Hardy, First Earl of Cranbrook. A
Memoir*, 2 vols., London, 1910.

Glover, Lady E., *The Life of Sir John Hawley Glover*, ed. by Sir R. Temple,
London, 1897.

Goodfellow, C. F., *Great Britain and South African Confederation, 1868–
1881*, Cape Town, 1966.

Gorst, H. E., *The Earl of Beaconsfield*, London, 1899.

Hall, H. L., *The Colonial Office*, London, 1937.

Hamilton, B., *Barbados and the Confederation Question, 1871–1885*, London,
1956.

Hancock, W. K., *Survey of Commonwealth Affairs*, 2 vols., London, 1942.

Hardinge, A. H., *The Life of Henry Howard Molyneux Herbert, fourth Earl of Carnarvon, 1831–1890*, ed. by Elizabeth Countess of Carnarvon, 3 vols., London, 1925.

Harrop, A. J., *England and the Maori Wars*, London, 1937.

Jenkyns, H. L., *British Rule and Jurisdiction Beyond the Seas*, Oxford, 1902.

Knaplund, P., *Gladstone and Britain's Imperial Policy*, London, 1927.

Koebner, R., and Schmidt, H. D., *Imperialism. The Story and Significance of a Political Word, 1840–1960*, Cambridge, 1964.

Lehmann, J. H., *All Sir Garnet. A Life of Field-Marshal Lord Wolseley, 1833–1913*, London, 1964.

Lindley, M. F., *The Acquisition and Government of Backward Territory in International Law*, London, 1926.

Lowe, D. A., 'Lion Rampant', *Journal of Commonwealth Political Studies* (1964), 2 (3).

McCullagh, T., *Sir William McArthur, K.C.M.G. A Biography*, London, 1898.

Monypenny, W. F., and Buckle, G. E., *The Life of Benjamin Disraeli, Earl of Beaconsfield* (revised 2 vol. ed.), London, 1929.

Moon, P. T., *Imperialism and World Politics*, New York, 1933.

Morley, J., *The Life of William Ewart Gladstone*, 3 vols., London, 1903.

Muir, R., *A Short History of the British Commonwealth*, London, 2 vols., 1922.

Newton, A. P., *A Hundred Years of the British Empire*, London, 1940.

Oliver, R., *The Missionary Factor in East Africa*, London, 1952.

Oppenheim, L., *International Law*, 2 vols., London, 1905, and 1955 edition ed. by H. Lauterpacht.

Pope-Hennessy, J., *Verandah. Some Episodes in the Crown Colonies 1867–1889*, London, 1964.

Pugh, R. B., 'The Colonial Office, 1801–1923', *Cambridge History of the British Empire* vol. iii, ed. by E. A. Benians, Sir James Butler and C. E. Carrington, Cambridge, 1959.

Schuyler, R. L., *The Fall of the Old Colonial System*, New York, 1945.

Stacey, C. P., *Canada and the British Army 1846–1871*, London, 1936.

Stembridge, S. R., 'Disraeli and the Millstones', *Journal of British Studies* (1965), 5 (1).

Taylor, A. J. P., *Germany's First Bid for Colonies, 1884–1885*, London, 1938.

Townshend, M. E., *The Origins of Modern German Colonialism, 1871–1885*, New York, 1921.

Tyler, J. E., *The Struggle for Imperial Unity*, London, 1938.

Uys, C. A., *In the Era of Shepstone: British Expansion in South Africa, 1842–77*, London, 1933.

Vetch, R. H., *Life of Lieutenant-General the Honourable Sir Andrew Clarke*, London, 1905.

Wemyss Reid, T., *Life of the Right Honourable William Edward Forster*, London, 1888.

Wood, Sir John, 'Treasury Control', *Political Quarterly* (1954), 25 (4).
Young, D. M., *The Colonial Office in the Early Nineteenth Century*, London, 1961.

(*b*) WEST AFRICA

Ade Ajayi, J. F., 'The British Occupation of Lagos, 1851–61: A Critical Review', *Nigeria Magazine* (1961), 69.
— and Smith, R. S., *Yoruba Warfare in the Nineteenth Century*, Cambridge, 1964.
— *Christian Missions in Nigeria 1841–1891. The Making of a New Elite*, London, 1965.
Allott, A. N., 'Native Tribunals in the Gold Coast, 1844–1929', *Journal of African Law* (1957), i (3), p. 163.
Anstey, R., *Britain and the Congo in the Nineteenth Century*, Oxford, 1962.
Biobaku, S. O., *The Egba and their Neighbours, 1842–1872*, Oxford, 1957.
Birtwhistle, A., *Thomas Birch Freeman, West African Pioneer*, London, 1950.
Bourret, F. M., *Ghana. Road to Independence 1919–57*, Oxford, 1960.
Catala, R., 'La Question de l'échange de la Gambie Britannique contre les Comptoirs Français du Golfe de Guinée de 1866 à 1876', *Revue d'Histoire des Colonies* (1948), 35, pp. 114–36.
Claridge, W. W., *A History of the Gold Coast and Ashanti*, 2 vols., London, 1915.
Coleman, J., *Nigeria. Background to Nationalism*, Berkeley and Los Angeles, 1959.
Coombs, D., *The Gold Coast, Britain and the Netherlands 1850–1874*, Oxford, 1963.
Crooks, J. J., *Records Relating to the Gold Coast and Settlements from 1750 to 1874*, Dublin, 1923.
Curtin, P., *The Image of Africa*, Madison, 1963.
Dike, K. O., *Trade and Politics in the Niger Delta, 1830–1885*, Oxford, 1956.
Fage, J. D., *An Introduction to the History of West Africa*, Cambridge, 1955.
— 'The Administration of George Maclean on the Gold Coast 1830–44', *Transactions of the Gold Coast and Togoland Historical Society* (1952–1955), i, p. 112.
Fuller, F. C., *A Vanished Dynasty — Ashanti*, London, 1921.
Fyfe, C., *A History of Sierra Leone*, Oxford, 1962.
Gavin, R. J., 'Nigeria and Lord Palmerston', *Ibadan*, June 1961.
Gray, J. M., *A History of the Gambia*, Cambridge, 1940.
Hargreaves, J. D., 'The French Occupation of the Mellacourie, 1865–67', *Sierra Leone Studies* (Dec. 1957), 9, p. 3.
— *Prelude to the Partition of West Africa*, London, 1963.
Johnson, S., *History of the Yorubas*, Lagos, 1924.

Kimble, D., *A Political History of Ghana. The Rise of Gold Coast National-ism 1850–1928*, Oxford, 1963.

Lloyd, C., *The Navy and the Slave Trade*, London, 1949.

McIntyre, W. D., 'British Policy in West Africa: The Ashanti Expedition of 1873–74', *The Historical Journal* (1962), 5 (1).

— 'Commander Glover and the Colony of Lagos, 1861–73', *Journal of African History* (1963), 4 (1).

Metcalfe, G. E., *Maclean of the Gold Coast. The Life and Times of George Maclean 1801–1847*, Oxford, 1962.

— *Great Britain and Ghana. Documents of Ghana History 1807–1957*, London, 1964.

— 'After Maclean', *Transactions of the Gold Coast and Togoland Historical Society*, i, p. 183.

Newbury, C. W., *The Western Slave Coast and Its Rulers*, Oxford, 1961.

— *British Policy Towards West Africa. Select Documents 1786–1874*, Oxford, 1965.

Robinson, R. E., and Gallagher, J., with Denny, A., *Africa and the Victorians*, London, 1961.

Sarbah, J. M., 'Maclean and the Gold Coast Judicial Assessors', *Journal of the African Society* (July 1910), 9 (36).

Schnapper, B., *La Politique et le Commerce Français dans le Golfe de Guinée de 1838 à 1871*, Paris, 1961.

Tordoff, W., *Ashanti under the Prempehs*, Oxford, 1966.

Ward, W. E. F., *A History of the Gold Coast*, London, 1948.

(c) MALAYA

Buckley, C. B., *An Anecdotal History of Old Times in Singapore from 1819 to 1867*, 2 vols., Singapore, 1902.

Cowan, C. D., 'Sir Frank Swettenham's Perak Journals, 1874–1876', *Journal of the Malayan Branch of the Royal Asiatic Society* (Dec. 1951), 24 (4).

— *Nineteenth Century Malaya. The Origins of British Political Control*, Oxford, 1961.

Gullick, J. M., *The Indigenous Political Systems of Western Malaya*, London, 1958.

— 'Captain Speedy of Larut', *Journal of the Malayan Branch of the Royal Asiatic Society* (Nov. 1953), 26 (3).

— 'Sungei Ujong', *Journal of the Malayan Branch of the Royal Asiatic Society* (1949), 22 (2).

Hall, D. G. E., *A History of South-East Asia*, London, 1955; 3rd ed., 1968.

Kieran, V. G., 'Britain, Siam, Malaya, 1875–1885', *Journal of Modern History* (March 1956).

Linehan, W., 'A History of Pahang', *Journal of the Malayan Branch of the Royal Asiatic Society* (1936), 14 (2).

McIntyre, W. D., 'Britain's Intervention in Malaya. The Origin of Lord Kimberley's Instructions to Sir Andrew Clarke in 1873', *Journal of South East Asian History* (1961), 2 (3).
— 'Disraeli's Election Blunder: The Straits of Malacca issue in the 1874 Election', *Renaissance and Modern Studies* (1961), 5.
Makepeace, W., Brooke, G. E., and Braddell, R. J., *One Hundred Years of Singapore*, 2 vols., London, 1921.
Maxwell, W. G., and Gibson, W. S., *Treaties and Engagements affecting the Malay States and Borneo*, London, 1924.
Middlebrook, S. M., 'Yap Ah Loy', *Journal of the Malayan Branch of the Royal Asiatic Society* (1951), 24 (2).
Mills, L. A., 'British Malaya, 1824–1867', *Journal of the Malayan Branch of the Royal Asiatic Society* (1925), 1 (2).
Parkinson, C. N., *British Intervention in Malaya 1867–77*, Singapore, 1960.
Purcell, V., *The Chinese in Malaya*, Oxford, 1948.
Sadka, E., 'The Journal of Sir Hugh Low, Perak, 1877', *Journal of the Malayan Branch of the Royal Asiatic Society* (1954), 27 (4).
Scott, J. G., *Cursed Luck*, London, 1908.
Sheppard, M. C. ff., 'A Short History of Trengganu', *Journal of the Malayan Branch of the Royal Asiatic Society* (June 1949), 22 (3).
Siang, Song Ong, *One Hundred Years' History of the Chinese in Singapore*, London, 1923.
Swettenham, F. A., *Footprints in Malaya*, London, 1942.
Tarling, N., 'British Policy in the Malay Peninsula and Archipelago 1824–1871', *Journal of the Malayan Branch of the Royal Asiatic Society* (1957), 30 (3), no. 179.
— *Anglo-Dutch Rivalry in the Malay World 1780–1824*, Brisbane, 1962.
— *Piracy and Politics in the Malay World: A Study of British Imperialism in 19th Century South-east Asia*, Melbourne, 1963.
— *Southeast Asia Past and Present*, Melbourne, 1966.
Tregonning, K. G., 'American Activity in North Borneo 1865–1881', *Pacific Historical Review* (Nov. 1954).
Wilkinson, R. J., 'Notes on Perak History', *Papers on Malay Subjects* (1908), 4.
— 'A History of the Peninsula Malays', *Papers on Malay Subjects* (1923), 7.
Windstedt, R. O., and Wilkinson, R. J., 'A History of Perak', *Journal of the Malayan Branch of the Royal Asiatic Society* (1934), 12 (1).
Winstedt, R. O., 'A History of Selangor', *Journal of the Malayan Branch of the Royal Asiatic Society* (1934), 12.
— 'A History of Johore', *Journal of the Malayan Branch of the Royal Asiatic Society* (Dec. 1932), 10 (3).
— 'Negri Sembilan', *Journal of the Malayan Branch of the Royal Asiatic Society* (1934), 12 (3).

(*d*) PACIFIC

Brookes, J. I., *International Rivalry in the Pacific Islands, 1800–1875*, Berkeley and Los Angeles, 1941.

Burdon, R. M., *The Life and Times of Sir Julius Vogel*, Christchurch, 1948.

Derrick, R. A., *A History of Fiji*, i, Suva, 1946.

Drus, E., 'The Colonial Office and the Annexation of Fiji', *Transactions of the Royal Historical Society*, 4th ser. (1950), xxxii.

Dunbabin, T., *Slavers of the South Seas*, Sydney, 1935.

Gordon, D. C., *The Australian Frontier in New Guinea, 1870–1885*, New York, 1951.

Henderson, G. C., *Fiji and the Fijians, 1835–56*, Sydney, 1931.

— 'History of Government in Fiji, 1760–1875', 2 vols. in typescript dated 1941. (Microfilm copy in the School of Oriental and African Studies, London.)

Jacobs, M. 'The Colonial Office and New Guinea, 1874–1884', *Historical Studies Australia and New Zealand* (May 1952), v (18).

Legge, J. D., *Britain in Fiji, 1858–1880*, London, 1958.

Lovett, R., *History of the London Missionary Society, 1795–1895*, London, 1899.

McIntyre, W. D., 'Anglo-American Rivalry in the Pacific: The British Annexation of the Fiji Islands in 1874', *Pacific Historical Review* (1960), 29 (4).

— 'Disraeli's Colonial Policy: the Creation of the Western Pacific High Commission, 1874–1877', *Historical Studies Australia and New Zealand* (1960), 9 (35).

— 'New Light on Commodore Goodenough's Mission to Fiji, 1873–74', *Historical Studies Australia and New Zealand* (1962), 10 (39).

Masterman, S., *The Origins of International Rivalry in Samoa, 1845–1884*, London, 1934.

Morrell, W. P., *Britain in the Pacific Islands*, Oxford, 1960.

Parnaby, O. W., 'Aspects of British Policy in the Pacific: the 1872 Pacific Islanders Protection Act', *Historical Studies Australia and New Zealand* (Nov. 1957), 8 (29).

— *Britain and the Labor Trade in the Southwest Pacific*, Durham, N.C., 1964.

Ross, A., *New Zealand Aspirations in the Pacific in the Nineteenth Century*, Oxford, 1964.

Rowe, G. S. (ed.), *Fiji and the Fijians*, by T. Williams and J. Calvert, London, 1858–60.

Ryden, G. H., *The Foreign Policy of the United States in Relation to Samoa*, Yale, 1933.

Scarr, D., 'John Bates Thurston, Commodore Goodenough and the Rampant Anglo-Saxons in Fiji', *Historical Studies Australia and New Zealand* (1964), 11 (43).

Scholefield, G. H., *The Pacific: its Past and Future*, London, 1919.
Tregonning, K. G., 'American Activity in North Borneo, 1865–1881', *Pacific Historical Review* (Nov. 1954).
Ward, J. M., *British Policy in the South Pacific, 1786–1893*, Sydney, 1948.

5. UNPUBLISHED THESES

Aderibigbe, A. A. B., 'The Expansion of the Lagos Protectorate 1863–1900" Ph.D. thesis, London, 1959.
Anderson, M. A., 'Edmund Hammond, Permanent Under-Secretary of State for Foreign Affairs, 1854–1875', Ph.D. thesis, London, 1956.
Burton, A., 'The Influence of the Treasury on the Making of British Colonial Policy, 1868–1880', D.Phil. thesis, Oxford, 1960.
Cumpston, J. H. I., 'Augustus Gregory and the Inland Sea'. Manuscript used by the courtesy of the late author's daughter, Dr I. M. Cumpston.
Eldridge, C. C., 'The Colonial Policy of the Fifth Duke of Newcastle 1859–64', Ph.D. thesis, Nottingham, 1966.
Gertzel, C. J., 'Imperial Policy towards the British Settlements in West Africa, 1860–75', B.Litt. thesis, Oxford, 1953.
Millington, J., 'The Career of Sir John Thurston, Governor of Fiji, 1888–1897', M.A. thesis, London, 1947.
Philpott, W. E., 'The Original Growth of the Protectorate System, 1800–1848', M.A. thesis, London, 1933.
Scotter, W. H., 'International Rivalry in the Bights of Benin and Biafra, 1815–1885', Ph.D. thesis, London, 1933.
Snidvongs, N., 'King Monkut's Relations with the West', Ph.D. thesis, London, 1959.
Thio, E., 'British Policy in the Malay Peninsula, 1880–1909', Ph.D. thesis, London, 1956.
Tyler, W. P. N., 'Sir Frederic Rogers, Permanent Under-Secretary at the Colonial Office, 1860–1871', Ph.D. thesis, Duke, N. Carolina, 1962.
Wolfson, F., 'British Relations with the Gold Coast, 1843–1880', Ph.D. thesis, London, 1950.

Index

'Abdu'l-Samad, Sultan of Selangor, 181, 188, 189, 190, 295, 296, 303
'Abdu'llah, Raja Muda, 176, 178, 179, 181, 193–4, 207, 292–6, 304–6, 308–9, 311, 313, 316, 381–2
'Abdu'llah Muhammad Shah, 176
'Abdu'llah, Raja of Klang, 181
Abeokuta, 89, 113, 114, 115, 117, 121
Aberdeen: George Hamilton-Gordon, fourth Earl of (1784–1860), 44
Aborigines Protection Society, 39, 41, 242, 256, 259, 330, 352, 379
Abu-Bakar, Temenggong of Johore, 174, 316
Abyssinia Expedition (1867), 313
Accra, 127, 149, 281
Accra Confederacy, 135
Ada, 127
Adansi, 277
Adderley, Sir Charles Bowyer, Baron Norton (1814–1905), *Review*, 10; Colonial Reform Society, 23; colonial affairs in Parliament, 38–39; parliamentary under-secretary for colonies, 57–9; frontier, 77; demands select committee on West Africa, 81, 99; supports Cardwell policy, 101; attitude to French near Sierra Leone, 105–6; Bulama question, 109–10; Anglo-Dutch negotiations over Gold Coast, 121–7, 129; attitude to Malay States, 161, 167; New Guinea, 342; Disraeli, 375
Admiralty, influence on colonial policy, 32–3; New Guinea, 347, 354
Ado Bofo, 128, 130, 131
African Times, The, 383
Age, The, Melbourne, 227, 246, 362
Aggery, King of Cape Coast, 133; banishment, 134
Akim, 87, 277
Akwamu, 127
Akyempon, 128, 130, 131, 132
Alabama case, 253, 333
Alabaster, Harry, 166
Alderley, Stanley of, *see* Stanley of Alderley
Ali, Sultan of Perak, 176
Amoafo, 277
Ampangan, 301
Angra Pequena, 368
Anson, Colonel Archibald, 173, 175, 184, 185; Selangor Incident, 188–192; and Clarke, 292, 305; idea of Resident, 363
Apia, 260
Arfar, 182
Asantehene, Kofi Karikari, 128, 131, 276, 277; Kwaku Dua I, 87; Kwaku Dua II, 128
Ashanti, British relations with, 84; attitude to Anglo-Dutch relations, 121–7; claim to Elmina, 125; hostility to British forts, 127–33; in Volta region, 129; defeat, 276–277; 1901 war, 285; 1874 expedition compared with Perak war, 313–14. *See also* Ashanti wars
Ashanti ring, 275
Ashanti wars (1863–4), 87–8, 127;

PRINTED IN GREAT BRITAIN BY R. & R. CLARK, LTD, EDINBURGH